PRAISE FOR HAROLD NORSE'S MEMOIRS OF A BASTARD ANGEL:

"Magically evocative and visual…fascinating! It can be read like a picaresque novel, horrific and hilarious. It's like an epic film. Every page breathes with the writer's presence." —William Burroughs

"Humorous and didactic…Norse charts a colorful life rich in literary affiliations…He emerges as a peripatetic Priapus…between belletristic concerns and homosexual escapades."
—*New York Times Book Review*

"I enjoyed the *Memoirs* tremendously. So well written . . . so honest . . . alive . . . powerful."—Anaïs Nin

"An important, moving testament to half a century of gay male lives, literature and culture [by] an original talent and cornerstone of both the gay and beat literary traditions." —*The Advocate*

Also by Harold Norse

Memoirs *of a* *Bastard* Angel

A Fifty-Year Literary and Erotic Odyssey

Harold Norse

THUNDER'S MOUTH PRESS
NEW YORK

MEMOIRS OF A BASTARD ANGEL: *A Fifty-Year Literary and Erotic Odyssey*

© 1989 by Harold Norse

Published by
Thunder's Mouth Press
An Imprint of Avalon Publishing Group Incorporated
161 William St., 16th Floor
New York, NY 10038

Library of Congress Cataloging-in-Publication Data is available for this title.

ISBN 1-56025-385-1

9 8 7 6 5 4 3 2 1

Book Design by Nicola Mazzella
Printed in the United States of America
Distributed by Publishers Group West

For James Baldwin
In fond memory of our twenties

Acknowledgments

Excerpts and sections of these memoirs first appeared, in earlier versions, in the following publications: the *Advocate*, *Antaeus, Appeal to Reason, Christopher Street, City Lights Journal, City Magazine of San Francisco, Exquisite Corpse, No Apologies, Semiotext(e), Harper's,* and *Queen* (U.K.).

For their valuable advice, encouragement, and aid in supplying forgotten incidents and details from the past, and for decades of friendship, and permission to quote from their letters and conversations, where I have done so, I express my gratitude to John Hagy Davis, Bonnie Golightly, Barry Benjamin, Frances McCann, Monica von Nagel, Neeli Cherkovski, and Ronald Chase.

I thank Professor Edward Mendelson, literary executor of the Auden estate, for his permission to quote from letters to me by W. H. Auden. I am also grateful to David Baldwin and Gloria Baldwin Smart, executors of their brother's estate, for their permission to use James Baldwin's Preface. I thank William Eric Williams and Paul H. Williams and New Directions Publishing Corporation, agents, for permission to quote from William Carlos William's correspondence to me. I also thank Ulysses D'Aquila for helpful conversations concerning his discoveries of early letters from Chester Kallman to W. H. Auden.

To my editor, Harvey Ginsberg, I express my sincerest gratitude for his indispensable editorial gifts, which he employed toward improving this book.

I also express gratitude to my attorney, Jerome Field, for his generosity with professional advice and friendship in the 1980s. In 2001, my immense gratitude to my new attorney, Pamela Pasti, for her crucial legal advice. Also thanks to her fellow attorney, Rufus Pichler, for his cooperation.

Also, without the assistance of friends who gave so generously of their time and labor, the task of printouts and copies would have been beyond my resources. Thus, I thank Virginia Shantell for furnishing me with early printouts of some of the material and, finally, I express my deep indebtedness to Gregory Moloney not only for his time and unstinting labor in the production of the entire manuscript, in successive stages, but for his ongoing moral support and valuable insights.

Fictitious names, used in many instances to protect the identity of the bearer, are indicated by quotation marks and/or a parenthetical phrase such as "name changed."

Preface
by James Baldwin

I've known Harold Norse so long that I don't remember when I met him. It was many years ago, anyway, in Greenwich Village, in New York. It's my impression that Harold was living then on Perry Street; the good Lord knows where I was living. We were quite incredibly, monstrously young, insanely confident—we were destined to do such things! Time passed—perhaps no time in the history of the world has passed so swiftly and so hideously—time passed, testing our assumptions, trying our confidence, breaking our hearts: and forcing us to work. For a very long time we saw each other not at all. But each knew that the other was somewhere around, and, in the peculiar way of poets, and to our peculiar gods, we prayed for each other.

All that I am equipped to recognize in the effort of any poet is whether or not the effort is genuine. The achieved performance, insofar as it is susceptible to contemporary judgment, can only be judged by this touchstone. And by genuine effort I do not mean good intentions, or hysterical verbosity, or frantic endeavor: the effort I am suggesting scours the poet's life, reduces him, inexorably, to who he is; and who he is is what he gives us. But he gives us much more than that, for his giving is an example that contains a command: the command is for us to do likewise.

That this example and this command are terrifying is proved by the lives of all poets, and that the example and the command are valid is proved by the terror these evoke. One is commanded to look on each day as though it were the first day, to draw each breath in freedom, and to know that everything that lives is holy. Neither the state nor the church approves of such blasphemy, banks will never knowingly loan it money, and armies trample it underfoot. So be it. It is themselves they are trampling underfoot, their hope, and their continuity: and one day all of us will know this, and be able to love one another and learn to live in peace.

Until that day comes, the poet is in exile, as Harold is now. But if light ever enters the hearts of men, Harold will be one of those who have helped to set it there.

Prologue

Who am I?
A wounded man, badly bandaged,
a monster among angels or angel among monsters . . .
　　　　　—TENNESSEE WILLIAMS, *"You and I"*

In the fall of 1975 I began writing my memoirs. I was working as contributing editor on Francis Ford Coppola's magazine *City of San Francisco*. The editorial offices were above the Little Fox Theatre, which he owned, on Pacific Street in North Beach. There were two floors, spacious, light-filled. Our boss, editor-in-chief Warren Hinckle, was a colorful, eloquent pirate with a black patch on one eye, who stimulated and drove us to exhaustion, and had the magic to imbue us with a sense of mission. One day an editor, having savored my yarns about famous people I knew, suggested I write them for submission and ampler reimbursement (which settled the matter). I wrote thirty pages on Allen Ginsberg, Tennessee Williams, and Marlon Brando. At 2:00 A.M. I handed it in while the magazine was being put to bed.

"Adventures of a Bastard Angel" was the fall literary feature. I supplied a half-nude photo of Tennessee in bathing trunks, which I had snapped on the dunes in Provincetown when we lived together, and a photo of myself at twenty-one. He was completing the final draft of *The Glass Menagerie* that summer of 1944, and as they say in show business, the rest is history.

An overnight success, my memoir was mentioned in every major newspaper in California. I had discovered a writing skill that offered instant feedback—and, more important, money.

Then Anaïs Nin wrote enthusiastically about the memoir and her letter appeared in the following issue. On February 7, 1984, the *Advocate*, a national gay journal, published my memoir on W. H.

Auden and again—this time with international repercussions—it caused a stir. On February 8 in England the *Guardian* ran a headline, AFFAIR MAD AUDEN "EMOTIONAL DOORMAT," with a caption, "New Disclosures." The correspondent, quoting me on Auden's acceptance of humiliation by Chester Kallman, comments: "Norse goes much further than Auden's biographer, Humphrey Carpenter, in assessing the relationship between the poet and Kallman as governed by sadness." My career as a memoirist was launched.

Greenwich Village in the 1940s and 1950s, loosely radical, nonconformist, and art oriented, was an oasis of liberation to which, from all over America, young men and women flocked to express their socially unacceptable life-styles. Some, like James Baldwin and Tennessee Williams, became global figures, but their early wounds still hurt. A friend once enviously said, "Well, Jimmy, you have nothing to worry about anymore. You've got it made." Jimmy's reaction was one of horror. "What do you mean I've got it made?" he exploded angrily. "I'm still *black*!" He might have added, for it was equally true, "I'm still *gay*."

More than a decade earlier, after his huge success with The Glass Menagerie, Tennessee Williams told me, "You know the first thing people ask when you're famous? 'Is he queer?' That's all they want to know!" He sounded bitter. Talent and genius were regarded as less important than what a man or woman does in bed.

Once, on a thronging subway platform of the Forty-second Street station, on my way to a movie with a male relative during the Christmas season, excited by the crowds, I let my eyes linger for more than a split second on the fresh, appealing face and figure of a handsome sailor. I was eighteen, a provincial virgin from Brooklyn, and the sailor, about my age, catching my glance, pointed at me and whispered something to his girl friend and they burst into mocking laughter. My stepuncle, a year younger than I, was amused. "He thinks you're a fairy," he said "because your cheeks and lips are so red. It looks like makeup." My lips and cheeks were indeed aflame—

crimson not with rouge but with burning desire; and they turned more crimson as my secret feelings were, for the first time, publicly exposed. Helpless against my need, with downcast eyes I mumbled, "I am." Amid the roar of the trains and the holiday crowd, my young relative gave no sign of having heard and the subject was never mentioned again.

Like Saint Sebastian, I didn't kick against the pricks; I licked them. Whatever the cost in shame and humiliation, I wanted to embrace my tormentors; they in turn wanted to respond but took refuge behind violence and contempt. An irresistible force met an immovable object: bigotry. I vowed to affirm myself as a person not defined by sexuality alone but with many sides and functions.

Addressing the Washington Press Club, the eminent anthropologist Margaret Mead once said, "I think rigid heterosexuality is a perversion of nature." A friend and basic admirer of James Baldwin, she uttered an unpopular but basic truth. As for myself, having intimately shared with Jimmy our youthful aspirations and reverence for sex and love, I decided to dedicate this book to him in memory of a cruel springtime when indeed, as budding bastard angels, in love with the divine in man and woman, we affirmed our right to worship physical beauty as we were born to do. We are not demeaned by sexual worship but by its suppression. If in many its highest expression is attraction to the same sex (and this has always been true of millions around the world), it has produced the best in art and thought, and proven its viability. Sexuality is not a choice; it is genetic.

In a *Vanity Fair* interview James Dickey allowed that he liked W. H. Auden but called his companion, Chester Kallman, a "creep." As Chester was my companion at Brooklyn College before we met Auden, I watched his metamorphosis, over the years, from angelic to diabolic, like the portrait of Dorian Gray—and for similar reasons. The longest section in this book is about Auden's entrance into our lives, a period that, at first hand, can be found in no other work on Auden and Chester. It is the paradigm for Chester's relationships during the rest of his life. I watched Auden's face crack and crumble into fissures like a parched mud flat as he became a noble ruin, dominated by his lifelong unrequited love for Chester. If he often behaved like Caliban, he offset this with the magic touch of Prospero.

An assessment of Auden and Kallman by Truman Capote (in *Conversations with Capote*), though bitchy, was entirely just. He called Auden a "dictatorial bastard...a tyrant," which he was. "And he had this dreadful boyfriend. What was his name?" He goes on to describe how Auden and Kallman "went miles out of their way" to insult Tennessee Williams on the beach at Ischia by walking past him and cutting him dead—because, according to Capote, they were so jealous of his success. This too was documented by others—Auden and Kallman had always refused to meet Tennesse (who persistently knocked on their door) with the tenuous excuse that "he won't do." Auden had "a terrific dull rudeness about him," said Capote, hitting the bull's-eye with that apt phrase. No one who knew Auden could honestly deny this.

But when it came to rudeness Tennessee and Capote were no slouches. They were spoiled monsters in their own right. Like Chester, Auden could at times be a generous, compassionate friend, which was more than I could say for Tennessee (with some justification Capote called him "cold-hearted").

A Village-born Italian, fresh out of Dannemora in his teens for armed robbery, Gregory Corso would sprawl on the grass in Washington Square kicking and screaming, "I got electricity in my bones! Electric currents are shooting out my ass! I'm on fire! I got in-spir-a-shun!" And at the San Remo bar Jack Kerouac and I shouted at each other, "Everybody's a genius in the Village! Where's your masterpiece?" I would go through some soul-trying experiences with Gregory, who would remain all his life the poet as voyou, the outsider, bum and angel.

One night I picked up the eighteen-year-old Allen Ginsberg, a student at Columbia. It was his first trip to the Village and I was the first writer he met. He came to my room a virgin and left intact. I collaborated with Ned Rorem on songs, lived for years in the Beat Hotel with William Burroughs in Paris. Anaïs Nin and William Carlos Williams became warm friends. Jackson Pollock and Dylan Thomas were my drinking buddies at the White Horse Tavern. I served as Auden's secretary, read Jimmy Baldwin's battered manuscript Go Tell It on the Mountain, and was the first to see the final draft of The Glass Menagerie by Tennessee Williams in the cabin we shared in Provincetown. I also played with little Bobby De Niro, a Village urchin seething with cherubic energy, when he was five; his father, Bob, was my friend. Some became sacred monsters, others fell by the wayside. We all paid a price.

This book is a patchwork quilt of my experiences, the life and loves of a poet in Bohemia, a behind-the-scenes peek at the people and the price. Though there may be some factual errors of detail here and there, the events I write about I remember clearly. Fact and fiction, however, like dream and reality, are divided by the thinnest of lines and overlap. And if each of us sees events differently, in one respect we are all the same: at every moment we live between being and nothingness; memory is a rescue mission to retrieve, as best we can, what is already lost.

So, for a few hours, dear reader, I put my life in your hands. Perhaps, like every life among us, it should be labeled: HANDLE WITH CARE. No other label will really do.

1

Bastard Angel

Call me bastard and I'll show you some of the greatest men who ever lived: Leonardo da Vinci, Richard Wagner, Ludwig van Beethoven, Alexander Hamilton, William the Conqueror. And remember—though he wanted to forget it—that Wagner was half Jewish. And that da Vinci and Hamilton were gay. I have always had a healthy respect for facts and a disdain for uncritically accepted stereotypes. Ethnic ones, for example: my family consisted of blue-eyed, blond Jews with small upturned noses and German Catholics with black hair and eyes. In some, like my mother, the cornsilk tow hair of childhood darkened into a fine ash blond, while in her siblings it remained fair or shaded into auburn or chestnut. My eyes are blue-hazel; my hair went from auburn to off-black. We were taken for Germans, Irish, Poles, and the like. Never Jews. We didn't have the nose.

In the Baltic country of Lithuania my grandfather, a tall blue-eyed blond, spoke twelve languages, owned an estate with servants, coaches, stables. My mother remembered horse-drawn droshkies, private tutors, peasants kissing her father's hands for his charity. It all disappeared in a flash when he died of pneumonia at thirty-six; my grandmother, swindled of everything, having known only luxury all her life, arrived at Ellis Island in steerage. A great-great-grandfather once came to America in the 1840s, looked around contemptuously, and spat, "Barbarians!" and returned home. The family stretched across Europe to Germany and France, had money and social position. So I had ancestors, after all—but never knew them.

In my family the drive to assimilate, to become completely American, was obsessive. Only the eldest, my mother and Aunt Ida, could recall the past, but they were children when they ar-

rived in 1905. The shock of these events led to my grandmother's early death. My uncles, who grew up in South Brooklyn
with the Irish, spoke like them and became cabbies, truck driv-
ers, bartenders, and bootleggers. Uncle Mike became a Florida
racetrack bookie when his bootlegging days in East Hampton
ended with the repeal of Prohibition. They melted into the ethnic pot, married German, Irish, and French-Canadian women;
my aunts married German men. My cousins have German, Irish,
English, French, Lithuanian, Finnish, and Jewish blood; all are
Roman Catholic. At first I felt like some kind of hybrid, with no
clear-cut identity or religion. My mother believed in God, not
religion; she feared but did not love Him. He had been brutal,
unkind: what sort of God was that? When things became more
than she could bear she raged at Him, accusing Him of unethical
behavior. She had every reason to: for years barely able to read,
write, or speak English, in her mind she was a princess sold into
slavery (the sweatshops), and she never recovered from it. Bewildered and anxious to solve the identity crisis, in my teens I
wrestled with the issues of race, class, and religion, so blurred
that I didn't know what or who I was. Feeling neither lower nor
upper class, Jewish nor Christian, I could be certain of only one
thing: I was American.

In my twenties the answer came: the great German philosopher Adolf Hitler said I was a Jew. And all my cousins, with
half or a quarter or one-eighth Jewish blood, Aryan-looking
Christians, were also Jews for the same reason. This simple logic
he backed up with great force: the *Wehrmacht.*

Thus the Nazis persuaded even the most stubborn thinkers
that they had solved the perplexing questions of race and religion: psychology, anthropology, sociology, abstract art, all were
perverted products of degenerate Jewish minds. This argument
was supported by a war machine you couldn't argue with; it
slaughtered twenty million people (Stalin added thirty million
more). One thing, at least, was certain: the human race wouldn't
come to an end because of sodomy.

Aunt Eva married a Pennsylvania Dutch electrician and
moved to Scranton. While still living with my grandmother, she
must have secretly converted before her marriage in order to be
acceptable to her fiancé's family. Perhaps she was overzealous, as
converts tend to be, and anxious about my state of grace, for

while my mother was at work Aunt Eva took me to church. I remember it vividly. All at once I entered a magic realm. At the age of five I saw for the first time a world of beauty and mystery: the holy water font, the statues and sacred pictures, the cross, the figure of Jesus, the fumes of incense and dazzling colors of stained glass, the rays of light crisscrossing dramatically in swordlike shafts, and the imposing organ pipes that swept me away with booming harmonies—all this penetrated to the depths of my impoverished little soul. My aunt solemnly sprinkled holy water in my face, touched my forehead, and mumbled something about the man on the cross, that he was God, and my flesh crawled. I was baptized. This was burned into my mind.

The lay baptism was made official when my aunt hung a gold cross around my neck. But my first exposure to religion was short-lived. When my mother saw the gold cross she was furious. She removed it from my neck and I never saw it again.

But the ritual drama of the church never ceased to fascinate me. It was a kind of theatre, not Shakespeare or Wagner exactly, but more like Cecil B. De Mille with a cast of millions. I felt the same way about Excalibur and Camelot—they gave me goose bumps. I grew up wanting to find the Holy Grail but, most of all, the young knights of the Round Table. It would become a life-long quest.

Aunt Eva was a raving beauty. In one of two surviving photos, wearing a cloche hat frilled at the brim with a veil drawn over the crown, and a coat with a fox-fur collar stylishly worn open in front, discreetly exposing a low V-neck gown (no cleavage showing), she was the equal of any film star. Gazing soberly into the lens with smoky violet eyes, whose velvet hue is lost in the sepia tone, she displays poise and elegance. She was offered a chance to be in the *Ziegfeld Follies,* but my grandmother wouldn't hear of it.

Had anyone told her that she was that rare, almost unheard of anomaly, a true Christian, with no pious airs and a heart of gold, she'd have exclaimed in that cheerful, melodious warble that I loved, "How nice of you to say tha-at! If it was only true! But I'm far from it, believe me."

But it *was* true. Saint Teresa, another Jewish lady (who became the patron saint of Spain), could not have been more gentle and kind.

I saw little of my uncles until they were married. Then, occasionally, I caught glimpses of them seminude or in the showers off the beach at Coney Island, and was seized with incestuous desires at puberty. Once I saw Uncle Lou, a shy, gentle young man who almost never uttered a word, silently lying in bed, his hairy chest and legs bare, arms folded behind his head on a pillow. He wore only boxer shorts. With his perpetually embarrassed grin, straight blond hair, and candid blue eyes, he looked like a boxer, rugged and handsome. I remember struggling in vain to keep my gaze averted from the well-developed biceps, the powerful thighs. I wanted to snuggle against him and feel his muscles. My uncles would have pounded me to a pulp if they had ever discovered my secret. They were tough, masculine young men and tolerated no deviation from the norm, and I agreed with them. I was ashamed of myself for such unmentionable thoughts.

Whenever I thought about my uncles in this way my mind would flash back to the age of four, to my first moment of sexual awareness. We had left downtown Brooklyn, my mother and I, to live near the beach in Coney Island. Aunt May, who had no children, looked after me when my mother went to work. She had a brown mole on her chin that she called a beauty mark, a tiny upturned bridgeless nose, a wide mouth full of close-set teeth, and large turquoise eyes. People said she looked like Gloria Swanson. She was certainly a comic version. Her sarcasm spared none, not even children. But I liked her because she made me laugh. She saw everything as a joke.

My aunt left me alone for hours. One day I stood at the window, my lips smeared with my mother's lipstick, cheeks aflame with her powder and rouge, my feet wedged into the toes of her black leather spikes. Around my head, wound loosely like a turban, I wore her chiffon scarf. When passersby stopped to stare I stuck out my tongue, dropped my knickers, and wiggled and shook my bare bottom for an appreciative audience. When they pointed and laughed I was so excited I nearly fell out of the window.

2
Original Sin

My birth was an unmentionable outrage. To my grand-mother, a product of czarist Russia, I was no less than the son of the Devil. She pronounced me dead before I was born and spat in the air three times, jabbing her thumb between her middle and index finger against the evil eye. In the years since then, obstacles thrown in my path with maddening perversity have made me ponder that curse. But in spite of her I managed to survive and prove that there was life after birth.

Today an unwed mother and her bastard raise no brows. But when I was born we were untouchables. My grandmother kicked us out, leaving a scarlet *A* branded on my mother's behind. During her long, tedious life my mother was unable to deal with the shame and guilt.

In the thirties being a bastard was considered glamorous. Illegitimacy was chic. After all, I was a slap in the face of bourgeois morality. But I knew nothing of my paternal forebears, had no legal name or status. Gingerly I'd ask my mother about my father, attempts that met with hysterical fits. Rolling her blue eyes heavenward, she would take leave of her senses, collapse in a flood of tears on the bed, and then, moaning and groaning balefully, she'd fall to the floor. There, exhausted from the emotional binge, she'd lie gasping, like a dying fish. Stricken with terror at having caused such horrible convulsions, I'd stand rooted to the spot, unable to utter a sound. Finally, with a set, immobile expression, she'd rise, wring a muslin cloth under the cold-water tap, and proceed about her household duties with an air of martyred resignation. I got the point: she was deeply hurt and the subject must be avoided.

As a teenager I was frustrated because I thought I was entitled to specific data about my genes. Would I go bald, have a heart attack, die young? Perhaps there might even be a homosexual gene or two, as I had begun to suspect. How else explain the fact that, in spite of myself, I kept gazing with burning desire at my male schoolmates? Try as I might, I couldn't control myself. I also fantasized tirelessly: my father was rich, handsome, aristocratic; he was a famous movie star, writer, musician. I dreamed I'd inherit a fortune. (I would catch my mother poring through names in the telephone book, which she'd hastily shut.) One day, I believed, he would find us, rescue us from poverty, make us happy. But he never did.

With the help of two aunts, I finally unearthed some facts. I would not have been surprised to learn that my father had played the piano in a whorehouse, but he didn't; he played it in silent movie theatres. He also gave lessons in classical piano (an activity hard to describe as diabolic). From this scrap of evidence I concluded that, like my mother, he had come from a genteel background but had no money. My aunts said he was either of German or German-Jewish descent and had been a doughboy in the war. They believed he was German, but he wouldn't admit it (Germans weren't at all popular).

My mother must have been too melodramatic for him. At any rate he left. After his desertion my mother crept to the Bronx, where, on the morning of July 6, 1916, at the Lincoln Hospital, weighing nearly six pounds, I reluctantly appeared. I didn't cry, I sneezed. She blessed me but blamed me for being born. I was blamed for being a bastard and a Caesarean; she couldn't give birth again. When soon afterwards all her teeth fell out she blamed me for "draining the calcium from her bones"— I can't remember how I did it—but despite all this, she reached her ninetieth year looking decades younger, and turned men's heads well into her seventies.

I have only the faintest recollection of the railroad flat in South Brooklyn where my grandmother and her brood established a foothold in the New World. In a corner of my grandmother's kitchen rested a golden samovar, alien and mysterious, like a time machine from another planet, full of strange knobs and devices that protruded from its highly polished, exquisitely embossed surface. In the drab kitchen it gleamed and shone metallically with the magical quality of an Aladdin's lamp. My uncles manipulated this contraption with the skill of engineers, extracting from its complicated depths endless glasses of strong tea. I never ceased to gaze in wonder at the samovar, which, it was said, was the only valuable heirloom rescued from the old country, although how they managed to transport this ponderous object is anybody's guess. At a rickety table decently covered by a clean oilcloth they sat for hours with sugar cubes between their teeth, sipping the strong brew from tall tumblers.

I could not have been more than five years old at the time of the only visit there that I clearly remember. Dressed in a white sailor suit with black booties, I caused a minor sensation among the passengers on the streetcar. They kept exclaiming, "What a beautiful child!" to the great satisfaction of my mother, who doted on me on Sundays. For my part I was intrigued by the clanging foot bell.

When we arrived my three uncles, all muscular teenagers, tossed me high in the air, to my shrieks of delight, and whirled me around in their arms until I was dizzy. My mother scolded them, snatched me away, and led me to a dark, gloomy room where, in the shadows, stiff and immobile in a Morris chair (with a shiny black button on top of the right arm that, when pressed, set the chair into a reclining position), an old woman sat upright, both hands held straight out in front of her, tightly clenched over the head of a walking stick. Her white unkempt hair fell bedraggled around her shoulders and she kept dully sucking her long yellow teeth with large gaps between them. Two prominent moles or wens, one on her left cheek and another on her chin, sprouted ugly gray hairs, which she absently fingered. She resembled every witch, minus the conical hat, that I had ever seen in storybooks, and I was afraid.

For quite a long time, her cold blue eyes icily piercing mine, she sat in glum silence. Longing to return to the kitchen with my boisterous uncles, I began to fidget and perhaps to fret. Laboriously, as if in pain, and breathing heavily, my grandmother raised the cane over her head and brandished it as if to strike me.

"*Out!*" she screeched in a high asthmatic voice. "Get him out of my sight! I never want to see the little bastard again!"

Screaming with terror, I was hurried away by my mother. Not long afterwards, at the age of fifty-two, my grandmother choked to death one night during an asthma attack, her years in America consumed by bitterness and despair.

I missed the fun of the roaring twenties and got stuck in my teens with the moaning thirties, a decade of dullness and discontent. It was a time haunted by the knowledge that another world war was inevitable; the Depression emphasized the futility of false hope. This was best characterized by two literary works that caught the corpselike tone and spirit of the times: T. S. Eliot's *Waste Land* (a long funereal coverup of homosexual angst) and Ernest Hemingway's *Sun Also Rises,* more or less about impotence, nostalgia for balls. Both of these masterpieces made sex, by implication, appear to be a nasty illness. Growing up in this arid atmosphere, I lived with a secret sexual longing that went unappeased until I was liberated by a college professor. I also adopted the prevailing faith of the era: that we would all be reborn in communism, a faith that promised an end to social injustice, war, racism, and inequality of the sexes. Without this ideal we faced boredom and masturbation. With it we masturbated to fantasies of the Noble Worker.

My mother did not appreciate my distinguished standing in the radical misfit community. Not being an intellectual, she remained unmoved by utopian ideals. To her it was all pie in the sky. She was a dead loss to my Marxist friends, whom she considered lazy bums.

But it wasn't communism or religion, finally, that made a difference—I had given up both by my early twenties. It was my personal relationships at college that changed my life. One day in 1937, a blond radiance called Chester Kallman illuminated the doorway of the Brooklyn College *Observer,* our literary magazine. I was editor-in-chief and he was a freshman of sixteen. Since I was a senior and a celebrity, he was too awed to speak. Months passed before I discovered that he was a brilliant conversationalist. His father once told me that he had never forced his son to study or read, but from the time the boy was four years old, Dr. Kallman left books and classical records around the house where he could see them. He would push them toward him inconspicuously, and out of natural curiosity, for Dr. Kallman had already taught him to read, Chester would go through the books and play the records. Thus began his omnivorous reading habits and insatiable lust for opera. This was the kind of father I had dreamed about. By the time Chester was six he was a prodigy.

When Igor Stravinsky met Dr. Kallman he asked in wonder, "How does one get a son like Chester?" The answer, I thought, should have been obvious. "You must first get a father like Dr. Kallman."

Even Mozart's father was not as suited as Dr. Kallman for the job of rearing a genius, for Leopold Mozart was a high-strung, disappointed man who viewed life pessimistically and attributed the worst motives to other people. Dr. Kallman, on the other hand, was cheerful, urbane, a marvelous raconteur. He enjoyed people and had a special gift of making them feel comfortable. His professional bedside manner extended well beyond the dentist's chair. His sympathetic attitude embraced just about everyone except his former wives. He loved wine, women, classical music, and literature, and knew a good deal about each (except, perhaps, women). Of all the parents I have ever known, if I had had the choice I would have chosen him as my father. I fell in love with both father and son.

3

Daddy

On the floor with the bright red fire engine that the strange man brought I grow uneasy. Looking up, in the dim light of the bare bulb suspended from the ceiling I can make out vague movements from beneath the blankets. I hear the man grunt, my mother whimper. I return to my toys thinking, That man is hurting my mother. A thickness and heaviness in my chest grows unbearable. Sobs rise in my throat. I chug the fire engine furiously across the worn linoleum.

One day he arrives and orders me to my feet.

"From now on," he commands, "call me Daddy!"

I look up at a fat cigar under a small black moustache and two hard black eyes, unsmiling, that fasten on me like buttons. "No, you're not my daddy."

I shake my head obstinately, clutching my toy soldiers and the green gas mask that Uncle Dave brought from the war.

"I *am* your daddy. Call me Daddy from now on!"

I refuse with clenched teeth. Bending down, he seizes me roughly—I can smell the stench of his cigar—and hisses, "Listen, you little bastard! Stand up when I talk to you! Call me Daddy, you hear?" I yell as loud as I can, *"No!"*

A stinging blow lands across my cheek. I howl with pain. The word *daddy* sticks in my throat like a bone.

A bespectacled clerk behind a teller's window at the courthouse made up the wedding ceremony. They didn't even have to say "I do." Merely a cut-and-dried signing of forms. In a yellowed photograph taken after their two-dollar notarized marriage (at which I was present), the three of us are on the beach in striped convict beachwear. Dark and handsome (he was only twenty-three), with slick black vaselined hair parted in the middle and a pencil-line moustache, Maxwell has one arm around my mother's waist. A heavily made-up flapper with vacant kewpie-doll features, blond hair, and thick legs, she stares vapidly into space. She was twenty-nine. In old age she cut his image out of the picture although he was dead and gone. Then she cut out her image. Only mine remains, a tiny tot with pail and shovel.

A mysterious photograph antedates that one: young doughboy with Teutonic features and short legs in khaki, seated beside a wistful Mary Pickford type, both in profile. This faded sepia postcard from World War I has an aura of innocence, of idyllic Rupert Brooke romanticism, untouched by bitterness. You can almost hear, on a raspy phonograph record, the strains of "Over There." The doughboy's resemblance to me is startling—head, ears, nose, eyes. It's my *father!*

"It's just an old postcard," says my mother with annoyance.

She will never grant others the satisfaction of knowing that they have hurt her feelings, that they have gained power over her. She will never admit that she suffers from wounded pride.

Near the sideshows and hot dog stands my mother rips his shirt with long lacquered nails, raking his shoulder and arm till they spurt blood. She accuses him of looking at a woman. Angrily he denies it. People stare. A calliope plays sentimental tunes. An hour later we're gliding through the Tunnel of Love in a gondola to *Tales from the Vienna Woods.* . . .

On the boardwalk we stroll past Steeplechase in the sweltering heat. Among thousands of striped Mack Sennett bathers we're jammed together on the blinding beach like one interminable body with countless arms, legs, faces, genitals—parts of a single organism. We devour red-glazed jelly apples and pink-blue clouds of cotton candy. Ices and soda pop are also sold by peddlers sweating on the sand. At Nathan's we buy hot dogs with mustard for a nickel. The air reeks of popcorn, peanuts, and chewing gum.

At night on teeming Surf Avenue we nosh salted pretzels and gulp root beer, sweating profusely as we watch the outdoor silent pictures at Feltman's. In inclement weather we sit indoors for the movies. The crowds are restless, the salt air heavy with seaweed, dead fish, tar, and the sea. The lights of Luna Park glitter like chains of diamonds . . . and the band plays on. . . .

These early scenes remain in my memory with the staccato speed and stiff awkward movements of silent flicker films . . . with blanks in between the scenes interrupting the flow when the film breaks and stops, leaving much of the story unfinished.

By the time my mother realized that she had made another fatal mistake it was too late. All her life she had fought a losing battle for self-respect. If she could not get a divorce without feeling disreputable, she could at least make life miserable for her hapless husband. Her second disappointment in the choice of a mate turned her into a shrew.

Max conned everyone. A bookkeeper and salesman with the gift of gab, in the end he wasn't even a good con man. Beneath the glib tongue lay a petty clerk without ambition. My mother never let him forget it. He had deceived her about his capabilities as a wage earner, handed her a line about his college degree in business. He had played on her intense longing for security, but we were always broke. Her resentment at being trapped never diminished.

We moved in and out of filthy holes that were all alike: a naked light bulb suspended from a cobwebbed ceiling, grimy walls, peeling wallpaper, iron bedsteads with creaky springs;

there'd always be a humpbacked straw mattress, rickety chairs and tables, the stench of stale piss, sweat, tobacco, and vomit. When the light went on cockroaches raced frantically under the icebox and into the walls. I can still smell the nauseating stench of mashed bedbugs, like bitter almond. Several times a night, drunk with sleep, we got up to destroy the fat black insects gorged on our blood. My mother squirted bug killer from an oilcan into the bedsprings—kerosene in those days—which stank as bad as the bugs. I didn't know which was worse. For the roaches we'd smear a whitish paste (probably a phosphorous compound) on slices of potato, which gave off a vile, nasty odor. I think this was also used as rat poison. My mother disinfected everything. We were always neat and clean but smelled like a morgue. Owing rent, we'd sneak out at night clutching a cardboard suitcase or two, hysterically shushing each other.

In summer mosquitoes would dive-bomb with a whining hum, striking for blood side by side with their comrades in arms, the bloodsucking bedbugs. The acrid odor of citronella, which my mother rubbed all over my body, mingled with the stench of kerosene. Although it disgusted me, it never seemed to repel the insects. On the contrary, they thrived on it. They attacked with increased ferocity. After an infernal night I'd wake in the morning soaked in sweat, piss, blood, tears, citronella, and kerosene. As an added torment the tap would drip into a green-stained washbasin. Plink, plank, plunk. There'd be violent eruptions, a volcanic belching of putrid matter from viscous depths, all in a ninety-five- or hundred-degree heat wave!

But in the morning my mother would hurry me off to the ocean front "to get a good spot," before the crowds came. She was right—if you didn't get there early you'd have to lie on top of somebody else, and I was not yet interested in that. She would spread white towels on the sand and inhale and exhale with loud sniffs and snorts. "AAAAhhhh! MMMMmmmm! Breathe! It's *good* for you! Clears up the sinus! The salt air takes away all sickness! Mmmmaaaahhhh, it's better than any medicine!" She believed in saltwater and deep breathing as fervently as others believe in God or Gold. She snuffed up handfuls of brine to cure all ills. Perhaps she was right. In those simpler times before pollution, pure seawater must have produced miraculous results. And it was free. The sea, sun, sand, and air bathed away some of the emotional stress of those godawful childhood years.

4

Scranton

U ncle Ed was the most colorless guy I'd ever seen. Even at the age of eight I regarded him as a dumb small-town hick with a wooden, faintly malevolent expression. Maybe he felt inferior to my aunt—he had every reason to. In later years, knowing how much they worshiped each other, I realized that theirs was another case of blind love, which I, for one, couldn't argue with, especially since I'd often awake with a hangover beside some bed partner and groan, "What on earth am I doing with *this*?" He or she probably felt the same way.

A small man in every sense, Uncle Ed smoked expensive cigars and drank bootleg whiskey. The nephew of an ex-mayor of Scranton, he belonged to a conservative German family with pots of money. He said little, drank much, and was a mystery to me, but whenever he opened his mouth I liked him less. When my aunt was out of earshot he'd lean toward me, his black eyes narrowing to slits, his breath reeking of booze, and mutter in a sly, stealthy way, "How's the little Jew-boy, huh?"

At dinner parties or during cocktail hour, in the presence of guests he'd tug at my earlobe and, in his flat, lifeless voice, speaking so that everyone could hear, he would drawl, "We're serving ham sandwiches, Harold. It's not poison, y'know. You won't croak if you eat ham." Then slyly winking at his friends, he'd snicker. His friends cackled without enthusiasm while I munched a ham sandwich that tasted like turds in my dry mouth.

Much worse than my uncle's provincial anti-Semitism (being was a disease, he believed, curable only by conversion) was my first anti-Semitic experience on the street. During an argument over a ball game with another boy, he suddenly screwed up his features and sneered maliciously, "Aw, yer a dirty Jew, anyways."

Flabbergasted, I retorted, "I am *not!*" "You are, too! You killed our God!"

Stung by this unfair accusation, I shouted, "Liar! I did *not!*" "You did, too! My mama told me you did!" "I didn't! You're a dirty liar!" "You're a dirty Jew!" Blind with rage, I bashed him in the nose and ran home in tears.

"Dirty bastards!" said my mother when I told her what happened. "Stay away from that lousy kid. God will punish him!"

"But, Mama, Uncle Ed says nasty things about Jews, too."

"Ed is a dumb klutz," she said disdainfully.

I asked my mother why my aunt went to church, not revealing that she baptized me. My mother began to shout. She always shouted when she didn't know the answers. "Uncle George and Mike and Lou—your own brothers—*they're* Christians," I persisted. "Like Aunt Eva. And my cousins wear crosses! Why are *we* dirty Jews?"

"God in heaven, that kid will drive me nuts!"

"Mama, if our relatives are Christians, how can they hate us?"

"Hah! What do you know?" She told me that Uncle Ed was sneaky and his family thought they were too good for us.

"Because we're Jews, Ma? And we're poor?" Again I burst into tears. *"I don't wanna be a Jew!"* I yelled.

My mother screamed, *"Look what you made me do! On account of you I cut my finger!"*

I was a closet Christian, a closet Jew, and later a closet queer.

Strange, wonderful, and awful things happened in Scranton. One day as I sat in the old wooden rocker on the front porch, like all the frame porches on the block, gray and weatherbeaten, it rained on one side of the street but not the other. In third grade Mrs. Carpenter read aloud Walt Whitman's "O Captain! My Captain!" I never knew that words could have such power. Then one morning I had a different experience. Seated at the desk in front of me was a black boy. Curious about his cropped woolly hair, I ran my fingers experimentally over his head. When he leaned back sensually and turned with a sweet smile, his soft brown eyes veiled and smoky with pleasure, an ecstatic feeling swept through me. I'd had no idea that he would respond with such a tender, loving look. We began to play together after class, but that soon came to an end when the other children taunted us. They called him nigger and me nigger lover. We gradually drifted apart, but I couldn't stop thinking about him.

The only other black person I knew was Aunt Eva's cleaning woman, Cindy. She was coal-black, quiet, and gentle. I had learned at school that Abraham Lincoln freed the slaves and wondered what Cindy would do if she saw a picture of Lincoln. Somehow I became convinced that she would fall to her knees and worship him. At that time boys circulated and traded little picture cards of baseball players, movie stars, and presidents. I got hold of a card with a picture of Lincoln and one day, while Cindy was cleaning the kitchen, I propped it up against a salt shaker on the table, hoping to see her fall down and cry with joy. She must have been an old woman, for she shuffled around awhile without noticing it. I held my breath when, finally, she came over, looked at the card, and said sharply, "Boy, get that off the table now! Cancha see I'm tryin' to clean up?" I remember my keen disappointment as I timidly responded, "Yes, ma'am," and removed the card.

One night I woke up hearing loud voices. I crept out of bed and hid behind the kitchen door.

"That's where you belong," my mother was saying angrily, "in jail. You bring only bad luck. I'll take the kid and leave."

Then, in a choked voice, Max said, "Call Uncle Willie. . . . I'm afraid—oh, he's *gotta* help— If he don't—"

More choking sounds, scraping of chairs. I padded noiselessly back to bed, frightened but elated. The bully had bitten the dust!

The following day my mother brought me to Aunt Eva's. Pressed against the wall near the parlor I learned that Max was in jail. He had gambled a thousand dollars of the company's money, a vast sum in those days. Having broken his bond, he could never be a salesman again. I thought of all the Juicy Fruit chewing gum I wouldn't be getting anymore. I thought of the big thick Havana cigars in colorful cigar boxes with fancy labels from Cuba. These were the products he talked retail store owners into buying, then squandered his commissions at cards. At some point he had bought a humidor of Russian cherry wood to keep his cigars fresh. This handsome piece of handicraft, remarkably enough, still remains in my possession, the only thing retained from childhood. After six decades, the aroma is stronger than ever, a rich, pungent odor of cherry and tobacco aged in the warm claret-colored interior of the oval box. It is hand-carved and looks like shiny mahogany. It was probably old when my stepfather bought it. In faded letters on the bottom you can barely make out the print: MADE IN RUSSIA. When I remove the knobbed lid and sniff the perfume of this heirloom my childhood emerges like a gigantic genie and confronts me, not with three wishes but Hydra-headed memories, some of which I still battle with and others of which I befriend. Held up to the light the interior shimmers with the silken sheen of dark rose, the texture of a wine-colored dove's wing. My mother kept it through the years. At her death it passed to me.

Uncle Willie swept into town from New York in his cream-colored Pierce-Arrow, paid the bail, gave my stepfather money and stern advice, growled that his delinquent nephew ought to get the hell out of this damn hick town and return to the City, where he himself would set him up with a good bookkeeping job, if Max promised to quit gambling and get some sense. He patted me on the head with hairy, pudgy fingers adorned with diamonds set in gold. "The boy deserves better, Max," he bellowed. "I'm gonna kidnap him!"

Max swore that he would go straight. He solemnly swore to quit gambling forever. "Uncle Willie," he said earnestly, "I mean it. I've learned my lesson."

Uncle Willie grunted approval but was not taken in. Short and fat, with blue jowls and sparkling blue eyes and a deep authoritative voice, he was a man of the world and probably knew that Max was incorrigible. Despite his gruffness he was kind and generous. Before whirling off to his real estate empire in New York he treated us to dinner at an expensive restaurant, waving bejeweled fingers under the noses of respectful waiters, who cast less reverent glances at Uncle Willie's poor relations. All charges were dropped when Uncle Willie reimbursed the company for the embezzled funds.

5

A Born Writer

Good as his word, Uncle Willie, procured a prestigious job for his ne'er-do-well nephew as an accountant at the legendary Waldorf-Astoria Hotel. Max took to wearing rimless pince-nez spectacles, looking "distinguished." We moved into middle-class respectability in Bensonhurst,

Brooklyn. The red brick apartment house in the Bay Ridge section, at 1770 Seventy-fifth Street near Eighteenth Avenue (now Bay Ridge Parkway), had an incinerator into which we dumped garbage down a chute from the fourth floor, and a "super" who was in charge. We enjoyed all the comforts of petit bourgeois life. Happiness was a job and a garbage disposal.

On Max's steel Underwood I hunted and pecked stories and poems as my mother sat at the window, chin propped in one hand, keeping watch. When she hissed, "He's coming!" I'd pull out the sheet and replace the cover with a racing heart. Thus from the beginning my career was that of an underground writer.

One day an older boy with blue eyes, wavy blond hair, and tortoiseshell glasses offered me some candy. He had acne but kept nibbling Hershey bars and Baby Ruths and offering me bites of his candy bars. He was seventeen and attended high school. One thing I didn't like about "Milton": he'd bend down and stick his tongue in my mouth. I'd secretly wipe my mouth on my sleeve. Otherwise I liked him. He lent me books and talked about writing. I showed him my poems and an adventure story.

"You must read this at our writers' club!" he exclaimed. So at New Utrecht High School I had my first success. Mr. Tarr, the English teacher who presided over the club, told the students I was a born writer: "This is how to write," he said, "simply and naturally."

Milton began teaching me French, which I had heard in Montauk, where I'd spend a few weeks every summer with my Uncle Mike and his French-Canadian wife, Aunt Mary, and cousin Georgie. The first French sentence I heard was *Le mort ne peût pas parler [sic]*. Aunt Mary's mother, a fat jolly woman, burst into laughter when I said it. They spoke patois. Whenever I asked them to teach me French they burst out laughing. Illiterate fisherfolk from Nova Scotia, they spoke English oddly. "He's some cute," they'd say. "Ain't he some cute?"

At four in the morning I went on fishing trips with Mr. Pitts, Mary's father, a dark wiry little man who made the rounds of his lobster pots. In the cold morning I watched the buoys bobbing in the sea as the men hauled in nets full of lobsters, crabs, and fish. The first time out I got seasick from the smell of motor fumes and the rocking of the little skiff, but after that I got my sea legs and never grew seasick again. I jumped around banging lobsters on the head with a stick until old Mr. Pitts caught me.

"Hey, Harold, whatcha doin'? Dat's some dumb! Dey gotta stay alive. Stop dat!"

He tossed me a fish and told me to scratch its belly. The fish expanded like a balloon. The men laughed at my dumbfounded expression. "Dat's a blowfish, Harold," explained Mr. Pitts. He was a quiet kindly man with a corncob pipe that was part of his face, like Popeye, whom he resembled. When the blowfish blew up into a great ball with a gleaming iridescent belly, I stabbed it with a spike and listened to the hiss as it deflated and became an uninteresting dead fish. I executed several of these clownish creatures before Mr. Pitts forbade me to play with this species, too. The fishing smack bobbed crazily and the crabs zigzagged around on deck or slithered in buckets of water. I amused myself by poking a stick at their claws and watching the big nippers close over it.

Evening meals consisted of fresh seafood and white French bread. Once Mrs. Pitts, shelling a lobster for me, extracted a strange object from its depths and held it up for my inspection.

"What does it look like, Harold?" she asked, laughing at my perplexity. "It's the Virgin Mary. *La Sainte Vierge.*"

The Virgin Mary inside a lobster? The red shell-like substance, as far as I could see, bore no resemblance to the holy lady on the bedroom wall.

Every morning Uncle Vitus, Mary's brother, would come into the kitchen wearing a hairnet. Tall and bony, with long horse teeth and a gummy smile (a family trait), he had a job as a waiter in New York. He would spend hours before a small mirror over the sink grooming his thick wavy black hair with gobs of sweet-smelling grease and lotions. His movements were effeminate. He was unmarried and showed up on weekends. After a few weeks in Montauk I'd return to Brooklyn, tanned and happy, looking forward to next summer.

Max reverted to his old ways as the stock-market crash of 1929, followed by the Great Depression of the thirties, descended on us. As bankers and industrialists hurled themselves from skyscraper windows, we returned to the squalor from which we came.

My childhood also ended dramatically. My mother, who was

a very jealous woman, constantly reproached Max for infidelity, though there was never any evidence of it. With a cold compress on her forehead, she shuffled around in a pair of cast-off men's sneakers refusing to speak to him, creating a deadly pall of silence. She'd relay communiqués through me while he sat there. "Tell him the chicken soup is ready," she'd rasp; then she'd add, "I hope he chokes."

Max would escape to his card games, but if he returned very late a fight would break out, her jealousy and suspicion at fever pitch. A jealous wife or lover can conjure up some very obscene images, at the same time regarding them as filthy and disgusting. She never said the *f*-word in her life. She was respectable and inhibited, and perhaps she feared that her husband sought more satisfying women. In retrospect, I'm sure my mother was frigid. She was devoured by jealousy, no doubt feeling inadequate for his needs. He was a gross, powerfully built man, short and very masculine. As usual, she tried to make him feel guilty and ashamed, her defense against powerlessness.

"He thinks I don't know he's got a skirt on the sly."

"She's nuts. She belongs in the crazy house."

"Dirty liar! I shoulda let him rot in jail! Filthy pimp."

"Aw, shut up for a change. Nag, nag, nag!"

"Drop dead, you louse! Good-for-nothing!"

The pattern was always the same, ranting, nagging, squabbling.

One night their voices grew so loud that the other tenants banged against walls and radiators, floors and steam pipes, threatening to call the police. Max raised a milk bottle to his lips in defiance of her household rule that this was reserved for me, to grow up healthy and strong (one quart twice a week).

"The last milk for the kid!" my mother screamed. She was like a tigress protecting her cub. Max responded spitefully, "You've spoiled him! He's a sissy!" He'd always taunted, teased, and belittled me, calling me a sissy, though it's hard to imagine how I could have been spoiled by squalor, malnutrition, and ridicule. It certainly spoiled the milk (I'm still allergic).

Suddenly my mother sprang and grabbed for the bottle; twisting his body slightly, Max swung and hit her in the mouth. She fell into a chair, her lip oozing blood, and began to cry. Something snapped in me. I loved my mother very much. I seized a bread knife, jumped on the bed, and clutched him by the throat. I stuck the blade against his paunch, tightened my grip, and held on like a pit bull. His face turned ghastly purple.

"I'll kill you, you sonofabitch!" I yelled hysterically. "If you ever touch her again I swear I'll kill you!" Half choked with rage and sobs, I tightened my grip. When I finally let go my fingers were stiff and numb, my teeth chattering like an ape's. I dropped to the bed, trembling all over. Max slumped into a chair and began to shrink before my eyes. Dimly I realized that I had turned the tables, shifted the balance of power. Still frightened but ready to put up a fight if necessary, I understood my newfound strength. Force had to be met with force. To prove that I was not a sissy I had become a giant-killer. I also saw with amazement that Max was a coward. As my mother used to taunt him scornfully, he was "brave only with women and children." I had struck my first blow against tyranny. I was thirteen.

Home was the most violent place I knew. Violence hung in the air, in the ominous silence. Once we lived in Harlem on 119th Street near Amsterdam Avenue, before the blacks crossed the color line at 125th Street. At the age of eleven I watched street gangs, boys from about ten to thirteen, battle with broken bottles, baseball bats, shivs, and razor blades. There was plenty of blood and guts. I was scared, but not half as scared as I felt at home. On the street I could defend myself. The worst blow I ever received was when a girl bashed me in the nose. Girls were even tougher than boys. At home I nurtured fantasies of murder, the kind you now see in animated cartoons, of kids pitted against monstrously cruel adults, destroying them. I cannot watch documentaries on child or wife abuse without identifying with the victims, without growing angry and tense.

When I was six I knew what it was like to fear for my life. Once my stepfather threw me across the beach like a ball, as hard as he could. I fell on my face, with sand in my nostrils, eyes, and mouth; I nearly choked to death. He watched coldly; he didn't care. Another time, he flung a corncob across the room at me with such force that when it landed in the pit of my stomach I threw up, unable to stop retching for half an hour. I was so bruised and battered I was afraid to talk. I wasn't *allowed* to talk in his presence. Punishment was brutal and swift. There was no appeal. So when I turned against Max he knew it was with murder in my heart. He was a lazy slob but not stupid. Never again did he lay a finger on me or my mother. When I learned that he had died of a coronary, I felt a rush of joy. I felt free. I was twenty-six and hadn't seen him in years, but it was as if a crushing weight had been lifted from my shoulders. For the rest of my life I could never control my rage at brutality against women and children, or against any living creature.

A friend once said to me, "The worst thing you can do to a child is to teach him fear and hate." Max taught me both, but later this became a feeling of commiseration. I identified with the suffering of others. Before I left home my mother warned, "You're too soft-hearted, too trusting. People will take advantage of you."

She was right. I wasn't well equipped to face the world.

6

Puberty

The bathroom window on the third floor of the apartment block overlooks a men's open-air shower. It has nothing to do with the house; it belongs to some beach concessionaire renting lockers, and my aunt happens to live next door. Amazingly, men shower in the nude *en plein air,* visible to whoever wishes to peep from apartment windows. Mostly old men with paunches and bald heads use the showers, but one afternoon the picture alters. As usual I am in the bathroom "abusing" myself. I peek through the bathroom window, parting the white chintz curtains. A gang of Italian youths, stark naked, prances on the sandy wooden boards, their bodies glistening in the sun. Under the cold showers they shout Italo obscenities, flicking wet towels on bare butts. *Va fongool!* My heart pounds wildly. I have an impulse to hide, but I'm rooted to the spot. Suddenly one looks up, his penis jutting in a long arc from his body. His streaming wet hair, dazzling smile, and hard belly ribbed with muscles hypnotize me. He can't be more than sixteen.

He catches my eye. With the flat of his palm he slaps his friend's glistening ass and leaps away when the other makes a dive at his balls. Their friends noisily join in. The one I've picked steals glances at me. I'm spotted as they follow his gaze and let out a whoop. My cheeks turn crimson. They wolf-whistle, horse around on wet wooden boards, nod, and make obscene gestures. It hits me suddenly: *They think I'm a girl!* At this thought another little thrill runs through me. I shudder. I'm only thirteen, my hair is thick and glossy, my pale skin velvet as peach fuzz. My lips tingle and burn. A flash bulb goes off in my groin, I go limp, and their voices fade into the surf.

A pale, bespectacled creature with a long razor nose and pinched features, his eyes gimlet through us as he nervously licks his lips, a snake's tongue probing the air for prey. We nickname him Mr. Slimeheart—our freshman biology teacher at Lincoln High. Although it's a coed class, he lectures on sex. You can hear a pin drop. Our heads are bent as if scribbling notes. I'm drawing male genitals, big, ripe, and hard. Now and then I glance at the illustrated colored chart pulled open on the blackboard. It shows a cross-section of a nude man and woman, with veins, arteries, guts, heads, all cut in half, half-assed, half-brained, half-sexed. Not very sexy, even for horny teenagers.

"In this cross-section of the male reproductive organs"—he indicates them with a pointer—"you will notice the fleshy protuberance known as the *glans penis*. Primarily a mucous membrane, it is extremely sensitive to touch, like the nerves of the mouth or anus. Notice from its bulletlike shape that nature intended it for penetration. Indeed, the terms *penis* and *penetration*, both from Latin roots (no pun intended, heh heh), are similar. Penis, tail, is made for piercing, and *penetrate* derives from the Latin verb *penetrare*, to enter forcibly, to pierce. The penis stretches from a few inches to, uh, fantastic proportions when erect, due to a rush of blood into the virile member. When penetrating the female sex organ, called the vagina, it reaches a state of acute excitation until a sudden ejaculation of sperm, or semen, a sticky white fluid . . ."

Out of the corner of my eye I can see my classmates squirming in their seats. A big foul-mouthed tough called Brodsky is stroking himself, sneaking meaningful looks in my direction. My heart races as Slimeheart's voice, undeterred by the sensational effect his words are producing, drones relentlessly on.

"'The testicles contain the spermatozoa . . . in a wrinkled hairy sac called the scrotum, which, like the glans, is *very* sensitive . . . producing instant sensations of exquisite pleasure. . . . The vagina is composed of a pair of fleshy lips perfectly adapted by nature to receive the penis, which is arrow-shaped, thus enabling it to force entry into *any* aperture—I mean, ahem, into the *female* pudenda, of course, heh heh. . . . A flow of lubricating juices indicates her readiness to receive the male organ. . . .'"

Tensing and stretching his thighs, Brodsky mutters hoarsely, "Hey, Harold, yer lips are white. No kiddin'. It's some sticky white stuff runnin' down yer chin." I touch my mouth, unaware of the meaning. He grins. "Cancha feel it? Lick yer lips—yeah, that's it. Don't show yer teeth! Good! Now open wider—yeah, that's it. No teeth!" He strokes himself faster, leans back (we're in the last row), and with a sharp intake of breath hisses, "You'd be some cocksucker, Harold!" I blush to the roots of my hair. At the sound of the bell we spring to our feet, gather our books, and race for the door. As I near the exit Slimeheart's voice rings out, "Harold, would you please stay a moment?"

He has witnessed a performance, he says, that I gave in the auditorium before some five hundred pupils, parents, and teachers. I hammed, mugged, and ad-libbed for an hour, keeping the audience in stitches. But in class, he says, I'm morose, silent, inhibited. "Your skill on the stage is almost professional. You have energy, inventiveness, talent. I've also read your poems and stories in the *Lincoln Log*. So what's your problem?"

I'm covering up my problem with strapped schoolbooks. It's a *big* problem for a kid.

"In class," he says, "you're introverted. On the stage you're an extrovert—the elements of a split personality. I'd like to help . . . if you want to talk about it."

I keep my eyes fixed on my shoes.

Slimeheart sighs. "Perhaps, Harold, you need"—his voice lowers and in soft, confiding tones he says—"a friend to lend a helping hand."

I watch with horror as a hairy claw grazes my arm. "Uh, excuse me, sir, I have to go to the boys' room." I wriggle from his grasp and flee down the hall. Yes, I need help. But not from waxy-faced Mr. Slimeheart.

7

My Life and Loves

When I was fourteen we lived in an attic. Bobby, the boy next door, lived in a rambling house with a baby grand and a library. He played George Gershwin on the piano and read all the books. His father was at work and his mother was dead. The boys I knew were my age, middle-class, and Jewish; they all lived in their own homes except me. We played handball, touch football, and basketball and stripped in the locker room of our high school gym. The stale smell of socks, feet, sneakers, jockstraps, and sweat both repelled and excited me. I found this confusing—how could they do both? I fell madly in love with Bobby and a tall pale boy called Jackie, whose gleaming honey-brown hair, combed flat, and sweet baby face with cute snub nose and cherry-red lips tantalized me. Once as we self-consciously hurried to change, one of the boys cried, "Hey, guys, look at Jackie! He's got a hard-on! He's thinking of a girl!" But Jackie had been staring at me; he blushed as they neighed and guffawed. (Flashback: Jackie in bed with a cold, the sheet sticking straight up between his legs while we jabber about sports, pretending not to notice anything unusual.)

In the garage behind Bobby's house we convened one spring afternoon with the scent of honeysuckle and hedges in the air. Our initiation into the mysteries as revealed by Frank Harris in *My Life and Loves* began there—six of us huddled together like outlaws with hot sweaty hands pawing a "dirty" book. There were no illustrations, but the words produced a frenzy of lust. Never before had we read phrases like "I spilled my seed into her" and "she greedily gulped it down." It sent shock waves through each boy. In cracked, wavering voices, some just beginning to change, breaking from deep bass notes to a reedy soprano squawk, we took turns reading aloud. I remember the panting exhalations, slightly sour, the moist lips and dewy eyes, the faintly rancid odor of armpits, and the musky scent of hair. We squirmed and fidgeted in tight summer pants, sweat streaming down faces and bellies, soaking shirts. Hands and voices shook. I kept ogling Jackie and Bobby and a sturdy athletic blond called Georgie, the most manly and handsome of all, who had hairy legs.

That night, unable to sleep, I gazed at the stars through the attic window. Boundless space. Infinity. My mind boggled. *Who am I? Why am I here? Where am I going?* As I stood stargazing, I began to rise and soar like a comet, speeding out of this world toward the astral bodies, beyond space and time. A circle of light engulfed me as I floated in some fifth dimension, in a tide of faces, arms, legs, genitals—a sea of human bodies—thousands, maybe millions, swirling around in whirlpools. Then, as I had once done under ether, I suffocated, losing consciousness. So this was death! But almost at once I lived again—a new life— feeling ecstatic. Again I was standing in the attic looking at the stars. It was no dream. I'd had an out-of-the-body experience.

Although it did not bring peace or faith in a divine being (I'd had no experience of this), it showed that mind and spirit were not restricted by physical laws. I saw that I contained forces I could not comprehend but that existed within me. I was part angel.

8

Brooklyn College

Before moving in 1937 to its present location in Flatbush, where in appearance at least it became Ivy League, the campus of Brooklyn College, which had opened its doors in 1930, only four years before I matriculated, consisted of five office buildings scattered through downtown Brooklyn: Fulton, Pearl, Joralemon, Willoughby, and Clark. The classrooms, converted offices outfitted with desks and blackboards, were old and run-down, like the buildings. While we obtained a free education, our surroundings reflected the lack of funds during the Depression. We had meager homemade lunches— peanut butter, salami, or cheese sandwiches and half-pint bottles of milk—consumed in vacant classrooms with the din of the street in our ears. College romances were conducted to the clatter of traffic. We made a mad dash through the streets, dodging traffic and pedestrians, to get to the next class within fifteen minutes. Doing this four or five times a day kept you in shape, though it frazzled the nerves. Along with City College in Manhattan, we were said to have higher IQ's (and lower incomes) than any college in the country except Harvard, whose academic standing we rivaled.

If our "campus" consisted of city streets, only a few blocks away lay an area venerable for its literary tradition: Brooklyn Heights. Towering above the waterfront and the Brooklyn Bridge, it faced the skyscrapers of Manhattan on the East River. There in 1855 Walt Whitman hand-set the first edition of *Leaves of Grass* on Cranberry Street; in the 1920s on Columbia Heights Thomas Wolfe wrote *Look Homeward, Angel,* and a few doors away Hart Crane conceived and wrote sections of *The Bridge* (in the same apartment where the engineer John Roebling, some years earlier, had observed from the rear windows the construction of his masterpiece, the Brooklyn Bridge, which inspired Crane). Whitman had lived there as a boy when it was called Clover Hill. Below the bronze plaque to Whitman on the worn brick wall of the diner on Cranberry, which had been a print shop in his day, in the 1930s lean alley cats hissed and fought over scraps in the garbage cans. Walt would have wondered, perhaps, at this sad sight.

Columbia Heights, the street whose brownstone dwellings overlooked the harbor, afforded a sweeping panorama of the East River, the bridge, and the Manhattan skyline. Here lived two English professors of mine. One, a sweet, white-haired old woman, had Hart Crane's old apartment at 110 Columbia Heights. Two years after Crane's suicide I found myself staring out of his windows at the bridge, as he had done. I was seventeen. Had Professor Miner not restrained me I might have floated out in sheer ecstasy, like Crane's gulls, "with inviolate curve." The other professor, David Blake (name changed), lived at number 138. He was to play a major role in my life.

Foghorns moaned from tugboats and ocean liners. Below on South Street lay the warehouses and docks, saturating the air with the pungent aroma of coffee beans—"firmly as coffee grips the taste," wrote Crane in *The Bridge*. Columbia Heights exuded an ethereal aura of the legendary poets. From Montague Terrace I watched the tugs and liners glide by in the distance, "as silent as a mirror is believed," and by night the Manhattan skyline shimmered with a soft illusory glow.

If spirit of place means anything, a case can be made for a literary line of succession that links Whitman, Wolfe, and Crane in a family of rhapsodic, visionary writers established there. I had found my literary place. There was another link, the manly love of comrades (even about the lofty head of Wolfe hovered hushed rumors)—the "adhesiveness" of brotherly love, as Whitman called it. My initiation into this brotherhood began there. I was inducted by David Blake.

9

Queer Professors

In high school I won the four-year gold medal in English and as a lower freshman at college I took first prize in the annual poetry contest, previously won only by upper classmen. For a boy with my background it was considered astonishing. The poem was about my childhood in Scranton; its depiction of the miners, with its imagery drawn from firsthand experience, exerted a powerful appeal on the class-conscious, leftist, Democratic majority of those Depression years. Overnight I found myself the bright young genius of the intellectual set, invited to the homes of prestigious scholars.

One of them, "Armand Reinhart," was our Shakespeare authority; his wife, "Grace Winter," gained best-seller fame as a writer of popular but scholarly books, written as novels, on the Rossettis and pre-Raphaelites. She was a dark, tiny, intense woman, while Reinhart, a leviathan of a man, whose resonant bass voice and flamboyant manner kept the students enthralled, heaped scorn on those who rejected the Communist faith. A less unlikely Stalinist, however, would be hard to find. In mustard corduroy suits with silk foulards beneath many chins, and three or four massive rings on each pudgy hand, which he flourished in sweeping gestures as he bellowed his epigrams, he intimidated his students. He minced about in quick little steps that gave his gargantuan frame the aspect of a gaudy hippopotamus. "I could never keep a straight face when this huge fat man boomed out Ophelia's lines," said Irwin Shaw, our only celebrated literary alumnus. We speculated on their sex life: how did the fat man and his tiny wife *do* it? The answers were spicy and indecent.

One bald little professor with a lisp, convinced that I was the reincarnation of John Keats, would bow in the hall with the greeting "How are you today, John?" He gave me a fine old dress suit. I looked like little Lord Fauntleroy (Keats was my height), but I had no use for it either. Then there was "Dr. Blunder," our American literature specialist. He would forcibly eject with upcurled tongue sharp jets of saliva that accurately hit the light cord in the classroom. "I'll bet none of you can do that!" he'd boast. He also dreamily ogled the freshmen as, darting paranoid glances toward the door, he crooned lasciviously, "All you freshmen have hot pants." We kept our heads lowered over a book. I remember my dismay when he sneered, "Walt Whitman had a high falsetto voice, like all of his kind." Not only blind to Whitman's stature, he felt the need to belittle him.

"Blunder" surprised us all when he married a tanklike middle-aged professor of biology and began to extol the virtues of marriage. Until then he'd had nothing good to say about women. At that time I had written a long poem on reincarnation, based on my out-of-the-body experience, which he gravely asked to borrow; he considered it a unique document. I never saw it again. Not long afterwards "Blunder" put a bullet through his head.

To this day I have no way of knowing what connection, if any, existed between my poem and Blunder's suicide. For all I knew, reading the *Bhagavad Gita* might have produced the same result. Perhaps there had been no relation at all. Although the tragic event disturbed me deeply, from it I learned that music, literature, and art, working with and through the feelings, have effects for which the artist can't be held accountable. At seventeen, while reading the life of Goethe, and discovering that the twenty-five-year-old poet's first novel, *The Sorrows of Werther*, triggered a wave of suicides among the romantic youth of Europe, I felt certain that the power of poetry, even in the grim America of the thirties, had not diminished.

10

Strange Fruit

David Blake was an aesthete with a huge library and a cultivated taste for the arts. Above all, he had the means to indulge his tastes. A member of the social and economic elite, he chose to teach English in a college with no campus, whose student body was predominantly Jewish, Communist, or pinko. An aunt of his once remarked in disgust, "David, how can you associate with all those Jews? They look like monkeys." His reply was typical: "I can't tell them apart from anyone else." "Hmph!" sniffed his aunt. "*I* can!"

At thirty-four he was stony bald with sunken cheeks and a skinny body. His father was governor of a midwestern state and the family had major oil holdings, but David's interest in the plight of the working class was genuine. He was an idealist and an unfailing gentleman, but also a fervent Communist. Though I lacked breeding, was coarse, defensive, and insecure, I was also fiery, imaginative, quick-witted, with a compassionate feeling for the intrinsic worth of human beings. In David Blake I found a courteous, considerate friend and teacher. Incredibly gentle, he was loved by students and professors alike.

If the *Harvard Lampoon* office, the Castle, was "an imposing hovel," the Brooklyn College *Observer* office was a decomposing one. At the cramped, scruffy two-by-four littered with scraps of paper and flakes of plaster from the walls and ceiling, I first presented myself as winner of the poetry competition. That is how we met. David was the faculty adviser of the *Observer*.

He offered me a job cataloging his record collection, but it was really a first-class education in the arts and behavior. I listened to French classical music and sophisticated songs that he played for me, such as Beatrice Lillie's "There Are Fairies at the Bottom of Our Garden," Noël Coward's "Mad Dogs and Englishmen" and "Mad About the Boy," Marlene Dietrich's "Falling in Love Again," and, totally different, Billie Holiday singing "Strange Fruit," which had just then made her famous. With the exception of "Strange Fruit," these were "camp" songs, but if they were meant to seduce me they failed. I was so innocent and dumb I saw no double entendres and enjoyed them for their style and wit.

We often dined at the Hotel St. George on Clark Street and swam in the pool. When he saw me in a swimsuit David remarked, "You wear clothes oddly. You have a fine figure but why do you hide it?" I explained that my mother chose my baggy pants ("lots of room in the seat so they don't tear at the seam") and knee-length double-breasted jackets. Impressed by the old-world elegance of the St. George, I wondered why David spent so much time with me. It never occurred to me that it might be sexual interest. Respectable people, I believed, didn't have such thoughts. A year would elapse before he'd attempt to cure the virginity so dangerous to my health.

In the summer of 1935 I hitched south for a course at Commonwealth College, a rural Marxist school in the Ozark Mountains near Mena, Arkansas. I grew my first tenuous moustache, wore jeans and a ten-gallon Stetson. The teachers commented that I looked like a local hillbilly. Like most young radical intellectuals, anxious to shed the stigma of "city slicker" and participate in the real world of workers and farmers, I was proud of my new look. The Young Worker was the hero, the sex symbol of the era.

At summer's end I hitched north, having arranged to meet David in Ohio and proceed with him back to Brooklyn. When he saw me in my jeans and cowboy hat he was astonished at the transformation. We were to spend the night at the governor's mansion, but reason prevailed. My folksy appearance and lack of social graces taken into account, David decided on a wiser course, made hasty phone calls, and we set out in his little Chevy coupé, named Maxim Gorky, on our homeward journey. I regaled him with my adventures, one of which bears retelling.

On a side road to Dallas one blazing August afternoon, with nothing but cotton fields stretching to the horizon, I stood mopping my brow and wondering if I would die of thirst when, about a hundred yards away, I caught sight of a small ancient white-haired black man emerging from a ramshackle cabin and beginning to fill a bucket from a pump. Heaving a sigh of relief, I ambled over with a greeting and requested a drink of water. He stared vacantly over my head. When I repeated my request he continued to stare uncomprehendingly. "I'd be happy to pay," I said. He shook his head and pointed to a distant house. "Them's white folks across the road a piece," he murmured. "All I want is a drink of water," I said. He shook his head and finally I understood. I was talking to an ex-slave! Jim Crow was very much alive and I'd endanger him by drinking his water.

As I returned parched and desperate to the dusty road, an old model-T Ford with a narrow running board slowly put-putted north in my direction and I hailed it wildly, but it passed me by. It was jam-packed with Negroes, who stared as if I were an apparition. I considered crossing the road to the white residence when the flivver coughed to a halt and chugged in reverse. It stopped and a fat black middle-aged woman called out, "Where y'all goin', boy?" "Dallas," I answered hopefully. "We ain't goin' that far, but you can hop on the runnin' board," she said, eyeing me curiously.

I jumped aboard and held on for dear life, the woman never removing her eyes from me in puzzlement. Finally she blurted out, "Is you a white boy or is you an Eye-talian?" Stunned by her question, I thought for a moment and, as if explaining to a child, answered slowly, "I *am* a white boy and I am *not* an Italian." She continued studying my face with the same puzzled expression. Then, in a challenging tone, she said, "If you is a white boy, let's see yo' hair! Take off yo' hat!" Clinging to the door frame with one hand, with the other I removed the Stetson, leaning carefully away from the frame. The sun shone on my auburn hair, silky and gleaming with coppery tints that I could see in the damp strands over my brow. She gasped and her face brightened into a smile. "Um-mmm, he's *white* as *white* can be!" she exclaimed, then added admiringly, "And gosh, ain't he purty, though!"

"Wait until the Italians discover they're not white," I told David. He shook his head sadly.

That night in a motel cabin in the Appalachians I sat on the double bed watching David shave. When I asked why he did so before going to bed he replied, "Oh, it feels clean and saves me the trouble in the morning. We must be up early." Drunk on Jack Daniel's, my head swam. He turned off the light and I began to doze when I felt a hand on my penis. With a shudder I withdrew to the farthest side of the bed against the wall, drawing my knees up in the fetal position and quaking with terror. My teeth chattered as, chilled to the bone, I clutched at the knot in my gut.

Next morning, continuing our journey, I grew convinced that my drunken imagination had tricked me; the cold, dark night in the cabin seemed distant and unreal. The late August sun was shining, the fields were full of flowers and farm animals. As we passed a herd of cows David told me of a young hitch-hiker he'd picked up on the way to Ohio who kept repeating as he gazed at the cattle, "Cows are nice." We repeated "cows are nice" and "a rose is a rose" for miles.

In Scranton we stopped to visit my Aunt Eva. Still beautiful and gracious, she served tea and biscuits on the front porch and I reminisced about my childhood there. She called David "professor." The conversation lagged and we stayed no longer than an hour. When we left, David kept referring to her as my "Catholic aunt."

We spent our last night together in a motel in Pennsylvania and again I watched him shave as we hit the Jack Daniel's. That night my state of virginity came to an end. And it became clear why he had shaved at night: so that his beard wouldn't scratch.

Afterwards as we lay in the dark, I stammered in little-boy wonder and apprehension, "How long have you been—that way?" "What way, Harold?" "Homo-*sexual*!" "Oh, all my life," said David nonchalantly. Then after a pause: "But I'm *not* homosexual, I'm bisexual." "You mean—you like men *and* women?" "Yes, I've fucked all four sexes." "*Four sexes!*" "Yes. Heterosexual men and women, homosexuals, and lesbians." Pause. "Isn't that—*abnormal*?" "Harold, if you love someone or are attracted to them, it can't be abnormal. It's abnormal *not* to." This man was no sex fiend like Leopold and Loeb. "Then it's not *sick*—or *evil*?" I said anxiously. "No," he replied softly, "it's not criminal, sick, or evil to love someone—or be attracted—even to your own sex. It's natural. It gives me great pleasure to be close to you. I'm very fond of you."

I thoroughly enjoyed the deflowering. My spirit rose with the flesh. Tension ebbed. If I couldn't reciprocate in kind, as I had no wish to, that too was natural. It was a relief for both of us. I remained the *puer eternus,* the object of desire, the loved one. He was an "older man"—thirty-four—and physically unattractive to me. He accepted his role with no visible signs of regret. I was still underage, jailbait—twenty-one was the age of consent.

Next day on the road we praised Maxim, whose dashboard we patted affectionately. "Harold, I don't suppose I have to tell you that I'd like to see more of you from now on," said David. I nodded. "Or that I trust you completely." I nodded again. He laid a hand on my thigh. "You understand that what happens between us is entirely confidential." "I understand," I said. He heaved a sigh of relief.

If I'd been mercenary, I could have profited from our association, but to me this was beneath contempt. Here was this flaming Red poring over the daily stock-market quotations, but when I asked about it, having never read the business pages, all he said was, "Oh, I have shares in Philip Morris and Texaco." All *I* knew about Texaco was the opera program on Saturday (or was it Sunday then?) with Olin Downes as commentator. The only time I ever asked for money—two dollars!—was when I thought I had the clap. I was nineteen and, except for David's occasional blow jobs, very much a virgin. Old Doc "Daly," a stout red-faced man, asked me to bend over and I blushed. "Don't worry, Harold," he said as he inserted a meaty finger into my rectum, "unless I have *both* hands on your shoulders, ha ha!"

As I pulled up my pants he remarked enviously, "With a pecker that thick no wonder you can't leave it alone!" The diagnosis was prostatitis. "It's rare for a boy your age. Sedate that function! No wine, beer, or alcohol," ordered Dr. Daly, eyeing me strangely. The homely young nurse stared with a dreamy look as I paid the two dollars and squirmed with embarrassment. "Oooo," she said, rolling her eyes, "where'd you get those peepers?" It was sweet, corny, suggestive. Nothing explicit. I never even wondered about Dr. Daly when he offered to put me through medical school. Perhaps today I, too, would have had a large practice on Clark Street, opposite the Hotel St. George, a hairy, smelly, dirty old man cooing over fresh young boys. "Now, Tommy, it won't hurt, it's just my finger. What? It feels much bigger? No, no, don't turn around, keep your head down, you might faint! Ahhh, that's better!" Old doctor jokes . . .

11

The Shock of Recognition

D avid Blake had gone off to fight as a machine gunner for the Loyalists in the Spanish Civil War and, unlike so many others less fortunate, survived without a scratch. On his return in 1937 we resumed our liaison, but unable to reciprocate and longing for someone my age, I began to take subway trips to Manhattan and hang around Times Square and Bryant Park. I'd sit in the New York Public Library reading strange works, like the Prophecies of Nostradamus, in which the name Hitler was foretold (anagrammatically) and World War II described four hundred years before it occurred. The great psychic physician saw the future like a Fox Movietone newsreel.

I'd stand in front of the cigar-store Indian on Broadway and Forty-second Street, watching the hustlers go by. They were seedy in those destitute times. My first experience with a boy my age was brief. He was blond, wore soiled dungarees and a denim work shirt. We ended up in a sleazy hotel room on Eighth Avenue, where I finally discovered the joys of homosexuality with another youth. But he was tired and wanted to sleep. I paid a quarter for the room and the same for him, and returned home for a nickel with a lighter step. I was twenty.

In the reading room of the library my eyes constantly wandered, picking out attractive young men who were totally oblivious of my Whitmanic love. Restless, I'd roam around Bryant Park behind the library, with the bronze statue of William Cullen

Bryant green with pigeon shit. There were mostly old men on benches, bums rummaging in garbage containers, and hayseeds from farms and prairies, lost in the big city where they tried to find jobs and ended up hustling. Times Square was overrun by young vagrants and clip artists, but I steered clear of them, frightened by their look of desperation.

One evening I was approached in the dusk by what I took to be a slim beautiful girl wearing slacks. But under the lipstick and eye shadow rang a deep bass voice. We rode the subway uptown, and in an old tenement we entered a pitch-dark room where he grabbed me and kissed me before turning on the light. A flash of lightning blazed from my lips with a sizzling sound; he jumped back as if he'd been shocked. It was static electricity, the kind that comes from touching a metal doorknob. "My God," said the drag queen, "just what I've always wanted—electric youth!" The room lit up with my desire.

Later he said there were lots of boys my age who would like me, but I mustn't look belligerent or scared. Because it was hard for me to relax, I frightened them away by looking straight and uptight. He said I had to overcome my shyness to get what I wanted.

In 1937 Brooklyn College moved to its present permanent site in Flatbush with new colonial red brick buildings whose bare exterior was adorned with ivy. We poked fun at the Ivy League pretensions, but having known only urban squalor, I secretly approved this "bourgeois" touch. Now editor-in-chief of the *Observer*, I had a devoted staff of neurotic editors who noisily convened in the new office with all the nervous energy fueled by our late unlamented quarters. My poetry, articles, and reviews had appeared not only in the *Observer* for nearly four years but also in literary magazines; I was the only student to achieve this distinction.

On a warm Indian summer day in 1937, when Chester Kallman, only sixteen, stood for the first time in the doorway of the *Observer* office, he had just matriculated and was hoping to catch sight of the prominent young poet and editor. In the afternoon light his golden hair gleamed, a chalky pallor accentuated the dark circles of dissipation beneath the hypnotic blue eyes, and his pouting lips were aflame. I had a déjà vu and thought I was dreaming.

Chester lived with his father and grandmother, whom he called "Baba" (Yiddish for *granny*), a swarthy old woman with thick blue lips, heavy features, and spiked white hair like a punk hairdo. She bustled around and stuffed us with bagels and cream cheese in total silence.

In Chester both sexes merged with androgynous appeal: willowy grace combined with a deep, manly voice. Not at all effeminate, just young and blond, he was tall, unathletic, with slightly stooped narrow shoulders, a spinal curvature, and a heart murmur from rheumatic fever in childhood. He disliked all physical exercise except cruising, which developed his calf muscles. He picked his nose with long spatulate fingers, dirt-rimmed, and thoughtfully examined the product—a sure sign of a Brooklyn intellectual. For months he uttered scarcely a word, listening with avid schoolboy interest. Once when I mentioned visiting the homes of professors, he cried with envy, "*How* do you get invited?" Socially naive, he didn't remain that way for long.

We'd visit his father's office at 29 West Fifty-seventh Street just east of Carnegie Hall. Its oak-paneled walls bore modern paintings, one of which was a framed portrait in oils of Chester at the age of ten by the Mexican artist Siqueiros. I can still see the child's huge eyes staring at the world with a pensive, petulant expression, composed but sulky.

Many examples of his composure come to mind. Once, at a literary club we attended, a tall blond boy named Joe Wershba made some lighthearted but slighting remark, whereupon Chester rose with unruffled dignity and in a tone of withering scorn said, "Let's go, Harold. That Joe Wershba is a ruffian." Nobody I knew was capable of such sangfroid. I was even more astounded when Joe (from whom I had expected a sharp rejoinder) reddened and looked sheepish.

Poetry was our passion. We committed vast amounts of it to memory: I could recite great chunks of Chaucer, Shelley, Blake by heart. The contemporaries we most admired were Auden, Spender, Eliot, and Hart Crane, to whose work I introduced Chester, but I failed to convert him to Whitman. Once he offended me by attacking the Good Gay Poet, reacting in much the same manner as had the young Henry James in 1865, with youthful arrogance and supercilious disdain. After reading *Drum-Taps* James concluded in his review, "This volume is an

offense against art." Well, nobody's perfect. But whereas James
in later life recognized his mistake and, after rereading *Leaves of
Grass*, according to a memoir by Edith Wharton, thought Whitman the greatest of American poets and said, "Oh, yes, a great
genius; undoubtedly a very great genius!" Chester never relented. Unwittingly he echoed James's earlier objection to Whitman's "vulgarity."

One afternoon at his father's flat, after I'd rhapsodized
about "Song of Myself" as more meaningful and inspiring (and
better written) than the Bible, Chester made a wry face and imperturbably retorted, "Oh, Harold, Whitman is a bore! He's ver-
bose and suffers from verbal diarrhea. And grandiloquence.
Those endless lists—like a Sears Roebuck catalog! That's not poetry, it's prosaic, tiresome, sentimental verbiage! And that fake
manliness! He's just a big fairy under it all."

One day in the *Observer* office as we were discussing Auden,
without thinking I chirped offhandedly, "Oh, don't worry, you'll
meet him. You'll get to know him well—in fact, intimately." I
shall never forget the look on Chester's face.

"What makes you say that?" he inquired with a fierce scowl.

"I can't explain," I replied defensively. "I know it—as if it
had already happened." His arched brows knitted violently, but I
needn't have apologized. In less than two years it happened. I
had inherited the gift of second sight from my mother.

I was the first to publish Chester in the *Observer* and introduced him to everyone, including a girl called Elsie who became
a lifelong friend of Chester and Auden.

In June 1938 I left home, a step I'd have taken much sooner
had it not been during the Depression. It was like stepping into
quicksand. There were no jobs and I was too proud and naive to
hustle. Before I moved out, in a brief man-to-man, Max said,
with customary subtlety: "Don't stick it into *any* hole. Use a rubber." It was the only confidence he'd ever shared with me. My
mother wept. Overnight I had become a man (I was twenty-one).

I got my B.A., then my WPA—my first job on the Writers'
Project. For five dollars a week I rented a room in Manhattan in
a dilapidated tenement on the northwest corner of Sixth Avenue
at 77 West Fifty-fifth Street. It contained a creaky cast-iron bed
with a lumpy mattress, a rocker, an armoire with a cracked mir-

ror, and a yellow-stained sink. The chain toilet was down the hall. I was used to this.

Chester visited daily, leaving notes in the battered mailbox. We attended the opera, ballet, movies, and bars, ate in cafeterias (Stewart's and Bickford's) and Horn and Hardart's automat on West Fifty-seventh Street—large, impersonal emporiums of mass-produced junk food. Lunch cost twenty-five cents, coffee and subway fare a nickel, beer a dime. Everything was so cheap that I saved on my twenty-two-dollar-a-week salary.

On New Year's Eve 1938, after parties uptown and down, we mingled with the crowds of Times Square at midnight (as we had done the previous year) in a drunken mob scene. Tightly wedged among thousands of youths under the *Times* building, with its revolving electric-bulb headlines, we laughed and bellowed, "*Hap*-py New Year!" and got kissed on the mouth by young sailors and civilians, even in the presence of their girl friends. Every year it was the same. A mass outpouring of erotic energy crashed the same-sex barrier. It was a Dionysian release, a license to love. For a few hours the god of ecstasy reigned. The rest of the year they pretended it didn't exist (if for one moment you stop pretending, you're queer). By no means restricted to Times Square on New Year's Eve, however, it was true of drunken youths in bars, men's rooms, parties, dark corners— wherever alcohol releases censored feelings. With horns blaring, bells ringing, and confetti swirling like multicolored snow in the brilliant lights, those few roaring hours of joyous deliverance from a bleak decade showed human nature at its freest and finest.

At about 4:00 A.M., blind drunk, Chester and I staggered to my room and fell into my bed. That morning, New Year's Day, we became lovers. We awoke in the afternoon with steam knocking in the pipes, then dressed, and watched the snow fall on icy pavements. People straggled in and out of the old Dover Hotel across the street. Shyly Chester confided that with each new boy he picked up he'd groan, "Oh, why aren't you Harold?" Neither of us had been able to break the taboo, to declare ourselves. When I mentioned my feeling of recognition and love at first sight, he confessed he'd had it also. Even as we talked we found it difficult to reveal these closely guarded secrets. The inhibitions against such sentiments were overwhelming. It was the first time either of us had confessed our love for another male, an emotion ridiculed and condemned. Though I'd had anonymous sex for six months, pickups were furtive, anxiety-ridden. You stood absently gazing into a shop window, and if they stopped, you asked for a light or the time; the signals were understood. Sex was usually conducted in secretive silence; even on parting, we rarely spoke. If by chance you met again they would often betray no sign of recognition. I felt like Typhoid Mary. In the forties, when I began frequenting the notorious "Everhard" Baths, I'd run into them, stripped of their fig leaves and false pretenses, in the most undignified positions ("If their wives could see them now!"). Old fags would shake their sequined wigs and mutter, "The trade of today is the queen of tomorrow." By then I knew from experience that sexual lines were drawn not by Mother Nature but by the apes of God (in the hay they waver and dissolve).

I'd had an affair with the famous dancer Jack Cole, an articulate talker, but not once did he refer to his feelings beyond an embarrassed "I'm very fond of you." The same was true of David Blake. We had grown up pretending that our strongest urge, buried beneath layers of disavowal, did not exist. At college Chester was convinced I was straight and I thought *he* was.

"How could I tell?" he cried. "Why didn't you give me a sign? For over a year I've dreamt of a night like this."

"I was afraid to let on I was queer," I said unhappily.

"Who isn't?" he replied. Unmentionable to family or friends, homosexuality was regarded as a lurid, criminal act, worse than murder. Cops, punks, blackmailers, pimps, and whores despised us. A beautiful youth with a famous name (his family was both socially prominent and eminent in the theatre) would pop into my room, have a premature ejaculation, and flee in guilty haste. Wham, bam, thank you, man. Our conversations existed before, never after sex. Our true feelings were submerged beneath fear of exposure.

This did little for my already battered ego, further conditioning me to hide my affectionate nature. I believe this restraint, plus early traumas with stepmothers, warped Chester's essentially benign nature, turning him against himself and evolving into sadomasochistic self-hate and self-destructiveness. It was also true of me.

When I asked about women he confided that he'd had sex only once with a girl. When I asked if he'd liked it he grimaced.

"I was bored—but not *stiff*, my dear. I went through the motions thinking of how I could get away and suck off a sailor."

I told him about my first experience with a girl. While wanting to kiss and fondle her breasts, I felt I was defiling her, degrading her, treating her like a whore. I was struggling with the rubber and thinking of when I was five and played with my mother's titties; this made me feel guilty and dirty. The girl kept moaning, which frightened me, and I kept thinking, "What would my mother say if she caught me?" I was still living at home. Full of sweaty anxiety and dripping wet all over, I was so nervous and afraid that my mother would burst in at any moment that I came all over the rubber while trying to put it on. I hurried the poor girl out of there.

I met many boys who were gay but unafraid. One stands out vividly—six feet two inches tall, with a cute baby face and an irreverent sense of humor, he looked and acted eighteen, but was fifteen. He came from a good family that traced its ancestry to John Jay, the first chief justice of the Supreme Court. He did not conceal his sexuality; on the contrary, he was assertive and defiant, spoke with an affected grown-up air, smoked cigarettes like a girl, and resembled Latour's Rimbaud. From his red, smiling, beautiful lips I heard the word *gay* for the first time, uttered with a boyish giggle. But he talked throughout sex. Most of the time we laughed and joked, poking fun at the straight, dignified world like two Marx brothers.

As a boy Chester was still capable of charitable feelings and would often say at a biting remark, "That was unkind." But such sentiments did not survive his teens. He soon became a bitchy, outrageous camp. His wit was an acid rain of mockery. Nobody was spared. Once in Central Park when I asked for a kiss he sneered, "It's like kissing a chicken's ass." "Well, kiss mine," I said, stung by his remark. We were drunk. Shocked at his own behavior, he quickly relented. I also discovered that I had to share him with the military, whose asses he slavishly kissed. Having from the age of twelve molested adults in subway toilets, he had notched at least a thousand and three conquests on his belt, which loosened so easily. We were inseparable, but I had to face it: Chester was the Queen of Tarts.

12
The Baron

One winter evening early in 1939, at a performance of *Der Rosenkavalier* with Elizabeth Schwarzkopf as the Marschalin, an old man in a tuxedo left his orchestra seat, squeezed himself next to Chester, and groped him at precisely the moment when the young Count Octavian in drag (disguised as a maidservant to the Marschalin, with whom he is in love) gets groped by the lecherous Baron Ochs von Lerchenau, who thinks Octavian is a toothsome country girl.

"Why didn't you push him away?" I asked Chester during intermission.

He laughed. "It was so *funny*—while everyone was breaking up at the grope scene onstage, he had his hand in my fly."

"What a hideola!" I said with a smirk. Pronounced *hid-ee-ola*, this was a word I'd invented for a hideous person. We attached the suffix *-ola* to words for comic effect: "My dear, he whipped out his big thingola—"

He grinned. "Diamonds are a girl's best friend!" (Anita Loos camp.) "And *anyways,* it's exciting to violate a taboo in public. He probably sees himself as the baron and me as Octavian."

In standing room we were the object of many furtive gropes under the exit signs, but unless the groper was young and attractive we gently but firmly removed the exploring digits. If "the baron" attempted to strike up a conversation in the lobby, Chester would pretend not to recognize him. Later it turned out he was not unmindful of the "baron's" presumed wealth, and was playing hard to get.

Shortly after the "grope scene" Chester began to visit him, regaling me with descriptions of "penthouse" luxury. When I asked what went on between them, Chester would protest with a shudder, "*Nothing,* for God's sake! He does make feeble attempts

from time to time, but I get annoyed and he stops. He's afraid
I'll walk out. But you should see his record collection! The whole
Ring, with Flagstad and Melchior; *Tristan,* ditto; Strauss, Verdi,
Bellini, Donizetti, *everything*! He's got *Salome, Elektra, Ariadne auf
Naxos.* And the gifts—like this burgundy sweater and this tie."
With absurd pride he pointed to his chest. "And he's getting me
an orchestra seat for *Lohengrin.*" He had bagged his first sugar
daddy.

One evening Chester invited me to meet his elderly friend at
his home in the West Sixties. As I left the elevator on the top
floor I was met at the door by the old man himself. Inside I
blinked in disbelief. The place looked like the Salvation Army:
tasseled dusty lampshades on floor lamps, overstuffed armchairs,
a clawfoot sofa with mangy cushions, a cumbersome oak side-
board with tasteless bric-a-brac. Bronx baroque. Not even a penthouse, it was a top-floor flat.

Pasty-faced, shriveled old Charlie! What a tough, mean old
bird he really was! He had sparse white hair, a toucan beak, and
evasive leaky blue eyes; Charlie sputtered clichés, mistaking
them for sophisticated wit. "Sit down and take a load off your
ass," he chuckled. "You want schnapps or maybe the houseboy
will bring something harder, ha ha." Charlie's only friend, a
mournful six-foot-six gentleman in his seventies called "Bullitt"
(name changed), dressed like an undertaker in black suits. I
never saw a houseboy or servant. Charlie served drinks, cracked
jokes at which nobody laughed, and talked of his Harvard days
in a German accent. He got us drunk, but I kept my wits about
me, having consumed much less than Chester by sneaking off to
the bathroom and pouring it down the drain. Charlie remained
abstinent, playing *Salome* over and over on his console RCA Victor radio-phonograph while Chester and I chorused passionately, *"Ich habe deine Mund geküsst, Joka-a-naan!"* whenever
Salome sang her macabre aria, with the bloody decapitated head
of John the Baptist held up by the hair.

Around midnight Chester passed out on the sofa and I gave
up trying to get him to go home. He looked comatose, but I
caught some eyeball flickers that aroused my suspicions. In any
case Charlie seized the opportunity, reached over, and groped
Chester, pressing his mouth greedily to his. The semiconscious
Chester, with tight-shut eyes, began to return the old man's
kisses in a blurred, drunken way. Charlie's fingers fumbled fran-

tically with Chester's fly and his bloodless lips found what they desired.

With glockenspiels dripping fin-de-siècle passions in my ears, I took my leave. The metallism of Mallarmé's *Herodiade* and Oscar Wilde's *Salome* materialized in the gold of Chester's hair against Charlie's frozen silver, caught in the amber glow of the Victorian lamp. It was like an old daguerreotype of wicked depravity so dear to the hypocritical Victorians.

In the cold night air I nearly threw up as I staggered across Columbus Circle, lonely and depressed. I couldn't doubt that Chester was a whore.

Chester continued to see Charles the Boring, as I dubbed him, and I became a frequent visitor to the dowdy top-floor fiefdom of decadence. "He is the last great love of my life," Charlie confided with obvious satisfaction one evening when we were alone in his apartment. He had invited me for drinks in order to pick my brains. Like a giddy teenager he went on about his obsession with Chester.

"You know, Harold, I'm sure he loves me. Has he said anything about it? I can offer him everything he wants and, heh heh, he can offer me the one thing I want, just one little—I mean *big*—thing, ha ha." He spoke of his plans for Chester's future: he wanted to take him to Europe. Would I intercede on his behalf with Dr. Kallman? His red-rimmed little blue eyes danced. "I'll make it worth your while," he croaked. "I want him to live with me, put him through Harvard. His father will understand. He is a man of the world."

"I don't think Dr. Kallman is a man of *that* world," I said.

"No, no, you're wrong!" he protested. "At your age you don't realize that older people understand you more than you understand them. He's a sophisticated man. He *must* know these things."

"Well, even if that's true," I responded sullenly, "I could never tell him about myself, let alone about Chester."

A cunning expression crossed the old man's face. "I said I will make it worthwhile," he rasped and put his hand in his pocket and extracted a fat wad of bank notes. More than I had seen in my life.

Ulysses S. Grant winked. Take me, he urged sincerely.

Chester was furious when I told him about my evening with Charlie. "He actually offered you money?" I nodded. He looked sheepish. "It took character to turn it down," he said. Bullitt had

said, "Charlie wouldn't know what character was if it snuck up
and bit him in the ass. If he can't buy and sell it, he'll piss on it."

I was no longer welcome at the "penthouse," but that didn't
bother me. Chester continued attending the opera and sitting in
orchestra seats until disaster struck. One afternoon Chester burst
into my room beside himself with rage. "I'll kill him!" he bellowed. "I swear, I'll put arsenic in his schnapps!"

Charlie had paid Dr. Kallman a professional visit and spilled
the beans. Ed Kallman thought he was crazy and coldly told him to
see another dentist. Then he confronted Chester, who admitted
his sexual bent. The world almost, but not quite, came to an end.

Chester knew two middle-aged men in Brooklyn who served
drinks, sandwiches, and various dishes—we were the main dish.
When I asked what was so alluring about it, Chester said, "There
are always about three or four of the most beautiful boys in
Brooklyn there. You can have any of them."

I found myself in a large pleasant apartment with three other
boys, a tall thin bald man and a short dark-haired one with a
German accent and intense gaze. I had been coached by Chester
that I must not touch any boy until I had satisfied the host, which
was, he assured me, a snap. On arriving I instantly singled out an
Adonis of about nineteen with flawless white skin and the athletic
beauty of a Greek god. His name was Hartman. I've never forgotten him. First I went into a bedroom with the little host, whose
fetish had to be satisfied: I arched my nude body with my rear
above his face while he sniffed, prodded, and masturbated. It was
over quickly and I went in search of Hartman. He was waiting. In
another bedroom a boy was buggering the bald man, whose
skinny legs waved in the air like insect antennae. He looked silly.
We found a bedroom, stripped, and wasted no time. Hartman's
Nordic beauty was that of the ideal Hitler youth minus the may-
hem. He was a Brooklyn boy. We shared a camaraderie as warm
as our passion for each other. He went to Brooklyn College, was
literary and bright—and also a champion swimmer and football
player. Chester, who'd had him a few times, agreed he was sensational, and looked jealous of us both. We pitied the poor straights
who never knew what they were missing, regarding them as incomplete in experiencing the full range of sexual potential in
nature's cornucopia. I saw Hartman only twice, but he remains
forever in my mind, an archetypal beauty like Cocteau's Heur-

tebise or Emerson's Martin Gay. I have always regarded beauty as a necessity, not a luxury. With food, sex, shelter, and clothing, it is a basic human need. A truly *good* society would protect the right to beauty and sex by law.

Although I'd have been content with only Chester, he opted for promiscuity, which resulted in competitive behavior to show off our conquests. What the underlying message really said was: Look, I'm so desirable that everyone is in love with me. It was a dangerous game with predictable consequences. But though in those late-Depression, prewar years life without the other was inconceivable, the number of young men we had was mind-boggling. Hooked heart and soul on Chester, I wanted him as my lifetime partner. In lieu of this, promiscuity appeased the desire to sample the wonderful variety of youthful beauties available at no cost. But, I would soon discover, as with everything else there *was* a cost: not disease—I never caught any—but *au fond* a deep dissatisfaction, a gaping void. It was loneliness.

13

A Change in the Weather

On a cold sunny afternoon on April 6, 1939, Chester and I strode briskly through the streets in high spirits. We were on our way to hear Auden and Isherwood read for the first time in the United States. A week or so earlier, in late March, Chester had stood before my mirror combing his hair. Measuring his words for effect, he said, "Did you know that Auden and Isherwood are reading on West Fifty-second Street next week?" He grinned impishly. "Let's sit in the front row and wink at them!" And that's precisely what we were about to do.

As we entered the large hall of the Keynote Club we hurried to the front row, about fifteen feet from the platform, where we obtained center seats. Some of the folding chairs were already occupied. I recall no familiar faces, though Chester may have spoken briefly with some classmates. I remember a long delay, caused by some mistake about the date or time, during which we began to fret as to whether it would take place at all. As a huge crowd of several hundred gathered, I did not budge from my seat, though I may have kept Chester's for him while he chatted with others.

Finally Auden, Isherwood, Louis MacNeice, and Frederic Prokosch arrived to sustained applause. We could barely contain our excitement. Our first impressions of Auden, slovenly in rumpled tweed, were of disbelief. His shirt was unpressed, heavy woolen socks bunched limply around his thick ankles, and untied shoelaces flopped over his shoes. "Miss *Mess!*" hissed Chester. Isherwood, on the other hand, looked "cute" and "spruce." MacNeice was "dapper" in blue serge with a blue polka-dot tie, a silk kerchief protruding from his breast pocket. Although there was to be a talk, arranged by the leftist League of American Writers, titled "Modern Trends in English Poetry and Prose," it was never given. Isherwood chatted amiably but nervously about his visit with Auden to China during the Sino-Japanese War and read excerpts from their collaboration, *Journey to a War;* MacNeice read from his *Autumn Journal* manuscript, his hands shaking so violently that the pages rattled; and Auden, who had absently strayed from the lectern, teetered perilously on the edge of the platform, to the consternation of the audience, making it hard for us to concentrate on his reading of the elegy "In Memory of W. B. Yeats," also in manuscript, written three months earlier. Leaning at a hazardous angle, he came quite close several times to falling some five feet or so below and thus joining Yeats before the reading was over. We held our breath. Totally oblivious of his predicament, only by sheer luck was he spared an ignominious fall. The room was overheated and during a pause between poems, as the poet was perspiring profusely, the actor Burgess Meredith, rising from his seat in the audience, offered to open a window. Auden shrieked, "Oh, I'd *love* that!" and we all cracked up. I clearly remember the sharp glare of afternoon sunlight as we turned our heads to watch someone open a window.

Auden's brisk Oxford-Yorkshire monotone was difficult to understand. With his sloppy clothes and awkward movements (not to mention his swift birdlike nods of the head) he was the star, the gauche comedian, the mad genius. He stole the show. Overcome by the situation, we stifled giggles and continued to flirt outrageously with Isherwood, winking and grinning, and he grinned back. We didn't know that Auden, who was nearsighted, never saw us.

The reading was followed by a question-and-answer period. Burgess Meredith queried Isherwood and Auden about when one could expect a performance in America of *The Dog Beneath the Skin* and *The Ascent of F6,* two verse plays on which they had collaborated. I remember the audience excitement when they replied that they would be performed soon. But it was something Auden said about his poetry that had the most significance for me. I had observed that the one element notably lacking in most of his work was feeling; some scoffed when I mentioned this, but Chester agreed. With a rush of pride I heard Auden publicly admit, referring to his entire body of work, that he was weakest in the faculty of feeling and was indeed unable to evoke it except through his intellect, his reasoning faculty. He said this in a tone of regret in response to a question. It was an ingenuous admission of a defect he deplored. Chester and I prized feeling above all other qualities in poetry, but I'm afraid we confused it a bit with overwrought rhetoric.

At the end of the reading we rushed backstage, where some students and other admirers were crowding around the writers in a cramped space. We stared at Auden, whose attention we wished to attract, but he was engaged in conversation. Isherwood kept glancing at us while talking to someone else. Finally when Auden had a free moment Chester told him we were from the Brooklyn College *Observer* (I had graduated the previous semester) and wished to interview him and Isherwood. In a brusque offhand manner Auden sort of trumpeted, "Oh, ah, see Mr. Isherwood!" and turned unconcernedly to another admirer who claimed his attention. This was no doubt Walter Miller, an athletic blond student (hetero) from Brooklyn College to whom Auden was attracted.

Fortunately Isherwood, whose eyes continued to meet mine, was interested. He presented a calling card on which he wrote his phone number (I was intrigued by the European cross-bar on the seven) and the Yorkville address on East Eighty-first Street. On the way to my room a few blocks east, Chester and I could not stop talking about the momentous occasion. With our uncompromising ideal of masculine beauty based on youth, virility, and athletic good looks, we were disappointed by Auden; we had expected the striking blond of the early photographs that we had seen in books and magazines. At thirty-two Auden was soft-looking, wide-hipped, narrow-shouldered, dough-faced; he lacked manly charms. By no stretch of the imagination could we consider him, as did some straight students, "extraordinarily handsome," but as adoring fans we were determined to visit him. Before returning to Brooklyn Chester asked for the card. When I reminded him that Isherwood had pointedly given it to me, he replied that he wished to show it to his father and would return it.

Two days later, April 8, not in the least disturbed that he had betrayed my trust, he visited them alone and never returned the card. Chester recounted the details of the visit. In the doorway Auden exclaimed with disappointment, "It's the wrong blond!" apparently expecting Walter Miller; he seemed bored and distracted. But Chester kept the conversation going, finally making a reference to the sixteenth-century metaphysical poet Thomas Rogers, at which Auden came to life. He admired Rogers and was impressed by Chester's mind and, even more, his wit. A lively conversation ensued and Chester was invited to stay for tea. Before departing he received an invitation to return. On the second visit, discovering Chester's endowment ("Thank God it's big!" Auden exclaimed fervently, clasping his hands), Auden was smitten. He later confessed that he had prayed to God that Chester would be "hung." God did not disappoint him.

On leaving Wystan's apartment Chester burst into my room that morning, flung himself across my bed, and in a voice filled with awe blurted out, "Harold, Auden is in *love* with me!" With unsteady hands he showed me an Oxford University Press edition of William Blake that Auden had just inscribed to him on the flyleaf with eight lines from a cabaret song he had composed for Hedli Anderson, a singer married to Louis MacNeice:

> *When it comes will it come without warning*
>   *Just as I'm picking my nose?*
> *Will it knock at my door in the morning,*
>   *Or tread in the bus on my toes?*
>
> *Will it come like a change in the weather?*
>   *Will its greeting be courteous or rough?*
> *Will it alter my life altogether?*
>   *O tell me the truth about love.*

My own prophecy, made less than two years before in the *Observer* office, had been fulfilled. (An English student we knew at Brooklyn College, who was a spastic, commented with grotesque twitches of the mouth and body, "Au-den—has fin-al-ly—found—his—*arse*—po-et-ica!")

The event was of unusual importance in the lives of four people: Auden, Isherwood, Kallman, and myself. It altered our lives altogether. I lost my lover and Wystan won him. Isherwood lost his closest companion and left for California, which changed his life.

Chester's schoolboy fantasy came true, but for me it would be at a terrible price. "He'll come between us," I said resignedly. "He'll separate us." "That's not true!" Chester cried indignantly. Unwilling to make a scene, with a reassuring grin I replied, "Well, I don't ever want that to happen." "It won't!" he said emphatically. "It should bring all three of us closer together."

The thought of separation disturbed us deeply, but with my troublesome gift of precognition, I saw it as a fait accompli. Already, instead of visiting me after class as he had always done, Chester saw Wystan first. As Wystan was ultimately to do with everyone close to Chester, including his father, he would weaken our bonds and drive a wedge between us.

14

The Auden-Kallman-Norse Triangle

My first intimate meeting with Auden took place at Lincoln Kirstein's apartment, where he stayed after Isherwood left for California. I recall that Kirstein, a very tall man, playfully stole behind Auden and sprayed the back of his neck and ears with perfume. Taken by surprise, Auden whirled around and screeched, "*Fuck! Stop that!* What on *earth* are you doing? I positively *loathe* perfume!" He rubbed his neck

as if he'd been stung. Kirstein, flushing deep purple, left shortly
afterwards.

Auden soon recovered his composure and began questioning me about my dancing, my writing, my life. "Chester has told
me a lot about you, Harold," he began. "In fact, he talks of almost nobody else. He's always quoting you." I grinned. "You
were voted 'the most literary boy' at college, weren't you? 'Coarse
jocosity catches the crowd; Shakespeare and I are often low-
browed,'" he quoted my lines from the yearbook to my astonishment. "You should talk to Lincoln about your dancing. I'm sure
he'd be interested in auditioning you." Then he asked about my
surname. "Was your father Scandinavian?" I told him about my
illegitimacy and that I had created Norse as an anagram from
my mother's Russian name. "Very clever," he said. "But why
Norse?" "My earliest reading was in Norse mythology," I said.
"My mother's family—like Chester's in Latvia—were Nordic
Jews, blue-eyed blonds from Lithuania." I had won his interest.
Because of Scandinavian origins on his father's side, he had been
influenced by the Norse sagas. Responding to a question about
religion, I revealed that my family was Roman Catholic and I
had German, Irish, Finnish, and French-Canadian cousins. My
religious views? Agnostic. From his look I saw I had won his
interest—a look I'd get to know, warm, intense, penetrating, the
blue-hazel eyes (same color as mine) focused like a high-powered
lens.

"Since you're both so good at English," he resumed, "let's
play word games. I'll give you a word and you supply the an-
tonym." He paused to think as Chester, his eyes beseeching
mine, grimaced with mock alarm. "Harold, be with me now," he
said, paraphrasing a line from Crane's *Bridge*. Since tests or
quizzes have the power to make me instantly forget what I know,
I went into a state of amnesia. "Epidemic," said Auden. The
word *endemic* immediately came to mind, but I couldn't speak.
Chester stared helplessly at me. Auden wore the look of an im-
patient schoolmarm. "Endemic?" I offered tentatively. Auden
grunted. We continued until Kirstein returned and offered to
drive me home.

An impressive six foot four, with glasses and an intense,
square-jawed face, Kirstein resembled Clark Kent/Superman of
the comics. About Auden's age, a poet and co-founder of the
New York City Ballet, he was said to be very rich. But to me what
mattered most was that he had known Hart Crane.

It was a warm spring day and as we drove through Central Park he asked about my ballet experience. I told him that without any lessons I had danced professionally. When I was nineteen, a friend who was even younger but already a principal dancer with the Ballet Russe de Monte Carlo was astonished when, imitating him in the park one day, I pirouetted, faked *entrechats,* took great leaps in *tours jetés.* "You have natural talent," he said. "If you want to make some money I can coach you for *Prince Igor.* You get ten dollars a night. The Yakovlev Russian Ballet needs a boy." So Valya—whose stage name was Vladimir Valentinoff—rehearsed me a few times and that weekend I found myself in a studio on Madison Avenue, facing an old woman.

I'd never had a lesson in my life and there I was, with about six professional dancers, all trying out for the part. She lined us up and the pianist began the music for the four bowmen. When it was over Madame Yakovlev studied each of us. Then she pointed her cane—at me! In her basso profundo voice and Russian accent she said, "I choose these boy because he has the bast tyechnyik!" A week later I made my debut at the Philadelphia Academy of Music and earned money!

Kirstein asked who my teacher was. I told him it was Mme. Duval on West Fifty-fourth Street. "Agnes de Mille practices with us," I said, to drop a name. He asked if I'd considered choreography, and I said my experience was too limited. He was auditioning for his new dance company and wanted me to try out. Wystan had told him I was a poet and Kirstein thought the combination might lead to something new.

Valya (who took Massine's role in *Union Pacific* at the Metropolitan Opera when the great dancer could not go on), had a girl friend called Sonya Robbins who mentioned that her brother Jerry was studying to be a dancer. "He has nobody to practice with," she said. "Maybe you two could get together." She gave me their home number and I contacted him. I was house-sitting for friends the summer of 1939 in a small apartment in the West Twenties when there was a knock on the door and a youth of nineteen with large blazing black eyes and straight black hair neatly combed, looking like a young Leonid Massine, said, "I'm Jerry Robbins." He had a nervous, preoccupied air and spoke little. We changed into our ballet duds and began practicing the bar routine. We immediately worked out with ferocious energy. He was studying with Mme. Dagonova, a legendary figure, and I told him about Kirstein's audition. Jerry went with me for the audition and was accepted. I was not. When Kirstein again asked if I'd consider choreography I told him that ballet interfered with my writing and I didn't think I could do both.

Obsessed with Chester, Auden literally adored him, regarding the relationship as a marriage. He mistakenly believed that Chester, who worshiped Auden's fame and genius but not his body, felt the same way. With the adulation of a famous poet Chester became more self-centered and spoiled. He may have been starry-eyed at being "the queen's favorite," as he referred to it, but he was merciless about Auden, whom he had begun calling "Miss Mess" and "Miss Master." His cruel if hilarious mimicry spared none, not even his father.

On Wystan: "His idea of religious worship is to kneel before the Great God Penis. Talk about groveling—he'd stay down all night if I didn't remind him that even *I* am not inex*haust*ible."

On his father: "For someone who's supposed to be Miss Lady's Man, he *adores* enemas." He fluttered his eyebrows suggestively.

One evening Auden, Chester, his father, and I had a memorable dinner at an Italian restaurant on MacDougal Street in the Village. The tables were gaily decked in red-and-white checkered tablecloths with straw-wrapped Chianti bottles. We had loads of spaghetti during which I grew stupefied on wine. The conversation was monopolized by Wystan with Ed acting as "straight man" in every sense of the word. He fed lines to Auden, who spoke animatedly. Chester made occasional remarks, but I was still awed by Auden, incapable of uttering a word. This was soon after he had begun to sleep with Chester. Polite and formal, Ed was also awed. I remember him saying, "Now that you're a master of the English language, Wystan, there's probably nothing you couldn't express. How does it feel to have achieved such mastery? I don't mean personal satisfaction so much as—well—" He faltered. "Do you have to grope for words as I've just done?"

Chester and I exchanged glances at the word *grope*, but Wystan exclaimed, "Oh, goodness, yes! My manuscripts are full of false starts, scratches, and blots. Although some poems come out whole, with only minor changes of punctuation, or a word changed here and there, others I have to work on, making substantial alterations. A line or stanza may not have conveyed what I wished. Or I've disagreed with what I said. I scrap entire poems because I no longer accept what I've said in them."

The conversation went on for hours, during which I found his accent, thickened by wine, impenetrable. Finally Wystan, beside whom I was seated, grew tired. He was doing his best to charm his lover's father (who was unaware of the nature of the relationship) and had obviously succeeded. Noticing my sodden condition, Auden remarked, "Oh, dear, Harold hasn't said a word all evening. Do you suppose he's recording it all in his memory, like Walter Winchell, and we'll read it someday in his memoirs?"

A few days later we took the subway to Brooklyn Heights to introduce Auden to David Blake, who had wanted to meet him. They were both leftists; Auden was the leading poetic spokesman in the English language for "the cause" and had also participated in the Spanish Civil War as an ambulance driver. He was immediately enchanted by Brooklyn Heights. It was a soft spring day. All three of us felt elated, chatting and laughing animatedly. Wystan kept staring at us with a look of happiness as we strode to David's new apartment on Clark Street.

"Terry McBride" (name changed) was a young English instructor at Brooklyn College, and David's closest friend. A striking black-Irish ex-Catholic, he was fanatic about his newly adopted Communist faith. We drank scotch and the conversation was pleasant. When we left, keeping up with Auden's long strides toward the subway, we asked what he thought of David Blake. "Oh, he's a real charmer," he said enthusiastically. "A lovely man. But his friend, I'm afraid, for all his good looks is a ninny." We laughed, but because I liked Terry I said, "Mr. Auden, why do you say that?"

"Please, Harold," he replied with warmth, "let's have no more of this *mister* nonsense. Call me Wystan. After all, you're one of the family." I flushed with pleasure. "All right, Wystan," I said, grinning. "What *is* wrong with Terry McBride?"

"He's tiresome, my dear, with a particularly Irish tiresomeness. He goes on and on in an emotional way about perfectly obvious matters. Of course the Fascists are unspeakable swine. But it won't do to harp on it. It doesn't make good conversation."

I was shocked at his remark about "Irish tiresomeness" but

hadn't the courage to challenge him. He used the word *tiresome* often, especially about the Irish. I soon learned that it was one of his quirks, not meant maliciously. He was snobbish and, in any case, loved to shock his listeners with outrageous pronouncements. Anti-Semitism, however, made him angry, yet on the occasion of awarding the Bollingen Prize to Ezra Pound, for which he was on the committee, he said, "Every gentile has at one time or another had anti-Semitic feelings." He was simply stating a horrible truth.

One of Auden's repeated shockers was: "I know what *I* was put on earth for, but what are all the *others* doing here?"

I had difficulty with his diction. Besides the native Yorkshire with the Oxford overlay, sentences came tumbling out of his mouth with great rapidity, word endings and phrases were swallowed whole, voraciously gulped down the way he gulped his food and wine. Chester professed to have no difficulty with his accent, but he spent much of his time close to Wystan. We had great fun mimicking him.

Chester once described a hilarious scene in the subway en route to his grandmother's for lunch. He and Auden were arguing loudly about the psychological roles they unconsciously enacted with each other, Wystan basing his arguments on Freud and Groddeck. "The passengers stared in disbelief," said Chester with that chuckling laughter so characteristic of him and his father. "We were yelling above the roar of the train, my dear, completely mad!"

The argument went something like this:

WYSTAN: I am *not* your father, I'm your *mother*!

CHESTER: You're *not* my mother! I'm *your* mother!

WYSTAN: No, you've got it all wrong. I'm *your* mother!

CHESTER: You're not! You're my *father*!

WYSTAN (screaming): But you've *got* a father! I'm your bloody mother and that's that, darling! You've been looking for a mother since the age of four!

CHESTER (shouting): And you've been obsessed with your mother from the womb! You've been trying to get back ever since, so I *am* your mother! And you're my father!

WYSTAN: No, you want to replace your father for marrying women who rejected you, for which you can't forgive him. But you want a mother who will accept you unconditionally, as I do. Which, my dear, is just what you've been looking for.

CHESTER: That's why you're my father, not my mother. You're the replacement, without the tits.

WYSTAN: But your father does not accept you unconditionally, don't you see. That's the mother's function, because the child's body is part of hers and she never disowns it in the unconscious. So because I accept you entirely in this way, I'm your ersatz mother, not your father.

CHESTER: *I'm your goddamn mother for the same reason!* You're always sucking on me as if I were one giant tit.

WYSTAN: I must always have something to suck.

CHESTER: Not now, Wystan, not now.

WYSTAN: Insufficient weaning. That's why I can't stop smoking.

CHESTER: You've got the sexes confused.

WYSTAN: Well, a tit becomes a penis in the unconscious, which does not discriminate between fleshy protuberances. The infant's need for oral satisfaction substitutes mother's breast and milk, as he grows into teen-age, for penis and cream. They are interchangeable symbols in the unconscious.

CHESTER: You're mad, Wystan, completely mad! That's the most awful psychological *dreck* I've ever heard. You know as well as I do that—

WYSTAN: No, no, my dear, you're simply uninformed. Read Lane, Groddeck, Freud.

CHESTER: And then I will see that you're my mother?

WYSTAN: Quite.

CHESTER: Well, perhaps *you* should marry my father. You'd make the best stepmother I've had!

WYSTAN: Darling, that would be bigamous! Actually polygamous, since you and I are married.

CHESTER: Wystan, you're nuttier than a fruitcake!

WYSTAN: Oh, darling, you're so earthy! And you look just like a sweet pea! A bit piggy, too.

CHESTER: Shall I inform my father that you're about to propose?

WYSTAN: Well, I *cahn't*, can I? I'm already married to Erika.

CHESTER: Don't worry, she'll make a better husband than my dad.

(Auden had chivalrously married Thomas Mann's daughter, who was a lesbian, so that she could obtain a British passport and leave Nazi Germany, where her life was in danger because her mother was Jewish.)

One time Wystan, Chester, and I, at Wystan's instigation, read aloud scenes from Tennyson's *Idylls of the King* at the Brooklyn flat. Since Wystan was the oldest he took the part of King Arthur, Chester was Guinevere, and I was Sir Lancelot. I can't imagine what Chester's grandmother must have thought, if she listened at the bedroom door. I can still see Chester on the floor as Wystan passionately intoned Arthur's last speech to Guinevere in the nunnery, a scene strikingly similar to Wotan's long denunciation of Brünnhilde before punishing her with the magic fire in *Die Walküre*.

Wystan, who loved Tennyson, said afterwards, "You must write as if Blake or Tennyson were looking over your shoulder. It's not your contemporaries but the illustrious dead we must please. Keep saying to yourself, 'What would Blake think of this?' or 'I wonder if Byron would approve.' They are the *only* competition."

He set standards so lofty that I developed writer's block—precisely the opposite effect of that intended—and wrote cramped imitations of Auden's prevalent style, while Chester turned out manneristic mimicries that Auden disliked. It would be years before I could shake off his stultifying effect. What I needed was something more than formal pedantry. I needed a voice.

15

The Honeymoon

Chester continued leaving notes in the broken mailbox making appointments, chiding me for not keeping them, or offering excuses for doing the same. These seem like hieroglyphic fragments from a distant past.

One day I returned from my job at the WPA Writers' Project and, having been up later than usual the night before, fell into a deep sleep. I was awakened by a terrific banging on the door and, feeling drugged, sluggishly opened it. To my utter amazement Chester burst in, gasping, "My God, I thought you were dead! I saw you through the keyhole—lifeless!" He was close to tears. Behind him stood his father, looking anxious. "I kept pounding, but you didn't move. So I ran to my father's office—"

"Probably a postmasturbatory sleep," said Dr. Kallman with a knowing grin. "The effect is similar to rigor mortis."

He was right. His remark, calculated to relieve the anxiety, was successful, and we all burst into laughter. Dear, funny, sensible Dr. Kallman. I was lucky, I felt, to have such friends. They actually cared about me. Except for my mother, nobody else did.

When Auden left in May to teach for a month, through the agency of the poet Richard Eberhart (at St. Marks School in Southborough, Massachusetts, a posh private school for very rich boys), Chester spent more time with me, as in the past, and I began to feel reassured. But this was to prove short-lived. Wystan sent love letters and new poems to Chester; one poem expressed his jealous angst at separation, indicating he was far from convinced of Chester's fidelity:

O but I was mad to come here, even for money;
To put myself at the mercy of the postman and the daydream,
That incorrigible nightmare in which you lie weeping or ill,
    Or drowned in the arms of another . . .

Hardly "weeping or ill," Chester was cruising endlessly and lay "drowned in the arms" of many another:

To have left you now, when I know what this warm May weather
Does to the city: how it brings out the plump little girls and
Truculent sailors into the parks and sets
    The bowels of boys on fire . . .

Our boyish "bowels," needless to say, were on fire all year round. But there were always plenty of sailors and volunteer firemen to quench the flames. As for being truculent, we didn't find the sailors so. On the contrary, since Central Park was our surest source of pickups, where sailors and civilians had easy access to one another, we rarely, if ever, went home alone. Indeed, we were in a permanent state of arousal—especially during those warm spring days and steamy jungle nights of summer that set us, more than ever, afire. Like animals on the prowl, we hunted and were hunted.

There was an endless parade of youth in the city, some as young as fourteen and fifteen. They came to New York from everywhere, refugees from the Depression or from Nazi oppression. They were castaways, throwaways, runaways. Auden used to say, "Sex is no problem. There are boys on every street corner." This was true. Poor, unemployed, nonviolent, they were available for a few cigarettes and a bed for the night. Drugs didn't exist for them. Mostly sweet-natured and wholesome, from poverty-stricken families, thousands of boys from rural America roamed the city in search of jobs and adventure.

Sailors were everywhere, looking like young ballet dancers in their fetching navy blue that clung skintight to taut muscles, especially to their thighs and buttocks, outlining their callipygian beauty. Those firm, full mounds seemed designed by Blake's Jehovah, leaning down from heaven with his calipers to carve them lovingly with divine precision. "Only God," said Chester, "could have created them." To which I responded, "Ah-men." They were irresistible among the leafing trees and bushes, the ponds with paddling ducks and swans, the stone bridges and sweet odors of flowers, mulch, and new-mown grass. The rank, stirring tang of rotting roots and fresh upturned earth mingled with the heady body aroma of healthy, vital young flesh, the musk of hair and sweat. We walked and idled for hours, sensually, sexually drunk.

> *O never leave me.*
> *Never. Only the closest attention of your mouth*
> *Can make me worthy of loving.*

Ah, yes, Chester's mouth: it had a distinctive flavor, a natural scent similar to slightly decayed gardenias, rich and intoxicating. When you got close, the same odor emanated from him. (Whatever happened to body odor? It used to play an enormous role in social and sexual attraction, but the age of electronic commercials has banished it. Instead a chemical stench assaults our olfactory nerves. We rarely get a whiff of healthy armpits nowadays except in a gym, but the men rush off madly to the showers and apply their synthetic deodorant, labeled "Musk," and spray on their cheap cologne and go off smelling like disinfectant.)

When Auden returned in June from St. Marks School, Chester informed me that they were leaving for the summer. "Wystan calls it our honeymoon," he said grinning. "*Such* a romantic girl." It was to be a cross-country trip to the West Coast. Before their departure they spent two days in Princeton as guests of Thomas Mann and his family, sleeping in his bed. Chester sent me a nude photo of himself taken by Wystan, requesting that I keep it for them, since he feared his father might see it. This black-and-white snap of Chester asleep on his belly on the rumpled sheets, his buttocks tilted upward at a voluptuous angle, was considered pornographic. He told me that Wystan would be furious if he knew that *anybody* had seen it. I had it for about a year before Chester reclaimed it and gave it back to Wystan.

They returned briefly from Princeton and, with a sinking sensation, I watched helplessly as Auden whisked Chester away from New York, from his past, from his father, from me. On June 20, 1939, they left and I tearfully smashed tumblers against the walls of my room in rage and desperation. I got reports from both, describing various stages of the journey. Wystan's state of bliss was somewhat marred by evidence of Chester's attempts, along the trail, to establish closer contact with sundry youths on the bus or at stops. Within eighteen months Wystan would be jarred by the knowledge of Chester's unrepentant infidelities and spend the rest of his life appeasing Chester rather than relinquish his friendship.

During the trip Chester kept quoting Hart Crane, among others, annoying Wystan, who disliked his work intensely. At Baton Rouge they met Katherine Anne Porter and her husband, who resembled a handsome biology teacher at Brooklyn College. Porter glowingly recalled Hart Crane in Mexico—Wystan, apparently, had not succeeded in toppling our idol, I noted with satisfaction. In Taos they met D. H. Lawrence's widow, Frieda; Chester, wearing sun goggles, lay on the ground pressing Kleenex to a bloody nose. He'd been examined by a doctor, who told him the altitude was not good for him because of a "severe" heart condition. Frieda rented them a house about two miles out of town, where Chester began writing a poem that he actually considered better than Auden's "Dover," which it imitated. Wystan, however, thought otherwise. Chester found himself unnerved by Auden's disapproval of his poems, something from which we both had to suffer. At most, Auden would comment only on meter, exact meaning of words, logic, and the truth or falsity of the premise.

The night before their departure, embittered by Auden's complete takeover, I warned that he would always live in Wystan's shadow, that it would affect his writing and ultimately his self-esteem. In the end, with the best intentions, Wystan would unwittingly blight Chester's talent, if not his personality. His influence was too strong to resist. As usual, my sibylline powers went unappreciated. Chester reacted defensively and left. But throughout the journey we maintained the closest touch, and Chester even apologized—rare indeed—for his behavior. He had begun to complain about talking with someone (Wystan) who is always right.

Their strict routine was ordered around Auden's work; Chester shopped, prepared and served meals (that is, opened the cans), and cleaned up. He also began complaining about the dullness of the food, enraging Wystan by refusing to finish dinner. Chester stubbornly stood his ground. Astonishingly, the thirty-four-year pattern of their lifelong relationship was foreshadowed here: Wystan's domineering authoritativeness and Chester's equally stubborn assertion of self-worth. Also his role of helper but not subordinate comes across clearly from the beginning.

In the final stages of the trip they rejoined Isherwood and his new boyfriend, Harvey, in Laguna Beach, where they settled in a room on the beach. This proved too much for Chester: he rhapsodized about the scantily clad young men everywhere and reported that Wystan accused him of addiction. Chester found himself barely able to cling to sanity because of frustration in such an intensely stimulating environment. But if Chester's addiction was boys, Wystan's was Chester. There was no known cure.

Through Isherwood they met Aldous Huxley and Gerald Heard, the British mystical thinker who brought Isherwood to Vedanta. Though superstitious, both Wystan and Chester were resistant to the temptations of metaphysical awe.

Wystan had been writing "a new marriage of Heaven and Hell" called "The Prolific and the Devourer," a long prose work influenced by Blake and Pascal, which would be his synthesis of the two works that influenced him most at the time. He was be-

ginning to veer away from politics as a solution to social problems and finding in religion a traditional base of intellectual
discipline that would allow a more ordered existence.

Through Chester, Wystan sent me some money during that
long hot summer of 1939. I had quit my job for the summer,
since I too was in heat, and resorted to incessant cruising as an
escape from loneliness. (I was almost always successful, but
mostly they were one-night stands.) Wystan could be incredibly
generous and, to be sure, a couple of months later I would have
further proof of his compassionate nature. In spite of his overbearing ego, he was almost saintlike in his prompt support of
friends in need.

In a letter to Chester and Auden, after thanking them for
the help, I speak of a "Commie rally" I attended with David
Blake:

> The girl at the door barked all the blunt manipulative
> phrases of "revolutionary" tail-wagging and I refused
> collusion with such slogans. When I asked her, "Do you
> speak English?" shock waves were perceptible. I fell in-
> stantly from Party grace. Well, I was never a joiner, and
> the Party, my dear, doesn't take kindly to writers and
> queers anyway. And what if they found out about David
> and me? To the salt mines, dear. But communism is the
> only thing he believes in. As for me, I believe in the
> Homintern; leave the Comintern to the Party.

The word *Homintern*, which I coined in 1939, is attributed to
Auden, who used it in an article in the *Partisan Review* about
1941, and has passed into the language. A takeoff on *Comintern*
(Communist International), it was meant to convey the idea of a
global homosexual community.

Meanwhile, I was not the only one who experienced growing concern. During Chester's and Auden's absence Ed Kallman
took the opportunity to deplore his son's new relationship. One
day he invited me to lunch at the Russian Tea Room, and although not given to displays of emotion, it was easy to see he was
upset. He urged me to persuade Chester to give up his affair
with Auden, insisting that it was merely an adolescent stage that
he'd outgrow ("a stage one goes through all one's life," mocked
Chester). Ed never spoke disparagingly of Auden, for whom he

had great respect and admiration, but until this meeting I had never really thought about his feelings. He was so debonair, so worldly, that I assumed he approved of the situation.

"After all," I said with a broad grin, "it's a brilliant match—even if Auden isn't Jewish." I'll say this for Ed Kallman—he knew how to laugh even when under pressure. But as Chester's best friend and confidant, I was placed in a painfully awkward position. Ed assumed I was straight and, having no knowledge of the true situation between Chester, Auden, and myself, unwittingly placed me in collusion with him, which I found unnerving. I felt powerless wearing a mask, pretending to be what I wasn't, unable to confess the truth to Ed or to any other straight man or woman. Caught between shame and the pressure to betray his son, I said that no one could influence Auden or Chester in so personal a matter. Besides, what future could be better for a young poet? At this, the hetero lobbying ceased.

16

We Must Love One Another or Die

At the end of August, when Wystan and Chester returned, Chester and I spent our first night at a notorious gay bar called the Dizzy Club on West Fifty-second Street, three blocks from my room. The dive was the sex addict's quick fix, packed to the rafters with college boys and working-class youths under twenty-five. From street level you stepped into a writhing mass of tight boys in tighter pants. On those sultry August nights it was a sexual experience just getting a drink. Like the subway at rush hour you were crushed against one another. It was quite a feat to hold on to your drink and keep it from spilling on your shirt or pants, or someone else's, though nobody seemed to mind. Amid the laughter and screaming and ear-splitting jukebox music, it was like an orgy room for the fully clad. Everything but exposure and nudity took place.

Having decided that he must see it, we told Wystan, who loved sleazy dives, about the Dizzy Club. The next night, September 1, without our knowledge he went alone. I can only imagine what occurred there. With floppy shoelaces, creased suit and tie, ash-stained, he must have looked out of place, though with his rosy California tan and sun-bleached hair he could, in the right light, pass for twenty-five. He didn't go to pick up a boy; however, aware of the age difference and quite shy, he would have selected one of the two unused corner tables at the rear of the bar, which was usually deserted except for those too drunk to stand, from which he could observe boys kissing and groping under the bright lights, packed like sardines pickled in alcohol. There he would begin to write the most famous poem of the decade. Surely he jotted notes, or even the first stanzas, for it begins with the immediacy of composition in situ. He did not write a detailed description of his immediate surroundings or his personal feelings but instead opened the poem outward into society at that historic moment, choosing the depressed mood of his isolation within the social drama. At precisely this moment, while Auden wrote tracing fascism and its "psychopathic gods" from Martin Luther to the birth of Hitler at Linz, the German Führer marched into Poland and started World War II. The poem was, of course, "September 1, 1939."

This remarkable elegy, which closes the decade, contains what may be his most famous line: "We must love one another or die." Unquestionably, it was the Big Truth of the moment as opposed to Hitler's Big Lie. At twenty-three Auden had ushered in the thirties with his first book, *Poems* (published in 1930 by Faber and Faber under the editorship of T. S. Eliot), and become its most famous poetic voice, with a new style for the times. His was the voice of the humanist, socialist, liberal Left. At thirty-two he summed up the decade and the future. If we hadn't sent him to the dive on Fifty-second Street he wouldn't have written it— despite the irony that he wished he hadn't. In a letter to a friend that he never sent, he called it the most dishonest poem he had ever written.

Much has been made of Auden's rejection of the poem. As its author he had every right to reject it. Like T. S. Eliot, Auden found some of his own work objectionable—as one feels, perhaps, about certain follies of one's youth. Ironically, of his most famous line he said, "It's a damnable lie!" For the later Auden the poem was too committed to a point of view and way of writing he no longer espoused as he became a religious conservative eschewing liberal humanism on the grounds that it accepted no moral absolute. Reason alone, he held, is flawed and inconsistent; only faith in the absolute could answer the problem of evil in human affairs. Therefore his poem was based on a lie, on a moral injunction to a world of innately immoral, unethical humans to behave in a loving manner when they were by nature incapable of doing so. He found no way out of the dilemma except to return to the church of his childhood. If people cannot be good through reason alone, they must accept a higher force, through faith in the mercy of God, as his reading of Kierkegaard taught, the only alternative being despair. It was always a mystery to me, however, that a man of Auden's intellect could miss the obvious: that faith in a moral absolute has never kept Christians or other religionists from behaving in the most abominable, irreligious way.

In any case, Auden's return to the church had no effect on his behavior. He was just as rude and unfair as ever. He remained gossipy, vain, arrogant, bitchy, and outrageous. He was a dogmatic tyrant who denounced personal confession and emotion in poetry but loved it in opera and movies, where he wept sentimentally.

In the space of about nine weeks, from the start of the honeymoon to the writing of "September 1, 1939," Auden's life was completely altered. He had shifted from the political to the religious point of view. He was to remain a devoted Episcopalian (Anglo-Catholic or High Church) for the rest of his life. But poems are artifacts that exist in the minds of others, and I cannot be convinced that "September 1, 1939" is not a great poem. It represents a point of view shared by millions of more or less compassionate, civilized, humane, if flawed, people. And when he wrote it he believed it. I continue to welcome its inclusion in new editions of Auden's work.

17

A New Genius

Auden never saw more than a few poems of mine. In each case his only comment, aside from grunting, was, "This line doesn't scan," or "This word is not used exactly." Once or twice he said of a line or entire poem, "This isn't true." Chester often complained in sheer frustration, "He never discusses the poem. It's maddening." But one poem of mine called "The Gift of Love" (now lost) he liked well enough to recommend to Thomas Mann's son, Klaus, then editing his new magazine, *Decision*. Mann was going to publish a poem of Chester's—his first publication—on Auden's recommendation.

I phoned Mann and was invited to his office on West Fifty-seventh Street. He was thin, flat-haired, and pale with deep-sunk eyes and a gaunt look, in his thirties. Chester had showed me a photo of Klaus that Wystan had recently taken, saying, "This is Klaus looking like a fiend." He was not at all fiendish, however, and liked my poem very much. Flushed with the heady prospect of an entrée into a major new literary magazine, I became exhilarated and was charmed by his cultivated European accent and manners. In my teens I had published in a few "little" magazines and newspapers but none of the caliber of *Decision*. We were seated on the couch in his office when Mann leaned over and placed a hand on my thigh. "Do I haf the honor of discovering a new chenius?" he breathed heavily into my ear. Publication was assured. "I hope so, Mr. Mann," I said, gently removing his hand and rising to my feet.

"Oh, please, *please* call me Klaus!" he said quickly, also rising. "We are going to be friends, aren't we, Harold? Wystan has spoken very highly of you. Perhaps we can go to lunch and talk some more. I would like you to be my guest, Harold, yes?"

He was perfectly charming, not formidable like Wystan, but

his intensity put me off. As always, older men did not attract me and I didn't wish to be unfair by leading him on. Since I had no intention of prostrating myself on the casting couch, even for a prestigious debut in a highbrow literary quarterly with an international reputation (it published such names as Auden, Isherwood, Spender, Thomas Mann), I politely thanked him and accepted his invitation but resolved not to sleep with him. Now my famous integrity was put to the test.

We had lunch at Schrafft's (which Auden loved and I considered fancy) and as we left I refused Mann's offer to return to the office. He looked as if I had slapped him. His face began to twitch, his eye developed a tic. With compressed lips he politely told me to look him up again. My poem never appeared in *Decision*, but Chester's did.

18

Montague Terrace

On his return to New York Auden stayed at the George Washington Hotel on Lexington Avenue and Twenty-third Street. There he finished the September poem. Some weeks later he moved into a small but elegant Brooklyn Heights apartment on the top floor of 1 Montague Terrace, a three-story brownstone. From the mullioned windows of this tower-shaped apartment the view of the Manhattan skyline across the East River was breathtaking. Its large living room, rounded bay windows, and tiny adjoining bedroom—an aerie with a single window like a cyclopean eye—overlooked the harbor. Every day Chester arrived after class, then visited me; he spent part of his weekends there, part with me. Occasionally I accompanied him to Wystan's.

On my first visit Auden asked about my WPA job, to which I had returned at the beginning of September as "archivist" at the

Historical Records Survey. This impressive-sounding bureau did nothing more than compilations of data about sewers, bridges, roads—riveting stuff—published as historical source material. All day I sat hunched over a desk writing "entries" that consisted of information from heaps of material that I summarized in precis form. When the entries were placed before me I'd lapse into a coma from which I'd awake abruptly when someone sounded the warning, "Wake up! The supervisor!" I'd pretend to be engrossed until the danger had passed, then I'd relapse into comatose boredom. At twenty-two I was the youngest member of the Writers' Project. "He's only a baby!" one plump young woman would chortle, pinching my cheeks. Some of the men surreptitiously pinched other parts of my anatomy, dropping unveiled hints that I tactfully ignored. One, a bald linguist in his forties who wore T-shirts during the scorching New York summer, complained one day that he'd been ordered not to wear them.

"I don't understand," I said. "I wear them all the time."

He laughed. "On you it looks good. But on me—well, they said I should wear a brassiere." His breasts shook like Jell-O.

I described all this for Wystan. He also asked about my dancing job at the Lama Temple of Tibet at the World's Fair, about which I'd written to Chester in the middle of August. It only lasted a month. I described how the first day we danced in our long-sleeved saffron robes, some cute teen-age boys kept giggling and flirting with me. Afterwards, on my way to the dressing room, one of them said, "Hey, do monks wear Ingersoll wristwatches in Tibet?" I'd forgotten to remove mine. Wystan giggled and asked, "How many twittles can you do?" "Pirouettes," interpreted Chester at my blank stare. Only Wystan would use a word like *twittles*. I've never heard it before or since. "Oh, five or six," I told him. "Let's see you do some," he said. When I informed him that crepe-soled shoes made pirouettes impossible he insisted, "Come on, no excuses." I was foolish enough to attempt it and failed. I would have stood a better chance in stocking feet. I felt embarrassed, knowing by his silence that he thought me incompetent, which was untrue.

One night I picked up a young Hungarian refugee with flaxen hair who was hungry and homeless. From my meager earnings I fed him donuts and coffee in an all-night diner, shared my cigarettes, and took him in. He had a courteous Euro-

pean manner and wholesome cheerfulness. He also had a hood-
lum friend with a harsh voice and no trace of wholesomeness.

"I don't like your friend at all," I'd complain.

Sandor would smile sweetly. "He only talks bad, Harold. He
is not bad. Hugo is my friend." One day Hugo swaggered into
the room, spat, tossed a cigarette butt on the floor, lowered his
skinny frame into the rocker, and in a conspiratorial whisper
said, "Listen, ya know the liquor store on the corner? Good for a
heist."

"You're nuts," I said. "They know us."

"Chickenshit," he sneered. "We go around closing time. I
stick my rod in the old man's mug. Sandor grabs the dough and
I bop the old guy on the bean with the gat. We get out fast."

"And you just walk away?"

"Aw, whadda *you* know? Hey, Sandor, remember Tony the
wop from Dannemora? He'll be waitin' outside with his Stu-
debaker."

Sandor nodded. I had a sick feeling in my gut. So they'd
been prison cellmates. That night I gravely informed Sandor
that he could not stay unless he gave up Hugo and such ideas.
He readily agreed.

Next day I found a note on the mirror of the armoire. In
block letters, scrawled in a wavering illiterate hand, it read:
HAROLD I EM SORY IT IS NUT MY FULT GOODBY SANDOR. I sat on
the bed stupidly staring at the brown scrap of paper torn from a
grocery bag. Then, with a sinking sensation, I fumbled around
in my secret hiding place inside the mattress. My entire savings
were gone.

When later that day I told Chester what happened, he said,
"They never intended to rob the store. It was a diversion to put
you off." At this I burst into tears. Chester tried to console me.
"I'm alone again and broke," I sniveled, feeling sorry for myself.
"Harold," he murmured, "that's not true. You always have me."
His eyes were heavy-lidded—with lust or compassion? I smiled
and washed my face with cold water. A few days later a letter
from Wystan, dated October 10, 1939, arrived with thirty dollars
in cash.

In 1939 thirty dollars was a lot of money. I had no way of
knowing that Auden, with a much higher standard of living, was
himself short of funds. In fact many years passed before I
learned that he had to do reviewing, teaching, and lecturing to

make ends meet. About a month or so later he lent some money to William Empson, who had been robbed and was unable to return to England. Empson recalled that all money from England was frozen and Auden could not at the time expect repayment. He did, however, repay him before leaving. Noble was the word for Auden's behavior, especially since Chester was also accepting money from him and using it as any teen-ager would—for his own pleasures. For my part, I couldn't repay Auden—whose fortunes, in any case, improved through constant hard work and increasing fame. Reassured by his gesture, I wrote a heartfelt thank-you note, convinced that Wystan and Chester cared about my welfare.

19

A Raw Deal

I had read William Saroyan's famous short story, his first publication, "The Daring Young Man on the Flying Trapeze," in *Story* magazine and identified with the starving young writer who lived on water from park fountains. Chester, who'd always spent Christmas and New Year's with me, now spent it with Wystan. On Christmas Eve 1939 I reached the nadir of my morale. I received a card with five dollars from my mother and an equal sum from my Aunt Eva and spent it all on food, bars, and movies, returning home in the early hours of Christmas morning to find my room filled with hissing steam escaping from the open vent of the defective radiator. I had forgotten to replug it before leaving (the valve had to be removed for ten minutes to get the steam up). In the rush to insert the valve I scalded my hand.

The following day a letter from Wystan arrived, undated, but from the Christmas greetings it contained I knew it had been sent a few days earlier. In it he revealed for the first time his awareness of the problem between us, namely our mutual love for Chester, but it also revealed much sympathy for me. As he put it, not without the preachy tone from which his letters would never be quite free (as if speaking from an Anglican pulpit), I was cheated out of my birthright (until then I didn't even know I had one). He also spoke of his own privileged life and, having seen a letter I wrote Chester when they were at Laguna Beach, about a scene with my dancing teacher who had struck me with her cane (I seized it and almost broke it in two and quit dancing for good), Wystan had wanted to write to me. He said that I must also feel bitter about his having taken Chester away from me. This was true. He spoke about suffering as something abhorrent to those who must endure poverty and deprivation, whose acceptance of worldly values, such as wealth and success, produces in them envy and revenge, which must inevitably lead to despair and self-destruction. He exhorted me to accept all that I had suffered as the true gifts of life, and to reject worldly values (I already had) as false. If I accepted my life as it was given, he concluded, he felt very deeply that I would be one of the few who realized the most difficult destiny of all, that of the saint.

His letter was shattering. He saw me as an innocent victim of circumstances and, unlike others I knew, was truly compassionate. I had no doubt that he believed every word he said. But, for the first time, it woke me to the squalor of my life. It also pierced my pride. I was appalled. For he saw no future for me as an artist—given the tremendous disadvantages, from the perspective of the Great Depression, that I would have to overcome: poverty, illegitimacy, no profession. He had consigned me to a life of suffering. The reader may imagine the effect this letter had on me that Christmas.

I had never shown him much of my work and, in any case, he had a negative attitude toward American writing in general. No American, he believed, had produced anything to compare with European literature. His attitude toward Chester's poetry, despite the great love he bore for him, was equally severe.

I could not shake off the feeling that his guilt about "taking Chester away" from me lay behind much of this. I also viewed the letter as religious rhetoric—inspired by euphoric sentiments of the season at a time when he had just converted back to the church—with its sacerdotal tone of an Anglican bishop (the career he would have chosen had he not become a poet).

He concluded by saying that he saw in me a great talent crying out to be recognized, a destiny I could not change: "to be a saint: one of those rare beings whom, when they die, the people who knew them remember . . . for their existence, beings whose presence was enough to make others convinced that human life has not been an entirely vain experiment." But this was not the talent for which I burned.

20

I Become Auden's Secretary

Wystan needed a secretary, and since I was an expert typist he hired me on a part-time basis. I typed his poems and correspondence with explicit instructions on epistolary salutations and farewells. According to degree of intimacy, which he indicated in pencil as "intimate" or "very intimate" after their names, friends were to be addressed as Dear or Dearest, and closed with Love, Much love, while formal letters, closed with Faithfully or Sincerely. Wystan was meticulous about such details. He wrote mostly in pencil, and his handwriting was for the most part legible, though at times he scribbled illegibly and I'd ask him to decipher it. After reading what I had typed he'd grunt approval. His correspondence, domestic and foreign, was large. He paid fifty cents an hour, I think, for about two or three hours at a time, no more than two days a week; and sometimes weeks passed without work.

I always went to Wystan's with Chester, and while they sat in the tiny bedroom I did the typing in the adjacent living room. Usually the bedroom door was left slightly ajar, but sometimes Wystan closed it. I could hear their laughter and conversation.

In early January of 1940 Auden started writing his long poem, "New Year Letter," which he finished in April. This was to become the central part of his new book, *The Double Man.* I clearly recall typing most of the book. One day, as I sat at work in the living room while Wystan and Chester caroused in the bedroom with a bottle of wine amid loud laughter and campy conversation, my fingers struck the keys like a pianist in the mad climax of an onrushing crescendo. I was eager to finish and join them. Finally I completed the ten or so pages of octosyllabic couplets and called through the half-open bedroom door, "Wystan, I'm finished." He emerged, took the penciled manuscript and typescript, remarking on its neatness and absence of erasures (I was, indeed, an expert typist in those days), handed me some correspondence to type, and returned to the bedroom. Again I heard the easy laughter and conversation. Then, abruptly, the laughter ceased, followed by a long silence. I assumed they were making love while I plodded on, when suddenly Wystan burst into the living room in a towering rage.

"You've ruined the manuscript!" he screamed. *"You left out a line! Why the hell didn't you go over it, for God's sake!"* His voice, growing more hysterical, rose in volume and pitch. *"The whole damn poem is in rhymed couplets so you could have easily detected a missing line! It's ruined!"*

This was too much. I leapt to my feet. "It was the only mistake," I muttered with choked resentment. "I can retype it, but I'm leaving!" I grabbed my jacket and put it on, my eyes blurring with tears. Torn between shame and fury Wystan glared nervously, puffing compulsively at his cigarette. He fumbled in his trousers for the wages, paid me, and I fled.

Although I was afraid that our friendship was compromised, he soon forgot the unpleasant episode and all seemed back on track; but bit by bit the close ties loosened until eventually they broke.

In the summer of 1940 Auden and Chester stayed on a farm in Williamsburg, Massachusetts, where Wystan was "getting on" with *The Double Man* and his sonnet sequence, "The Quest." A surviving letter from Chester dated July 2 indicates that little had changed between us. They had been together over a year and Chester had suffered an attack of impotence, which seems to indicate boredom with the sexual aspect of "marriage" to Wystan. He enclosed a new poem, asking me to get two copies made at his father's office, then rhapsodized over the country and its young men.

The next communication, dated July 9, is an exhortation to write him. The face of the penny postcard, to the right of my name and address, contains a verse scribbled in Wystan's hand:

The people of Spain think Cervantes
Equal to half-a-dozen Dantes:
An opinion resented most bitterly
By the people of Italy.

21

The Bawdy House on Middagh Street

After their return from Williamsburg Wystan began looking for a larger apartment so that Chester could live with him. At the end of the month an invitation came from George Davis, a friend of Wystan's who was fiction editor of *Harper's Bazaar*. He had rented a brownstone at 7 Middagh Street, a few blocks from Montague Terrace, and was filling it with friends. Chester raved about his literate wit, his inexhaustible supply of funny stories. In his late thirties, George was short and plump, with a chalky skin under dabs of makeup, his prominent feature consisting of two swollen buns thrust out aggressively in tight-fitting chino pants. "Born to be browned," he crooned airily, "that's what your mother's ass was made for."

George was what in those days was called piss-elegant. He had published a novel, had a stylized, campy wit, and moved with a slow, haughty, disdainful air, like an aging brothel madam. Once, responding to an interviewer querying him on the Middagh Street establishment, George said he was running a boardinghouse, which the reporter heard as "bawdy house." That's how it appeared, to the amusement of the boarders, in the *New Yorker*.

One of the famous boarders was Gypsy Rose Lee, the striptease burlesque queen. With George's help she wrote her best--selling whodunit, *The G-String Murders* (it was rumored that they were married). Carson McCullers, Auden, Paul and Jane Bowles, Benjamin Britten, Peter Pears, and a trained chimpanzee were some of the other famous or soon-to-be-famous inhabitants. One of the lodgers, nicknamed Lazula, an eccentric pundit I knew from the Writers' Project, could smoke a cigarette through his ass and puff out smoke rings. Once he holed up at the "Everhard" Baths for three weeks, subsisting entirely only diet of cocaine, Coca-Cola, cigarettes, and boys. He sent out for whiskey—all, presumably, on his meager WPA salary. Actually, this was impossible; he supplemented his income by writing reviews and pulp fiction under various names.

On my first visit to the "bawdy house" George gossiped with Chester (who, as Auden's boy, had earned George's approval). Then, without offering us refreshments, he launched into a long, hilarious account, in his southern-belle style, about how he had met his man:

"My dear, when I spotted this *gorgeous* hunk of seafood in a Sand Street bar I said to myself, 'Miss Davis, you have met your piece of trade for life . . . so get to work, girl, and literally charm the *pants* off your future husband!' And that's what your mother did. He never said a word—how could he, *pooor* dear! Your mother was blindingly brilliant, as usual. Well, Missy . . . he just listened in his strong silent manly way . . . mmm, the very *thought* of him [shriek]! Sooo, at some un-*god*-ly hour your mother guided him through the unbroken ranks of tiara-studded queens camping shoulder to shoulder—Scylla and Charybdis they should call *that* joint—and we tippy-toe through the juleps right out of there when suddenly your mamà . . . well, dear, you know, finding herself alone in the dark with this big muscular brute—de-*vine*!—gets shivery second thoughts . . . tsk tsk, this *could* be a homicidal maniac, darling, a mad *queer basher* for all *she* knows . . . sooo, 'Mademoiselle Davis,' she says, '*Miss Bazaaar!* get hold of yourself, girl . . . are you out of your cottonpickin' mind? Have you forgotten the first law of cruising? Never . . . *never* . . . [shriek] . . . *never-lose-control!* . . . Just talk the big hunk out of his skivvies before he gets any bright ideas.' And, honey, that's just what your mammy does as we stagger through the deserted streets—not too steady on our pins—towards my bohemian bordello . . . your mother talking for dear life. . . . Sooo . . . next thing she knows her legs are in the air . . . and—she's a respect-able married lady. . . ."

Throughout this outrageous performance Chester giggled and snorted while I sat with a frozen smile, chilled to the bone.

"So what happened? Did he move in?" said Chester, still gig-gling a trifle hysterically.

"Lock, cock, and jock," said George coolly.

"How old is he?" I asked. I hadn't said a word till then.

George looked at me distantly. "Twenty-eight."

"Twenty-*eight*!" I heard my voice sounding shocked, as if he had said eighty-eight.

"Is there anything wrong with *that*?" His tone dripped acid.

"Oh, no, nothing—I—uh—just thought he was younger."

"Oh, you *did*? Well, we're not interested in kiddies, you know."

At this point I was saved from further embarrassment when a big muscular man ambled into the room. He had close-cropped, sandy, thinning hair, a strong rugged face, and a shy manner. For a moment he stood awkwardly playing with his hands and slowly gazing at Chester and me with a puzzled grin. This was clearly George's "husband."

"This is Mort," said George, and we all stared.

He looked like a manservant awaiting orders. George mut-tered something and he answered softly and left.

My debut into the camp world of small talk and effeminate behavior was not a success. I did not like the word *gay*—at that time used only by homosexuals—any more than I liked the word *queer*. Both terms seemed false and degrading. "Femme" types seemed a grotesque parody of both sexes. Then as now mas-culinity was cherished and idealized; we loved the way men walked, talked, looked, smelled, tasted. We worshiped strong, simple farm boys, servicemen, workers. I did not yet understand the courage and heroism of transvestites, who dared to assert what they were in the face of the world's (and their gay brethren's) hatred and contempt. Unwilling to accept being gay, I was a sexist, ageist, sizeist, and looksist—who wasn't? Such words and concepts had to wait another thirty years to be born.

22

Flesh and the Devil

In late winter of 1940 Chester fell in love with "Tom Drew," an attractive, virile Englishman with literary ambitions. A merchant seaman on his first dangerous mission across the Atlantic, Tom arrived in New York with a letter of introduction to Auden (whom he revered) from a mutual friend at Oxford. Intrigued, Auden put him up at Middagh Street, where Tom met Chester, who was even more intrigued. The rest was predictable: both succumbed to each other's considerable charms and I watched it happen from the beginning.

During this affair Chester, who was sexually versatile, specialized in anal passive sex, but although he could be shameless in the meaty details of steamy sex, he was at times paradoxically prudish. Once when I showed him a piece of prose I had written describing two youths in erotic action he was mortified. "Harold, burn it immediately, for God's sake!" he gasped. I was so dismayed I destroyed it.

Auden knew nothing of Chester's new affair, nor did Tom know of their relationship. When Chester revealed it the seaman was horrified and insisted that either Wystan be told or it must end at once. Frightened, Chester begged him to remain silent. Whether George Davis or Chester himself revealed the secret is unclear, but some time before December 1940 Chester may have confessed to Wystan and also announced that he would never sleep with Wystan again. Mad with jealous rage Auden lost control and, while Chester slept, his soft, pudgy fingers curled around Chester's throat in an attempt to strangle him. Chester awoke, furiously pushed Wystan away, and fled. No one was more shocked than Wystan, who wrote a friend: "I was forced to know what it's like to feel oneself the prey of demonic powers, in both the Greek and Christian sense, stripped of self-control and self-respect, behaving like a ham-actor in a Strindberg play." To Chester he later confessed, "On account of you I have been in intention, and almost in act, a murderer." It was the most intense suffering he had ever known. But realizing that life without Chester would be unimaginably bleak, in order not to lose him Wystan was forced to compromise. He submitted to long periods of separation and forms of humiliation and submission whereby Chester would always have the upper hand: "If equal affection cannot be/Let the more loving one be me" became Wystan's motto—a sad but enduring one for the rest of his life. Chester never slept with him again.

Wystan must have suspected Chester of infidelity from the start, but his self-delusion was so great that for a year and a half he had lived convinced that their "marriage," as he called it, had been made in heaven. It was a cruel delusion. Chester had been dazzled by Auden's poetry and fame and at first tried to convince himself that he loved Wystan. His early love letters reveal a schoolboy infatuation and some self-deception, but though he was not physically attracted, he couldn't get over the feeling that the whole affair was "utterly fantastic," as he told me.

That fall Wystan left to teach at the University of Michigan in Ann Arbor. I received a letter dated November 1, 1941, in response to one of mine, in which Wystan goes on in his preachy manner for three handwritten pages, at the end of which he makes a startling confession of grief at losing Chester: "Dear Harold, I shouldn't dare . . . say anything if it weren't for Chester having gone to California, to find his own life. What being without him is like for me, I think you can guess. I feel as if I were scattered into little pieces. And if the Devil were to offer him back to me, on condition that I never wrote another line, I should unhesitatingly accept. Much love, Wystan."

For the next thirty-two years of his life Auden created an astonishing body of work, one of the great oeuvres of any age. Perhaps we owe it all to Chester's cruelty. But I could indeed guess, as Wystan well knew, what it was like to lose Chester. The truth was simply that Chester could not be faithful to anyone. The affair with Tom continued, with Wystan's knowledge, for another year, and then broke up disastrously. Chester returned to promiscuity.

Tom's big mistake was to protect Chester by confirming Auden's obstinate view of his "innocence," (that Chester had slept with only the two of them!—a preposterous distortion of reality on which Wystan continued to insist). Chester had also depicted our affair as a schoolboy romance, an intimate friendship like that of Auden and Isherwood (though Wystan's letters show that he knew better).

After the affair with Tom broke up, Chester introduced him to a very good-looking boy whom he immediately set up: he told him Tom had fallen for him at sight. Then he encouraged Tom to pursue him and they were smitten. What Chester had neglected to tell Tom was that the handsome youth was one of Wystan's new boyfriends. When Wystan discovered this—through Chester?—he asked to see Tom and informed him that he had again usurped one of his lovers. Again Tom protected Chester by not revealing that he had set the whole thing up. Wystan behaved in a rude and disagreeable manner and, to his horror, Tom realized that Chester had poisoned Wystan against him. Then both Wystan and Chester united in blackballing him forever.

Privy to many of Chester's imbroglios, slowly I grew aware that my days as a principal player in Chester's or Wystan's life were numbered, hastened by Chester's deceits, Wystan's gullibility, and Pearl Harbor.

23

Greetings!

During the summer of 1941 I received from my draft board the dreaded greetings card. Although President Roosevelt had assured us that America would stay out of the war, young men were being called up for conscription. Partly intrigued by the prospect of being a commissioned officer, thanks to a college degree that had served no useful purpose until then, and partly repelled as a pacifist who, in the name of humanity, condemned all wars, I found myself morally and emotionally torn. How could I justify being a conscientious objector when the plight of Jews and gays became more desperate in Germany and the Nazi-occupied countries of Europe? I had to deal with entering a global conflict where, with luck, I might be killed or, worse, returned home as a basket case.

I remember a middle-aged man in the tenement where I lived—a leftist writer and composer—who saw me extract the familiar greetings card from the mailbox and slapped me heartily on the behind. "Well, well, if it isn't the cute bit of cannon fodder," he said, beaming with savage humor, "getting called up by his Uncle, at last. Just the right age, boy. Didn't you always say you'd love to see Europe?"

What would it be like, I wondered, as a raw recruit in the army or navy? The answer was clear: like a pasha in a harem forbidden to touch the naked girls. A well-informed pacifist friend dissuaded me from any inclination to join up, recommending Dalton Trumbo's book about the first war, *Johnny Get Your Gun.* If the draft board believed I was not suitable military material, she said, they would grant a deferral. I decided to be myself, whoever that was.

Days later in a high school gym with hundreds of other naked youths, like government-inspected hunks of meat we waited in line and watched "short-arm" and "brown-eye" inspection, bending over and spreading our buttocks for Uncle Sam. When the finger probed deep into the anal recesses every head turned away. The whole scene screamed *Queer*—but it was a case of the emperor's new clothes. The men played it with a straight face. I was afraid I'd get an erection, but to my relief found the probe painful. This proved I was a man. I had always felt like one. Our totem poles in this extended family of brothers under the foreskin were not supposed to stick out lest we show that we loved one another better than our country, which was unpatriotic.

So many conflicting emotions arose within me that I could hardly think. I was directed to a row of cubicles and at a signal from a guard, I entered one. A bespectacled snowy owl at an oak desk motioned me to a seat opposite him. After perusing some official papers, he began questioning me.

"Do you think you could adjust quickly to the armed forces?"

"I don't know, doctor. Maybe not quickly."

"Is there any reason why you might not adjust?"

"Well, I—I might find army routine hard to take."

"I see." He scribbled something as a faint cloud of suspicion crossed his features. "Do you consider yourself normal?"

"I—well, yes, I guess so," I stammered. He shot me a penetrating look.

"What do you most enjoy doing?"

"Writing and reading poetry." I watched his eyebrows arch.

"Poetry?" I had blown my cover. "Do you—dream of women?"

"Oh, yes, yes!" I tried to sound enthusiastic.

"And do you"—he lowered his voice—"also dream of men?"

"Uh—doesn't everyone?" I mumbled.

He looked stern. *"Intimate* dreams, young man?"

I nodded.

"By intimate I mean of a—a *sexual* nature." He barely whispered.

"Sometimes," I said softly.

The pen scratched rapidly. When he looked up his face had set. I was trapped by the machinery of government into an admission of the most personal, confidential sort. I hadn't, however, confessed to an overt act of "perversion." With an air of finality the shrink stamped the documents, coldly instructing me to present them at the outside desk.

As I stumbled through the gym in a daze I glanced surreptitiously at the nude bodies of the silent young men, so exposed, so vulnerable, such fresh, tender meat on the government rack, and I was almost swept away by a wave of brotherly lust. They were so silent, obedient, cowed, and ashamed that I felt like kissing and licking them all back to shape, saying, "There, now, doesn't it feel better?" Before reaching the desk I glimpsed the top page of the report. It bore a large red stamp: PRE-PSYCHOTIC STATE. 4-F. DEFINITELY NOT TO BE RETURNED. Beneath was scribbled F-REACTIONS. Feminine reactions? Fag, freak, funny reactions? Officially, I was a borderline case in a prepsychotic state. But I was free.

24

Pilgrim's Progress

S ince Auden had recommended one of our friends for a scholarship toward a master's degree at the University of Michigan in Ann Arbor, I wrote him requesting a similar recommendation. As the war drew closer, only weeks before Pearl Harbor, I found myself hankering for the cloistered walls of ivy. Wystan's response ended this dream. In his letter of November 1, 1941, I received yet another homily. For self-imposed moralistic reasons he could not recommend me for the scholarship. As a result, a new chapter in my life was about to unfold.

25

World War II

T he Alabama Drydock and Shipbuilding Company in Mobile was a humid inferno of mud, shrieking machines, and death. That men fell from towers and bulkheads to be smashed like bugs on metal decks went unreported in the press, hushed up, presumably, for the sake of the war effort. Each day saw at least one body falling into the depths of holds, halting work for a few minutes. With three shipyards operating at capacity, the town had tripled its population. Most of the men came from other cities to make money and avoid the draft. They came from neighboring states, from the hills and prairies. They came from lumber camps in Washington and offices in New York. When the town could hold no more they spilled over on the banks of rivers, living in tents and along the roads in trailers and lean-tos. For the first time since the bank holiday of 1930 jobs were to be had for the asking.

I lived with three men in one room, shared the same bath, gas stove, refrigerator, and party-line phone. Each slept in a corner on a cot, partitioned by screens, blankets, and bed sheets. If anyone complained of cramped conditions, the others said we were lucky to be at the "home front" instead of in combat. Secretly we felt guilty about earning money while "our boys" were dying overseas. We lived in a fine house with a wrought-iron balcony in a quiet neighborhood. It was the lesser evil.

At night, when I walked the warm, oak-lined streets after the day's work was done, I could hear in the darkness soft voices uttering oaths behind the flickering glow of cigarettes on frame porches and grillwork balconies. In the downtown district loud jukebox music, mostly wheezing mouth organs and country guitars, blared from the bars. Oaths and curses came from within, harsh and violent. The drinkers could not disburden themselves—through liquor and sex—of confusion and loneliness. The music reflected their dilemma in sentimentality for wide-open spaces, for escape. Love and sex dominated the songs, but the void could never be filled, yearning haunted each note. Nasal voices and the twang of the jew's harp sounded sorrowful in the night. I felt lonely and out of place.

If it hadn't been for Eric I might have shipped out to European ports (tankers were sunk by German U-boats whose periscopes could be spied in the gulf off the coast of Mobile). A twenty-year-old cornsilk blond Norwegian from New Jersey, Eric was the only other "Yankee" in the house. At the end of the day when he removed his grimy work shirt, revealing a wet muscular torso that glistened like alabaster, and fell heavily on his cot clad only in boxer shorts that clung stickily to his thighs and crotch, it was all I could do to keep my hands off him. But he thought of nothing but girls. He'd dwell on the spicy details of what he was going to do to his latest pickup that evening. Then in sheer animal spirits he'd grab me and we'd wrestle, hot and sweaty in our shorts. Afterwards he'd collapse on his cot complaining of the heat. Though soaking wet we were unable to use the bathroom—the "Chief" always occupied it. Eric would leap to his feet chattering like a monkey, swearing under his breath. "The fat slob! He's been in there at least a half 'n hour, ain't he? The fuckin' hog. Let's bang on the door!"

The "Chief," a cockney who had been chief engineer on a British battleship in the first war, had settled in Texas, married, and raised a family. Stodgy and set in his ways, he was short and chunky, with sparse white hair, a pendulous paunch, and the most enormous low-hanging balls we'd ever seen, like an old bull's. He shuffled about the house grumbling and monopolizing the bathroom and refrigerator. We all dined at a boardinghouse across the street where latecomers received minuscule portions of food, for point rationing had recently begun. Unless we got home before the "Chief," we'd get leftovers: small hard bits of dry beef, pea soup turned into green concrete, and stale, bitter coffee.

Mr. "Noll," assistant superintendent in the Outfitting Department where we worked, came home last. A tall, lean, taciturn ex-lawyer in his fifties, he read Rupert Brooke and shyly hinted that in his youth in World War I he too had written poetry.

The "Chief" left no room in the fridge for our butter, milk, cheese, and Coca-Cola, which he'd place outside to spoil in the heat. One evening he found three of his bottles of cream—which he drank before retiring—on top of the fridge and our food inside. Infuriated, he confronted me and I confessed. "You're not the only one here," I said coldly. "We have equal rights to the refrigerator *and* bath."

The old man gasped, turned purple. "Ahrrr," he growled. "We shall bloody well see about that! Just you wait, you—you—"

My eyes fell on a large, colored map of Europe, the middle page of a Sunday rotogravure section spread on the *eau de Nile* wall. The year on the page was 1942. The room was full of shadows, its single long window with thick lace curtains filtering the light of the waning day. It was a beautiful room, with a high sculptured ceiling and neoclassical moldings. "Scale: 1 inch equals 50 miles," I read. "Shaded area indicates German-occupied territory." France was in the shaded area. I concentrated on France. The old Brit was fighting another war—to occupy the refrigerator, bath, and kitchen table and, out of sheer malice, also the Winthrop desk where I wrote letters, a journal, poetry, and fiction. Once a week he wrote his wife a letter that took two minutes, but he'd remove my papers from the desktop, crumpling them carelessly into a bottom drawer. He was fighting World War II against the barbarian hordes of youth, but I had won the Battle of the Fridge.

This little war continued until disaster struck. One hot day I returned home early, my teeth chattering violently. Mr. Noll asked if I had a pain in the right side, which I had, and said gravely, "Young man, you've got to see a doctor at once."

"But why can't I just go to bed?" I objected. "I'll be okay."

"I've seen this before," he insisted. "We're taking no chances!" He hustled me into his Pontiac and drove to a doctor, who placed me on a gurney, palpated my side and said, "Not a minute to lose. Surgery. Sign here." He shoved an official form at me. I hesitated. "Young man, you have minutes to go!" he snapped. I signed. Peritonitis had almost set in as I went under the knife. Like any other boy, I was just another piece of meat in the meat grinder of war. This was my war wound, my Purple Heart, my Croix de Guerre. I would wear it forever.

The deep McBurney incision had to be drained. A ribbon of gauze yards long kept turning viscous yellow and was replaced until the wound was entirely clean. No mere routine appendectomy, no one-inch incision and a day in the hospital; this was a rescue mission. Mr. Noll had saved my life.

A week later I was back on the job, moving slowly and delicately. In a month I was walking upright and the red stitch marks had paled to pink. One warm Sunday Eric and I visited my favorite recreation spot, the "world-famous" Bellingrath Gardens, which, I believe, claimed the largest azalea beds in America: seas of purple, lavender, and cochineal stretched in boundless profusion. The lush tropical verdure and sweet heady odors intoxicated me. There were also hydrangeas and camellias and from the live oaks hung Spanish moss in hazy tresses. Lazily we trod the flagstone paths with the scent of gardenias behind boxwood borders as brown thrushes fussed among dead leaves. Seated on an iron-grillwork bench on a luxuriant parterre with a marble fountain, we looked out over a broad glassy lake. There were surprisingly few strollers in the quiet bowers and sudden steep descents. Eric chattered mindlessly of girls and fistfights and of the knives he owned, to subdue any assailant. His lank yellow hair fell over his merry blue eyes and his Jersey accent sounded foreign there. He took a snapshot of me ("Smile for the birdie!") seated on a white railing with two-toned Thom McAn shoes and striped T-shirt, the garden lake behind me.

26

A Lesser Evil?

One blazing afternoon in the shipyard I witnessed a coldblooded murder—a black man among hundreds of crazed whites beaten to death before my eyes with fists and lead pipes. His crime: he had been "sassy," they said. Talked back to a white man. *"Lahnch 'im! Kill 'im!"* they screamed. *"Lemme get a whack at 'im! Gimme a lick at the nigger!"* Jostling and shoving to get close enough to hit him, their features twisted with rage and hate, they howled insanely. I saw a sheet-metal worker bashing the black man, who was on his knees trying to shield his bleeding head and face with both hands. His hair, peppered with gray, was oozing blood. Then I saw a worker from our group, a brutal, handsome blond of nineteen who had threatened everyone in the shop, including me; once he stomped a kitten to death as if snuffing a cigarette, drawling, "How'd ya lahk mah boot on *yore* face, mashin' yew, Norse?" Now he was raining blows on the hapless black man. When I screamed, *"Stop! For God's sake!"* his lip curled. "Shut up, Norse," he snarled, "or we'll lahnch yew, too!" Then two more of our religious Baptist boys savagely attacked the man. My stomach churned. Sweat poured down my back and chest. I heard the heavy breathing, the shouts and grunts, the thud of blows on bone. It seemed unreal. On his knees the black man looked up from a broken, bloody face. How can I ever forget that look? The look of a martyr, of the sacrificial lamb, the innocent victim of popular delusions of the madness of crowds. The rolling eyes were no longer wide with terror but glazed with shock, the look of prey in the lion's jaws. He died before my eyes. They had bashed in his brains, these true believers in God and the Bible. Even as they fought the Nazis, the racist fundamentalists were in the grip of their own mass psychosis. The two-headed eagle of ignorance and prejudice spread its wings over America. Karl Marx was wrong: religion was not, as he thought, the opiate but the mania of the masses. I came to the realization that if these crazies gained control, the United States would be as evil as Nazi Germany.

At the office of the leading newspaper in Mobile I showed the editor my article on the shipyard murder. "Are there any other witnesses?" he asked. "I couldn't get any." "Then it never happened," he snapped, shoving my story across the desk.

27

Crimes Against Nature

The "Chief" remained on the warpath, and the landlady had a vacant cot upstairs with two boys about my age. "You'll like the boys," said the landlady—a terrific understatement. One was a tall creamy blond of eighteen with a cherubic face and flame-red lips; the other, about twenty, was a body builder with incredible muscles. For two nights I tossed and turned, unable to sleep, their bodies drawing me like magnets. Then a remarkable thing happened. Bud, the blond, beckoned. Doubting my senses, I sat up; sure enough, he whispered, "C'mere!" Naked in the moonlight he lay invitingly, aroused and ready. I got up and hovered over him; his hand lightly brushed my leg. I bent down and he grabbed the back of my neck and drew me on top of him. Arching his pelvis, he ejaculated as I came on his thigh. He lay still awhile, then hoarsely whispered, "Don't *ever* do that again, hear?" I was thunderstruck: *he* had made the advances. "Why? Didn't you like it?" "It's a crime against nature," he said smugly. "It *is* nature," I said indignantly.

"You asked for it!" "Never mind!" he replied sharply. "Jest stay in yore own bed, hear? And leave Warren alone!" "That's *his* business," I said, angrily rising to my feet. "It's mine!" he snapped. "If I ketch yew touchin' him it'll cost yew yore job!" He probably helped kill the black man, I thought bitterly.

Next night I heard Bud snoring. The full moon burned like a torch in the starry sky, flooding the room with silvery light. I dozed fitfully in the intense heat, then heard a flapping sound and saw Warren's nude body glowing in the moonlight. He was masturbating. I crept toward him and stretched out my hand, ready to risk a hostile reaction, if necessary, and felt the taut bands of muscle near his groin. He started violently, stared a moment, then reached out and stroked my chest and belly, feeling the hair. In the moonlight we devoured each other like starving cannibals.

Pursued by wrathful demons, I had to keep moving. In a doorless room between parlor and kitchen I bunked with a fifteen-year-old boy in another house. The new landlady and occupants sauntered in and out of the kitchen all night, turning on lights, rattling cups and saucers as the boy thrashed like a sex-crazed octopus. Occasionally I peeked under the sheets; as I suspected, the Great Need had reared its lovely head, but I was not about to dally with a minor in Dixie, the strains of Baptist righteousness still fresh in my ears. I dozed fitfully, hearing the Christian saints in the shipyard chanting, "Kill him!" and Saint Bud snarling, "Crime against nature!" as he pressed me to his sweaty bosom. At dawn I found the boy wrapped around me like an anaconda. Gently disengaging myself from his smooth limbs, I went to work red-eyed and that night requested another room, only to be paired with an overweight Cuban clubfoot with an aggressive interest in my rump. Again I changed partners, this time with a blond eighteen-year-old protected by an invisible cloak of Christian virtue.

One day he drove us in his shiny Chevy to a laundress who was so busy she made us wait two hours. She'd never taken this long before, Jamie told me. When we left it was dark. Across the road in the dirt and gravel of a run-down shack with a wooden sign reading BAR with an inverted R, stood some young blacks who stared with drunken hostility. A big stone whizzed past us. "Bad news!" muttered Jamie under his breath. "Run, Harold!" He scampered down the dirt road with me after him, holding my right side with one hand and my laundry with the other. From the sharp pain I knew that the incision had not healed entirely. The youths took after us and I saw myself murdered by a black mob in a black ghetto, a martyr to race hatred, like the old Negro in the shipyard. "I'm a friend!" I wanted to shout, but I was only another white face.

As I scampered blindly in the direction Jamie had taken, suddenly my path was blocked by a big black man whose hand shot up before my nose. "*Stop!*" he ordered in a deep voice. A street lamp shone in my eyes. "Two bits, white boy, and yew pass!" he muttered with a fierce scowl. I dug frantically in my pocket, fished out a quarter, and plunked it into his outstretched palm. He broke into wild, echoing laughter and, with a theatrical sweep of his arm, waved me on. Miraculously I found Jamie just as he was scurrying into his car. The boys were almost upon us when I scuttled in, lungs bursting, and off we roared in a puff of smoke.

I had no divine call for sheet metal. In fact, I loathed it. I couldn't wait to see the last of that filthy shipyard. All day the workers drilled and hammered and caulked, they welded, rat-proofed, and sheared. They spat and pissed on the ground and talked only of "pussy" and "keepin' the niggers in their place." At the end of 1942, after about ten months of my season in hell, having saved some money, I sped as fast as I could back to the Big Apple.

28

Cruising

On the third floor of the old West Side YMCA on Sixty-second Street I had a monkish cell over Central Park with the standard bed, chair, desk, and Bible. There was a housing shortage, which grew more acute on weekends when servicemen arrived from their bases like invading troops, their pent-up erotic needs demanding immediate attention.

Greenwich Village and Times Square were the main targets; YMCA's were another. In a discreet way men surrendered to the pressures of loneliness and transience by making contact under the bright lights. With the stress of dislocation and impending doom, almost anyone in uniform was available, although some young men, mostly from farms and small towns, retained their sexual prejudices until, having firmly voiced their objections, their bigotry died hard. A significant number thus became sexually liberated. Toward this end I performed my patriotic duty.

My experiences ranged from quickies in hot showers or behind park bushes to one-night stands. Straight boys, facing the threat of extinction, quickly yielded to the gods of nature, Priapus and Bacchus (who never die). Far from their home communities, unhindered by what others thought, most responded willingly to homosexual acts. With a cross-section of young men from the entire country overrunning the city, it became apparent that our sexual behavior could hardly be regarded as "different"—if anything, it seemed very much the norm. When thrown together en masse American males indulged in same-sex acts in overwhelming numbers, indicating that, at least under wartime conditions, such behavior is natural. In the all-male atmosphere at the Y, whether in the lounge, washrooms, or showers, this was conspicuously evident. During the war one might safely assume that those who resisted homosexuality were perverts. But we were tolerant, setting out with moral zeal to convert the heathen. Here is a poem I wrote then:

YMCA Lounge

Behind the daily papers and cigarettes
they relax. Some read, most sit
and stare at The Three Fates *on the wall*
while Tschaikowsky's Hamlet *overture*
grieves. Eyelids droop. Talk rises, falls.

In the corridors boys leap
clutching small bags with the odor of keds.
Old men rasp to sailors stretching jersey thighs.
House phones ring at the desk. The Spanish motif
of hanging iron holders for flame-bulbs sheds
an embalming, funereal glow, reflects

the baldness of one with a turquoise ring
and pointed black shiny shoes. Odors
of hot athletes pervade the lounge, armpits
tangy with musk. The young men watch
each other with studied indifference, rise
and leave and return under stained glass
windows and porticoes. Eyes sometimes lock
and, with significant glances, the youths go
into the hall together murmuring
and ride the elevator to a room
or lavatory. The grieving overture
switches to Gaité Parisienne.

I saw some old friends, including Chester Kallman, who, back from Ann Arbor in 1943, sent a postcard from 792 East Twenty-first Street, inviting me to his apartment. We remained cordial for years.

At the Y I met an unemployed actor in his thirties with small twinkling blue eyes, sparse blond hair, and a campy wit. "Sid," as I'll call him, was one of those queens who couldn't even bid you good evening without a lewd double entendre. But by some inexplicable twist of fate, he proved to be the agent of a significant event in my life. One day we visited a friend of his in a small but charming apartment in the East Seventies. Also a blue-eyed blond ex-actor, he now worked for the post office. About Sid's age, Larry had a square jaw, dimpled chin, horn-rimmed glasses, and a forced gaiety. They gossiped, quipped, and throatily mimicked Tallulah Bankhead, Greta Garbo, and Marlene Dietrich, the pop goddesses of camp. Sid displayed me like a trophy, as if to impress on Larry that I was his catch (which I wasn't). Finally, when I rose to leave, Larry stared intently. "Your face is *very* familiar," he said. Memory stirred. At that moment we both remembered. "Larry" was Milton Lazarus (not his real name), the high school boy from the Bay Ridge apartment house where I lived when I was eleven. That night the recognition scene stole the show.

For fifteen years, with a morbid intensity bordering on the pathological, Larry had retained the image of me as an eleven-year-old boy lost among the city's millions, clinging to it like a delicate glass menagerie from his vanished youth. Now I materialized before him as a blue-jawed young man, sturdy and robust. And with him I remained for well over a year, settling into my first experience of being kept. I needed roots desperately, and this was as close an approximation as I was likely to find, serendipitously dropped into my lap. Fortunately, Larry was a kind, generous soul with a cultivated literary style, sensitive and nuanced, but he did not develop the gift. Fragile and vulnerable, he clearly lacked sufficient confidence for the insecure life of an artist.

At thirty-two, withdrawn and bitter after dreams of the stage had dwindled into disappointment, his existence as a civil servant was empty and meaningless. But though he lacked the determination required to pursue a career, his great passion for the theatre, which he faithfully attended, never died. Until I entered his life he'd had no love or, indeed, sexual experience. True, we had a history, a shared past, but the relationship was built on sand. He lived a sequestered life, I wanted the free love and artistic community of a young Bohemia. Thus it was like any marriage: two deluded individuals vow to deceive each other till truth do them part.

The one-room-kitchenette apartment had a large bath and railed balcony in the rear overlooking a garden, giving the illusion of space. It sparkled with Depression moderne, neat, clean, with light, sun, and air when available. Larry labored at the post office while, in my blue flannel ski suit (a gift from him), I labored at loafing. In the morning I wrote poetry and sunbathed, weather permitting, and in the afternoon I cruised. Although good-looking (he bore a strong family resemblance to Leslie Howard and Kirk Douglas, Anglo-Saxon superstars who, like him, in private were blond European Jews), Larry had an air of defeat about him. Marriages have ended for less, but impotence has destroyed most on the wedding night. As the young phallic god I performed my duties well, but even I could not raise this Lazarus from the dead. Once I hypnotized him and raised the member in question as, dazed and perspiring, it stood up under posthypnotic suggestion, but soon passed away never to return. Though forced to betray our nuptial vows, I did not betray his secret. Somewhere in his youth he had embraced defeat with an energy others brought to success. With a demeanor of mourning (was it Jewish Orthodox guilt and lamentation?) he faced the world as one who did not belong to it. His heroes were heroines, chief of whom was the misanthropic Garbo, whose fallen-woman portrayals of Anna Christie, Anna Karenina, and Camille struck a resounding chord in his disillusioned soul. *"Ay vant to be aloone,"* he crooned, and I realized I had come between them; I'd made a brilliant entrance into the wrong script. He was better off with Garbo: she at least would not deceive him.

We moved to various rooms on the city, ending in the Village, where I finally left him. He had showered me with gifts and endearments, asking nothing in return but understanding and fidelity. The former I could supply in abundance, but the latter put me on a leash. Larry's bouts of morbid gloom drove me to compulsive cruising—in bars, subway T-rooms, movies, and the Village.

One night on Sixth Avenue and Eighth Street a Danish baron picked me up and in his elegant apartment displayed my nude body in a wall-length mirror, rhapsodizing, "You are ballet! Sculpture!" as I struck Nijinsky attitudes from *Spectre de la Rose*. Next morning I woke from a wet dream, ejaculating; his lap dog was lapping it up.

"Suki, you *bitch!*" screamed the baron. "You have stolen my trade!" For a moment I considered hustling, but I had scruples I couldn't afford. The baron begged me to stay, offering luxury, travel, income; but he had gray hair and, though handsome, kept his head artificially tilted forward to prop up a sagging chin. Besides, I knew I'd never be a match for Suki, his true love.

29

Greenwich Village

One day a friend called Johnny Talayco brought me to a slum of decaying tenements on the Lower East Side, on First Avenue and Eleventh Street. Through a rusted iron gate we entered a courtyard of wash-laden clotheslines and reeking, overflowing garbage cans; it was known as Paradise Alley. In a cold-water flat with a grimy skylight lived a young man called Harry Herschkowitz. Scotch-taped on the walls were original watercolors by Henry Miller and pages of the outline for Harry's novel, *Alfred's Younger Brother*. Tall, emaciated, with a heroic, handsome head of curly brown hair, Harry was the stereotypic bohemian. He was the protégé of Henry Miller, had traveled many times around the globe as a merchant marine, and had endless, fascinating tales to unfold about the Persian Gulf and the Shatt al-Arab. With a single published story in *Circle* magazine, called "The Bulbul Birds" (Miller, Anaïs Nin, and Lawrence Durrell had also appeared in the first issue), Harry had gained legendary status. Three poems of mine had also appeared and caught the eye of Miller and Nin.

Harry had published the first issue of a magazine called *Death*. Hearing that he needed a poetry editor, I volunteered, and having admired my poems in *Circle,* he said, "You're on." All he knew about poetry, he said, he had learned in bed from women poets. "I introduced Miller to Lepska, my old lady, and they got married, which relieved us both, ha ha. I can't be tied to one woman. I want to fuck them all."

Miller and Harry flaunted their machismo, their lack of formal education, their domination of women, whom they treated with arrogant contempt. Harry repeated Henry's remark: "If you can't fuck it, eat it. If you can't eat it, piss on it." Sensitive guys. Though I'd had few sexual relations with the opposite sex (mostly prostitutes), I would soon have an affair with a woman.

I never had a chance to exercise my editorial skill—*Death* died with its first issue, although *Life* almost revived it with an article; Harry's face also appeared on the cover of *Newsweek:* as spokesman for a strike of the Maritime workers. He had a natural gift for publicity. A decade later *Death* became reincarnated in Allen Ginsberg's *Howl*—"who ate fire in paint hotels or drank turpentine in Paradise Alley, death"—surely a reference to the magazine, although the footnote in Ginsberg's *Collected Poems* (Harper & Row, 1984) mentions only "PARADISE ALLEY: A slum courtyard N.Y. Lower East Side, site of Kerouac's *Subterraneans,* 1958." It would come as a surprise if Kerouac had *not* been drawn by the magnetic madness of Harry, for we all drank at the San Remo, where Kerouac and I traded drunken insults and perhaps they traded women. Harry was a Jewish Neal Cassidy, also born and reared in Denver. The works of Dostoevski, Miller, Nin, Michael Fraenkel, and Nietzsche (from whom Fraenkel had derived many ideas) cluttered the orange crates that served as bookshelves. But Harry had set too high a goal. Overwhelmed by too many concepts, he talked much and wrote little.

We'd meet around the fountain in Washington Square, where he knew everybody. One day he introduced me to a slender young man with a small boy in tow. "This is Bob De Niro, a talented painter," said Harry, "and his son Bobby." The boy, around four or so, jumped in and out of the watery basin making a mess. An Irish-Italian, Bob was separated from his wife, Virginia Admiral, also a painter. Broke like the rest of us, how he managed to bring up the boy I don't know. He was dreamy and bland. The other day I saw a full-page 1947 photo in *Vanity Fair* of Bob and Bobby in his lap seething with cherubic energy, just as I remember them, Bob with his wavy blond hair, handsome, languid, and wistful. The cover story, of course, was on the young De Niro, a famous film star.

Another painter I met at the fountain through Harry I had read about in Miller's monograph *The Amazing and Invariable Beauford Delaney*. Short, stocky, bald, a middle-aged black man with the face of a shaman and an air of being in touch with unconscious forces, Beauford stared as if I were a talisman or painting, never removing his large sad eyes from mine, making slow, elaborate gestures as he spoke, showing his palms as if smoothing a canvas. Beauford, said Harry, was wise and kind. Years later, after many attempts, he finally succeeded in committing suicide in Paris.

Then, one long winter night in January 1943, which began at the San Remo and ended near dawn in Bickford's Cafeteria on Fourteenth Street, I met someone who would become a very special friend. As we left the cafeteria in the fog and bitter cold, a small black youth loped swiftly toward us through the mist, a woolen navy watch cap pulled down around his ears, his wild eyes bugging out alarmingly, giving him the crazed look of a junkie about to kill for a fix. Wearing only a torn blue sweater over a thin shirt, he was shivering. He looked as if he'd gladly cut our throats for a quarter. To my surprise Harry greeted him warmly.

"Jimmy! How the hell are ya? I thought you were a mugger!"

"I was worried myself," said Jimmy with a radiant smile. "Two white men skulking in the mist in the early hours can only mean trouble for a defenseless black boy." We laughed.

"Jimmy, I want you to meet a friend of mine, a poet," said Harry. "Jimmy Baldwin meet Harold Norse."

We smiled and nodded, stamped our feet, blew into our frozen hands, and rubbed them together. "Have you been published?" Jimmy asked with interest. I had—in *Poetry, Accent,* and *Circle.* He was impressed. In those days it was hard to break into print.

"You look very young," he said archly, "no more than twenty."

"Twenty-six," I said.

He stared in fascination. "You look absurdly young," he repeated wistfully. He was nineteen. With his half-starved, gaunt face he looked much older—in the misty light of the cafeteria window his brown parchment skin reflected a silvery glow like an ancient African mask. It was impossible to imagine that in ten years this starved, threadbare black ragamuffin would become a major spokesman for the civil rights movement and that his fiery essays and novels would help change the world.

Deciding on more hot coffee, we returned to the deserted cafeteria, where we talked and smoked till dawn. Jimmy had a concise, accurate way of putting things, with a rapid delivery and no trace of a southern accent. His mind was nimble, he spoke with conviction and made his points. One thing I clearly recall: Jimmy said that he felt estranged from Harlem, with its poverty and limitations and, except in the Village, felt alien in the white world. In either case he was in a ghetto, outside the mainstream, he said, an oddity in Harlem, which he had left two years earlier. Small and slight, he sounded like an educated white man and was regarded with suspicion and hostility in Harlem. "Hey, nigger! Ya wanna be white? Black ain't good enough for you? You must be crazy, boy!" Except for bohemians and radical intellectuals, with whom he lived and slept, he was discriminated against by both races. "Ya gotta disarm the enemy," Harry said. "They call you nigger, become 'the crazy nigger of Harlem.' Deal with them on *your* terms, not theirs, or you'll despise yourself. Let go like Miller, Artaud. Don't be trapped by their idea of you!"

Harry's solution held little appeal for Jimmy. He was too realistic to adopt the bizarre behavior that was common both in the Village and in Harlem, the flight into a fantasy world. He made a few conciliatory responses like "uh huh," and "perhaps," but his brows remained furrowed with concern. His protruding eyes glittered, darting from mine to Harry's. He looked to me rather than to Harry for support. I felt that I understood his predicament better, could empathize more. As the night wore on we knew that we had something in common that Harry couldn't share. When he said, "All right, Jimmy, so you're poor, black, and queer, but that's what will make you strong," Jimmy and I exchanged a look of understanding. Being queer was even worse than being black, Jewish, or poverty-stricken. Among bottom dogs gays were the bottom.

Jimmy and I saw a great deal of each other, managing to cadge drinks at the San Remo, Minetta's, and MacDougal's Tavern. The latter, a basement dive in MacDougal Alley, was a dark seedy gay bar run by Italians. A couple of doors south was a lesbian bar where drunken sailors tried to pick up women and got beat up by tough bull dykes. The sailors never understood why. A few doors north, Jimmy waited on tables for tips in a tiny restaurant called the Calypso, serving spicy, mouth-watering West Indian food. Connie Williams, the owner, was a hefty, chuckling Jamaican black woman whose motherliness and sweetness gave warmth to our lives, as did her food. Like so many others, mostly whites, she took Jimmy under her wing and fed him, clucking and chuckling like a mother hen. In the red-bulbed dim cellar the tables were always full.

One night Jimmy introduced me to a boy called Russell Edson whose father, Gus, drew the syndicated cartoon strip "The Gumps," which I had followed in childhood. Russell was only sixteen and, as I recall, had long hair, unheard of in those days. He was extremely bright and precocious and went on to become a master of the prose poem, achieving fame in a genre he made entirely his own. Whenever Jimmy, Russell, and I arrived Connie would call out in her ringing contralto, "Here comes de Gumps!" Then, even if only Jimmy and I arrived, she'd call it out anyway, followed by a rippling cascade of laughter.

Another friend of Jimmy's was Mason Hoffenberg, a cantankerous youth who drank too much and had a sharp tongue that kept you laughing—if it wasn't directed at you. Like most of us, Mason was well read but indulged in the Village pastime of putting down writers with a contempt that couldn't mask ill-concealed envy. His blue eyes danced with malicious humor. Small, with a ruddy face that revealed bad temper, Mason, although not exactly ugly, was simply unbeauteous. His nasal, unpleasant whine grated on the nerves, and his merciless wit drew blood.

Years later in Paris, where he had lived since 1948 with a French wife, he still greeted me with derogatory remarks. "Everybody I know has been mentioned in *Time* magazine at least once," he snarled in an encounter on the Boulevard Saint Germain. "I'll bet even *you* have been written up." I hadn't been and he was then known as the coauthor, with Terry Southern, of the best-selling novel *Candy*. Until he died he remained an old hand at making success sound like a social disease. Once, in a violent argument with Jimmy, who had just received a Saxton Fellowship to complete his first novel, Mason belittled the event and Jimmy shouted furiously, "I haven't seen *you* break into print yet!"

Even in the Village Jimmy was by no means immune to racist attacks. One night, an hour or so before he waited on tables at Connie's (meals didn't begin till about 9:00 P.M.), we went to Mac-Dougal's as usual and ordered two beers. The thickset barman stared at Jimmy a trifle sheepishly. "I can't serve you, Jimmy," he said. We thought we hadn't heard him correctly. "Two beers, Tony," Jimmy repeated. Pushing a beer toward me Tony shook his head. His face was set. "I don't understand, Tony. What have I done?" Tony ignored him. "I asked what I've done, Tony." Jimmy started to shout. "Don't make no trouble or I'll have to throw you out," growled Tony. "Come on, Jimmy," I urged. "Let's go!" But Jimmy was out of control. Fearing for his safety I seized him with both arms and pulled him kicking and screaming out the door.

30

Crying Holy

Jimmy would stare into my eyes, grasp my hand in both of his, and say, "You know I'm very fond of you," or "I think of you all the time." One evening he invited me to an apartment where he was staying and put a bulky, battered manuscript into my hands. "Tell me what you think," he said. As I read he watched nervously, chain-smoking and blinking. I read about a boy in Harlem called John, whose father, a deacon in a storefront Baptist church, tyrannized the family, especially the boy. Jimmy let me borrow it and I took it home, reading it through without stopping. Besides the gift for cadenced prose, for bringing characters to life in a convincing, dramatic way, he was also daring. It was the first time I had seen the subject of homosexuality in a contemporary novel. Each scene and character, each sentence and paragraph, powered by biblical and Negro spiritual cadences, resonated with authenticity. When I returned the manuscript I conveyed my enthusiasm and Jimmy basked in the glow of my appreciation. But he also wanted to bask in my arms. That night, amazed at the tenderness, gentleness, and depth of feeling of this extraordinary young black man—similar in intensity only to Larry—I yielded and stayed over. But, sad to say, I wasn't attracted to him.

Jimmy had written his novel when he was fifteen, had revised it more than a dozen times, but despondent over the improbability of its acceptance by a major New York publisher, he was at loose ends. "Who'd ever take it?" he cried. "Who wants a novel about a black boy anyway, much less a queer one?"

He was right. No publisher would touch it. They flatly rejected it or suggested massive cuts, primarily of the homosexual content. We despised those who "sold out" to the establishment by purging style and content to conform with standard norms of taste and decorum, taking a dim view of writers who compromised their ideals. Henry Miller was our role model of the rebel and outsider who succeeded in spite of the literary establishment (he was certainly an influence on me but not on Jimmy), and except for Walt Whitman and Kenneth Patchen, no other writer had shown such independence of style and thought, such determination to supplant tradition-bound conventions of language and subject matter. Jimmy, on the other hand, would never shatter any forms or break new stylistic ground, but a blind man could see that his style was superb, brilliant, and he had something new to say.

I knew a young woman who was a junior editor at Doubleday and may have brought her the manuscript, or perhaps Jimmy did, but I introduced him. This was his first submission. Duly impressed, she recommended it to the senior editors, who, in turn, pulled long faces. From the careful wording of their rejection slip—acknowledging the achievement of the novel but regretting that they could make no offer without seeing extensive revisions—we had a preview of the reception Jimmy could expect for the next decade. He would, in the end, make the desired changes, purge all controversial content from the book, and under the new title, *Go Tell It on the Mountain*, it would finally be published by Knopf in 1953. His life, of course, would never be the same. With that book Jimmy became James Baldwin.

31

Drossie's

In a little basement restaurant on Greenwich Avenue near Tenth Street, in 1943, I discovered my first real (yet tenuous) community. Against two opposite walls were ranged wooden benches before a long pine table where, in an upbeat, cheerful atmosphere, the clientele, young and gay, ate good food and entertained one another. Wit and humor spiced every dish; Drossie herself, a diminutive Jewish pixie with a droopy nose and bovine complacency, contributed no small share. Dumpy and of a certain age, she dropped one-liners that kept us laughing.

A few older women known as "fag hags" (like Drossie herself) frequented the place. Fag hags ran to type then as now. Such women not only feel more comfortable with homosexual than straight men but also develop deep attachments and infatuations, recreating an extended family of narcissistic males and incestuous mothers. Only dominant, aggressive males were out of place there; I never saw one. Greenwich Village, by its nature an asylum (lunatic to those outside), attracted refugees, mostly from the United States, fleeing persecution from inflexible norms.

I remember three fag hags at Drossie's: a German and an American diseuse and a waitress called Jenny. Maria, the German, wore black, had dyed black hair cut in a short bob, and sharp features, her flour-white skin accentuated by purple eye shadow and liner. No longer young, she was smitten with a waiter/busboy whose wheat-straw hair and muscular arms with tiger tattoos made him the darling of the establishment. He was a wholesome-looking depraved youth from the corn belt whom Maria relentlessly pursued.

"Ach, Peter, when are you coming home with me?"

"Now, Maria, you know my dance card is full for the week."

"*Ja*, but Peter, I am not talking about dancing. I haf something else on my mind. I can show you some new tricks."

"Sorry, Maria, but you're not built like a trick. You don't have the right gadgets."

"Peter, at home I haf *all* ze gadgets."

The American singer was a small woman who had been a nightclub star. Jenny the Pirate was a flaming Irish redhead, about forty, and fond of the bottle.

There I met a nineteen-year-old composer—Ned Rorem—whose luminous beauty and heavenly music were irresistible. But he was intoxicated on more than music: he drank too much. Dreamy and self-absorbed, he would smile his crooked little smile and in a languid foghorn voice remark on how "delicious" I looked, as if he could order me for dessert. I'd have come on a platter, but he was always accompanied by his lover, a short, dark, muscular man.

One night, during the Christmas season, we all met at the flat of a poet I often visited, an odd gentle youth with the worst case of acne I'd seen. He spoke with a nervous giggle and wore tortoiseshell glasses. A former novitiate in the Franciscan brotherhood (he was originally Jewish), he had assumed a monastic name and a tragic look. We'll rechristen him The Saint. To add to his affliction he spoke with a painful stammer but had a beautiful baritone voice. All smiles, he welcomed me to an evening of music and poetry. In the flickering candlelight Ned and his lover huddled on a couch by the window, drunk; on another couch lay Jenny, dead to the world, one arm hanging loose by an empty bottle of Seagram's as Debussy's *Nuages* played on the record player. Wicker-covered, tallow-dripping Chianti flasks, serving as candlesticks, were strewn among soiled heaps of laundry, books, and manuscripts. The Saint handed me a tumbler of wine. This was the soul of Bohemia—sex, love, wine, music, poetry, and poverty. Finally, The Saint said, "Why don't you read 'Key West'?"

From the couch Ned and his lover nodded in agreement while Jenny snored. "Key West," my first publication in *Poetry*, had just appeared (November 1943) and caught the attention of

Theodore Roethke, I'd been told by one of his students. Eager to be part of a group of young artists with similar interests (French music and men), I requested Ravel's string quartet *Introduction and Allegro,* drained the wineglass, filled another, and when the music started, quietly began reading my impressionistic long poem. I raised my voice with the crescendos, lowered it with diminuendos—pure ham, but my little captive audience loved it. When I finished, without releasing his grip on his lover Ned cried, "Bravo! That was de-*vine!*" There was always a hint of mockery in his tone and crooked little smile, but he was smashed enough to be sincere and his friend nodded vigorously. The Saint was beatific. "Please read some more," he begged. Jenny moaned in her sleep. "Since she asked me I will," I said.

By this time the wine, music, and poetry had aroused everyone. As the lovers kissed and groped, The Saint gaped at me with heavy-lidded lust, but only Ned attracted me and he was off limits. Jenny moaned again and half in jest I said, "I'm so hot I could fuck *her.*" Missing the irony, they egged me on. "She'd love it," said Morris. "That," said Ned, "is precisely what she wants. And we'd love to watch." His lover nodded vigorously and The Saint's jaw went slack. Jenny stirred, her bare heavy thighs spread in a short cotton skirt raised almost to her crotch. She had always dropped unveiled hints, but disheveled and drink-sodden, she was not exactly a lovely sight. She had often said, "I'm perfectly safe among a bunch of faggots, damn it!"

The Saint put on Ravel's *Bolero,* and with the mock-heroic air of a bullfighter approaching a bull, I took a few daring steps in rhythm toward the inert redhead on the couch and began to stroke her bare thigh. I knew at once I couldn't go through with it. I was no rapist. What had begun as bluff had turned into a bad joke. As I crouched halfheartedly beside her, Jenny gave a start and opened her eyes. They were so bloodshot and bleary that I recoiled in disgust. She mumbled something and then in her raucous fishwife voice shrieked, "What the fuck's goin' on?"

"Harold was about to rape you, Jenny," said Ned casually. She blinked. "Well, what the hell's holding him back?" A gust of laughter swept the room. "Ain't anyone *man* enough?" she sneered, sitting up. Everybody laughed. The party was over.

I myself was victim of a mock rape at a party thrown by a Drossie habitué, a stage director in his forties who had always said, "I'm gonna rape you one of these days." With the help of friends who held me down while I pretended to struggle, the director fellated me on his couch. A very civilized rape, it was all in the spirit of good clean wholesome sex, with lots of laughter.

But once, at the age of twenty-two, I was raped in earnest. It was neither civilized nor funny. One sunny spring afternoon as I lay on the grass in Central Park, two British sailors, one extremely handsome and the other fat and piglike, kept winking at me. They didn't have to lure me behind the bushes and into the trees. I went "under my own recognizance," so to speak, bent on criminal joys. But I didn't expect the party to become rough. I thought I could somehow handle the fat one, but when we reached the underbrush he suddenly pinned me down on my belly with all his weight on me, held a knife at my back, and twisted my arm. "If you yell, mate, you're dead!" he snarled in a cockney accent and proceeded to have his way with me, grunting like a hog. I gritted my teeth and endured the pain until he finished. Then the beauty, pressing his face to mine, began to soothe my anxiety, whispering, "Awfully sorry, mate, but you shouldn't be so damn attractive, so why not relax, mmm, yes, that's it, unnnngh, yesss," and proceeded so considerately that it became pleasurable. That afternoon I knew I had come close to being murdered or maimed and learned what women had to fear.

32

Waverly Place

Since one-night stands and pickups could not provide the satisfaction of a steady relationship, more and more the wish for security, for enduring domestic ties such as I'd envied among straight friends, captured my imagination. I wanted to be "normal," to be accepted, to belong. True, women did not attract me as powerfully as men did—I liked muscle not makeup—but I was fascinated by the clearly defined sexual roles. I'd been with several whores and enjoyed the act, but I wanted an affair. This, in a somewhat devious manner, I now proceeded to pursue.

In the Park Bookshop on the corner of MacDougal and Waverly, one entered a hushed world of young, literate bookworms where James Joyce, Gertrude Stein, and Dorothy Parker were quoted and where you could run into William Carlos Williams, Kenneth Patchen, or Paul Bowles (then a composer) in the flesh. In this oasis of culture, browsers were encouraged to sit in colorful little Mexican chairs and read as long as they liked. The owner, a slim, diminutive blonde in her early twenties, sat hunched at her desk reading or working at mail-order accounts (she specialized in rare and scarce editions) or holding quiet conversations with some of the young men and women who hung around. She was a debutante from Murfreesboro, Tennessee. Even before Truman Capote pirated it for *Breakfast at Tiffany's* her name, Bonnie Golightly, never failed to produce a reaction, the most recent of which, when I tried to obtain her telephone number, was the operator's response: "Is that a business name, sir?" I assured her it was legitimate.

One of the young men who hung out was cute, sandy-haired, and boyish. Attracted to him, I hopefully frequented the bookstore until I learned that he was Bonnie's husband and they had a child; I immediately began indulging in fantasies of being "a member of the wedding" (in Carson McCullers's phrase), wanting to "lie down between the bridegroom and the bride" (in Walt Whitman's poem of bisexual longing), expressing an urge deep within my nature.

Before long, however, the bridegroom and the bride were divorced and the child was placed in custody of Bonnie's parents in Tennessee. She began inviting me to her homey railroad flat on Waverly Place. It had an antique wooden love seat flanked by two bookcases topped by Mexican ceramic pots; a sofa, an antique armchair, a spinet desk, and a big black tomcat called Willie who scratched. Cigarettes, liquor, and wit were plentiful. Fortunately, she never wore makeup or high heels or painted her nails, all of which turned me off. I enjoyed those late evenings in her cozy flat and began to fantasize about a pleasant literary life together. We frequented the San Remo and Minetta's and I'd walk her home and return to my frigid little room. Then one night she invited me to stay over. At last I had a girl friend.

Overnight, like a born-again Christian, I went straight. Like a reformed addict, I lost interest in my previous life-style (for a while) and regarded young men without lust. I recall my amazement and delight at feeling free for the first time from the nagging ache of humiliation, though I later discovered that the old addiction would inevitably resurface. But I no longer felt totally, fatalistically scripted into one sexual role. The conflicts I couldn't resolve as a homosexual, such as self-rejection and low self-esteem, seemed to dissolve like magic. Suddenly the feeling of being despised vanished. In the never-ending struggle for acceptance and approval, internalized self-hatred (a feeling familiar to every member of an oppressed minority) seemed over. But of course this was an illusion. Social acceptance involves much more than sexual orientation.

For most, homosexual desires remain undetectable unless we choose to reveal them. Since I never had the guts to reveal this to anyone, I now began to play my straight role to the hilt, behaving like any "normal" young man; contentedly smoking my pipe, I minded the store when Bonnie had other things to do, enjoying the irony of the situation when men eyed me furtively as they pretended to peruse some book or other, just as I had behaved with Bonnie's former husband. Especially during the war years, I was careful to conceal my homosexuality. It was difficult enough just being a healthy young male without a uniform. People stared accusingly and often snarled, "Why aren't *you* fighting overseas with the rest of our boys?" As the war dragged on I grew more defensive and, feeling guilty about not being in uniform, occasionally snarled back.

One afternoon as we were strolling down Eighth Street between Fifth and Sixth avenues, just outside Mary's Bar, we saw a large crowd partially blocking traffic in the middle of the road. A white-haired bearded old peddler, trying to defend himself from a big drunk, was throwing up his arms and covering his face. His pushcart was half overturned; brooms, buckets, pans, and clothespins—hundreds of clothespins—were scattered in the gutter. His black fedora lay dented beside his wares on the street. The drunk kept trying to hit him in the face but staggered wildly with each swing. He'd pick up a dish, smash it, then grab handfuls of clothespins and scatter them, yelling, *"Goddamn kike! Kill all the kikes! The only good Jew is a dead Jew!"* Nobody made a move to help the old man. The crowd's passiveness and the helplessness of the old peddler at a time when millions of innocent Jews were being exterminated in the gas chambers of Europe proved too much for me. I pushed my way forward through the throng and hovered a moment indecisively. Then, almost without my knowing it, my fist shot out of the crowd and the drunk went down, flat on his back, his head thudding on the asphalt. A cheer rose from the crowd, which began to disperse, many thanking me warmly, shaking my hand. Why had no one acted before, I wondered? I had made no conscious decision. I didn't even feel as if I had punched the drunk. It seemed to be someone else's fist, not mine. It was a reflex action. In my teens I'd been trained to box by my tough Uncle Mike.

I grabbed Bonnie's arm and said, "Let's get the hell out of here!" As we were leaving, the drunk picked himself up and stumbled off, blood trickling down his chin. The poor peddler pathetically picked up his battered hat and rummaged about in the rubble of his wares, hoping to salvage some. The scene was pitiful and degrading.

At that point a woman onlooker stared and asked, "Did you lose your wristwatch?" She was right. The watch was gone. "How did you know?" I asked. "Well," she replied, wreathed in smiles, "everybody figured it must belong to the brave young man who knocked out the drunk. They're holding it at the shoestore across the street. Good luck!" she cried emotionally. At the shoestore I was welcomed effusively. "A war hero!" cried the Jewish owner. "Fighting Hitler at home! Y'oughta get a medal!" I got my watch.

Back at Bonnie's apartment I downed in quick succession two shot glasses of Vat 69, which was always at hand, and was finishing a third when I turned to catch Bonnie undressing. "Honey, that was a mighty *fine* thing yuh done," drawled Bonnie in her mock country accent, which she turned on when she was pleased or horny or both. "I'm *real* proud of ya!"

Her eyes shone as she spoke, looking at me in a way I hadn't seen before. Still feeling soiled by the sordid event, I felt a quick wave of pride. So that's what it felt like to be a hero, to be a *man*. It warmed me like the whiskey, heated my blood. For once I didn't have to apologize for not wearing a uniform, for being a 4-F—for fag. I grinned, swallowing my third shot glass and lighting another Lucky, which I'd been chain-smoking since the incident. A few smoke rings circled Willie's whiskers, which he flicked disdainfully. He was the only creature who remained un-impressed. Smart cat. Then, as I began undressing, everything seemed all right: the nude woman, the cat, the fight between good and evil, the war, yes, even the war. Suddenly I thought: I'm drunk. How can the war be all right? I can't stop the stinking war with one punch in the mouth, can I? But I felt terrific—young, drunk, sexual, strong, and alive. I was on top of the shaky world.

One evening a bald old man with a big red-veined bulbous nose and a ghastly pallor puttered among the titles, stealing glances at me. Finally, he said, "You bear a startling resemblance to Hart Crane." My hair stood on end. But thinking it was a come-on I coldly replied, "How do you know?" "Oh, he was a very close friend," said the man. "I used to live with him." It was Samuel Loveman, onetime lover and later companion of Crane. He said that Crane was called Harold before he used his middle name, Hart. He described how he'd get drunk and rush up to the roof intent on jumping and, on each occasion, Loveman saved his life, dragging him back to the apartment. On one of these suicidal binges Loveman found Hart on the roof weeping bitterly. "Rhetoric!" he blubbered. "My damn poems are nothing but rhetoric!" Crane was an alcoholic who would break down and sob uncontrollably at his miserable state of poverty and love-lessness and, like Sylvia Plath much later, attempted suicide sev-eral times before he succeeded.

Paul Bowles often came into the shop. Our paths had crossed earlier, though we didn't know each other, when he and his wife, Jane, lived on Middagh Street. Twenty years later we would become friends in Tangier.

I had often seen Kenneth Patchen, whom I greatly admired, walking around the Village, and one evening, leaning heavily on his walking stick, there he was—a big man, thickset, handsome, with black eyes, black eyebrows that joined above the nose in an inverted *V*, and a leonine mane of thick black hair. He talked with Bonnie about his books, which he carried in a large cloth bag to sell to the bookshops—some with his colored hand-drawn covers. As they stood conversing she finally drawled, "Mr. Patchen, here is a young poet who'd love to meet you." He turned and began staring with great interest at my brown cor-duroy jacket, quite worn and weathered, and fingering its velvety texture, he murmured, "That's a beautiful jacket—very beautiful." He emanated a warm, sympathetic humanity that also distinguished his work, set it apart as only Walt Whitman had done before him. This quality of compassion infused his work with a pantheistic glow. At that moment our jackets seemed like saintly garments of a holy order—he was wearing a black velour jacket that I thought far more impressive than my threadbare corduroy. I thought he looked like a Hebrew prophet or Italian Renaissance master or ancient Welsh bard (he was of Welsh ancestry). His eyes engulfed me in a mystical embrace as his deep, resonant voice and measured speech set a slow cadence that put me into a meditative mood, almost a trance. A gentle giant, with his impressive bulk, massive head, and slow movements he stood out in the Village landscape. There was nobody like him in American poetry. Years later, recalling these events, Bonnie wrote me: "He'd limp into my shop on his cane to deliver copies of his book for consignment. I felt very sorry for him until one day I happened to watch after he'd painfully scaled those two-steps-up and when he thought he was out of sight, proceeded along the sidewalk with a jaunty air, not realizing I was watching."

I too had seen him limping stiffly with his cane but at other times noticed he walked quite normally. He was unquestionably an invalid, suffering from a spinal injury sustained while playing college football, for which he'd had repeated spinal surgery that actually caused the condition to become chronic. Most of his life was spent flat on his back. I visited him several times on West Fourth near Hudson, a few blocks from my tiny room on Horatio.

After about four or five months of heterosexual bliss I found myself looking at boys again. This was intensified by trouble in paradise: we had eaten the apple or, to be more precise, had taken one too many sips of Vat 69—by courtesy of Bonnie, who was nothing if not generous. In short, I liked her and thought I loved her. But she had her faults: no fact or detail was too small for her to quarrel about. She also had a southern defensiveness that, too often, manifested itself as condescension.

One night (I seem to remember it as Christmas Eve, 1944) we celebrated with a turkey or duck at her flat, with a few friends, and when the smoke had cleared, found ourselves in the wee hours smashed as can be. Her head drooped forward as she slumped over the bottle, and I heard her mumbling to herself. In those days I drank a good deal, but even when dead drunk I remembered everything up to the point of passing out, which I rarely did. Leaning forward to hear what she was saying I froze: like a witch's incantation she kept repeating T. S. Eliot's malignant words:

> *The rats are underneath the piles.*
> *The jew is underneath the lot.*

I shook her. "What the hell are you saying?" I yelled. "Do you know what you're saying?" Her head lolled as she slumped forward, repeating the venomous verse. I think I pushed her away, for she fell to the floor. I turned and walked out.

A couple of days later she stood at my door, pleading with me to let her in. I glared with a coldness that she later described as "the most chilling look I've ever seen." Somehow we patched it up; I accepted her heartfelt apologies. But it was never the same again. We had lost our innocence.

33

The Glass Menagerie

In 1939 I had met Joe at Mme. Duval's dance studio on West Fifty-fourth Street. He was not gay but had a faunlike grace and feline suppleness. He was reading *Swann's Way* and practicing yoga and meditation, and he spoke of an unknown writer called Tennessee who was homosexual. I asked to meet him, secretly hoping he was beautiful, but he was always out and when we finally met we were not attracted to each other. Joe, who was married by 1944, had convinced me to spend a month or so in Provincetown, where, in 1940, he had introduced another young dancer, Kip, to Tennessee, who fell for him. Kip resembled Nijinsky and like him had a mysterious fey charisma. Before Tennessee ever saw him I was wild about Kip but never showed it. He had an affair with Tennessee but broke it up to marry a young woman who depicted for him the "horrors" of homosexuality. Not long after their marriage he died, the victim of brain surgery, at twenty-six.

Joe met me at the bus station that August day in 1944 and introduced me to Tennessee. For a day or two I stayed in some dim room, then Tennessee offered me his lower bunk in the cabin he was staying in. We moved within circles stretching from New York to Provincetown and the Ivy League universities, mostly Harvard, Princeton, Yale, and Columbia. From Brooklyn College Chester Kallman and I were part of this Homintern through which gay writers and artists met. With no agenda or design, sharing only the common denominator of sexual feelings, we kept crossing one another's paths. It was like a family.

Tennessee was working on the final draft of *The Glass Menagerie.* The small rustic cabin we shared for the next six weeks belonged to the painter Karl Knaths, a gentle gray-haired man who lived with his wife in a large clapboard house in front. As Tennessee's guest I paid nothing, slept in the lower, Tennessee in the upper bunk. He rose early, usually around dawn, brewed endless pots of strong black coffee, and wrote all morning. On the door he tacked a sign he had printed in red and black crayon: WRITER AT WORK—DO NOT DISTURB. There was no telephone, no electricity, no water; from a garden tap behind the Knathses' house we drew water. At night we lit candles.

Tennessee's output was prodigious: plays, stories, poems. He worked from morning till midafternoon. He also drew freehand in an art sketchbook as we sat outside the cabin in the sun. We'd smoke and talk as Tennessee sketched. Slim and boyish, he was thirty-four but pretended to be twenty-nine. I had just turned twenty-eight going on twenty-four. We exercised poetic license, you might say, over the dictatorship of time, to which we made as few concessions as possible. It was too scary, too inflexible. Youth was rapidly slipping away, we were broke, and had not attained success. Tennessee had worked at various jobs as shoe salesman, busboy, waiter, movie usher. He had waited on tables in a Greenwich Village bistro on Morton Street called the Beggar Bar, run by Valeska Gert, a dance-mime who had fled Nazi Germany. With two others (one was Judith Malina, who was also the hat-check girl), he earned money on tips.

From dirty street steps with an iron railing, cluttered with overflowing garbage cans by day, you entered a tiny ill-lit smoke-filled cellar, crowded and noisy, where coffee and beer were served. You ran into every poet, painter, actor, and intellectual in New York. The lights would suddenly go out, plunging you into darkness, and after a long delay Valeska would appear in a blinding white spotlight, her puckish face carefully smeared in flour, with mauve eye shadow and glitter on her lids and cheeks (anticipating hippies and punks), and some outlandish harlequin costume. In a German accent she delivered political satires in singsong poetry to thunderous applause.

Derived from Berlin cabarets of the 1920s, Valeska's style was called *Sprechstimme* (Arnold Schoenberg had used it in *Pierrot Lunaire*), characterized by musical speech, rather like the tone of wonder and awe that grown-ups employ when narrating fairy tales to children, but heightened and intensified by sudden dramatic variations in pitch, volume, and duration, punctuated by eerie cries. Its spooky appeal went over big in the 1940s. The New York press wrote her up in glowing terms. She became a celebrity, and the tiny foul-smelling dump was packed nightly, including the uptown carriage trade. Tennessee did well on tips and was, perhaps unconsciously, influenced by her handling of mood and speech. Valeska's influence on young writers, actors, and playwrights—including Julian Beck and Judith Malina, who later founded the influential Living Theatre—was considerable.

Tennessee had brown, crew-cut hair and large, dazed blue eyes—definitely walleyed. Except for delicate features and a dreamy expression he was quite insignificant-looking. When he was particularly nervous, his high-pitched laugh, walk, and manner became conspicuously effeminate. With more than a shade of disapproval people inquired if he was "that way" or "minty." "He's a big fag, isn't he?" "No," I'd respond coldly, "a small one."

When Tennessee spoke at all, he'd attempt to be funny, which usually led to embarrassed silence. Too shy and unsure of himself to utter more than a few hesitant one-liners, he was no talker—not then, at any rate. His woebegone, hapless personality made you feel sorry for him. You wanted to pat him on the head with a few reassuring words: "There, there, it's gonna be all right." But beneath this ineffectual exterior lurked a literary giant. Some of his plays had been performed by small theatre groups, but the important Theatre Guild had produced *The Battle of Angels,* starring Miriam Hopkins, which was a dismal flop. Expecting his first big success from the production, he seemed crushed by this defeat.

Extremely short and slight, Tennessee looked like a lost beagle among strangers. As I got to know him better I discovered that he was quite shrewd and practical, and I never heard him utter a hostile or arrogant word to anyone's face, though when they were barely out of earshot he could be very cutting. Still unknown, he was an underground figure whom some writers and poets were aware of. That year James Laughlin, publisher of New Directions, had included his poetry in the prestigious series *Five Younger Poets* (for those under thirty, but Tennessee, as I've mentioned, was adept at faking his age). Laughlin had accepted a volume of mine for the series, which I was busily revising (he gave up the series before publishing me).

One afternoon a thick typescript in the center of the desk caught my attention and I began reading, growing more and more excited as it dawned on me that here was a play of the utmost delicacy, deeply moving in a way that only music can be. It was a masterpiece. Of course it was *The Glass Menagerie* and I was probably the first to see the final draft, which he had finished only a day earlier, exploding with relief, "At last, I've finally got this damn thing over with!" He sounded fed up, having labored on many rewrites and expressed disgust with the entire project.

"My God, Harold, I've worked on this draft all summer. I can't stand looking at it." He was experiencing writer's burnout but also, without saying so, probably out of uncertainty and fear of criticism, he was divided between self-doubt and the need for approval; he seemed to want me to see it. A writer's most vulnerable, least objective stage in the creative process occurs at such times, soon after completion, the point at which you simultaneously crave and fear a reaction. Adverse criticism is painful, another rewrite sheer agony. So when I heard his footsteps on the gravel and saw him enter the cabin, I made no effort to replace the play. "Sheer magic!" I said. He blushed. The more I enthused, the redder he grew. Finally he blurted out, "Oh, Harold, it's only a potboiler!"

Shocked, I replied, "You're wrong, it's a work of art!"

After a lengthy, thoughtful pause, as if unconvinced, he sadly drawled, "I've been getting nowhere for so long with my poetry and poetic drama that I figured I'd have to write something to boil the pot!" He gave his short nervous laugh. He expressed no faith in the play. Partly autobiographical, it portrayed the squalid life of an impractical, once genteel family during the Great Depression. Tennessee was terrified of poverty and failure; anxiety emanated from him like a physical substance. In spite of his many social relationships he was a tormented, isolated loner—something I knew all too well myself.

That night, before going to sleep, as we lay in our bunks in the darkness, we discussed the problem of being "queer." "It's a curse," I said, "the worst fate that could befall anyone. We have to hide our need for love and sex, never knowing when we might be insulted, abused, attacked, killed. Just for loving other guys."

Under cover of darkness our voices grew more emotional.

"Homosexuals," said Tennessee in a choked voice, "are wounded, deeply hurt. We live with a psychic wound that never heals."

This was an accurate if overwrought statement from the gut of how it felt to be "gay," a word dripping with irony. Our need to conceal our powerful feelings was relieved when we camped, ridiculed everyone, even ourselves. At the basis of this black humor lay the pain caused by contempt and rejection. My journal notes:

> As I lie writing in Tennessee's cabin, by the flickering light of several ebbing candles and a kerosene lamp, the incessant shrilling of crickets creates a numbing effect on my mind. I think of how I happened to come to P-town and meet Tennessee. Eva Hindus persuaded me to leave New York a day earlier than I had intended, simply to accommodate her husband, Milton, who didn't like traveling alone.
>
> "What do you want to meet Tennessee Williams for?" he said. "He's not an important writer. And he's queer."

One evening, having dined with Tennessee at a seafood restaurant and silently watched the other diners laughing and having a good time, I began to feel depressed. Tennessee had said little during the meal and I fell into a glum silence. Having had too much wine, on leaving I staggered to my bicycle and we started back to Captain Jack's Wharf on Commercial Street, where some friends of his, who were visiting in Boston, shared a studio. We spent a few hours there every night listening to music surrounded by Picasso reproductions and fishnets on the walls.

As I weaved drunkenly on my bike Tennessee chuckled.

"Harold Norse, author of *The Drunken Bicycle*," he said.

I executed a few turns, swaying the bike. "Tennessee Williams," I joked, "author of *The Pickled Menagerie*."

We were almost in good spirits as we neared the studio when a very handsome blond youth, about eighteen, nearly made me lose my balance. I turned to get a better look and whistled softly. "Did you see that? That's the most *beautiful*—"

I caught up with Tennessee, who lowered his voice. "Stay away from him!" he whispered. "He's bad news!"

"He's beautiful! He smiled at me! What's wrong with him?"

"That boy is nuts," said Tennessee. "He's dangerous."

Provincetown was full of handsome young gay boys and Portuguese fishermen, but while living with Tennessee I had no sexual outlet and was in a state of feverish excitement. "I don't care," I said with drunken bravado. "He's looking back."

"Don't say I didn't warn you," said Tennessee.

I turned and caught up with the boy, who showed no signs of unbalanced behavior. Soon we were off the road in the darkness of the beach, a shallow where the waves were mere ripples. I could hear the sound of wavelets lapping the shore. We dropped our slacks in the darkness; I recall the crisp damp air on my bare skin. I remember the rancid fishy smells as we fell on each other like pent-up, sex-starved maniacs . . . and then I didn't know where I was. My head felt wet and cold, but the feeling was not unpleasant. I made no effort to move until it grew colder, and then I tried to raise my head. Pain. Slowly and tentatively I moved an icy leg. Cold waves lapped my face. I don't remember getting to my feet or finding my way to the studio. At the screen door I clutched the jamb for support. As through a scrim I saw Tennessee from a distance. "Is this real?" I said.

"Oh, my God! You're drenched in blood!" exclaimed Tennessee.

He led me to a studio couch and helped me lie down. He applied several towels to my face. Instantly they turned crimson. He phoned a doctor, but it was past midnight and there was no answer. I lay in shock as Tennessee made black coffee and gave it to me. I drank the coffee and went completely gaga. He didn't know that you don't give coffee to shock cases, no stimulants. This, I thought, is not happening. I'll be all right in the morning. I'm probably dreaming. Then I suspected I was a character in a play by Tennessee, acting my part while he wrote it. He kept hovering over me, looking scared, feeding me black coffee. I was knocked out a second time.

Next morning, badly shaken but no longer in shock, I went with Tennessee to a doctor he knew. "Tell him you fell off your bike," said Tennessee. The doctor, a gray-haired elderly German, looked at me. "Hmmm," he said knowingly, "there haf been a lot of bizycle accidents zis season. You are ze sixth case in five veeks." Tennessee and I exchanged glances. But the doctor was no dummy. "Concussion," he said. "It could haf been vorse, young man. *Himmel!* Zat's a very ugly cut under your chin. Looks like you fell on brass knuckles. Funny bizycles, *ja, ja.*"

With my face swaddled in cold compresses, I lay recuperating in the studio for three days. Like a male nurse, Tennessee bustled about helpfully, adjusting pillows, making meals, and guzzling gallons of coffee. He couldn't write or think without it. He would sing strange southern songs I'd never heard:

> *Underneath the bamboo,*
> *Underneath the bamboo tree,*
> *Room enough for you and me,*
> *Yes, room enough for one, two, three, four . . .*

He drew neat little still lifes in pen and ink. Once he drew a cluster of grapes, each grape so perfectly rounded that I saw a Matisse-like ornamental mastery in it. I told him he had a fantastically developed aesthetic know-how and predicted great artistic success as a writer. "How can you tell?" he said, intrigued.

"I dunno. I just see it. Success. Inner balance."

"*Balance?* If you knew how unbalanced I feel—"

This was years before I'd read Carl Jung's mandala theory about individuation through art or meditation. I made an ink drawing of Tennessee under which, in large block letters, I wrote: GLORY TO THE HIGHEST! I'd forgotten about the drawing until Julian Beck showed it to me decades later, first making me promise I wouldn't claim it. I have no idea how it came into his possession, but I probably left it behind in the studio, for he was one of the two young men who rented it. On Julian's return Tennessee introduced us—I lying on my back with blood-stained towels on my face. Julian was nineteen, tall and thin, blue-eyed with wavy red-gold hair. He leaned over with a look of compassion—later his friends would say, "Julian is a saint!"—and clasped his hands. "Oh, you poor kid!" "Julian," said his friend, "you can't have sex with a concussion case." Everyone thought this very funny, but I couldn't laugh, the pain was too severe. Julian ministered to my needs and I recovered.

One day as I rode Tennessee uphill on the handlebars of my rented bicycle he exclaimed, "What powerful legs!" I told him that was why I had become a dancer.

The rest of the summer was spent on the beach and attending parties, at one of which I met Marlon Brando. At eighteen he was indescribably attractive, but shy and tense. Two years later we met again at a party of Tennessee's in a ballroom on Irving Place in New York, just before Marlon got the role of Stanley Kowalski in *A Streetcar Named Desire*. Hundreds of people milled about or danced to the all-black jazz band. I was standing alone when Marlon approached. "Don't I know you from somewhere?" he drawled, sizing me up with intense interest.

"Yeah," I said with a grin. "Provincetown. We met once."

"Are you Italian?"

"No."

"You look Italian. Are you a friend of Tennessee's?"

"Yeah. I stayed with him in Provincetown."

"Oh." He seemed to think this over. "Uh, well, what are you doin'—I mean, uh, after the party?" He was fishing around for a clue, perhaps, to my relationship with Tennessee. "Are you stayin' with him?"

"Oh, no," I said quickly, "I live alone."

"Are you goin' to Tennessee's private party afterwards?"

"He invited me," I said.

Stuck in our macho roles, I couldn't tell if he wanted to fuck or fight. "Wa-aal," he drawled in the sexy way that he would make famous, "maybe you'd like to, uh, get together. . . ." His eyes wandered around as if searching for other game. I hesitated.

"I'll think it over," I said with a tight smile.

"I wouldn't think too long if I were you," he snapped and swaggered out of my life. I had let Marlon Brando get away.

Before we left Provincetown, Tennessee had a visit from Lynn Riggs, who had written a play called *Green Grow the Lilacs O* from which the musical *Oklahoma* was adapted. He invited Tennessee for drinks and I tagged along. Riggs was pleasant, middle-aged, with glasses and an unassuming manner. He reminisced about D. H. Lawrence, whom he had met twice. He was staying at the summer house of Ida Rauh, a former wife of Max Eastman, and, as a close friend, one of those present at Lawrence's death in Taos. Ida came in and sat with us. She was elderly, with a strong, intelligent face. She joined the conversation about the Lawrences, growing rather passionate about Frieda, whom, she said, she had always disliked, not because she was earthy and crude but because she was indifferent to others, hurting them constantly, displaying an almost monstrous unconcern for them. She and Riggs invited us to join them any afternoon to go swimming. I had a glimpse into the passions of the literary generation before ours—no difference.

In early September, before leaving for Harvard, where he was to stay a few days with Bill Cannastra, a sexy law student he had met in P-town shortly before my arrival in mid-August, Tennessee collected his manuscripts and few belongings into one small handbag. Very absentminded, he would have forgotten his cigarette holder had I not reminded him of it. I don't suppose he would have survived without it. He'd have felt amputated. I had to lend him a dollar for the trip to Cambridge—he was flat broke.

I stayed on for another week in the now abandoned summer resort. He had left behind some stray pages of a short story and some notes, all of which I kept for years. My last surviving journal entry of that period, dated September 1, 1944, about a week before his departure, reads:

It is a gloomy Friday. A heavy mist hangs over the cape and hordes of gulls, like little old women, huddle together on sand barrens, or fly low in irregular, spotty indecision. The entire village has taken on, suddenly, a wintry bleakness. Now, for the first time, it becomes apparent that Provincetown is a serious place after all where bulky men go sloshing in great boots down narrow streets, dangling strings of lobster, perch and mackerel, and where Portuguese women, swarthy and houseworn, lean heavy arms on wooden fences, eyeing strangers with indifference and distaste. It is not so much a resort, after all. It seems to have been made so from outside, by imposition, as there is no express shaping of this village by intention as a pleasure spot. Artists and writers have forced, as it were, on a resistant, provincial population their unwelcome presence, their money and city manners.

But the trend, as in everything else, seems to be going against the vacationers. Reports of "cleaning the town up" are common, and the bohemian set, with its loose morality and elastic wit, may have to go elsewhere to practise the Utopia of amoral freedom. I grope for the words that express my disappointment in Provincetown since that serio-comic day when Joe met us at the bus station and I almost fainted with fatigue and disgust in a sea-food restaurant.

I can't remember the cause of my disgust. As for my disappointment with Provincetown, it was caused by sheer sexual frustration. Except for the episode with the psychotic beauty, I was unsuccessful in hooking a young Portuguese fisherman. Perhaps it was because I looked like one myself. Gays reeking of suntan oil tried picking me up. I acted dumb and straight and they bought me drinks, thrilled at cruising local trade. But I didn't put out.

Shortly after my return to Horatio Street, Tennessee began to visit every evening. Silent and distracted, he worried about his play. Then, one evening in early fall, he showed up in a state of great excitement. "Harold!" he exclaimed. "Eddie Dowling has taken *The Glass Menagerie*!" But as the weeks passed he grew anxious. Dowling, the director, had cast himself in the role of Tom. "He's too old, too goddamn old!" wailed Tennessee. "I wanted a handsome young seaman!" Then I'd get reports like this: "Harold, he knows it himself! Guess what he's doing to hide his double chins? He's wearing a turtleneck sweater! He *looks* like a turtle!" He expected the play to flop if Dowling persisted in his madness. Tennessee grew more and more desperate. I got all the news about rehearsals, blow-by-blow descriptions: Dowling was dreary; Laurette Taylor, an old woman, had been snatched from obscurity to play the role of the mother, Amanda Wingfield. "If we can keep her off the bottle!" Tennessee fretted and prayed. One of the grandes dames of the theatre, with Katharine Cornell and Helen Hayes, Taylor had been in retirement for twenty-five years because of alcoholism. Although he worshiped her, Tennessee entertained the gloomiest forebodings, seeing no sign that she had reformed and worrying because she never knew her lines. The young Julie Haydon as Laura, however, was superb.

One evening Tennessee said, "Do you know Charles Henri Ford and Parker Tyler?"

"Yes," I said, "they rejected some poems of mine."

"Well, they've asked me to do a book review for *View*," he said, rolling his eyes. "I wouldn't know how to begin. Why don't you write it and sign my name?" Tickled pink, I agreed. I'd have my revenge on Parker Tyler, who'd never know he'd published me! I wrote the review (I can't recall the subject) and they published it. A friend said they showed no respect for Tennessee and ridiculed him behind his back. A descendant of President John Tyler, Parker was an insufferable snob. In 1942 I had submitted some poems to *View* and was elated when I received a note requesting an interview. In high hopes I hurried to their office in the West Fifties. The first surrealist magazine in America, it had considerable prestige. But again, as luck would have it, it was hate at first sight, as with George Davis. Tight-assed, with prim pursed lips, Tyler began criticizing one of my poems with icy disdain. "Now, what in the world does *amaranthine* mean? You can't use it in a poem!"

"It's a common garden herb and appears in Rimbaud's and John Milton's poetry," I retorted. This infuriated him. "What makes you think you're a poet?" he said, angrily shoving a typescript page at me. "Here's a real poet we're publishing—Dylan Thomas!"

I stood up. "If my grandmother had balls she'd be my grandfather," I said, reverting to Brooklyn surrealism. As I walked out Ford detained me in the outer office, making some friendly remarks to indicate that he was interested if Tyler wasn't. But they never accepted the poems and I wondered why they had wanted to meet me—unless they were cruising via their magazine, which, I decided, was the case. Apparently I was not Tyler's type. About a year later, when I began to appear in leading literary magazines, Tyler behaved in an amiable, even sheepish manner whenever I ran into him at literary parties. Ford later became a friend.

At its premiere in Chicago, *The Glass Menagerie* had been unusually well received, but only Broadway could make or break a playwright. Tennessee was petrified. His whole career, his future as a writer, depended on Broadway. The evening before the New York premiere he showed up in a terrible state.

"Harold, I'm so nervous I must get smashed," he said.

We went to Mary's, a gay bar on Eighth Street, frequented in those days by just about everyone we knew, and sat at the counter drinking Cuba Libres. It was a hot night, and the iced rum went down cool and smooth. It didn't take long to get thoroughly plastered. In no time Tennessee was mellow and relaxed and started looking around at the handsome young men. At the end of the bar near the door sat three or four young toughs, conspicuously out of place. In Little Italy, south of Washington Square, I used to pass the dingy storefronts, catching a glimpse of young Italians shooting pool or lazing around, but I had never seen any of them in a gay bar before. This was a line they did not cross, especially during the war, when gangs of Bleecker Street Goths, as we called them, went about beating up any male who wore glasses or carried a book. There was an uneasy truce between the intellectuals, gays, and bohemians and the Italo hoods, who nursed an inferiority complex that flared up in violent pogroms from time to time.

Tennessee kept smiling at them. "For God's sake, Tennessee," I hissed, "quit smiling!" It was too late. "Hey, you, wot da fuck ya lookin' at?" snarled the one nearest us.

Hypnotized, Tennessee stared with a glazed expression.

"Aw, dis place is fulla queers!" rasped another, typically astute. "Let's beat 'em up!" With alley-cat belligerence they got to their feet. Still smarting from my Provincetown incident I was drunk enough to be foolhardy. *"Hey, punk!"* I yelled in my tough Brooklyn manner. With a black turtleneck, deep tan, and two-day stubble I looked like a hood myself. I was also sick to death of queer bashers and thirsty for revenge. The bar grew still. "Get the fuck out of here!" I yelled. "Beat it!"

Nobody moved. The bartender reached below the counter. Then the hood who had started it growled, "Ah, shit!" and turned to his gang. Slowly they swaggered out the door. Tennessee exhaled forcefully. "Whew! Thanks, Harold." He wiped the sweat from his face. "How would I look at the premiere with a black eye?"

The play was a smash hit and Tennessee was famous over-night. If I'd been an early riser—I was a night owl and he was an early bird—we would have remained close. When he started liv-ing in deluxe hotels and inviting me for a morning swim, I could never make it. His evenings were taken by events in which I played no part. Once I wrote him requesting a loan but received no answer. I heard stories about the startling change in his per-sonality. He had become loud, arrogant, aggressive; at Broadway premieres of other writers he sucked Cokes noisily through a straw (his friends began calling him a cokesucker), interrupting the performance and making obnoxious remarks in a loud voice. The *Life* magazine accounts bore little resemblance to the man I knew. But beneath the ballyhoo and hoopla he had changed lit-tle, beset by the same morbid fears and anxieties. The wound he spoke of in the cabin of his obscure, penniless days did not heal.

While *The Glass Menagerie* was in rehearsal in New York, Ten-nessee and I were walking along West Eighth discussing poetry on our way to visit Lynn Riggs when he said, "Harold, why don't you write prose? You'll never get rich writing poetry." I didn't have to think for an answer. "Because," I replied laughing, "poetry is the air I breathe, Tennessee." He regarded me out of the corner of his whitish-blue walleye to see if I was joking. "It's my food and drink," I said firmly. "Long ago I decided that poetry—not money—was my reason for being. If the choice is between making money and writing a good poem, I'll take the poem." He looked shocked. He was really a shrewd, practical person.

As we crossed Sixth Avenue to Greenwich opposite the Women's House of Detention, we heard some cries from the old brick building. Looking up to the top floor of the gloomy edifice, we saw the women prisoners huddled in groups at the windows, calling to us, "Hey, sweetheart! Daaarling! Where ya goin'? C'mon up! Wanna lay? *Youse got a big one? Ha ha ha!*"

Waving and gesticulating frantically, they made obscene ges-tures and kissy sounds. We waved back. Then, breathing on the windowpane, one of the inmates wrote backward with her index finger in large block letters: I LOVE YOU. Touched and astonished by the episode, we lingered on the corner to wave and blow kisses back to the frantic women in the grim penal institution. Speculat-ing on their sexual frustration, we decided they were lesbians.

"Baudelaire and his flowers of urban reality," I commented. "E. E. Cummings lives around the corner from the prison in Patchin Place. A Cummings poem is being lived out here."

In the elevator of a vast apartment house across the street Tennessee cautioned, "Riggs thinks of himself as a great playwright. We mustn't let on that we might think otherwise." I admired Tennessee's tact—some might call it hypocrisy—but with the passage of time I learned that tact spares feelings.

Riggs welcomed us effusively and we sat drinking his expensive whiskey. I got noisily drunk and the evening grew boring (the other side of being too polite). Tennessee started to tell the story of the women in the prison across the street but fumbled for words, turned red with embarrassment, and blurted, "Oh, Harold, *you* tell it!" I told the story with relish, racing off into an interminable monologue about the theatre and the Faustian hero—schoolboy stuff—but on my way to the bathroom I heard Tennessee exclaim, "Brilliant boy! A genius!" We were all pretty sloshed.

The last time I saw Tennessee in New York, although we met several times many years later in Tangier—and I spent a wild night with him in his palatial rumpus rooms in Rome—he was having one of his eye operations, to correct strabismus and a cataract. I entered a small private ward in the hospital where a vase full of American Beauty roses stood on the night table beside his bed. The odor of the bedpan mingled with the odor of roses. He had a bandage over one eye. Two visitors, a striking young man and a glamorous woman, probably actors, were unbelievably good-looking.

Although our paths did not cross often over the years, before I left America I had a memorable experience related to Tennessee. One night I went to the Eberhard Baths, to which Tennessee had introduced me. The "Everhard," as it was known, was a vast dingy structure honeycombed with a rabbit warren of cubicles, showers, and steam rooms on three floors, with a dark spacious loft full of single cots. The Seventh Circle was another name for it. Men of all ages wandered like ghosts in tattered white cotton smocks encircled by a frayed cloth belt, probing, groping, seeking, yearning. Fantastic sex scenes took place there. An old college professor of mine, "happily" married, stepped into my cubicle and, pretending not to recognize me, asked if I cared to "wrestle" with him. He was huge, fat, and deceitful, and I did not care to. He had turned informer during the McCarthy era and denounced his colleagues for what he himself had been, a Communist. While still a Commie he had once attacked me in class for my apostasy from that secular faith. He had also said, "The right woman will solve your sex problem." Apparently it hadn't worked for him.

Later that night a small wiry young man entered my cubicle. He had a rock-hard, hairless body and a hawklike Italian face. His name was Frank Merlo and he was Tennessee's lover. Astonished to discover that I was a friend of Tennessee's, he begged me never to mention our escapade at the baths, which was quite sensational. I assured him that I would keep his secret from Tennessee and I did until, years after Frank's death from cancer, I showed this memoir to Tennessee, then in his sixties, in his hotel suite at the old El Cortez on Geary in San Francisco. I had no idea it would upset him, but it did, and he behaved badly. He accused me of lying. He threw a dollar bill on the floor, saying, "I don't remember borrowing it from you but if that's what you want—" I picked it up. I'd been practicing some spiritual exercise in which one of the principles was to turn away nothing that is given to you. Perhaps it was an exercise in humility, but the reader can imagine Tennessee's interpretation when I put it in my pocket. My impulse was to tear it into tiny pieces and throw it in the air like confetti. It would have been futile; no matter what I did I'd never have regained his approval. Tennessee had not been playing with a full deck for years.

34

Allen Ginsberg

In my tiny room on Horatio Street I froze in winter. In the wee hours when the streets were deserted I'd go on sorties to gather orange crates for firewood around the corner at the slaughterhouse. Old bums wrapped in newspapers slept on concrete platforms that by day held bloody beef carcasses. The gloomy racks stank like a stockyard and the meathooks glinted menacingly in the moonlight. When it snowed the bums were covered like sacks of garbage with the cold white stuff.

In my unheated two-by-four on Horatio Street I was visited by Tennessee Williams, James Baldwin, and Allen Ginsberg. Far from being monstrously famous, they were all obscure, gay, unsure of themselves. In that arctic winter of late 1944, one night I was riding the IRT subway to the hole in the wall I called home, drunk and dispirited. I can't remember where I'd been, some dull party or other in Brooklyn, where I hadn't succeeded in dragooning into service a bedmate for the night. There was nobody else in the car and I was lonely, dreaming of love and sex, which I needed every moment and had to forage for, like firewood, to keep warm. The yellow lights glowed eerily, the empty train rattled and roared—an empty train speeding to an empty room, to empty nights and meaningless days. It was a time of total war, total hate.

.With a feeling of desolation stifling me, I fought back my despair. A charter member of the "Beat Generation," which would be named some ten years later, I didn't feel like a generation. I felt like a scared drunken kid in a terrifying world of murderers.

A tall skinny youth wearing a red bandana around his neck entered and took a seat directly opposite. He carried a book from which he kept reading aloud; occasionally he'd shoot a glance in my direction, not really seeing me. Always curious about people carrying books, I wanted to see the title—was it a piece of crap or the real thing? In my romantic way I hoped to meet an undiscovered genius, some teenage Rimbaud who would become my lover. Meanwhile the youth across the aisle began babbling louder, his head lolling around, glazed eyes rolling wildly behind horn-rimmed specs. But the clatter and roar of the train drowned out the words. He had thick black hair, sensual Jewish features, smooth olive skin, and a slender body— definitely attractive, I decided, at least on a cold night at three in the morning. At station stops, when the roar of the train died down, I could make out what he was reciting. It was in French. "Rimbaud!" I said at a stop. "'The Drunken Boat'!"

"You're a poet!" said Allen Ginsberg with open-mouthed astonishment. Here was the genius, though neither of us could swear to it then. I always thought there was something prophetic about the meeting. For instance, he might have sat at a far corner of the car and it wouldn't have happened. I was the first writer he had met. ("I met Kerouac about a week after I met you," Allen told me in San Francisco in 1974. "I met Burroughs ten days later.")

A virgin of eighteen and a student at Columbia, studying poetry with Mark Van Doren, Allen had nervously come to the Village to pick up a boy for the first time in his life and ended up with me. I was twenty-eight. We both wanted the same thing—a teen-aged "angel-headed hipster." I had found mine (though not a hipster) six years earlier, but Auden had taken him from me. It only happens once. I would never again find quite the same thing, and I'd never again be that young.

For Allen, as for us all, the Village was an oasis in the puritan desert, a watering place for the soul. The Village offered freewheeling sex. The closet cases of America were drawn to the bars and hangouts of Bohemia, longing to fulfill their secret desires and sneak anonymously back to conventional niches. Ginsberg was no exception. The scared willowy boy came to my room and sat primly and self-consciously, and somewhat stiffly, beside me on my single cot, anxiously showing me his rhymed four-line poems, seeking my praise and approval. His quatrains, however, were in my opinion ordinary. Ironically, in view of what he would become—this was eleven years before *Howl* was written—I found his efforts too tame, too feeble, too conventional. Both in his personality and his poems he was too restrained.

Obsessed with Hart Crane's visionary homosexual mysticism and Dylan Thomas's inebriate incantatory style, I spoke of them and of Whitman, the obsessions of my youth, as masters of the spontaneous, intuitive flow of language. As we huddled together I held forth about Dionysian breath, as evidenced in "Song of Myself" and *The Bridge*, by two great "fairies" who wrote the two greatest long poems ever written by Americans. *The Waste Land* (we didn't know that Eliot wrote it for a drowned young Frenchman he was in love with) was no model for succeeding generations—like Pound's *Cantos*, it was too hermetic. It may be hard to imagine now, but during World War II almost nobody read Pound except to attack him. While Hitler was devastating Europe it was impossible to read without bias a rabid Fascist who made violent anti-Semitic harangues from Mussolini's shortwave Radio Rome. Pound praised the dictators and slandered American writers and politicians as "yids" and "kikes" or in the pay of Jews. Tennessee referred to him as "the unspeakable Mr. Pound," which summed it up.

Perhaps I influenced Allen a little that morning and perhaps I didn't. I showed him my poem "Key West" in *Poetry*, which was greeted by some critics as a neoromantic breakthrough in a concrete wall of academic dullness. Apocalyptic poetry, however, enjoyed no vogue in America. Anything British was highly regarded by the establishment, as Oscar Williams's *Little Treasuries* proved, but with the sole exception of Dylan Thomas and the surrealist David Gascoyne, the other so-called Apocalyptics produced no stylistic departures to speak of.

Allen listened, agreed, said little. Around 7:00 A.M., when I began hinting that he could stay over if he wished, he glanced at the hard narrow cot, which could comfortably accommodate two if one slept on top of the other, and with a look of alarm jumped to his feet. "I've got to get back to New Jersey," he said quickly. "I'm leaving tomorrow for Murmansk!" We both held union cards from the Maritime Commission. So Allen, who had arrived a virgin, departed a virgin. If I had resembled Peter Orlovsky, this memoir would have been longer.

That little room was a turning point in my life. There I would soon take a wrong turn that I've regretted ever since.

35

Watershed

David Blake was an infrequent visitor. One evening as we sat on the floor before the fire—I stark naked under my bathrobe—he solemnly spoke of his love for me. He wanted only three things in life, he said: the revolution, a long life, and "most important, you." As we stared into the fireplace he asked me to live with him. I recall thinking, "If I say yes it wouldn't be honest. I love him, but I'm not in love with him." He was forty-four, had brought me out, shown respect and kindness, was mild, considerate, and—a millionaire. I'd be free from want forever. A heartbeat away from security, complete independence, I turned him down for the sake of independence! Unable to deceive a friend (who would have been happier anyway with me beside him) and having recently left Larry because I could not be fulfilled with him, I decided against David and missed the chance of an easy life. Within months he was dead, leaving millions to the Communist party. He also left a fortune to "Terry McBride" and a large sum to a boy who'd fought beside him in Spain. McBride told me that I'd have inherited the bulk of the money. His death was caused by a heart attack in his private plane while he performed stunts called chandelles (in Spain he had learned to fly and use a machine gun). But who knows, I might have been in the plane with him, my life cut short at twenty-eight, had I accepted him. At his death he had attained none of the things he desired.

On my return from Provincetown I asked Jimmy Baldwin to introduce me to Paul Goodman, and one afternoon we went to his cold-water flat. Paul had thick brown hair with a cowlick, glasses, an aquiline nose, and a quick, nervous manner; he was a genuine Jewish intellectual. Easygoing and shy, he spoke softly, with a diffident grin, blue eyes flashing, and looked like a waif. He asked if we cared to hear him translate a passage from Genet's *Our Lady of the Flowers,* which had appeared in a limited French edition the previous year and was not yet available in English. Pacing beside the window over the street he began to sight-read, with amazing fluency, the section where Divine, blowing a young convict, experiences the orgasm as a pistol shooting off in his throat. It is one of the most shattering and exalted passages in literature. It raised homosexual experience to the level of high art in defiance of an oppressive conspiracy of silence. I was grateful to Paul for introducing me to Genet but did not take him up on his invitation to see him again. I knew what he wanted. He kept asking Jimmy, "Where's your handsome friend?" One afternoon we revisited Paul and when Jimmy rose to leave I also stood up. "Stick around," said Paul. When Jimmy left Paul put a hand on my thigh.

"Sorry, Paul, but it won't work," I said.

"At least you could give it a chance," he said, turning red.

"No, Paul. I'm sure."

If hell hath no fury like a woman scorned, look again. A man scorned makes a woman seem saintly by comparison (women have too long served as scapegoats for the flaws men dare not face in themselves). Paul, who was bisexual, was mean when rejected. For nine years I continued seeing him, but though amiable face to face, he made bitchy, untrue remarks behind my back. On the other hand, most writers I knew didn't score much better in the ethics department. Virtue existed in their work, not in their lives. Paul, who was married and had two children, never ceased pursuing young men relentlessly. Grudgingly he once said of me, "He's a talent."

In the spring of 1945 I met a young Englishman, two years my junior, in Washington Square Park. A commercial artist, he was no bohemian. Twenty-six, handsome, clever, and eloquent, he dressed well, maintained standards of hygiene and neatness, and spoke with what he called a "mid-Atlantic accent." His voice was as beautiful as Chester's, his wit more polished. It amazed me to see how people fell all over him with admiration and lust. Graham Rackham (name changed) had a cool Noel Coward wit that sliced through brains like a knife through butter.

Graham asked me to move in with him and I accepted but waited until the end of summer, which I spent on Fire Island in a cabin at Ocean Beach. I wanted to sort out my life—a goal I have not yet achieved. My affair with Bonnie was ending for a variety of reasons, not least because she confessed to plans of marrying a writer in his forties who, she unflinchingly said, was good for her social position. I liked and respected the man, who lived in the Hotel Earle, a small but elegant establishment (now a welfare hotel) of which the bookstore occupied the street-corner basement, but Bonnie's implication that I was socially of no account stung me. In my déclassé way I had assumed that I was above such trivial concerns as social position; for the first time I saw that I was beneath them. My egalitarian ego was piqued; hammers, sickles, and guillotines swam before my eyes. How dare this southern Marie Antoinette treat me like a common plebe? Having only recently discovered the joys of heterosexuality, I now stumbled upon its horrors. So she would dump me for a man she didn't love? Well, I'd show her. I would dump her for a man *I* didn't love. Her look was unforgettable. She made a face as if she had stepped in dogshit and, in a tone of aggrieved discovery, exclaimed, "Oooh, I *see!*" The dirty little secret was out. I was a fairy.

36

Fire Island

If I was not good enough for Bonnie's social level I decided that Fire Island was good enough for me. Like most college-educated idealistic bohemians, I was a malcontent, a homeless radical, and a snob. The vacationers were vulgar, mindless, and rich, so I could look down on them. In a bar I met the greatest hairdresser in the world, Antoine de Paris. "How you do?" trilled the white-haired old Pole in a silvery voice. "You are Italian decent?" "Neither Italian nor decent," I said. He and his boyfriend discussed the weather and a blister on Antoine's foot. Their sunny thoughtlessness acted like a sedative on me. What a relief! I didn't have to think. Antoine sent Reuel on an errand and no sooner had he left than the old man boldly inquired, "What you like better, mens or womens?" to which I replied, thinking to put him off, "Women." I couldn't get rid of him after that. The old man's brain was no bigger than a postage stamp, but his bank account was colossal. Like other moneybags in that Mecca of chi-chi, he followed me around, but I was not for sale: with a thorough disregard for self-preservation I treated my body as though it were not a commodity. From brothel to brothel the wires hummed, "Mr. Strength and Health is straight."

On the beach I worked out doing calisthenics, swimming, and masturbating. One hot afternoon I stretched out in a cavernous dune hidden from view, removed my trunks, and fell asleep. I was dreaming of an overheated teen-aged bellhop who had eyed me ever since my arrival when I awoke abruptly and, to my horror, saw Antoine bouncing up and down on my erection with wild abandon as I climaxed. Extricating himself with difficulty, he hissed, "Sank you, sweetie!" and sailed off with a toss of his silly old head. Suki, the baron's lap dog, was more delicate about it.

As for the teen-aged blond, an all-American boy (I could tell from his furtive interest in me), I kept seeing him with different girls, whom he displayed ostentatiously while staring significantly into my eyes. Even when I tipped him after he showed me my room he hovered expectantly. One evening I ran into him with a girl in a gazebo. "Hello, again!" he called with bluff heartiness, then disappeared with his date.

The following afternoon as I lay sunbathing nude in a sand dune he appeared at the crest alone, stared in silence, then slipped beside me and removed his trunks. I enfolded my arms around his tan body and submitted to a few moments of sheer lust.

Meanwhile I was receiving letters from Bonnie, Graham, and Jimmy Baldwin. Jimmy's letters from Woodstock, where friends put him up so that he could work on his novel in a peaceful atmosphere, were full of fears about his future, about poverty, obscurity, lack of love. "What's going to become of me?" he'd write in hopeless despair. He would always mention his feelings for me. Bonnie's letters were chatty and amusing, her anger at my breaking off sexual relations barely concealed beneath a debonair manner. On July 28 her best friend married the socially prominent writer and Bonnie was left out in the cold. (That was the day an airplane hit the Empire State Building.) She wrote me an aggrieved letter about the marriage as a betrayal and "dragged home" a handsome decorated war hero she had met at the wedding party. If until then I had believed that straights were different from gays in their sexual behavior, I found I was mistaken. Both behave with equal absurdity. *Les liaisons dangereuses* by Choderlos de Laclos was a cult novel Bonnie had introduced me to; now ironically I watched life imitate art.

July 11

Strong wind across the bay. The sea plunging and crashing on the shore. . . . Spoke to Graham and Bonnie long distance. They're having dinner together tomorrow. They will devastate each other with charm.

July 13

Full moon, ochreous and mellow. Soft deep sky. Scrub pine raises bony fingers, silver-tipped. Foxtail dark and shadowy. The island is now magical. The boardwalks glow, dunes rise by the shore like gibbous shadows. Filigree webs brush my face as I pass, my heels too loud for the hush. Small slimy creatures rustle in the foliage. At the beachfront the surf is a muffled roar, eerily aglow with spume and spindrift like spun glass. I feel tired, irresponsible. My mind is numb.

Reading Henry Miller's *Tropic of Cancer,* for the second time. Its insolence, arrogance and sexual candor are energizing; he strips language and people bare. On the other hand, there's a foul stench about it, not so apparent on first reading—because of its fresh approach—that leaves a bad taste. He repeats preposterous lies about Jews—the usual redneck crap. Jews, he says, are so neurotic that they enjoy Gentiles because the latter are so healthy. When Gentiles suffer they suffer differently, because they do not become neurotic. Dreck, Henry, dreck. No amount of fresh air can make shit smell like perfume.

July 17

Bonnie showed up and stayed till Sunday night. I confessed all about my sexual nature, for the first time to a woman. She was understanding but, as she said she still loves me, she could not forgive me for throwing her over. Who was dumping whom? I wondered. She manoeuvred it so that we were compelled to fuck—for the last time. I must admit that I was super-horny. We had what I can only describe in Hollywood superlatives as torrid, tropical sex. We ran along the beach, plunged into the waves, sweated in the sun. She had a peach pink tan and called me her "golden boy." She came into my room where I sprawled across the bed in khaki shorts. "I'd like to lie down beside you," she said softly, "but my bathing suit is wet." "Take it off," I said facetiously. She did. "Didn't think I'd do it, did you?" She lay beside me. Our hands met. She touched my face and I got an erection. We kissed. I slipped my shorts down. She went into the small room, inserted a Norform lozenge that smelled like cocoa butter into her cunt, came back and lay close to me and we fucked three times that afternoon and again at night and all day Sunday, lying down and standing up. I kept feeling her small breasts and fingering her orifices and she kept murmuring that I was the most beautiful, sexiest boy. . . .

Her cunt boiled and I screwed in a sexual frenzy, unable to stop. Weeks of solitude, sun, blazing beaches, exercise and daily exposure to beautiful young bodies, none of which became a human to whom I could relate or have sex with, had stored up in me a fierce energy that a few days with Graham did nothing to relieve. In fact, it only made matters worse. He was recuperating from circumcision and was out of commission. His cock was bandaged and stitched around the foreskin. Erections caused excruciating pain. "It looks like a powdered donut," he joked.

Bonnie told me how hard it was going to be to give me up. "This is the last weekend," she said sadly. We had tears in our eyes.

In mid-September I moved into Graham's first-floor flat at 62 Perry Street, an old Victorian two-story brownstone. Before leaving for Fire Island I had moved from my room on Horatio and on my return had to unpack all the suitcases and cartons I had stored at Graham's and help arrange a bachelor's apartment to accommodate two bachelors. The apartment was a floor-through consisting of two high-ceilinged rooms separated by double doors that, when open, made one spacious parlor stretching from the street to the rear garden. Two charcoal-burning fireplaces (one in each room), topped by marble mantelpieces, were kept supplied with bricks of soft coal that glowed and crackled in the grate on cold or rainy evenings, sparkling with bursts of starry flame and creating warmth and coziness, although we also had steam heat. On the papered wall above the mantelpiece in the front room hung two gilt-framed rococo mirrors, and another in the back room. Graham had installed an intricate system of lighting on tracks and dollies, which he built himself, with bulbs in black cone-shaped metal shades that could be turned in any direction; dimmed or brightened they focused on paintings of geometrical designs, all cleverly executed originals by Graham. It looked like a downtown gallery.

When we arrived the disarray was appalling. We bore heavy suitcases full of my books, notebooks, and clothes, and faced the job of unpacking and arranging everything. Worn out by heat and fatigue, Graham grew more touchy by the minute. Paint cans and brushes lay strewn about on newspapers, my cartons and suitcases were everywhere. In a grim, silent, determined way, Graham tidied up without stopping. At one point he spoke sharply: "Harold, you *must* keep some semblance of neatness here this week. If you don't I shall go mad." Later, by way of apology, he explained that when fatigued he worked even harder on nervous energy instead of collapsing. It took me a week to clean up.

37

Auden Revisited

One fall evening in 1945 I ran into Auden in a Village restaurant, wolfing his food and his wine, engrossed in a book. I thought it odd that he dined alone. Where was Chester, not to mention all the admirers—the students, writers, poets? And the friends, where were *they*? The war had changed everything. When I greeted him I was surprised at the cordial invitation to his new apartment, only a few blocks from Perry Street, where I lived.

In tan trench coat and gray trilby worn at a rakish angle in the best Bogart manner, I arrived one rainy evening at 7 Cornelia Street. Wystan's voice crackled on the intercom. New but drab building, sandwiched between sweet-smelling Italian bakeries and *salumerias* on the narrow street. Elevator too. Apartment E, fourth floor. Auden opened the door, soiled shirt hanging out of baggy pants and stained pullover, lank blond hair unkempt.

"Oh, you're soaking wet, poor dear! Let me fix you a martini. It's ab-so-*lute*-ly *fil*-thy weather."

Inside the bed-sitting room in my dripping raincoat, drops

falling on my nose from the brim of my hat. Pensive, Auden gazed at me a long moment. "You look like Joe College," he said softly.

"After all these years! I wish it were true."

"Oh, but it *is*, my dear! You haven't changed at-tall!"

A note of nostalgia crept into his voice. He took my wet clothes and shuffled down the hall in carpet slippers, like an old auntie, and deposited them in the bathroom. He must have seen me almost as I first appeared to him, fresh from college. Nearing forty, he looked much older, pudgier than I remembered, that egg-white pasty face much less severe. I thought I detected something I had never observed before, a trace of loneliness, of suffering. He seemed chastened. I didn't know that he had recently returned from a tour of duty in the uniform of a U.S. Army major with the Strategic Bombing Survey in Germany at the end of the war. Surveying the ruins, human and material, he had witnessed firsthand the effects of war, of untold havoc on human lives.

The martini, served in a murky tumbler, was strong. Others followed in rapid succession. Not dwelling on the subject of Chester, whom I saw from time to time, we talked like old friends, seated at opposite ends of the sofa bed against the beige wall smudged with grease and fingerprint stains. This apartment, unlike the one on Montague Terrace, lacked the remotest hint of charm or elegance. It was small and squalid, boxlike, ill lit by garish overhead light bulbs in a tacky chandelier at the center of the dusty ceiling. Brass wall brackets above the sofa shed paltry light from little flame bulbs. Against one wall in the untidy living room stood a smallish worktable, overflowing in monumental disarray: books, magazines, manuscripts, cigarette cartons and packs, ashtrays choked with butts, a portable typewriter.

Did I know of a good restaurant nearby? I did. The one where we had met served "dismal food in a dreary atmosphere, my dear." I recommended one on Barrow Street, where he became a regular with his books and cigarettes, imbibing vast quantities of meat and fowl, Valpolicella and Riesling, and spiritual sustenance from Kierkegaard and Reinhold Niebuhr with equal voracity at the candlelit table. I saw him there often, a solitary diner. Barely looking up, he would grunt hello or merely nod and return to his book as if it demanded every precious moment of his attention. The name of the restaurant has faded from memory, but the golden glow of the candles on white tablecloths remains as clear as Wystan's bent head, tousled and shining, nose buried in a book.

I got smashed on those strong martinis as we conversed animatedly about everything by way of catching up, until I realized at some point that the conversation had ground to a halt. Wystan was watching me owl-eyed through cirrus wisps of cigarette smoke from his end of the sofa, near the windows facing the street. Only the sound of the rain pelting the panes was audible. We puffed our Luckies as, from my end of the couch, next to the hallway leading to the bathroom, I stole glances at him to find him staring at me. I recalled this look from earlier times—thoughtful, calculating, probing. Why doesn't he say something? I thought uneasily.

Then, without warning, he pounced. He hurled his hulking frame from his end of the couch to mine like a football tackle, groped me clumsily, and growled, "Let's have a little romp, shall we?" rolling his British *r*. It sounded like *rump*. And that's what it was. In total confusion I protested weakly. "Hey, wait a minute! Stop! *Wys*-tan!! For God's sake!"

Wystan was all over me, unbuttoning my pants, fumbling under my shorts, breathing hotly down my neck. Ineffectually, I kept pushing him away, not applying force, but he pressed harder, muttering, "Come on, now, don't be a ninny, dear," huffing and puffing with exertion.

My head reeled. I had just begun to feel comfortable with him and now, once more, he was behaving with total disregard for my feelings. He had written several letters about "feeling guilty for having taken Chester away from you." How had he dealt with his guilt? No attempt to iron things out, no friendly overtures. This seduction was yet another monumental piece of clumsiness. By using a little tact and subtlety Wystan could easily have redressed the grievance. But he possessed less talent for diplomacy than even I. In the harsh glare of the overhead light, and with a spinning brain, I knew this was going to be difficult.

"Turn out the light," I said with resignation.

"Yes, yes, of course," agreed Wystan hastily, jumping up and switching it off.

A pool of light still shone from the bathroom at the end of the hall. In the dimness I could see Wystan frantically stripping down; it unnerved me further. His body, a massive blur in the half-light, was unappealingly soft and plump. Wystan's sudden unappetizing nudity shocked me into near sobriety, so incongruous was it with our past relationship of wary détente. Then, too, to complicate matters, this could only create further problems between me and Chester. My feeling for Chester, if one can quantify feelings, was as great as Wystan's. He had altered that camaraderie, leaving me to get over it as best I could.

Now, hovering over me like an amorphous hulk, stark naked, he was again behaving like a klutz. There had been no transition from the varying degrees of distance and estrangement, except for the brief hour or so of casual conversation that ended abruptly with his sexual assault. "There's still some light down the hall," I said hoarsely, with uneasy foreboding.

"Oh, sure, sure," breathed Wystan, and galumphed to the bathroom, doused it, raced back, and fell upon me like some huge animal falling upon his prey in the dark. I lay back feeling frozen, detached from my body and from what was happening. On the other hand, Wystan was completely carried away. Oblivious to everything but his pleasure, he surprised me both by the force of his passion and by his clumsy attempt at fellatio (a word Chester and I first learned from him). He was certainly no master of *this* art, I thought with exasperation. The more feverishly he labored, the less I responded. Finally, exhausted and panting, he raised his head and gasped, "Uh—my-my-my *deah*—you're—*ausgespielt!*"

I mumbled some excuse about being dog-tired after a sleepless night, staggered to my feet, and pulled up my shorts and pants. I could not very well let on that his inept performance, following the Groucho Marx seduction scene and, not least, the unfinished emotional business that had gone unresolved for years, scarcely made for instant sexual turn-on. I also told him that I was a bit nervous, to which he didn't respond.

Only a few times in my life, when drunk or emotionally upset, had I experienced impotence. This time I felt annoyed as well as bewildered. I still very much needed Wystan's—and Chester's—friendship and approval. That night I gained a clue to Wystan's sexual insecurity and, perhaps, to his compensatory gruffness and curtness of manner. Chester and I had a friend in college who made up our triumvirate of leading undergraduate poets. Good-looking, athletic, and heterosexual, he behaved with adolescent arrogance to everyone but us. We were deeply attached to one another. At nineteen he committed suicide—because of his small penis. He left a suicide note to that effect. His death was the worst shock we had at college. Although not suicidal, Wystan may have felt similarly inadequate. He was convinced that nobody could love him because he was unattractive and underendowed. Penis size meant nothing to me if attracted to the person. Bigger was better as a rule when cruising, but face, body, and personality came first with situations more intimate than quickies. I could even have given Wystan what he wanted had he given me time.

Wystan switched on the light and threw a tatty old bathrobe over his fleshy frame. His carpet slippers, which never left his feet, were the worse for wear. I went to the bathroom to wash up. When I returned he was fussing with a teapot, looking very homey and human. There was even something pathetic about him, a word I would never before have applied to Auden. In any case, it was a fleeting impression, which he soon corrected. But there was no mistaking his air of loneliness. I declined his offer to stay for a hot cup of tea but invited him to a party that Graham and I were throwing. He accepted eagerly, then added shyly, "I hope you'll come back again, my dear." Several times he repeated anxiously, "Don't mention any of this to Chester, Harold." "Of course not," I reassured him. I kept my word.

Wystan, who had not had sex with Chester for four years, had gradually grown resigned to Chester's promiscuity since *l'affaire* Tom. He simply could not face life without a constant—or inconstant—companion. He even boasted to friends about Chester's sexual prowess. I remember him telling me, with both envy and pride, of Chester's successes. To another friend, referring to the period at Ann Arbor, Michigan, in 1942 when Chester lived with Wystan (who was teaching at the university and paying for Chester's graduate school studies, besides keeping him), he confessed to having let "*le faux* Chester . . . shit on my face." Auden had turned into a complete doormat, living with him without the satisfaction of sex, putting up with Chester's incessant pickups, some of whom he brought home, and swallowing his pride. He made huge sacrifices so that they would remain together. Wystan had always expressed his belief that the chief problem with homosexuality was that it produced no family ties, lacked permanence and social acceptance.

Perhaps Chester's cruelty was his way of taking revenge. Stephen Spender has pointed out that since Chester was a very competitive person, he had begun to believe that Auden had destroyed his personality (which is what I had warned about from the start).

Later, Auden regarded Chester's refusal to sleep with him as "providential." God, having bestowed on him a divine gift for poetry, did not bestow the gift of happiness as well. It would have been ungrateful to expect it. Genius and happiness in love seldom go together. Rationalizing in this manner, Auden became more, rather than less, confirmed in his belief in Christianity and in his poetic mission.

It was a marriage made in hell. Mephistopheles was never far off in the wings. Chester had sold his soul to the devil for fame—even if it was mostly reflected fame. He had struck a hard bargain for immortality and paid the price. Wystan dutifully plucked him from obscurity in the nick of time—thus saving the relationship when all seemed lost. One day we met by chance in the street and with barely restrained excitement Chester said, "I'm going to collaborate with Wystan on the libretto of *The Rake's Progress!*" Stravinsky knew nothing about it yet. It was the end of 1947, shortly before Chester's twenty-seventh birthday. Auden saw this as the means for reuniting them through artistic collaboration—the relationship was at its lowest ebb. In fact, Chester's looks had already begun to fade. He had put on weight and his face was puffy.

The subject matter of the libretto was perfect: an opera based on Hogarth's "Rake's Progress" engravings. Chester, whose trashy histrionics and need to hog center stage at all costs made him behave like the stereotypical prima donna of grand opera, had a remarkable knowledge and appreciation of that art form and, in fact, had been single-handedly responsible for instilling in Auden a love and respect for it. "Wystan Auden's devotion to Chester Kallman was . . . the real subject of the libretto (the fidelity of true love)," wrote Robert Craft, Stravinsky's friend, secretary, and biographer. The story fit their lives perfectly—Wystan thinly disguised as Anne Truelove and Chester cast in the role of the Rake, Tom Rakewell. A travesty, if you will, but a great one.

Chester's career was a stupendous gift from Wystan. Without it, he would have remained an obscure minor poet writing impenetrable verse in metrical feet of clay. His cryptic poetry rarely left the ground, competent though it was in rigid traditional forms and tricks of language. Auden put him on the world stage.

Is it justifiable to conceal the sex life of a major artist without distorting the truth? I believe that such concealment causes great harm to the homosexual image. (Freud once psychoanalyzed da Vinci, who was arrested for having sex with a fifteen-year-old boy.) Homosexuality being a fact of nature, we do not serve truth by bowing to false morality. Auden once said he was a normal man except for his homosexuality. He should have said *because* of it.

Nobody who knew Auden could think of him as a typically pious Christian. I am certain he enjoyed Ronald Firbank more than the Bible. "As organizations, none of the churches look too hot, do they?" he once remarked. He was never prudish or reticent about sex, nor did he subordinate his pleasures to his religious convictions. You might say he indulged in homosexual acts religiously.

Once, at the beginning of our stormy friendship, I confided in Wystan my sexual frustration when, as a virgin of eighteen, at Commonwealth College I bunked one summer with attractive students who walked naked in the dorm in the intense heat. I nearly went mad.

"For God's sake, why didn't you just announce, 'I'm a cocksucker'?" said Auden. "That's what *I* would have done." I was astonished. I could never have declared myself so blatantly. For his part Wystan was amazed at my reticence, unable to understand my fear of open declaration. "You might have had at least *hahf* the student body, my deah," he added with a wistful look.

"The *whole* body or nothing," I bantered, shaking my head in disgust at my virgin folly.

Always candid about his gayness, Auden behaved outrageously even for the 1920s. At Oxford the historian A. L. Rowse, who was also gay, was revolted by Auden's "frank and meaty accounts of his amours." He would approach any young man who attracted him, gay or straight, and boldly declare his intentions. More often than not it ended in bed. Yet Auden's life, paradoxically, was governed by a bizarre sense of propriety or, more narrowly, by what *he* considered proper, based on his strict Anglican upbringing. His pious mother dominated his childhood with parochial standards of conduct to which, all his life, he adhered. These arbitrary rules had little to do with sexual prudishness but much to do with "good form." He was despotic about punctuality to an absurd degree, insisting on modes of dress to which he himself never adhered, condemning inappropriate behavior while behaving in an appalling manner. As with so many of his beliefs, Auden was never prevented from ignoring them when it suited his convenience to do so. He insisted, "I don't care what people say about me when I'm dead."

The night of the party Graham and I were throwing, Auden arrived with customary punctiliousness at precisely 8:00 P.M. when only a Viennese music critic and Paul Goodman were there. With a beatific smile of adoration, showing his gappy teeth, Paul reverently shook Auden's hand when I introduced them, then sat himself on the thick carpet at Auden's feet. All year Paul had pestered me for an introduction. Wystan promptly plunked himself down on the couch, where the music critic sat. I served cocktails (Paul took fruit juice; he detested alcohol and drunkenness) and almost immediately Wystan and the critic were at loggerheads in a heated discussion of *Der Rosenkavalier* and *Salome*. They argued about the librettos and the music, about which they grew technical, in the jargon we called "musicalese."

The critic, a middle-aged friend of Graham's whom I had never seen before or since, was obviously a heavyweight in his field. He exuded supreme self-confidence behind black horn-rimmed glasses with thick lenses that distorted his eyes into a sinister leer accentuated by a more sinister German accent, like a movie Nazi biting out phrases with blade-thin lips. Anybody but Auden would have given up—the man was a pro—but Auden, who couldn't stand contradiction, kept at him doggedly in what sounded like a losing battle. He started shouting shrilly, and I kept jumping up and greeting the guests as the contest grew hotter and hotter. The flat filled up with handsome young men as we played jazz and bebop records: Billie Holiday, Duke Ellington, Thelonious Monk, and Benny Goodman. Auden kept eyeing the young men and growing more belligerent. He shouted at the critic, "You're wrong! You don't know what you're talking about!" Ignoring his rude outbursts with unflappable authority, the critic countered evenly with obvious erudition, further inflaming Wystan, who yelled, "Shit! Absolute bullshit! *Scheisse!*" which everyone thought hilarious.

Red-faced and angry, Wystan stood up, helped himself to more drinks, and tried to engage some youths in conversation. But they wandered off with others and he stumbled back to the couch, at a respectable distance from the critic, and talked laconically with Paul Goodman, who brightened. But Auden continued playing the boor even with Paul, while shooting swift glances at me. I smiled reassuringly. Since he did not direct his ill humor at me I found him more ludicrous than fearsome. Perhaps, having experienced the *heimische* vulnerable Wystan a few nights earlier, I no longer found him so formidable. But he was a very convincing ogre.

I realized that for him I was the only familiar face and that beneath his monstrous behavior Wystan was like a shy, scared child in a crowded room full of desirable goodies he was unable to have. He seemed even more like a naughty child when, at exactly 11:00 P.M., he suddenly stood up in some alarm and loudly announced to nobody in particular, "It's way *pahst* my bedtime!" as if expecting to be punished. This was greeted with laughter. The night had just begun. Booze had done its work, inhibitions began to dissolve, the music and voices grew louder. I got mobbed by some of the young men, thrown on my back in the bathtub on a huge pile of coats, and next thing I knew a heap of bodies were squirming and writhing on top of me, all of us drunkenly kissing and groping each other. I still retain an indelible image of Wystan, bleary-eyed, comically peering down at me and clucking, "Oh, *deah!*" I laughed and shouted, "Join us, Wystan!" He lingered awhile, only his head visible above the bodies, regarding the orgy with a wistful expression. Then he was gone.

38

"Make Me Chaste, Lord, But Not Yet"

Soon after the party I invited Wystan for cocktails. He arrived punctually at 5:00 P.M. and Graham, who served martinis, sat composed and silent while we chatted. When Wystan rose we escorted him to the door, where he announced brusquely, "Harold, I want to see you Wednesday evening, eight o'clock—sharp. My place." Without waiting for a reply he shuffled down the steps into the street.

Above left, a formal portrait of Mother as a young woman (marred by her scissors and my childhood scrawl), before her two unhappy experiences, with my father and stepfather, soured her disposition. *Right,* Aunt Eva in a studio pose. She turned down an offer to be in the *Ziegfeld Follies.* AUTHOR'S COLLECTION

Below, in the bosom of Irish and German Catholic aunts, age two. Aunt Eva, lower right. AUTHOR'S COLLECTION

This mysterious faded sepia photograph Mother kept for years, refusing to identify the young doughboy—my natural father? The resemblance is too strong to be accidental. AUTHOR'S COLLECTION

A Photomat snap of Mother pushing sixty
AUTHOR'S COLLECTION

My stepfather, Max, Mother, and me, age nine, always glum in his presence—in a Coney Island studio AUTHOR'S COLLECTION

With Max's little brother, Seymour (right), a tender camaraderie that lasted into our teens
AUTHOR'S COLLECTION

Above, staff of the Brooklyn College *Observer,* our literary magazine, of which I was editor-in-chief. I'm seated, second from right. AUTHOR'S COLLECTION

Left, portrait of the writer as a young man (twenty-three), *War and Peace* weighing heavily on my heart and hands; by Marcus Blechman, great-nephew of Sarah Bernhardt, New York, 1940 AUTHOR'S COLLECTION

Right, taken in Miami Beach, days after Pearl Harbor, December 1941, just before entering the shipyard in Mobile in the Maritime Commission. My mental and emotional state are symbolically indicated by cracks across head and pelvis. Remarkably enough, two months later I underwent surgery for a bursting appendix. I did not, however, undergo a lobotomy, though my feelings were strongly negative. PHOTOGRAPH BY A FRIEND, AUTHOR'S COLLECTION

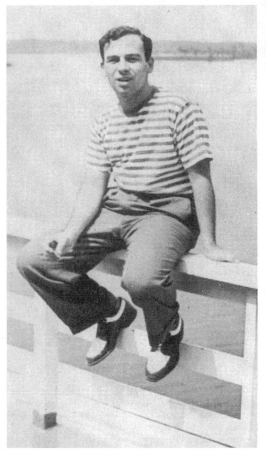

Left, in the Bellingrath Gardens, Mobile, Alabama, sporting two-tone oxfords on my day off from building Liberty ships, while Nazi U-boats roamed the Gulf, 1942 PHOTOGRAPH BY A FRIEND, AUTHOR'S COLLECTION

Above, living it up with some sweet servicemen more interested in me (center) than in Dorothy, a Brooklyn College girl friend. This faded snap was taken by a wandering photographer in MacDougal's Tavern, Greenwich Village, during World War II. AUTHOR'S COLLECTION

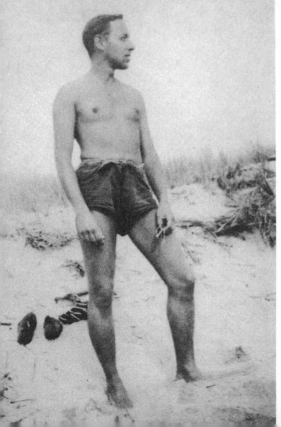

Left, Tennessee Williams on the dunes in Provincetown, where we bunked in a cabin during the summer he wrote *The Glass Menagerie,* August 1944 PHOTOGRAPH TAKEN BY ME, NORSE ARCHIVE, LILLY LIBRARY

Right, Tennessee in the doorway of the cabin, look-ing like a Southern sharecropper. We were relying on the kindness of strangers. PHOTOGRAPH TAKEN BY ME, AUTHOR'S COLLECTION

Below, the 1809 colonial farmhouse in Canter-bury, Connecticut, bought for $1,000 in 1951. It had one hundred acres of woodlands, marshes, fruit trees, every other kind of tree, wildlife, rockwalls, etc. To my lasting regret, I sold it a few years later for very little. PHOTOGRAPH TAKEN BY ME, AUTHOR'S COLLECTION

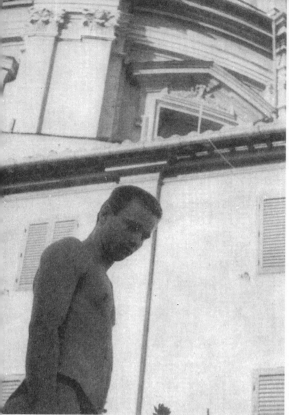

Left, a memorable young Roman friend (of German parentage) on the terrace of my last residence in Rome, via Santa Maria dell'Anima, behind the Baroque dome of the Church of St. Agnes in Piazza Navona PHOTOGRAPH TAKEN BY ME, AUTHOR'S COLLECTION

Below, in Rome with Frances McCann (on my left) and Giuseppe Ungaretti (on my right), the great Italian poet, in Frances's Rome–New York Art Gallery, Rome, about 1955 PHOTOGRAPHER UNKNOWN, COURTESY OF MONICA VON NAGEL

I realized that Wystan loomed as a threat to Graham. Again I was enmeshed in the Eternal Triangle. Knowing that Graham was my lover, Wystan must have felt awkward demanding a date in his presence, but as always, in a situation that required the utmost delicacy, he became gruff and bossy. Graham's silence was his defense against arrogance. "It's hard being a British colonial administrator in darkest Greenwich Village," said Graham.

I didn't show up for the command performance. A few evenings later, when Graham and I saw Wystan in the restaurant on Barrow, he nodded curtly, his nose buried in some ponderous Protestant tome. We took our seats at a nearby table. *"Brideshead Revisited* is more entertaining than *Fear and Trembling,"* I said. At college I had dealt with weighty Germanic concepts, but as far as I could see, the Second World War had kissed goodbye to all that. Goodbye to arguments on predestination, goodbye to original sin and immaculate conception. Goodbye forever to Good and Evil. The hard and fast line between them had vanished, blotted out by Hitler and Mussolini, blown up at Pearl Harbor and Hiroshima. There were no good guys anymore. Neither Reinhold Niebuhr nor the church, synagogue, or mosque could bring them back. It was goodbye to religion—at least the organized religions. They were warlike and clinically insane. They hated love and sex; they loved control; they punished good and rewarded evil. Their leaders, like Nazi, Fascist, and Communist leaders, were certifiably nuts. As far as I was concerned, God was the Big Bad Guy in the sky, no better than His constituents, who were munitions manufacturers, politicians, ruthless businessmen. They were in the business of killing. God had always been in that business. By comparison the Marquis de Sade was a pussycat, a benign philosopher who unmasked the real culprit for what He was, an omnipotent bully. God had sentenced us all to death, sudden or slow. We were not about to throw away our youth while millions were tortured and slaughtered in His name. No, we had seen through the religious hoax. It was totalitarian: the innocent were guilty, the guilty innocent.

Wystan had repeatedly said, and had written in a letter to me, "Live every moment as if it were thy last," quoting an Anglican hymn he had sung in childhood. And although the context of this line was religious, I could believe the thought without the religion. There was no other way to live. Certainly not if you were in your twenties and the most devastating war in history had just ended. I was lucky to be alive. I was lucky the government did not have room in its military machine for young men designated 4-F because of "feminine reactions." The government *was* a psychotic state. Blind to the masses of servicemen who rushed into the arms of gay men as fast as they could, it rejected gay men as unfit for military service, unaware that there'd be no military at all if they drummed out everyone who'd had sex with men. So I said no thanks to war and no thanks to God. Let Him occupy His psychotic heaven. *Our Father which art in heaven—stay there!* said Jacques Prévert, the French poet of the *Résistance*. And Auden quoted Saint Augustine: "Make me chaste, Lord, but not yet."

At eighteen I had discovered Billie Holiday singing "Strange Fruit." It was not a song about gays; it was about black men hanging from poplar trees in the South. It was about lynchings, about genitals severed by white racists. It was about young white women who lopped off fingers, ears, toes, and dicks from black corpses and kept them as souvenirs. They were not imprisoned or committed to mental institutions for criminally insane behavior. I had personally witnessed such a murder in an Alabama shipyard during the war. Like the Nazis who made lampshades from Jewish skin, the good Baptist Christians saw nothing wrong with it.

Our black friends meant a lot to us: Jimmy Baldwin, Billy Strayhorn, Aaron Bridges, Gordon Heath, Ruth Ellington (Duke's sister). We shared an intimacy, warmth, and mutual sympathy that I have not experienced since with black friends in America. Perhaps, because we were young and struggling for liberation from oppression, we shared a community of feeling that gained intensity because we could entertain little hope, realistically, for improvement of our condition. Jazz and blues provided the expression of these feelings.

Auden had nothing to do with this world, which was such an integral part of our lives. As whites we felt privileged to participate in the intimate life of black musicians and writers, while as an American with Jewish blood at a time when Jews were massacred in Europe, I identified with the predicament of blacks. Oppression of women and gays was identical with that of blacks and Jews. I believed that the fate of all minorities was inseparable.

Consequently, Graham and I may very well have regarded Auden with some generational hostility. Black music meant nothing to him—only opera and classical mattered. Wystan was on the wrong side, I told Graham. After his flirtation with the Left he retreated to the High Church of his childhood, which I regarded as an intellectual evasion, a copout. Nor did I think it did his poetry much good. In my opinion, he had surrendered his intellect to custom, bigotry, and tradition. From homosexual communism he had gone to straight Christianity. Wystan was no mystic, like Blake or Hopkins. He was a dyed-in-the-wool hedonist, a pragmatic realist who enjoyed the lusts of the flesh, against which, sensibly, he never launched judgmental attacks except for occasional assertions that excessive promiscuity weakened one's ability to love (which is arguable). Yet he secretly had more young men than anyone could keep track of. He showed unabated sexual interest in meeting them while, with the same secrecy he displayed with regard to our own abortive affair, he kept his friends apart, presumably so that they could not compare notes, whatever other private reasons he may have had—not least being the fear that Chester might discover the extent of his promiscuity. This lack of monogamous intent seems to have gone largely unexplored by biographers. If he considered his relationship with Chester a marriage, and promiscuity a weakening of the ability to love, nevertheless he fully indulged his desire for sexual partners.

39

Pimping for Auden

Wystan inquired if I knew of any young college boys interested in meeting him. I knew several and told him about one of them.

"What does he look like?" asked Wystan, all ears.

"Rather homely, I'm afraid. But a brilliant lit. scholar."

"Oh. How old?"

"Twenty-one."

"Mmm. Yummy."

"Glasses. Crew-cut. Funny nose. Italian. Nice body."

"Ya-as? Well hung?"

"Nine inches. Real thick."

He gulped a quick martini and clasped his pudgy hands. "De-*vine!*"

"Rather tiresome, I'm afraid. In an academic way."

"Oh, that's all right! I'd *love* to meet him!"

"Very opinionated."

"Who isn't?"

"Quotes the Trillings. Empson, Ransom, and—Auden."

"Ahhh," he purred. Nothing could dissuade him now.

"So you want to meet?"

"Oh, for God's sake! Of *course!*"

Next, I told John I had fixed him up with Auden.

"Great!" he said. "But—no hanky panky."

"Are you crazy? You're setting up roadblocks?"

"But I'm not attracted to him," he objected prissily.

"Would you turn down Walt Whitman?"

"Wait a minute—"

"Listen. There'd be no graduate school without the likes of Auden," I snapped. "Here's your big chance with a great master. But he's human, too. We all have the same needs. You could establish a friendship. Without poets like Auden where would the Trillings be? Teaching home economics, no doubt. Where would English lit. be? Ya wanna teach English?" He nodded quickly. "So if he wants a nibble of your Italian salami," I said, moving in for the kill, "what's the big deal? You're not exactly a 'still unravished bride of loveliness.'"

He did not correct my emendation of Keats, which was a good sign. He was thinking hard. He nodded. I had scored my point. Like so many friends who had asked to meet Auden, including some who would later become celebrities like James Baldwin and Paul Goodman, he would definitely not risk losing this opportunity. He was taking a Ph.D. toward a university career and wanted to tell his students one day that he knew Auden personally. Besides, a friendship with Auden might help advance his academic standing.

"Well, if you won't cooperate with Wystan," I said casually, "we'll call it off. I know at least *ten undergrads*—and they're beauties—dying to meet him."

"I—I'm sure I can handle it," he stammered.

I winked and gave him Wystan's phone number. My God, I thought, I have a hidden talent for pimpery. We stripped, as we had so often done, and got into bed. He had a very beautiful body and a most impressive endowment. Auden would be mad with joy.

John phoned a few days later.

"What happened?"

"Oh, you mean with Wystan?" I noted his use of the first name. "We got along fine."

"Then everything's okay?"

"Well, uh, I don't know. That's why I called. Have you heard from him?"

"No. You mean you haven't seen him again?"

"No. Everything went fine until he got me drunk and—made a pass. . . . God, he's clumsy! He fell on me like a raging bull!"

"So what happened?"

"I—I—well, nothing. I couldn't get it up!"

I gathered courage and phoned Wystan to tell him I was sorry if John had been a bore. Wystan welcomed the call and I said another friend, an attractive young blond, was dying to meet him. He expressed pleasure at the prospect of a new recruit.

Dennis, also a graduate student in English lit., was witty and bright in a campy way. He had blue eyes, blond hair, buckteeth, and boyish charm. But he dressed like a dandy, in serge blazers with a breast-pocket emblem and loud ties. He affected a clipped English accent—phony but part of the act. He had picked up a British persona along with a rolled umbrella during a year in England on an Oxford scholarship. I arranged the meeting at my apartment, but Wystan was aloof and taciturn from the start.

"He won't *do!*" growled Wystan in his death-sentence voice when Dennis had gone. "He simply won't *do!*"

"But why, Wystan? Too nellie, or what?"

Wystan's dreaded judgment fell like the blade of a guillotine. "Wearing school *ties!*" he exclaimed in a voice filled with horror. "How *fright*-fully vulgar! It's not *done* if you're an American. And that *accent!*"

"But Wystan, he *lived* in England! He went to Oxford!" I remonstrated, not fully grasping the point.

"My *deah,* unless you've *been* to an English public school, you don't do it." He pronounced it *bean.* "You don't wear an *Eton* tie!" Horror and shock mingled in his expression. Dennis was never mentioned again.

I gave up trying to please Wystan. I was not much as a call boy and even worse as a pimp. After the fiascos our stormy friendship petered out. It was doomed anyway. Some people you can never please and, for me at least, Wystan was one of them. I was both passive and at the same time resistant to Wystan's fiercely assertive, tyrannical personality. I had learned in childhood to bide my time as a budding giant killer and then strike for the jugular. Under pressure I would do it verbally; if goaded, physically. The chemistry between us was wrong. Perhaps, and it is a real probability, I was a repressed bully myself, at times tactless, blunt, and overbearing, yet I shrank from cruelty to man or beast. Unless sorely put upon I dealt gently with others. I could not put up with Wystan's tantrums—or even with my own.

40

Tomorrow

Eileen Garrett occupied a spacious penthouse on West Twenty-eighth Street. Tropical plants grew in lush profusion everywhere. Fat Persian cats lounged luxuriously on hassocks and divans. Parrots and parakeets shrieked and twittered amid orchids, datura, and passion flowers. It was a miniature rain forest in mid-Manhattan. Mrs. Garrett was a student of Frank the linguist, who brought me there. If in my world many were negative and despairing, in hers not the slightest gloom was tolerated. All was power and light.

Before such opulence I felt intimidated. As we stood on the terrace overlooking the street far below, she slipped a bank note into my hand and extended an invitation to visit her again. I didn't know how to refuse the money without giving offense. Later Frank said that she loved helping young people and that I should not be proud. He said she was favorably impressed by my humility, commenting on its rarity in a young poet. But I had not felt humble, merely out of place.

It all started when her prestigious, large-circulation magazine, *Tomorrow,* accepted two poems. I had received an enthusiastic letter from the editor, saying, "Your poems rang all the bells here." I also received a fat check, which rang all my bells. Mrs. Garrett's publishing company was called Creative Age Press and she happened to be the greatest living trance medium. For many years she was being studied under controlled conditions by Professor Rhine at Duke University, whose studies concluded that she possessed genuine paranormal abilities. As a girl her remarkable powers had come to the attention of William Butler Yeats, Oscar Wilde, and George Bernard Shaw. Later she was befriended by Robert Graves. After her conquest of England she came to America and made her fortune advising senators, presidents, and their wives. On my second visit she asked if I would like a palm reading and I readily accepted. In her lilting Irish brogue she crooned, "Dear, you have a beautiful, tender heart. But you give it away and it causes you grief. Your heart rules your head: fine for poetry but disastrous in life. You must discipline your passions. You will make a name for yourself. More sherry, dear?"

She possessed uncanny psychic gifts. Not long before, I had received a letter of praise from William Maxwell, the fiction editor of the *New Yorker,* to whom I had submitted a short story about a wounded army lieutenant. He said I had a rare sensibility and that "even a blind man can see that you have talent," but I lacked discipline—precisely what Mrs. Garrett had divined. Even more remarkable was her clairvoyant power to penetrate secrets that I had told no one. Gently stroking my palm in a sort of caress, she said, "Illegitimacy does not trouble you, but you have always felt the absence of your natural father. He was a pianist, wasn't he? From his side of the family you've inherited artistic gifts. They were wealthy once."

To earn money I began writing reviews for *Tomorrow.* I had done reviewing for other magazines, but they didn't pay. I was also writing a novel. On February 27, 1946, Mrs. Garrett accepted the novel for publication. I was twenty-nine and envisaged a bright future. The Depression, the war years, and my ghastly background were at last safely behind me—or so I thought. I received a note from Mrs. Garrett with a hundred-dollar check, asking me to see her at the office of Creative Age. I'd been in bed with the flu and the weather was cold and nasty. With a motherly gesture Mrs. Garrett felt my forehead and said I had fever and had better go back to bed. We discussed my novel, which she thought very ambitious. She would send the advance, she said. Meanwhile she whipped out a checkbook and wrote a check for fifty dollars. "I think you can use this little sum," she said. It was not little to me. She asked if I had done reviewing for the big magazines. "That's a way of picking up more money," she said, "and getting your name around. It's important to have people hear more of you. You should publish as much as you can." I said I knew no one on the other magazines. She got up, went into the office of John Richmond, the editor, and came back with the news that he was writing four letters of introduction for me. The magazines were the *Nation,* the *New Republic,* the *Saturday Review of Literature,* and the *New York Times Book Review.* I was to return with my manuscript on the second of March. "Be sure to get me then, as I am going away," said Mrs. Garrett, "and want to begin payments of your advance the first week in March."

It was all too rosy, too dreamy, too Hollywood to be true. The huge Wurlitzer organ in the Paramount theatre played "Stardust" over and over again in my brain as I collected the four letters of introduction from John Richmond, who said expansively, "Well, here they are, boy. You're in!" Then he leaned over and, in a confidential tone, said, "Go to Harrison Smith first at the *Saturday Review.* He's old and sort of gruff but really a great feller. We know him well and you're sure to get something. Just drop in—it's around the corner." Richmond said that it was impossible to crash any of them unless they knew you.

At home I had a few jiggers of rye and when Graham returned I broke the news. We went out to dinner to celebrate. That evening Jimmy Baldwin phoned. He had also received an advance to revise his first novel. He wanted to come over with Russell Edson to celebrate. About an hour and a half later Jimmy arrived, alone. We sat and discussed publishers, writing, and luck. "It's been so lousy all along it's *gotta* be good from now on," said Jimmy, chuckling. We discussed the remarkable turn of events.

Jimmy said he had to see an artist who had a place in Woodstock and we went to his studio on Cornelia Street. He was out, but his roommate, a sculptor, gave us some beer and we sat on orange crates in a mess of sculptured objects, canvases, frames, clothes, a gas stove in the center of the room, lamps without shades, dust, and garbage, talking about art.

Next day—Friday—Miss Davison, Eileen Garrett's secretary, phoned. "Mr. Norse," she said, "I'm afraid Mrs. Garrett won't be able to see you Monday at three-thirty as we had arranged. We try to keep her out of the office as much as possible, you know. She still hasn't sufficiently recuperated from her illness. But she won't be going away for quite some time. She wants you to call at the end of the month."

In utter astonishment I repeated, "At the end of the *month*?"

Miss Davison's voice did not waver. "Yes, dear," she said. "Give me a few rings before then, just as a reminder. Then we'll get you an appointment late in March."

"Right, Miss Davison." I tried not to sound disappointed.

I phoned Graham and he said I was losing the hundred dollars Mrs. Garrett had promised to start payment with in early March.

"Don't try to cheer me up!" I said bitterly.

"Oh, what do you want me to say?" Graham replied in a tired voice. Reality had reared its ugly head. We were bickering and snapping at each other. We consoled ourselves with the fact that she hadn't reneged. By Saturday I had sufficiently recovered from shock to return to the novel. Saturday evening we visited Barry Ulanov, an old high school friend, and drank a lot of whiskey. Barry's wife was the film star Barbara Bel Geddes. Ruth Ellington and her husband, Danny James, arrived.

Shortly after my conversation with Miss Davison, on March 15, I received a letter from Mrs. Garrett. She was indeed "going away"—she made it sound like a trip to the moon—and wanted to assure me that although she had a great deal of faith in me she must be truthful and say she believed I was not yet ready to write a novel. She did not think I had sufficiently developed the story line or created credible characters. It was terribly revealing about the poet rather than the novelist, she said (whatever that meant). For this reason she could not "go ahead" on her "commitment." But she had no doubt that, with discipline and work, I would succeed. She enclosed a check for $250 drawn on Creative Age Press as an advance until I could show more of the novel, "to preserve your own dignity as well as our sweet impersonal relationship." I reread the letter a dozen times and each time found "impersonal" ambiguous. Graham thought if I'd been more "personal" she'd have gone ahead on the commitment.

Mrs. Garrett did leave New York, and anxious to learn when she would return, I phoned Creative Age. Miss Davison answered. She'd be back around the beginning of May. "I hope you weren't disappointed by Mrs. Garrett's letter," she said, trying to gauge my reaction. "Well, I was, a little. But," I added hastily, "I think she was right when she said she didn't think I was ready for the big job." "Then she'll help you!" exclaimed Miss Davison, sounding relieved. My answer had a remarkable effect. "It's those who take the *other* attitude she doesn't help." Her tone, which had been cautious, became friendly again.

Jimmy Baldwin had suffered a similar reversal. All his work on the first novel came to naught. It was rejected, which plunged him into despair. He had no income, no hope of making money. I recall one of the many parties we attended at this time. From our first meeting Jimmy had professed feeling more than friendship and when drunk he became insistent. When some young men displayed interest in me Jimmy thrust himself frantically between them and me. Finally, seizing me by the arm, he positioned us before a mirror. "Look at me! Just *look*! What do you see? I'm queer, ugly, and black! What future can I possibly have?" His desperation was so intense that I felt guilty for being annoyed. "Jimmy," I said consolingly, "you're only twenty-one, you're very gifted and have lots of friends." "Friends!" he exploded. "But no lover! And no money! What good is talent without recognition?" "I'm in the same boat," I said. "Oh, no, baby, we're in different boats!" he cried. "You're *white*!" I longed to leave with one of the handsome young men, but after his outburst I felt his situation so keenly that I left with Jimmy. It was like taking care of a sick friend. Besides, he had ruined the party.

In a letter of November 5, 1946, at the age of twenty-two, he indicates just how desperate he felt about his life and unpublished novel. He continued to cling possessively to me, constantly complaining until I began to avoid him. On receiving the letter I was astonished to learn that Jimmy thought he was avoiding me.

Jimmy was full of contradictions. Although convinced that he was unattractive, he could never tear his eyes away from a mirror. At parties he would gaze enthralled at his reflection, as if mesmerized, turning his head this way and that. Once, to my astonishment, he said, "I look very much like Hart Crane, don't I?" I smiled without responding. Self-deception is unanswerable.

Deciding that I was not a novelist, I abandoned my novel and the "sweet impersonal relationship" with Mrs. Garrett. The great lady kept "going away" to England and other countries and my phone calls, intercepted by Miss Davison, met with repeated but unfulfilled promises of a rendezvous on her return. At length, tiring of the grandeur of it all, I gave up. Many years later in Paris, long after she had "gone away" on her final trip to the Beyond, with which she had always maintained close diplomatic relations, when I mentioned her to Brion Gysin at the Beat Hotel he exclaimed, "Oh, I knew Eileen! Did she bring the *mooon* down on the terrace?" He waved his arms about. "One night as we stood on her terrace she said, 'Now, Brion, get ready to catch the moon in your arms!' It fell through the sky and landed at our feet!" I missed that act, but I did get to write some reviews for the *Nation*, the *New Republic*, and, I think, the *Saturday Review*. Which was quite a miracle for me.

41

A Clockwork Mouse

One balmy spring afternoon in 1946, a handsome youth who was following me on Fifth Avenue caught up. "You're a fast walker," he said a trifle breathlessly. "Are you a dancer? You look like one." "I *was* a few years ago." "Now what are you?" "A writer." "So am I! My first novel has just been published!" Since pickups will say anything—I'd heard all sorts of lies and fantasies—I challenged him. "But you can't be more than twenty," I said, unable to keep the skepticism from my voice. "I *am* twenty," he said. "I wrote it when I was eighteen." Now I was sure he was lying. He had been first mate on an army freight supply ship in the Aleutians during the war, he said, and his book, called *Williwaw,* was based on this experience. I told him I was a poet and had done reviewing for the *New Republic* and the *Nation.* He was in turn impressed.

As we talked animatedly on Fifth Avenue the young, strikingly handsome Gore Vidal spoke oı Guatemala, a country that might have been in the Aleutians for all I knew. "Look," he said, turning the lapel of his elegant gray suit. "It's vicuña—made in Guatemala by my favorite tailor. All my clothes are made there." "You go to Guatemala just for clothes?" I asked incredulously (I bought used clothing at the Salvation Army). "And other pleasures," he replied archly. Aha, I thought, another con artist—the kept boyfriend, no doubt, of some rich old queen. Again my tone must have betrayed skepticism for he said, "My book's on display at the Gotham Book Mart. Let's go see it."

Well, it wasn't on display. The owner of the Gotham, Frances Steloff, a white-haired ogress with pale blue eyes, stared blankly when he introduced himself. Since I was a frequent browser who bought copies of the magazines in which I appeared, I knew her well. She had an overworked, harried air at all times, and was usually cross and irascible. But she was also a sweet, beautiful lady in love with great literature and metaphysical pursuits. Her bookstore—a musty shrine of the avant-garde—had back issues of every little magazine in America. Autographed photos of the illustrious hung in black frames on the grimy walls: Eliot, Joyce, Stein, Forster.

"I don't see my book, Miss Steloff," Gore complained in an aggrieved tone. "Well, look around, young man," she said distractedly. "We have thousands of books." Gore's face fell; she didn't recognize him. "I'm *Gore Vidal*, Miss Steloff," he said self-importantly. "Gore who?" She turned to bark an order to a cowed subordinate—employees didn't last long. "Gore *Vidal!*" he said imploringly. He was met with a blank stare. "Can't you see I'm busy?" she snapped. "My *book*, Miss Steloff. *Williwaw!* I'm the *author!*" He looked desperate. She blinked. "Well, why didn't you say so? Come with me, young man!" We followed her to another aisle of tables heaped with new books—also in disarray. "It's here somewhere," she said, waving her hand, and hurried off.

Gore found it at last and held up a copy, beaming. From the flap of the dust jacket his photo also beamed in an officer's uniform. He stood before me like a young father holding up his firstborn, searching my face for signs of approval. I beamed back, touched by his pride—who can deny a young author this once-in-a-lifetime joy in his first publication? I felt a pang of envy. I steered him toward some issues of *Poetry* and other magazines containing my work. I'd had two poems accepted by a prestigious anthology called *Cross Section*, edited by Edwin Seaver and published by Simon & Schuster, which would not appear until the following year. More than seven thousand manuscripts had been submitted and of these some fifty short stories, novelettes, and poems had been selected, among them works by Richard Wright, Gwendolyn Brooks, Nelson Algren, and, in the previous volume, an unknown called Jane Bowles. Gore read some of my poems and looked at me with keener interest. "Let's go!" he said excitedly. I'd have followed him anywhere.

As we left, Gore went on about himself and his rich, powerful family: his grandfather was a senator from the South, his father a general in the army. His colossal vanity and conceit made me feel my own wretched poverty keenly. He had everything: youth, beauty, money, talent, brains. I wondered what else he could want and found out soon enough. He wanted me.

Just as two years earlier I'd been powerfully attracted to Marlon Brando, I was attracted to Gore, but in both situations I passed. When Gore invited me home it was with a sort of airy amusement, as if it were no more than a diversion, or so I imagined. "We can spend the rest of the day in fun and games," I think he said—a harmless phrase, to be sure, and perhaps, under it all, he was really driven by intensity. At that age I never revealed my feelings either. But thinking him too frivolous, I declined.

From time to time I'd run into him on the late-night "bird circuit," as the East Fifties gay bars were known, and whenever I saw him he wore a tense, compulsive look. I felt the same way and knew, or thought I knew, that his quest was as quixotic as mine, and wished I had seized the opportunity when it was offered. But there was the mocking tone, the supercilious air. When I shied away with the excuse that I had a prior engagement, which was true, his face fell and he said something so strange, so bizarre, in so glacial a manner that after forty years it still mystifies me. "In that case, Harold, you'll miss receiving the gift of a clockwork mouse. I always present one at the end of an affair."

Ever since I have wondered about the symbolism of that mouse. He played cat-and-mouse with lovers and made them his toys? Perhaps. There was much cruelty in the debonair remark.

42

St. Mark's Place

Graham and I were not made for each other, and in 1947 I left and moved into a rear cold-water flat at 28 St. Mark's Place on the Lower East Side. Larry Rivers, a young painter-saxophonist, helped me adjust and another painter, Jan Mueller, a tall intense young German in his twenties, occupied the flat next to mine. They were studying with Hans Hoffmann, a white-haired old German who had fled Nazi Germany. Around him Willem de Kooning, Jackson Pollock, Franz Kline, Herman Cherry, and others were forming the New York School of Action Painting. I got to know most of them.

The tenements were slatey brownstones with stoops and iron railings, inhabited by Poles and Ukrainians. In winter they shuffled through the snow like czarist peasants. Once I saw a blond, blue-eyed drunk swearing and shouting in *Yiddish*! Another stereotype bit the slush.

In my new abode a friend—let's call him Jack—who visited occasionally came over one evening to moan about the breakup of his affair with a girl he loved. He was so lonely he asked if he could spend the night with me. In the dark he confessed to being curious about sex with a man. He was willing, he said, to try it because of his disillusionment with women. I assured him that, as a good host, the least I could do was satisfy his curiosity. Jack had a firm, slender body and an exciting intensity. We slept in each other's arms and I made love to him, but when I began to doze I heard weeping. "My God, Jack," I cried, "was I that bad?" "Oh, no, you were wonderful!" he sobbed. "But I can't help thinking about Sue—I love her so much!" He confessed that although he enjoyed sex with me he could not be interested in a man that way. He knew Paul Goodman but had never yielded to his advances because he felt Paul wished to dominate him intellectually while using him sexually. They were both anarchists and of the two Jack, an obscure poet in his early twenties, refused to become a pawn in Paul's intellectual games, as he put it. Jack later became famous for his experimental poetry, but I will always remember him as the youth who wanted to experiment with me in bed.

Another penniless young artist, who was gay, spent several nights as a bedmate. A tall, witty, talented sculptor who had just arrived from the Midwest, he needed a place to stay. He brought back all sorts of junk that he found in the streets—tin cans, nails, wire, broken watches—and made from it what he called, appropriately, junk sculpture, for which he would be famous.

In 1948 I landed a full-time teaching job at the Cooper Union College of Arts and Engineering, less than a block away on Third Avenue and Cooper Square, at the foot of St. Mark's Place. I was hired because of my published poems and reviews. I taught in the Humanities Department: freshman English, poetry, and Greek drama.

That year the Kinsey Report came out, revealing statistically for the first time the high incidence of homosexual experience in the male population. It came as no surprise. Some of my students flirted outrageously with me, but I had a self-imposed code of ethics not to become sexually involved. One, a stunning Armenian with thick black hair and huge dark eyes with long lashes, loudly announced in class one afternoon during a discussion of homosexuality in ancient Greece, "Mr. Norse, according to Kinsey one out of three males is queer." He looked deliberately at the youths beside him and then at me. "This means that one of us—you, me, or John—is queer. Which is it?" The all-male class broke into jeers and laughter. "See me after class, Aram," I joked to hide my embarrassment. At this they whistled and whooped.

"Professor," Aram continued, "if so many males are queer, and maybe more are bisexual, and most don't confess it, then

homosexuals are normal and heterosexuals abnormal, right?"
More laughter.

"Neither is abnormal," I said. "The problem is in defining
normal. It's subjective, not scientific. We can't force nature to
comply with our definitions and prejudices. According to Jung,
all men and women have both the animus and anima in the
psyche—male and female in both—which must be expressed for
a proper balance of the individual and society as a whole. If the
feminine in man or the masculine in woman is not permitted to
express itself, we get an imbalance, a distorted personality. The
Greeks recognized this fact of nature. We don't—to our detri-
ment."

"Maybe," said Aram flashing a dazzling smile, "that's why
they were so great that we've never equaled them." I'll never
know why I didn't take Aram home with me. That boy had
guts—as well as beauty. His smile and winning ways neutralized
the taboo and had the students laughing good-naturedly with
him, not at him. He demystified the subject by coming out in the
classroom while I hid behind my desk like a coward.

I looked so young that when I first tried using the faculty
elevator to class, the operator, a bored old man who sat reading
the *Daily Mirror,* rudely ordered me to the student elevator. I
had to bring the chairman of the Humanities Department to
convince him of his error.

In a short time I became the most popular teacher in the
college and remained for three years, till 1951, when I was terminated, so that the board would not be required to offer me
tenure. The students revolted, demonstrating by the hundreds,
holding placards and chanting as they marched around the
building for two days, threatening to bring all classes to a halt.
The chairman asked me to address them, to explain that I had
wished to leave. When I did so he thanked me. "You are the
most popular and best instructor we've ever had," he said. The
reason for my dismissal was my nonparticipation in faculty social
functions. "There's more to being a professor than teaching,"
murmured the chairman regretfully. "It was always clear to me
that as a poet you never gave teaching top priority." I ac-
quiesced. With that sort of record he could not offer me tenure.
The teaching schedule had absorbed all my available time and
left none for writing. I had no ambition to rise in the hierarchy,
feeling compelled instead to resume a writing career. I welcomed the dismissal.

Since then, however, I've often questioned my judgment—indeed, my sanity—in sacrificing a life of academic security for a desperate gamble, a dream of stardom and literary immortality. Was it worth it? I still don't know.

43

Love Story

One drunken wintry night at the San Remo I met D., an apple-cheeked, ruddy-faced youth who looked like an English public school boy. He had chapped, flaming lips, doelike brown eyes without lashes (a Flemish touch), and a robust frame. He had spent three years in prison as a conscientious objector from the age of eighteen to twenty-one and, at twenty-two, was a talented composer. The statistics came from Jimmy Baldwin, who was trying to get over a crush on him. My journal for November 1948 records: "Not since Chester have I had such a full relationship . . . this time monogamously reciprocal." The love affair, the longest in my life, lasted nearly five years.

In the few remaining journals of that period random notes surface like fragments of ancient papyrus, revealing clues to long-forgotten events. Baldwin received a fellowship and sailed to Paris to finish his novel. Having had strong feelings about both D. and myself, perhaps he felt embittered about his failure with each. Our friendship endured, though we were not as close as before.

Ned Rorem, in a flurry of postcards outlining his needs, requested lyrics for a song cycle, allowing little more than a day to produce each poem. With my heavy teaching schedule plus graduate work at New York University for a master's degree, the extra pressure cramped my style. During the five years we had known each other I felt an affinity with Ned's music. I wanted a "Lordly Hudson" success (he had won his first prize for a song he set to the Goodman poem). I delayed on the lyric, having always needed time for perspective and revision, and received a note saying, "Please hurry with the lyric. I will immortalize you." I wrote it in one sitting and mailed it with my reply: "Thanks, but I will immortalize myself."

Coaxed into existence by Ned's urgent demands (he had specified the subject, "Penny Arcade"), the six hastily dashed off lyrics were with equal haste set and a performance given—by mezzo-soprano Nell Tangeman, with Ned at the piano—at the MacMillan Theatre of Columbia University on May 19, 1949. Virgil Thomson, who sat in front of me, never turned his head. Onstage Ned handled questions smoothly (I admired his poise) and called out, "Harold, are you in the audience?" when they referred to the poems. Lacking confidence in my lyrics, which seemed stilted, I responded diffidently. "Much of the musical material used therein I incorporated into later works," Ned wrote recently in response to my queries about the fate of the cycle. "But perhaps I should look at the whole suite again. It's been years." He reminded me that during that period (circa 1948–49) he had set other poems of mine to music. After his departure for Paris the following spring, except for some communications from Fez and chance encounters in Venice and Rome, we lost touch for many years.

From St. Mark's Place I moved to a railroad flat comprising the entire top floor at 573 Third Avenue between Thirty-seventh and Thirty-eighth streets, and D. moved in. We bought an old upright piano and installed it in a small side room facing the street. The El thundered below. A few years later we celebrated its demolition.

In Ned's dark little room on West Twelfth Street I was entertained by his latest pieces or by his throaty moan in imitation of Ida Lupino or Marlene Dietrich warbling their torch songs. When sober he had a sardonic wit, but too often he was a falling-down drunk. We frequently met (years before I lived with D.) at a little Italian restaurant on West Twelfth Street called Beatrice Inn on the facade of which, above the descending stone steps, was carved a blue-and-white ceramic bust of Dante. Invariably I carried a book. Years later Ned said, "I educated myself by reading the books you brought to Beatrice Inn." I didn't know then about his diaries—that masterpiece of self-revelation, which must rank with contemporary classics. Few writers have given us their life and times with such exquisite style and self-revelatory candor.

D. visited Ned for composition studies. We sang, or rather howled, a Poulenc song called "C" that influenced both Ned and D.: *J'ai traversé le pont de C, Cest là où tout a commencé.* . . . The internal rhyme woven throughout the lyric, perfectly matched by the score, had a haunting melancholy that poignantly conveyed the nostalgia of a long-vanished love affair.

After the war Paris was the mecca for Village intellectuals. Harry Herschkowitz had met André Gide and Jean-Paul Sartre via an introductory letter from Henry Miller; Jimmy Baldwin wrote about meeting Richard Wright. Those of us who hadn't the funds to go to Paris huddled around reading letters by those who had. My journal records one such evening at the San Remo in the winter of 1949:

> We sit in a booth passing around [Milton] Klonsky's letter. Anatole [Broyard], who admires Klonsky and the *Partisan Review,* praises the style; Paul [Goodman] mutters in an undertone, "Klonsky is pretentious and ignorant;" Grace [Baldwin's sister] shows us Jimmy's story in *Zero* but can't forgive him for not writing her; Paul and I discuss *Poetry* Magazine, now run by Hayden Carruth, how after 37 years it is in danger of folding by December. The economic recession is hitting the little mags, sponsorship is falling off, and soon, bad as they are, the mags may not exist; the non-commercial writers will have no poetry market (this is oxymoronic) to speak of.
>
> The juke-box is playing Verdi and Donizetti, behind us a huge black dog is licking every face in sight, which people find extravagantly funny, and Mason [Hoffenberg] has been crowned the American king of bang and hash—the phrase is Klonsky's—and represents our culture [in Paris]. (Klonsky is good at naming—his phrase for the Italo hoods in the Village, "the Bleecker Street Goths," in a *Commentary* article, has stuck.) Klonsky is still lonely, has nasty things to say about Europeans and Americans in Europe and writes that leaving America is like your first lay—you lose your innocence and, suddenly sophisticated, you begin to

subside, after the initial shock, into your former naiveté. This is the substance of his letter which Anatole proudly exhibits to the intelligentsia as a breath of Worldliness, Travel, Enlightenment. Night after night we sit in the Remo envying the expatriates, expressing our frustration. We are in a bohemian ghetto—analytical, suffocating, miserable. So-and-so is talented but needs depth analysis—feels his orgasm in the spine and then in the head, where it bursts. He falls on the floor, has fits— sexual epilepsy. Should he go to a Reichian or Freudian? Goodman recounts this with a wan smile.

7 May 1949

This evening Paul Goodman told me I was *sanguine*. Because I expressed hope, the notion that one could be successful in love. "Marriage is the proof of disillusionment in love," he said. I disagreed. His pessimism is founded on being rejected in sex. He admitted that he had never *had* those people he wanted most. As one of those who rejected him, I feel guilty.

At first, life with D. was joyous. We went to concerts and movies, bars and grilles, visited people and had open house. Two friends, a painter from New Zealand and Walter, a poet-scholar from California, occupied the floor below. We established a close community. My teaching job was going well, although the hours were demanding—morning, afternoon, and evening classes, all for less than sixty dollars a week. But my energy was boundless and at the time my goal was tenure. D. did odd jobs before getting one to his liking at Carl Fischer's music store on West Fifty-seventh Street. We were happy and it seemed that the relationship might succeed. Through D. I met avant-garde composers John Cage, Lou Harrison, Alan Hovhaness. I started a poetry group that met every two weeks at our flat, attended by Paul Goodman, Jean Garrigue, and others. Paul said his best poems were written a few years earlier, in the mid-1940s. The young surrealist poet Philip Lamantia, visiting from San Francisco, said he felt nothing in common with any poet in New York but me. I was feeling my way in poetry where others stood still, he said. He disliked Goodman's baroque academicism. We had first met in 1942 at Drossie's when he was fifteen, a prodigy praised by André Breton.

Soon it became clear that D. complained of everything. He accused me of indifference, of not trying to help with his problems. When I tried to help he accused me of telling him what to do. "Stop impinging on me! I'm a personality, too!" Goodman said, "He's eaten up with envy. He must have thought he was a great genius once; whether or not he was isn't important. Now he's afraid that if he writes music it won't prove him to be what he thought he was. So he has writer's block and envies you."

When D. was not attacking me for heartlessness and egotism, he attempted to humiliate me with gibes, taunts, and put-downs. Simmering with anger over imagined slights and infidelities, he'd scream, "Kill me! kill me!" or, "Call Bellevue!" (nut ward), kicking and screaming on the floor.

Once on a steamy July day I heard the sound of glass shattering in the kitchen and found D. with hunched shoulders wailing on the mattress. On the floor were strewn crumpled bits of blood-stained Kleenex. "What is it you want? What can I do?" I asked. "Why this end-of-the-world attitude whenever we have a spat?" In answer he slowly unclenched a fist revealing a deep laceration across his palm, from which protruded a jagged fragment of glass. I extracted it, disinfected the wound with peroxide, and bandaged his hand with gauze. As D. whimpered I swept up the pieces of glass and a shattered clam shell we had used as an ash tray.

In the winter of 1949 I met a millionaire at a party given by Walter and Glyn in the flat below. He fell for me with a dull thud heard round the room. The flat was full of painters, poets, wives, and lovers: Theodoros Stamos, Bill Baziotes, Julian and Judith Beck, Oscar Williams and his wife, Gene Derwood, Johnny Myers, Paul and Sally Goodman, Ruthven Todd, Howard Griffin (who lived around the corner), and others. Before the millionaire passed out he asked me what I most wanted. "I'll give you anything you want, dahling," he said in his campy Oxford accent. "I know you haven't a bean, deah, but I have enough beans to feed the army and navy."

Taking it as a big joke, I blurted out with drunken laughter, "How about a Picasso?"

"Is that *all*?" he screamed. "*Daahling,* it's *yours!*" Then he dropped like a stone. His friend caught him as he sagged. I dismissed the incident as drunken chatter but was assured by my hosts that "Cyril Reed" (name changed) would make good on his promise.

Four days after the party, as D. and I looked out the front window, a black limousine drew up to the curb and a uniformed chauffeur emerged. The doorbell rang. "Mr. Harold Norse?" inquired the chauffeur, removing his hat. "Yes." "Mr. Reed has asked me to deliver this." He handed me a small package in brown wrapping paper. "Any message, sir?" "Just thank him." I tore open the package. A Picasso. And a calling card. "Hope you enjoy this little token of my esteem." A genuine Picasso gouache about ten by sixteen inches, 1923, *The Dancers*. A study for the great canvas. Certificate from the Pierre Matisse Gallery. Some little token!

Under the smoke-stained, cobwebbed, corrugated tin ceiling it hung for years, an icon we stared at till our eyes watered: the stark cubist gestures, the fractured features. This prize had come from a cynical jest, a few words of disbelief and scorn. And so I befriended the mad Maecenas, was wined and dined in the best restaurants (Le Pavillon, the Chambord, the Plaza), drank champagne and ate food with impenetrable French names never learned in high school. Cyril spoke twelve languages and wrote light verse in all. "Listen to my Croatian poem, dahling! It's about absolutely nothing!" Once I had to meet him in the Semitic Room of the New York Public Library, where he spent hours reading *War and Peace* in Arabic. "A girl has to do *some*thing with her time, my deah!" He insulted maître d's, who smiled as if he had complimented them. At galleries he made disparaging remarks about paintings in the presence of the painter. I wondered why he wasn't pounded to a pulp. I didn't know that great wealth shelters one from all but flattery. If my life depended on it, however, I doubted if I could flatter anyone convincingly unless I meant it. Cyril found this irresistible. I never asked for anything but a Picasso. "Who could ask for anything more?" I'd quip.

Books and objects, mostly of little value, were stolen from my flat, but not the Picasso. Everyone thought it was a reproduction, like Van Gogh's *Sunflowers* on the wall. Two cardboard cartons with five hundred letters from Henry Miller to Harry Herschkowitz, left in my safekeeping while Harry shipped out, mysteriously disappeared. The letters were chiefly about Miller's schemes to raise money. They were hilarious. One was about starting a chain letter among writers and painters to submit one dollar to a fund for Miller in return for which the winning numbers (it was a kind of lottery) would receive an original water-color by Miller, who was living in a cabin in Big Sur. I was very upset at the loss, but Harry took it philosophically.

My most valued possession was an old desk-model Underwood. Returning one evening with a huge Native American who, like Queequeg, was covered with tattoos and equally loyal, we encountered a young man I had put up and fed, descending the staircase with my Underwood. Outraged, I yelled, "My typewriter!" With incredible speed "Queequeg" lunged, seized him by the throat, punched him in the face, wrested the machine from his grasp, and threw him downstairs. The "friend" did not come around again.

44

Dylan Thomas

In January 1950 my friend the Scottish poet Ruthven Todd phoned to say that Dylan Thomas was coming to America. "Can you put him up? He won't burn the house down." "Even if he does," I said, "it would be an honor." Ruthven (rhymes with "driven") was a rapid, rabid nonstop talker-smoker with nervous energy to burn. He had an inexhaustible supply of anecdotes about luminaries, like "Uncle Tom Eliot," on both sides of the Atlantic and, given sufficient booze, he could go on for hours cackling away until you were exhausted. "Have you heard how Victor Gollancz turned into a camel?" and off he galloped on a "true" story about the English publisher who had helped so many writers and Jewish refugees during the war. Ruthven and Dylan had been close friends since their teens. "I can think of no better place for him to stay," said Ruthven. "He wants to be near Irish bars and *not* near stuffy academics." Dylan and Ruthven were straight, but Ruthven would quip, "A hard man is good to find, right, Harold?" followed by a cascading chuckle-choke-cough. With his black horn-rims he looked like a tipsy owl. He became a best-selling author with a pioneer children's book called *Space Cat*—the first cat launched into space.

When I conveyed the extraordinary news to Walter, Glyn, and D. they were thrilled. "We'll have to lock up the liquor cabinet," Glyn wryly remarked. "And get fire insurance," observed Walter. D. blinked thoughtfully. "Mmm," he murmured. I was accustomed to such wild demonstrations of enthusiasm; but to tell the truth, Dylan's reputation for wreaking havoc while on interminable binges was legendary. I knew they were immensely pleased, however—it was fashionable in the postwar poetry milieu to be Anglophile. The role models still came from the United Kingdom; Oscar Williams's "Little Trasheries of American Poetry," as Ruthven called them, featured academic imitations of British verse. I'd pitch my baritone an octave lower, roll my *r*'s, broaden my *a*'s, counterfeit a sonorous lilt and phony resonance, and with a sudden Celtic persona recite by heart, "In my craft and sullen art" and "It was my thirtieth year to heaven," feeling very Anglo-Welsh. And so the pudgy little god of British poetry himself was going to find his American home with us. Green valleys would bloom on Third Avenue; Irish bars would become pubs.

When Dylan arrived at Idlewild Airport on February 21 I got another call from Ruthven. "Dylan's staying at the Beekman Towers. John Brinnin has arranged it all. I can't go to meet him, so give him a ring and tell him you're a friend of mine. He wants to be rescued." John Malcolm Brinnin was director of the 92nd St. Poetry Center of the YM-YWHA.

Immensely excited, though disappointed that Dylan would not be staying with us, I phoned the posh hotel. From the other end came coughing, hacking, choking. Then silence. "May I speak to Mr. Thomas," I said. Gut-wrenching coughs. "Mr. Thomas?" Pause. More gagging. Then a deep resonant voice groaned into the receiver, "Ooohhh . . . I wish I was dead! Who's this?" "A friend of Ruthven Todd's, he told me to call—" "Any friend of Ruthven's is a friend of mine. For God's sake, come right over!"

I grabbed my duffel coat, rushed out in my jeans, hailed a cab, took the elevator to the penthouse floor, and there, seated at a table in the bar with Brinnin, was Dylan Thomas. When I got to the table Brinnin looked up and blanched. "What are *you* doing here?" he said rudely. Blue jeans and rough clothes were inadmissible, but so was I. Dylan himself was frowsy, blowsy, and rumpled. "Sit down!" he said. "I want to talk to you." He seemed acutely bored, eager to welcome almost anyone who would provide relief from Brinnin. When I sat down beside him he leaned close and in a stage whisper meant to carry, said, "How the hell can we get rid of this bahstard?" I rejoiced at the put-down. Brinnin's mean behavior to me had reached epic proportions—I never knew why (about which more later). White as a sheet, Brinnin rose, to our mutual relief, and announced that he'd be back in half an hour.

Seated alone with Dylan Thomas, who never stopped guzzling and ordering beers for us both, I felt enclosed within a cocoon of misery and miracle. He goosed the waitress, who gave a muffled shriek, almost dropped her tray, and grinned! He dropped ashes on the table, the floor, his rumpled clothes. Everyone stared, spellbound, or was it my imagination?

His was the only living, electric presence in the crowded bar high above the city, his voice and accent the most beautiful I'd ever heard. He could have read the telephone book and made it sound like Shakespeare. He had the power to enthrall. Yet he was merely a very short, very stout, pig-faced drunk with curly, unkempt sandy hair and brown spaniel eyes—a kind of defiant soulfulness distinguished those eyes from the flat surface of most eyes and drew you within their fearless depths. I wanted to listen to that voice forever, to drink myself insensible with him, to roar with irreverent laughter at the stodgy, catatonic zombies.

"Y'know, people asked me why I was going to America, as if it was Outer Mongolia," he said in a confidential tone. "'To make money,' I said. 'What else would I be doing there?' I've got a wife and three kids to support. America means only one thing—money." He made a moue of disgust with pursed lips. His caramel eyes swept the hushed mausoleum. In a softer tone he said, "You're a poet, I suppose?" I nodded. He looked at me with sympathetic appraisal. "It's tough even when you've got a reputation," he went on, "but, oh, God, it's absolute hell without one. Listen, the truth is, I can't write anymore. I mean, not the good poems, the poems that made my reputation. That's over, finished. I've been imitating myself for the past three years or more. Singing the same song, playing the same tune. But nobody knows, least of all the Americans. I want to cash in on my fame while I have it." He downed a tumblerful of beer, pinched the waitress's bottom, and winked. She smiled and swept off to another table. He was entirely natural, ineffably sad, a sorrowful tragic clown. I was warmed by these confidences, so intimately disclosed to a total stranger. He spoke with the intimacy of an old friend—with no sign of drunkenness—and seemed as familiar as a cousin.

When Brinnin returned the atmosphere altered. Dylan became rambunctious, raised his voice, and suddenly behaved with drunken abandon. "We've got to go," said Brinnin with compressed lips, avoiding my eyes.

In the elevator we pressed against the wall while Dylan, who was my height, stood behind a tall distinguished gray-haired man in formal dress who, with his back to Dylan, held a homburg reverently over his heart as if at a funeral. Dylan began to make doglike growls deep in his throat in the silent elevator. Two elderly women in evening gowns stood frozen with shock. Teeth bared, Dylan snarled, his lip curling like a cur's. Then he bit the man's back, several times. The man squirmed but maintained his dignity, never turning his head. I was reminded of Groucho Marx cutting a caper with Margaret Dumont, the tall dignified society lady in the Marx brothers films. Stiff with embarrassment, Brinnin wore a look of utter exasperation, but I enjoyed every moment of the farce, the "biting" satire, if you will, against conventional decorum. As a teen-ager, to the discomfort of my friends, I had often behaved in this manner.

We trudged to Brinnin's car over ice and snow, Dylan clinging to me in near stupor. He slumped in the backseat dragging me beside him like a security blanket. Brinnin stood outside glowering. "We're late for the party to meet Allen Tate and the *Partisan Review* crowd," he said, more icy than the weather, "and you're not invited, Harold." "If Harold doesn't go, I don't go," muttered Dylan thickly and promptly passed out. Brinnin and I glared at each other. Facing him alone, I had no defense except my pride. I got out of the car. "Fuck you," I snarled, and left.

Brinnin represented the academic bloc of poetry in the 1940s and 1950s while, with no reputation to speak of, I represented the intruder. I had briefly but warmly been embraced by the King of the Misfits and Rebels, but he might just as easily have embraced a baboon. Dylan could do no wrong. He had conquered the world with his genius, become a sacred monster. He could commit any social outrage and maintain his position as the foremost English-speaking poet; he would even find it enhanced.

My poetry had been highly praised by prestigious scholar-poets like Allen Tate and John Crowe Ransome. Why did Brinnin leave me out? A year later, in 1951, William Carlos Williams wrote, "You are the best poet of your generation." I was discovered—again. In 1952, Brinnin himself—unaware that I was the author of a group of poems anonymously submitted in keeping with the rules of the YMHA poetry contest (of which he was a judge)—awarded me first prize but withdrew the award when my name was disclosed. It was bestowed on a lesser-known newcomer: John Ashbery.

The deception might have gone undiscovered but for two revealing occurrences. When the manuscript was returned by the Poetry Center I found an erasure in the top right-hand corner. The words *First Place* had been written in pencil, then erased. Around this time some poems of mine appeared in *Poetry* magazine, to which I was a frequent contributor, with a brief biographical note that I had sent. Imagine my astonishment when I read: "Harold Norse is the winner of this year's Discovery Prize in the New York YM-YWHA Poetry Center Contest." I wrote Karl Shapiro, then the editor, informing him that there was some mistake and inquired how he had come by this information. It had been sent, he replied, by the judges, John Malcolm Brinnin and Kimon Friar, to be announced in the section on prizes and awards. There was no mistake. I *had* won the contest!

I called Friar for an explanation. "It's true," he said. "I was very unhappy about what happened but couldn't persuade John to change his mind. His argument was false—he said that since you had been a student of mine a charge of nepotism would be leveled against me." I almost shouted into the phone, "What about the charge of *prejudice* by Brinnin? He deliberately violated the ground rule of anonymity!" "I argued with him for days," said Friar. "We had already sent the results to Shapiro. But John wouldn't budge. Ashbery was the second choice, and split the prize with another. You were definitely the single winner. We had both agreed on you but not on Ashbery."

In the spring of 1951 William Carlos Williams singled me out—as did Dylan Thomas, E. E. Cummings, and Anaïs Nin. I was being discovered like crazy. Years later Kimon Friar, who had meanwhile achieved distinction for his translation of Nikos Kazantzakis's *Odyssey,* said that of all his students only James Merrill and I had achieved major status. But whereas Merrill and Ashbery won just about every prize and award, I won nothing. It seemed like a dirty trick of fate.

Dylan did not stay long at the Beekman Towers. It was too posh for him. He moved into a tiny room at the Hotel Chelsea. Never alone, he was surrounded by hordes of adoring fans, mostly women, in an endless round of parties, bars, and gatherings. He loved the Third Avenue bars and the White Horse Tavern in the Village. Oscar Williams, a spidery little man, followed him everywhere. One night as Dylan got up to go to the men's room at the White Horse, Oscar rose to follow. "Are you gonna hold it for him, Oscar?" I shouted, but nobody laughed. Well, I thought, that leaves me out of the little trasheries forever. I was right. But when I got up to stagger to the "loo" Dylan called out in an affectionate, boozy voice, "There goes another little Lord Byron!" and everyone laughed. Dylan and I were the same height, and Byron, who was five foot eight, walked on tiptoes in boots to appear taller. Vain little bastard. I loved him beyond all poets.

Vanity is not the madness of poets only, but I've never known one—good, bad, or mediocre—who was not sick with it. Oscar Williams once told me that as a boy he had to read and write poetry secretly in bed using a flashlight so that his father would not catch him at it. "That's genius," he croaked modestly. Genius for self-delusion, I said to myself. For sixteen years Oscar gave up poetry for advertising. When he had made enough to retire he published a book of poems on the back of which he wrote something like, "After a sixteen-year silence he returned to his first love, poetry." On learning this from me, Tennessee Williams remarked, "Time for another silence, Oscar."

Geniuses ran around loose in the Village, but few made it to fame and fortune, like Jimmy Baldwin and Bob DeNiro. Dylan became the rage, was written up in *Life* and *Time,* his antics reported with relish—all that is history. When it became known that I was a friend of his, the chairman of the Humanities Department at Cooper Union asked if I could get him to read there. It was arranged by Dylan's agent and one afternoon, cold sober and somewhat late, he showed up with a hangover. Before the reading, while awed professors fluttered about the lecture hall, we joked together in an undertone. The chairman glorified Dylan with lavish praise and Dylan muttered, "I get the feeling I've been dead a long time." I was assigned the task of carrying a tray with a tumbler and beaker of water, at which Dylan wrinkled his nose in distaste, and after the orotund introduction we walked together to the platform to the sound of deafening applause. "Hebe, cupbearer to the gods," muttered Dylan. "Pronounced Heeb," I whispered and he chuckled as he stepped to the podium. He gave an awesome reading, after which, with some students and professors, we withdrew to Clarke's, an Irish bar nearby.

Much has been written about the lionizing of Dylan in America—how it spoiled him and led to his early death at thirty-nine at St. Vincent's Hospital in Greenwich Village (I wasn't there, I had left for Europe). I clearly recall that Dylan did on occasion behave badly, like a pampered idol, and could be a mean, nasty drunk. Once, at a book party in the Gotham Book Mart for his *Collected Poems,* he was so intoxicated that, surly, bleary-eyed, and contemptuous, he stood apart, snarling and sneering at everyone who approached for his autograph. Balefully casting his gaze around the room with open hostility, he was like a bear at bay. Since he had never turned on me, I was foolish enough to approach with a greeting. "Hello, Dylan," I grinned. With total lack of recognition he snarled, "Who the hell are you?" Blind drunk on cocktails and looking miserable, he stood swaying, the center of attention, while people stared nervously from a distance. I seem to remember Stephen Spender at that awful party and some painter who made an uncomplimentary remark, at which he bridled. Customarily polite and mild-mannered, Stephen grew abusive toward his antagonist. Dylan had set the tone.

Three months after I left America (on August 3, 1953), Dylan died. I was living in Rome and one sunny, glorious day in early November I ran into Allen Tate on the Spanish Steps. "What made him drink so much, I wonder?" he asked, perplexed. "I think he drank himself to death because he couldn't stand himself. He knew he was washed up. Sheer frustration." "You know," said Tate, as if he had never realized this, "I believe you're right!"

Years later I heard a ghastly story about Tate from a southern writer who had known him well and, like myself, liked him.

Tate, who'd been a close friend of Hart Crane's but who made nasty remarks behind his back about his homosexuality, received the news of Crane's suicide by getting drunk with his wife, the writer Caroline Gordon, and repeating jubilantly, with thigh-slapping glee, "Well, what do you know, the sharks ate 'im!"

In 1946, the only other young poet I remember in Kimon Friar's poetry class was the nineteen-year-old Jimmy Merrill, who had also studied with Friar at Amherst. Impressed by his talent and youthful good looks, I was too shy to show my interest, but one fine spring day we met by chance in Central Park and walked to the zoo. He invited me to an evening at his town house in Sutton Place, where, throughout dinner, his friends ignored me. Not one had drawn me into the conversation. I'd seen better manners among laborers. At my departure Jimmy tactfully suggested a rendezvous for another evening when we would be alone. Not taking him up on it remains on my long list of regrets. I was simply too thin-skinned.

I remember when Kimon Friar first inaugurated the series of solo readings in the YMHA lounge; these were sparsely attended by no more than thirty or forty people in an intimate, informal atmosphere. Anaïs Nin, the first time I had seen the lady, read from her as yet unpublished diaries to a small spellbound audience. Robert Lowell read from *Lord Weary's Castle*, which had been recently published (Randall Jarrell greeted him loudly, "Here's the genius!" and Lowell visibly cringed). I was struck by his shy, self-deprecating manner. When James Agee read he was so stricken with stagefright that he had a convulsive seizure: his rolling eyes showing the whites, his tongue cleaving to the roof of his mouth for several dreadful minutes. Then, to the intense relief of an audience agonized with empathy, he recovered as if nothing had happened and finished his reading. Dame Edith Sitwell, clad in a red-and-gold brocade cape and gown, as if she had stepped out of a medieval tapestry, read among other poems "Still Falls the Rain," about the bombing of London, elaborate with wordplay and tonal inflections. I remember Paul Goodman approaching her with his gappy grin and being regarded with cold hauteur.

Then in 1949 Friar stepped down and passed the Poetry Center on to Brinnin, who brought it to the auditorium and large audiences, making it pay. It became institutionalized.

Though part of its history, I've never been asked to read there in my whole career.

45
Journal 1

1 July 1950

Last night I learned from Joe Wilson, an occultist, some basic procedures for conducting a seance. When he left I acted as medium and four of us—Julian and Judith Beck, Dick (with a cold) and me—sat around the rather Gothic black table in our flat.

Nothing happened for about an hour. Then the table moved. Dick's cold forced him to leave the table and Julian, thinking we would stop temporarily, removed his hands; but Judith and I kept our hands on the table, our little fingers barely touching. Though there were only two of us in physical contact with it, in answer to my question, "Will New Directions publish my poems?" it responded, "Yes." "Will the book be a success?" Reply: "D—E-V-E-N-T." Disastrous Event? I dared not ask.

No sooner had Julian re-entered the circle by joining hands than the table began to rock. It tipped three times in Julian's direction. It was his Uncle Leon who died in 1937. He said he was happy and that Julian would have his Living Theatre when he was 26. He responded to various personal matters. Then, for about three hours until dawn, we received the tapped-out message: TURN RIGHT TO LOOK TO PEACE, JULIAN. RUSSIA PLANS WAR. WHO POSTPONES THE SIZE OF ROYAL GOLD VOTES RUSSIA. YOU TOUCH M. . . . whereupon it broke off.

As the room grew lighter we could see Dick snoring

on the couch. My fingers were paralyzed, my limbs stiff, incapable of movement. Everyone looked deep-eyed, as if emerging from a trance. We'd experienced nothing like this before.

Although impressed, the Becks could not willingly suspend disbelief. Judith thought the subconscious had a lot to do with directing impulses to the table. Julian could neither believe nor disbelieve in the existence of a spirit. I felt that I had communicated with a mysterious entity.

11 July

Fooling around again with table-tapping at the Becks'. The spirit's name was Anne. With each letter the table moved a foot off the ground and came down with a smart, decisive rap. First message: WAR—FLEE NY. We should leave before Autumn. When asked where to go she replied: NOWHERE. Dick giggled and joked with Judith about the paradoxical directives, finally became insulting and called the spirit a "bitch." At this the table refused to budge. "It's wounded! Its wooden feelings are hurt!" sniggered D. "Maybe we should smooth it down with sandpaper."

At this point a very irate spirit took over, rapping the floor harshly and refusing to identify itself. It spelled out the word HATE. Annoyed, I broke up the seance.

The ceiling has been leaking from heavy rains. Streams of water course down the gray cobwebbed walls, leaving vertical stripes in the flat paint. The water drips onto the floor, sounding like a leaky faucet. I phoned the landlord, who is on vacation.

13 July

The Korean War is the big news. Regimentation, the draft, high prices, bloodshed, fear of the Bomb—all within five years since peace broke out. Downstairs Glyn Collins, once married to Muriel Rukeyser, now to Walter, is painting bright, happy pictures. He says it's the function of the artist to paint joyously as a criticism of the times.

D. is of draft age. In fact, he is among the first to be called. If he can manage to stay out until his 26th birthday in October, he will be beyond draft age. Having already served time as a CO doesn't exempt him.

17 July

Sides are being taken. The sphinx-like iron man of Russia is seen smiling on the covers of periodicals and in the grim cartoons of the press. The equally grim faces of American politicians stare at us from everywhere. No nation can win. Now the smallest is equal to the largest. A bathtub culture of botulinus can wipe out all life on the planet.

46

Journal 2

28 August 1950

Paul Bowles has become a writer. His story, "Pages from Cold Point," about a 16-year-old boy who seduces his father, turned a new page in writing.

31 August

The Becks are giving up their apartment and vast expensive library to raise money. They want us to form the nucleus of a group in an invulnerable area in the West—live off the land, solve money problems, create, etc.

Last night we had a seance at their place with Michael [Fraenkel] present; he raised a fuss about how "surprising" it was that such "developed" people could really believe the table moved through some extra-human agency. Big argument on the subject. I'm regarded as the mystic (Yeats' influence?). It got so late we all stayed over.

When I awoke in the early afternoon I saw across the courtyard in another apartment the naked back of a woman, ass and all. When she turned, her front was entirely covered by some bead-like garment. In the next room a naked man kept masturbating, pouring himself drinks, turning the pages of a magazine. Judith and Robin, singing at the top of their voices, were improvising a song based on the theme of Ibsen's *Ghosts:*

> *I've got the ve, ve, venereal disease,*
> *I want the sun, mama.*
> *He's a gone, gone, gonorrhea guy, etc.*

Judith cleared up the incident of the naked lady and masturbating man. The entire house next door, she explained, save for two apartments, is a brothel.

I marveled at this phenomenon in the very stronghold of middle-class Jewish respectability—West End Avenue.

English lyric poetry begins with a fart:

> *Sumer is a-cumin in,*
> *Lude sing cuckoo,*
> *Bullock sterteth,*
> *Bucke ferteth,*
> *Sing cuckoo.*

The buck farted about five hundred years ago when no Englishman thought it unmentionable. Why worry about taste and prudery that has strangled the language and individual liberties since Cromwell's criminal dictatorship 300 years ago? He was the Anglo-Saxon Hitler and his legacy remains in America. This legacy is the result of ignorance and greed, not holiness and faith. Ignorance of the flock, greed of the ministers. It seems incredible that in these personal pages I should be enslaved by the laws of censorship.

Wonderful line from the "spirit" last night: YOU TOUCH MONEY WITHOUT LOVE. The first seance with the Becks at my flat two months earlier ended with the mysterious, incomplete message: YOU TOUCH M. . . . Spirit or unconscious, it works in marvelous ways. . . .

1 September

I rise late, about noon or 1 P.M., feeling as though I hadn't slept, dog-tired. Muggy heat of Indian summer. I spend a few hours at the piano, make some headway with the first prelude from *The Well-tempered Clavier*. Haven't finished Mikrokosmos I of Bartok, however. D.'s a good teacher.

Howard Griffin phoned and said Bill Goyen had invited him to stay in Taos. But Howard has no money. He sits in his bare cold flat around the corner, on 37th Street, playing Hawaiian music and writing his journals.

Dwight P.O.'d because a *New Yorker* profile of his cousin omitted mention of him. "The least they might have done was to write: Dwight Ripley, a first cousin, is an expert taxonomist, although he knows nothing about birds."

4 September (Labor Day)

We were to have gone on a trip to Bearsville, N.Y. yesterday visiting Holly Cantine and Dachine Rainer. But Gary, the Becks's baby, became suddenly ill with trench mouth and instead of starting out at 10 A.M. the Becks rolled around at 1 P.M. Everything had gone wrong—first the baby's illness, then waiting for the doctor, then a slight collision with a taxi, etc. So we drove out to New Jersey instead, had some food on the road, sang songs, returned in the evening. We stayed late, discussing plans for "the colony," and finally held a seance. The message was: Tontusstoo, QUEETZACA. The spirit advised us to go there. We rushed to maps of Mexico and Central America, hoping to find it but to no avail. We put it down to automatic writing.

"But if we should find there *is* such a place," said Julian, "I'd go without a moment's hesitation."

We all agreed. With a name like that, who wouldn't?

Stayed over at the Becks, rose late, read copies of *Flair,* told jokes, played with the baby's toys, looked over the library.

Problem remains: where to go? We are ready to leave.

One year left to write my Master's thesis on Dylan, who is no help. His father wrote from his sick bed to say that he cannot be much help as he has been ill since January. He does not know his son when he adds that Dylan will write me to help with the subject. Dylan will never write.

6 September

I'm tired of sweeping up broken glass. He sits on the floor, screaming. With a mad shriek he crushes the fragment of glass in his hand.

4 October

The face in the library, engrossed in a call slip . . . the sturdy form disappearing down the black hole of the subway . . . the furtive, answering look of a hauntingly beautiful youth—

2 November

Howard Griffin tells me that Tennessee has just thrown a party for Edith Sitwell. Children with painted faces kept ringing the doorbell—it was Halloween—and one of them cried, "What a modern apartment!" and thought Dr. Sitwell was wearing a mask. She wasn't. The front page of the press is equally bizarre—surrealist collage of disasters. A photo of the Pope proclaiming the first dogma of the 20th Century: the *physical* body of the Virgin Mary is in Heaven. Catholics who do not believe this live in mortal sin. More papal bull.

Isadore From, just returned from Europe, recounts the following: Kenneth Rexroth, unhappy in Paris, had gone to find a lover but could only observe of French women: "Their breasts are too small—not like American girls!" The other incorrigible straight, William Barrett, had no sooner left the ship and arrived in Paris than he breathlessly demanded, "Where can I find some women?" to which Isad replied, "At Pigalle—for a thousand francs!" Both rabid homophobes, Rexroth hoots maliciously at "fairies" in his poems and Barrett makes a fool of himself in a preposterous *Partisan Review* article in which all "fairies" lisp, swish, reek of perfume, and wave limp wrists.

22 November

We throw a farewell party for Donald Pippin, who is leaving for California. He is another of D.'s talented musical friends. The Becks, Richard Miller and a wonderful contralto called Isca, who sings Bizet's *Habañera,* make it a warm sweet moment in a sea of turbulence.

1 December

World War III. The U.S. government may use the atomic bomb on China. Our worst fears confirmed.

2 December

In a telephone conversation Lore Perls has backed down. She no longer considers the moment urgent enough for action. Only two days ago, at my instigation, she was ready to hold a big caucus of friends, at her house, including Fritz, to discuss plans for immediate action. But she retreated from her position. My urgency she regards as containing neurotic elements. The world is in a state of frenzy, the capitols of Europe are stunned by the President's lack of diplomatic brilliance, the turmoil precedes a possible world conflict, perhaps "the final conflict," and this is *my* paranoia!

After 4 years of successful analysis, Julian must be even more paranoid than I. If anything, he seems under greater compulsion to act. Lore and Fritz Perls, after one successful escape in their lives (from Nazi Germany to South Africa), in middle age no longer seem to possess the same urgent sense of survival. This confirms my suspicion: a little neurosis is good for the health.

12 December

On a quick decision I put my mother's hard-earned savings into a home and property, to provide a stable base in an unstable world. A friend told me about a Colonial farmhouse in Canterbury, Connecticut, with 60 acres for $1000! Built in 1809, with the date on a cornerstone, it sits on top of a knoll about a mile from the highway, accessible only by a dirt road. The clapboard is unpainted except for a streak of white in front. There's a central chimney in fair condition and a good gabled roof, shingled about 9 years ago. Of the original 9 rooms the former owner tore up the entire attic floor and second floor ceiling underneath to build a garage with wide oak timbers! He left 3 rooms on the second floor practically intact, but the squirrels and woodchucks ate holes into it and built nests. The house once had an L but it was destroyed, perhaps by Ames, the former owner. Windows and frames are missing but the ground floor is in good condition with solid oak flooring. The deed reads "60 acres more or less" but is closer to 100. This was a way of paying less taxes in the old days. Grapes, cranberries, blackberries, oak, pine, butternut, sugar maple, birch and appletrees grow in abundance. Dozens of lichen-covered green-gray rockwalls zigzag on the land. Most of it except for 10 tillable acres is heavily wooded. There are 2 wells and 2 marshes which can be converted into ponds. There is a great deal of wildlife and hunters are fond of shooting on the land. I'll soon put a stop to that.

25 December

Returned last night from a sleepless weekend, the Becks and I having slept on the floor, in the dead of winter, in the old abandoned farmhouse, wrapped in overcoats and blankets. For 2 days our food consisted of sandwiches and coffee. 5 hours of driving in the ancient jalopy that let in the cold, 5 hours back in blinding rain. My job was to bring the second instalment on the farm, sign mortgage and deed papers. All this to provide a home and sanctuary not only for myself and my mother but for the Becks and their child and for the two Richards, Miller and Stryker.

We arrived in Canterbury Saturday, wind cutting through open spaces under the doors and through the flooring of the car. The footbrake had never functioned and the emergency brake would not work unless struck with a hammer. Every time Julian started, Judith grasped the hammer with both hands and asked in an anxious voice, "Now?" "Now!" said Julian and bang went the hammer on the emergency brake. We went roaring down the road like an old airplane. But it got us there.

To sleep in the empty house we had to borrow two kerosene lamps and kerosene stoves from the Ameses down the road and close off one room with plywood and a towel. As we lay on the icy floor like opium eaters in our blankets we watched a vision of circles within circles, monkey faces, petals of light—shadows cast upon the ceiling by the kerosene stoves when the lamps were dimmed.

"Three interlocked circles are an engram of mine from childhood," said Judith.

Then she couldn't sleep. She tried writing in her journal, paced the floor, kicked the stove, looked out the window at snow falling in the Christmas white fields.

Earlier yesterday we saw a speckled deer bound beautifully across the snow. We were in the car at the gas station and we all gasped. "A deer! a deer!" The redfaced chubby gas attendant said blandly, "Yup! If I only had a shotgun right now!" He was met by what Judith called "a deadly silence" and what Julian and I corrected to "a lively silence." Then when we later told the Ames family of the deer Mrs. Ames, smacking her lips, said, "Mmmm, venison." She, too, was met by a lively silence.

When we first arrived I took the Becks for a walk in the snow-filled woods. I kept repeating, "Whose woods these are I think I know." Judith laughed and added, *"All mine, mine, mine!"* clutching my hand tightly. "How I envy you! It's the best investment of anyone I know." I smiled, not knowing an investment from a mudhole. When I saw animal tracks in the snow I vowed that nobody would kill animals on my land.

On my return to the flat, dog-tired and hungry, D.

was in bed. "I'm sick," he said. I nodded, put down my
bag, stripped and lay down. From those two words,
without greeting me, I knew he was wrapped up in himself, resentful. My first impulse was to upbraid him for
his selfishness but I realized that this was what he
wanted so he could turn self-rejection into self-righ-
teousness about the cruelty of others. It would also turn
another Christmas Eve into a *Walpurgisnacht* of bitterness and despair. So I did what Lore suggested I do
with automatic reactions—experiment. To avoid the
compulsive habits of my own behavior which perpetu-
ates unhappy situations, I transformed my annoyance
into an interest in his condition. Knowing how disturbed and insecure he was, especially now that analysis
has shown his own defenses to be the sources of his un-
happiness, I inquired solicitously, "What's the matter?
Don't you feel well?" (I conquered my own tendency
toward self-pity, thereby lessening my annoyance at *his*
tendency and realizing how similar our patterns were.)
It worked. Instead of producing wounded antagonism I
produced a desire to lean, to express his grievances to a
sympathetic listener. "Ooh, I feel sick! I have aches and
pains all over! I think it's the flu." He got up, hobbled
about, picked up some gifts he had bought and brought
over a soft little pony that, when wound, played "Pony
Boy" in a music box that tinkled when held close to the
ear. It was for a niece. "I always wanted one myself," he
said, pressing it against his face. He looked so young
and vulnerable I kissed him, which he ignored. "I
bought gifts only for those I like. I didn't get one for
my mother." "What about mine?" A guilty look. "I'm
getting it tonight." "Christmas Eve? No stores are
open." "Oh, yes, they are! I'm going to get it." I wondered what had happened to his disabling "flu." I
walked away, unable to disguise my hurt and consequently felt more exhausted. He reacted with a scared,
resentful silence that continued through a Christmas
meal at Horn and Hardart: dry slices of turkey, canned
cranberry sauce, and greasy mashed potatoes. I sat near
the window staring at the neon letters of the sign: MAT.
After dinner D. said in a choked voice, "I'm going

now—to find your gift." I nodded, went home, lay down and fell asleep. He woke me at 2 A.M. to say he couldn't find an open bookstore that had Pound's *Letters*. He asked where I was going to sleep, my bed or his. Mine, I said. He swore and left, slamming the double doors.

This morning, somewhat refreshed, I experimented again, without emotion, with fairly good results. D. knew he had behaved badly and said so, complaining that he was entirely confused, "left without a personality" through analysis. We ate in the Village after seeing Cocteau's *Orpheus*.

22 January 1951

D. has gone to live with the Becks. I have twice as much time at my disposal. Lonely; hunger of the flesh.

Undated

Got to know the composer, Lou Harrison, who wants to collaborate on an opera, *Cupid and Psyche*. Lou is the nearest thing to a Renaissance man that I've encountered. He was written up in *Vogue* by Peggy Glanville-Hicks as one of the six most important artists expanding the musical vocabulary. He writes prose and poetry, paints well, was once a dancer. He invited us to dinner at his cold-water flat in the Village; we bought noodles, pot cheese, butter and bagels. Lou played his compositions on the piano and on records, then showed me his verse and Noh play. I was overwhelmed by so much Blakean activity. He writes his scores in red and black ink in Gothic script. His work on counterpoint is not a mere textual account but poetic prose, as if Swedenborg or Blake had applied their vision to a textbook. As Yeats pointed out Swedenborg applied the technical mind of a man of science to his descriptions of Heaven and Hell and was at great pains to maintain accuracy and precision in his account. Lou also saw angels, during which he wrote a mass.

Lou whooped, gasped, and guffawed, waving fingers adorned with huge rings. A big heavy man, he was reminiscent of the young Orson Welles, with a theatrical, flamboyant personality—always amusing, keeping the conversation going at all times.

On March 12 I attended a Patchen benefit at the Community Church with an all-star cast to attract a large audience and make money for the ailing poet. I had never seen such a large audience for poetry. The stars were Auden, Cummings, William Carlos Williams, Marianne Moore, Edith and Sir Osbert Sitwell, and Archibald MacLeish. As usual, Auden read in a monotone (two notes at most), MacLeish keened, Cummings was waspish, Moore flat, Williams also flat with a tendency to rant, Edith Sitwell histrionic, Sir Osbert foppish. It was a unique event in New York. D. reintroduced me to Miriam Patchen, who exlaimed, "Oh, I've read your poems!" She had completely forgotten me in the six years since I'd visited them.

Miriam told D. that besides arthritis, which kept Patchen supine, he had developed ulcers and a mysterious black fur on the tongue that baffled the doctors. In the past year he had left the house only twice, hobbling with two canes through Old Lyme, Connecticut, where the townfolk removed his books from the shelves of the local library and hid them in the cellar (protecting youth from corruption). One of the books, called *Memoirs of a Shy Pornographer*, they wanted to burn. I wrote the Patchens a compassionate letter.

Lore Perls on homosexuality: "It's inconvenient because of social prejudice, but I see nothing inherently wrong with it. Once a pleasure principle is established in sex it can be more harmful to change it than to accept it." How civilized she was!

"You're all so young-looking," she once said to her therapy group of lesbians and gay men, to which I belonged. "It must be a refusal to grow up." In my mid-thirties, I looked mid-twenties. The way we dressed, talked, walked, and felt was adolescent.

At the end of April Chester invited me to attend a cocktail party at the Gotham Book Mart for his small chapbook, *Elegy*. It was his first book. The day before I had received William Carlos Williams's letter of praise for my poetry, but I hadn't yet published a first book, nor would I get a prestigious party at the Gotham Book Mart. As it turned out, this was Auden's doing.

He pulled strings. *Elegy* was a poem for Chester's mother, whose death when he was four was never forgiven: "In our feelings we are always 4 years old," I wrote in my journal.

Around the same time I participated in a performance of John Cage's "Imaginary Landscape No. 4," a musical collage of chance sounds. This was at a New Music Society concert, which began at 8:30 P.M. The program was devoted mostly to musical "jokes," a "fun concert," Lou called it. But because not all the pieces were intended to be amusing, the tone of the concert was uncertain. Stefan Wolpe, a Hungarian composer, detested dodecaphonic and aleatory music but attended the concert with his clique, apparently not to miss a golden opportunity to hiss and boo throughout the evening. The composers ran around the stage before each piece, moving pianos and other instruments for one another.

Virgil Thomson's setting of Gertrude Stein's "Capital, Capitals" recalled the dadaist era, as the words, in delightful combinations of sound and nonsense, were emphasized mostly by notes running up and down the scale. Thomson banged these out on the piano. "Thomsoniana" by Peggy Glanville-Hicks was a setting of reviews of Thomson's music followed by satires of Satie, Schoenberg, and Stravinsky (the three S's?), all of which produced a paroxysm of howls, hoots, boos, and hisses from the Wolpe section.

For Cage's "Imaginary Landscape," set for twelve radios and twenty-four players, a mob scene took place onstage. Among the twenty-four players were the two Richards (Stryker and Miller), myself, the Becks, Lou Harrison, Remy Charlip, and others, mostly musicians. Cage conducted with great seriousness from his score based on random selection of notes or silences from the *I Ching,* whereby at each radio we turned the dials on or off at a sign from John, who waved his hands conducting silences. The effect was similar to an automobile ride at night on an American highway in which neon signs and patches of noise from radios and automobiles flash and disappear in the silence. Picking up snatches of music and speech, with lengthy silences in between, it had a disturbing effect. Lou's piece, Canticle No. 3 for Five Percussionists, included brake drums (automobile parts), Indian bells, cowbells, ocharina, and more. It created a beautifully exotic mood and was the only piece not hissed or booed by the

Wolpe mob. The huge audience received it with bravos and applause.

After the concert we helped remove the instruments to the street in a procession. Every minute someone would pass in the hall with an armful of instruments and deposit them on the curb. It looked like an Egyptian panel depicting a funeral. In fact, as if the whole evening of Dada had been planned by a master impresario (perhaps John Cage), when all the weird instruments were accounted for, a long gray hearse drew silently up to the curb and they were deposited inside and carried away—to a music cemetery?

47

William Carlos Williams

On December 6, 1946, my ex-girl friend, Bonnie Golightly, threw a party at her bookstore on Waverly Place for William Carlos Williams, celebrating the Williams issue of the *Briarcliff Quarterly*. Norman MacLeod, the editor, promptly passed out in the back room of the shop, on a studio couch, and the Briarcliff students acted as handmaidens, rushing back and forth to help. One hundred twenty-five guests attended that party, including Babette Deutsch, Randall Jarrell, and other "names." Williams and Auden, ignoring everyone else, stood by the Waverly window rapt in earnest conversation. I wondered what they were saying. In a letter years later Bonnie explained:

> The reason Auden spoke to no one but Williams was that they had been carrying on a literary feud and hadn't seen each other for years. The party reopened genial terms. . . . One of the interesting things about that party was that Mr. Rafferty, the manager of the Earle (which catered the party) got the dates mixed up,

and had his staff down in the shop a week early, complete with zillions of pre-mixed Manhattans and martinis and trays of canapes. Never did know who quaffed and munched all that stuff.

The "literary feud," as it turned out, was basic to Auden's and Williams's entire approach to modern poetry: they were exploring opposite means in measure, cadence, language, and material. What I did not know was that on April 12, 1940 (a year and a week since Chester and I had met Auden at his first American reading), Auden and Williams participated in a joint reading at Cooper Union and Auden stole the show. Williams was fifty-seven, Auden thirty-three. Williams, whose sense of inadequacy and harsh personal judgment of his own worth gnawed at his self-esteem, recalled experiencing a great sense of failure. "Auden's success before the audience as contrasted with the rest of us was the feature of the evening," he reluctantly admitted in his notes scribbled after the event. "The rest" were Malcolm Cowley, Alfred Kreymborg, and others. Williams was choosing commonplace themes and situations in natural speech and cadences, whereas Auden stuck to "the old excellences"; the audience felt comfortable with formal cadences and language using new materials in old forms, reported Williams—who was searching for a new measure, which he, though nearing sixty, had not yet found.

The significance of all this did not strike me for years. By what seems purely the laws of chance, my work caught the attention of Williams in March or April 1951 while he was in the hospital with his first stroke at age sixty-eight. My career, which hardly existed until then, had been stuck between two poles represented by Auden and Williams. But the Muse works in mysterious ways.

Auden did not believe in chance and I did not believe in design, yet four decades later, with so many extraordinary intersection points in place and time over the years, I wonder if it was not design: Cooper Union, St. Mark's Place, Bonnie Golightly. She had conducted a correspondence with Williams since 1945. Her enthusiasm for *First Act,* the first two parts of a novel that New Directions had published, stimulated him—six years after he had written the book—to begin the last part.

Another six years later Williams and I intersected—the most

important literary relationship of my life. It happened this way: in the winter of 1951 I received a request from a Canadian poet, Louis Dudek, to join a round robin of about a dozen unknown young poets, which involved submitting two or three poems and criticizing one another's work in detail. It was to be sent to Ezra Pound and Williams for comment; if they saw fit, they would select one poet they felt had forwarded the tradition of the "new." I submitted a long poem about childhood in Scranton called "The Railroad Yard" and two short lyrics. One poet, Paul Blackburn, caught my attention; his poems and comments seemed the best of the group—and he in turn gave me his vote.

We never heard from Pound, but in early April I received a postcard from Dudek, who said that although Williams was in the hospital with a stroke, he had singled me out and would write when he felt up to it. Soon a letter came, now lost, in a shaky scrawl saying, "You are the best poet of your generation." Weeks later another, dated April 21, 1951, arrived, also in an unsteady hand:

> Dear Harold Norse:
>
> I admired your poem "The Railroad Yard" for two or three simple reasons: first it was a *poem,* i.e. it MADE a thing out of words that said something by the way the words were used. But the thing that struck me most forcibly was the language which determined HOW the words were to be used. You *worked* with the language, your language, that *gave* the elements out of which you *made* the construction.
>
> If more of the instruction that is forced on us could be forgotten and more that is here to be seen and heard could *possess* us—we'd come off much better. We do not realize how far back we have to go before we find good wood. We have tried to start too far UP the scale. We have not gone back to the language itself, letting it dictate its forms.
>
> You have been one of the few to go back far enough and to use the direct image on its own. I was very moved. Good luck with your book—but it will be a hard tussle to get it printed and harder still to sell it. Readers are years behind you, only a very few know what it is all about.

It is all right to enjoy Eliot but remember, he ran away from the thing which you have to realize to come out whole. Watch your step.

I was thirty-four years old and felt plucked from obscurity at last; but when the elation subsided I began to fret: his comments seemed too simplistic. The first paragraph sounded inarticulate, even banal. Could it be the effect of the stroke? I wondered. On the other hand, the second paragraph, in which he spoke as a navigator steering in uncharted seas, was as original as Pound minus the ruffles and flourishes. Still, a phrase in the third paragraph, "the direct image on its own," bothered me: what else could an image be? But the important thing, the vital thing, was that I'd been recognized by a major poet on the basis of quality, not cronyism. The warmth and wholeheartedness of his appreciation meant more to me than any reservations I might have had about his vagueness of expression. "Readers are years behind you, only a very few know what it is all about."

Since 1941 I had been struggling to abandon strict forms and rhyme, choosing assonance and accentual verse, writing in natural speech rhythms, using line breaks determined by breath, as if speaking personally to someone. My themes were childhood experience, the quest for love, the pain of alienation in an urban environment. All three themes came together in "The Railroad Yard." Through Williams's recommendation the poem appeared that year in James Laughlin's *New Directions No. 13,* an annual anthology of new and experimental work. The volume was dedicated to Tennessee Williams and contained a poem by him; an article by Céline; prose by Jean Paulhan; Kenneth Rexroth's "The Dragon and the Unicorn, Part II"; Charles Olson's "Introduction to Robert Creeley"; prose by Creeley, Paul Goodman, Lorine Niedecker, Niccolo Tucci; poems by Edouard Roditi, Charles Henri Ford, Max Jacob, Francis Jammes; and Kimon Friar's translations of Kazantzakis, Sikelianos, Seferis, Engonopoulos, and the great surrealist poem "Amorgos" by Nikos Gatsos. It was a superb anthology and I was thrilled to be represented. This was my literary debut. But in the mistaken belief that it was more "literary" I had changed the title to "Warnings and Promises"; in my collected poems I would restore the original title. Here, slightly revised, are some excerpts:

Two storeys high were violets
In a window-box. Soft coal ash
Blew gently, wafted
Into the room. Downstairs
The fat landlady in a calico dress
Hung washing on the line. Heat
Punched and pounded her dress
As it pounded the walls.
In the room with the violets
I listened to **Waltz Bluette.**
O room with the whirl of **Waltz Bluette!**
—The phonograph winding, winding—
That summer madness of the poor.
Over the dirty violets
My father flung the machine.
                         *

Grey woofs of smoke muffle the clouds—soft
Fabric of cinder and dense fire
In the engine's larynx—coughed
Out, spewed from the funnel in a bolt of wool
Floating, unspooled, on rooftops and windowsills
—Geraniums wrapped in wool
Like the clouds. Something else—
Wool on the memory, hooding
The approach—is happening, a
Scene, two figures, in the dawn, dare
Under cover of wool, mysteries
*Of motion, undulant—*pain . . . ? Or
Possibly, as the window cools to pearl
Panes, clearing, it is—shuttling
There, in the lump of shadows
Parents weave—a bobbin in
My eyeballs, till they purl hot flame!
—Pulling the warp down over shame. . . .
                         *

Now recall . . . factories, knitting mills—
Where sewing children's bathing suits
My mother sat behind the frosted glass.
Peddlers with forget-me-nots
And ice cream vendors by the gate
Joked with the girls who laughed
And ran when the factory whistle blew.

Summer brought assorted smells
Of locomotives, beer, gardenias. . . .
We walked home, knitting hands,
Through traffic, vendors and newsboys.
And Peter Rabbit, in the din,
Hopped chicken wire to the cabbage patch.
Jump, Peter, Brother Fang is hiding
There, behind that briar—where
Could Peter go? The woods are dangerous.

At his written invitation I visited Dr. Williams in Rutherford, New Jersey—the first of many visits. As the large buff frame house on the hill at the end of the main street hoved into view I began to tremble with excitement. To add to my nervousness I had acute bursitis—low back pain—and could hardly straighten up. When I rang the bell at 9 Ridge Road Williams appeared with a big lopsided grin (his facial muscles paralyzed by a stroke) and, putting an arm around my shoulder, greeted me warmly.

"Here's the poet! Come in! Drop your hat and coat and let's get a good look at you." The warmth of this reception immediately dispelled my anxiety. He motioned me to an armchair, exclaiming "Here's the man!" with such cordiality that I positively glowed. We sat looking at each other, grinning. Although one side of his face was paralyzed, his blue eyes were keenly alert. The parlor, where we sat drinking cold beer, was homey, old-fashioned. He was still a handsome man, tall, narrow-hipped, and with no pot belly; his movements were agile and youthful. He was not overly impressed by the poetry scene, he said, caring little for scholarly formalism, and even Robert Lowell, who *had* something, was too academic. Though my chief influence was Hart Crane grafted onto Walt Whitman, I too had fallen into evil ways—primarily the legacy of Auden—but he didn't know. I could not break completely out of the old mold except in some poems like "The Yard." Thanks to this first meeting, a seed was planted, ultimately to flower through the complete abandonment of fixed forms.

But after a while his vim and vigor fizzed out. He sat wringing his hands. Finally he blurted, "I don't know what to *do* with myself. I just sit most of the time, read a little, and twiddle my thumbs. Never in my entire life have I been so inactive!" He ejaculated, "Aaarrghh!" just as he did in his poems. "Right now I feel that all of my work is lousy—I've done nothing worthwhile!"

"But that's not true! It's just one of those periods of doubt and despair that come to every good writer."

"And probably every bad one, too," he said disgustedly.

"After you've finished something don't you always feel as if you can never write again?" I persisted.

"I *know* it, I *know* it!" he yelped in his curiously high, adolescent voice. "But in that stage it's real. You believe it. It *can* be true. That's the nature of doubt. I may snap out of it, but right now I'm just—" He puffed out his cheeks and forcefully exhaled. I was amazed that so accomplished an artist experienced doubts I knew so well. Only the year before at our first meeting Dylan Thomas had also confided the same thing and believed he was washed up. What a precarious calling poetry was! A continual search for renewal and discovery ending in despair.

He leaned forward with clasped hands and I was struck at how much he resembled a football star who has sustained an injury and must sit out the game on the sidelines, fretfully watching lesser players on the field. About a year later, when I asked E. E. Cummings what he thought of Williams, he remarked, "Oh, I've always thought of him as a college football coach!" He must have seemed that way in his youth. The stroke, having partly paralyzed one side of his face, left one eye glaring, lifeless, the muscles rigid. This imparted to his expression a sinister touch but could not rob him of his candid, straightforward look. We drank more beer and he showed me the garden at the back of the house. "Isn't it pretty?" It was full of purple, red, and yellow flowers and silky grass. He was the emperor of flowers. I had seen them in his poems and could not say which were real and which imaginary.

Seated once more in the large comfortable living room overlooking a noisy intersection of buses and cars, we talked until it was so dark I couldn't see a thing. "Since my stroke the light is a strain," he said. "It tires my eyes."

His wife, Floss, entered with coffee, milk, and homemade apple pie. I liked her at once, as I had liked him; her flat gray hair and stern, set features had the look of a Grant Wood primitive. Although she lacked the exuberance of her famous husband, she seemed cordial. (On later visits I discovered that as my admiration for Bill's critical intelligence grew, so did my respect for his wife's. His reliance on her criticism was not misguided.)

Williams looked tired and I began to worry that he might not have the energy to read the manuscript I had left in the hall. As if reading my mind he suddenly said, "Well, I noticed you brought a portfolio with you. Are they your poems? Let's have a look!" As I went for my folder he switched on a floor lamp and indicated a place beside him on the couch. He began reading slowly, like a doctor carefully diagnosing a patient. I had a sense of the thoroughness of his analytical mind, trained in medicine. He read at random—it would be a matter of chance whether he picked the good poems or the stinkers I hadn't the heart to reject, a fault of the inexperienced writer; but luck was with me. He read some of the best and spoke enthusiastically about what he considered my "special talent," my "creative use of language," without which, he said, no one could call himself a real poet. "And *you* are a real poet!" he exclaimed. "You have the language. I can't see these traditional poets—a poem is language, not fixed forms."

Then he put it so beautifully I wished I could have written it down. About how out of the concrete experience the words come up from nowhere and shape themselves, and if the poet is completely honest and doesn't conform to preconceived hand-me-down concepts of form, the form more or less takes care of itself. Yes, there must be form, the shape is important. But the form is not a rigid mold prepared by others in the past—it grows out of the language and the sense. The form is created anew with each new experience.

"Don't worry about how many feet a line must have! Who the hell cares? What people want, when they read a poem, is to be arrested immediately. Stopped in their tracks—held by the words. Get their attention in the first line—then hold it! The form can't do that. Only the words, the words in new, surprising combinations, can do it! You have to shock and surprise! They won't be interested if your words are used conventionally—or if you have a riot of words. That's just verbiage. Garbage. You've got to *see* things. Make others see afresh. You can't write without *seeing*. Ah, here's a good one—"

With the nail of his index finger he scratched several times under the image "sea-swell in hard loins" from "Key West." "A good intuitive insight," he said. When he came to the words "heavy with aimlessness" he laughed. "That's me right now. Heavy with aimlessness." At several other images he grunted approval. "You've got it, no doubt about it," he mumbled appreciatively. "You've got the power of words, to make us see in a new way." The so-so poems he said little about. He carefully examined "Postcard" and covered up the last few lines with his hand, squinting like a painter drawing a sketch. "If you say *too* much," he warned, "you can spoil the poem. I wonder if this wouldn't be improved by stopping at 'artifice'?" I trashed the poem.

He read about a dozen more, then closed the cover and bridged his nose with thumb and forefinger. My heart sank. So much, I thought, depends on—luck. "I can't praise it highly enough," Williams had said about "The Railroad Yard." With closed eyes he said, with an effort, "I'm afraid I can't read much more. You understand. It's a big book—I mustn't tire myself."

"Of course," I said softly. "I understand." But I didn't. I'd never been seriously ill—or old—and miserably, selfishly, kept thinking, Perhaps most of the poems don't come up to "The Yard," when suddenly he jerked open the binder and it fell on "I Remember Papa"—the poem I'd most hoped he'd read! Very carefully, as he had done with all the poems—for he was not a man given to empty gestures—he read and then, nodding vigorously, exclaimed, "Whew! This is as good as Cummings at his best!" Then, with finality, he shut the book and, turning toward me, said, "You have a flair for words that only the best poets have. All you need now is to get your foot in the door—" He pushed his foot against an imaginary door. "Brush up the book a little. Cut out the earlier poems, most of the stanzaic ones. Make it tight. Satisfy yourself. Keep the ones you like best. I'd abandon the sections." I had divided the book into sections with subtitles. He said he'd write his editor, David McDowell, at Random House about me. I can still hear his words, still recall how eagerly he expressed his pleasure at my visit: aside from wanting to meet me, he said, my visit energized him, made him feel better.

I visited him many times and corresponded until he died. It was fashionable to regard Williams as a minor imagist, not in the same league as Pound or Eliot, at best a "primitive" who did not employ the academic jargon associated with literary criticism and book reviewing. Yet far from being an unsophisticated naif, he was, if anything, far ahead of his critics as well as his times—ahead of Pound, even. In 1946 he saw that Pound's time was over, that he had been eclipsed by new events. It was Williams, not Pound, who would become the spearhead of the new in poetry. Pound had reinvigorated a stagnant literary scene, starting around 1910, but by the 1940s, when he was incarcerated for treason at St. Elizabeth's Hospital, his politics and views disabled him. He remained stuck in the past, an antiquarian. "My final diagnosis of that guy," said Williams bitterly at the time, "is that he's got a blank spot in his thinking which he has exploited all his life as profundity." He wrote Pound angrily about his "egocentric irrelevances" and "assumptions of knowledge which I know you well enough to know you do not have." A fair assessment indeed.

Time and scholarship have proven Williams right. He never pretended to more than he knew—and he knew a great deal. When in 1946 Randall Jarrell wrote a long, favorable review of *Paterson 1* in the *Partisan Review,* saying that if Williams could keep up that level in the succeeding books it would be "the best very long poem that any American has written," Williams came into prominence among the "serious" critics who had excluded him from major status until then. He *did* keep up "that level" and *Paterson* ranks with *The Bridge, The Waste Land,* and *The Cantos.* No primitive or naif could have accomplished this. When the first major biography by Paul Mariani appeared in 1981 the reviewer in the *New York Times Book Review* wrote: "[It] succeeds in placing him . . . as the single most important American poet of the twentieth century."

A series of poetry readings at the Museum of Modern Art had been initiated whereby a well-known poet introduced three unknowns, who would read twenty minutes each. The first group was chosen by Auden and, no surprise, Chester was among them and I was not. The second group was chosen by Williams, who wrote me in November 1951, asking if I wished to read. Nothing could have stopped me. The museum was prestige with a capital *P.* In December Williams wrote that he hoped I'd read "the Scranton poem which I first admired." The date of the reading was March 26, 1952. He enlarged the group to five, explaining, "It's quite a crowd but I think that as an introduction it will be better to . . . give more men a chance to appear." It was characteristic of his generosity.

I recall only two others, Kenneth Bowdoin, an experimental southern poet, and Eli Siegel, who founded a school of writing called Aesthetic Realism, which, among other bizarre claims, professed to "cure" homosexuality. Thinking of Siegel, a man in his fifties whom I had known from the WPA Writers' Project as a mirthless, self-important intellectual, made me wonder who would discover a cure for heterosexuality. He enjoyed, if that is the correct word for a grim-faced maven whose long nose sniffed disdainfully at everything, a minor notoriety for a poem called "Hot Afternoons Have Been in Montana," which in the 1920s or 1930s won a prize in the *Nation*. Based on long Whitmanesque lines, it was actually about the weather. But Williams was right to include him; the poem defied existing norms with a flat, bland insouciance that mocked conventional taste.

The auditorium was packed to capacity. Onstage I sat listening with the other poets to Williams introducing the group in his high-pitched voice. I believe Siegel read first and Bowdoin second and then I heard Williams introducing me from the lectern. The blood drained from my face as he turned, his arm extended toward me. When I rose and stood at the lectern, my nose barely above it, Williams kicked the podium to me hissing, "Use it." I thought I'd look more grotesque towering above the lectern, so I kicked the podium back to him. More decisively he kicked it to me again, muttering, "They won't see you!" Again I shoved it back with my foot. A soft ripple of laughter rose from the audience at this Laurel and Hardy routine. It broke the ice. The dignified tone of the proceedings dissolved in the laughter. Williams grinned, shaking his head helplessly, and sat down. With my nose barely above the lectern I began to read "the Scranton poem," still panic-stricken but sensing that the audience was with me. At the end there was a burst of sustained applause. When the evening was over I was the center of attention. Even Oscar Williams came up and croaked something complimentary. Most significant to me was meeting E. E. Cummings, who approached with congratulations for the Scranton poem: "You've transcended your background and transformed it in your work." He handed me his phone number. I was a hit.

In spite of Williams's recommendation, my book of poetry was rejected by McDowell at Random House. By way of explanation I was told that they published only the best-known poets and could not afford to risk unknowns. Farrar, Straus, on the other hand, offered to publish it if I submitted a novel they liked, but I had no novel. Williams made other suggestions and tried to "wangle a grant" for me, but with no book I didn't stand a chance. On April 5 Williams wrote: "There were many favorable comments on your reading and you'll have one [a book] in time. I know, 'in time' is what gets us down but we've got to face it—until we're damned near 70 at times." He also said that he was "going to be at the Library of Congress next year. I don't know what it amounts to but you can count on it, I'll be pushing for you younger men who write as I think one *must* write today." That never panned out either. He was investigated by the FBI, who decided he was a "pinko" because he had signed petitions for Communist front groups in the 1930s and 1940s. The House Un-American Activities Committee was carrying on its witchhunt under Senator Joe McCarthy, and the FBI was citing his poems "The Pink Church" and "Russia" as evidence of the poet's leftist leanings, which were nonexistent. In danger of having another stroke from this irrational persecution, Williams resigned as consultant to the Library of Congress. The loyalty investigation was called off.

Meanwhile things had begun to happen. My book was accepted by Alan Swallow, Publisher, in Denver and I wrote Williams about it. Publication was set for spring 1953. I also visited Cummings in early May. He was nothing like the public perception of him as a feisty racist with a shotgun ready to blast all trespassers off his property. He was a rugged individualist and independent artist and thinker, member of no school, cult, or coterie. He stood alone, charming, witty, amusing, and above all candid. His house on Patchin Place, the little mews off Greenwich Avenue by the Women's House of Detention, was one of the old frame dwellings there, a slice of rural New England collaged into the urban stone and brick of downtown Manhattan. In fact, entering the house was like stepping into a surrealist collage. The living room with the colonial windows on the dead-end street had weird paintings by Cummings, easels, and sagging bookshelves; there was an old coat rack, an upright piano, a baroque mirror over an eighteenth-century fireplace with a blazing fire, a parrot in a cage, and objets d'art. Cummings had a cubist face: a lopsided nose and misaligned features. His fingers were gnarled with arthritis. When I admired the mirror he said, "Dylan Thomas, who was here recently, kept staring at himself, then said, 'Who is that distinguished Lesbian writer?'"

After about an hour I plucked up the courage to ask about

those of his poems which seemed anti-Semitic and anti-Negro. Did
he feel that way? "Not at all!" he said. "I've never been a racist. I
dislike groups, including my own, and can only relate to individuals.
Groups destroy them." His poem about Olaf, the conscientious objector, satirizing American militarism, is one of the harshest denun-
ciations of war, racism, and blind patriotism ever written.

I continued visiting Williams and his wife, whose rhubarb
pie was fantastic. He said I cheered them up and in January
1953 proposed that I live with them. I needed money and he
needed a typist. Living with William Carlos Williams—what
more could I ask? But for a number of reasons I declined. Williams was moody, ill, and depressed, and I was given to rages
and depression myself. I could not sustain indefinitely a cheerful
attitude and I knew the atmosphere would present problems.
Floss, whom I liked immensely, had a silent air of stoical resignation, which, I felt, would put a strain on me. My stint as Auden's
secretary served as a warning. I could not afford to risk losing
Williams's friendship, as I had lost Auden's, which I still regret.
Besides, who would feed my cats? D., who had taken to drink,
was no longer reliable.

Through the round robin I had gotten to know Paul Blackburn, a slight young man with clean-cut features and a bass
voice. He was a scholar and poet who would eventually earn a
reputation for his translations of the Provençal troubadours and
his own verse. One day he told me of a party for the poets of the
round robin who wanted to meet me. Having earned the kudos
of Williams, I was a phenomenon to them. Blackburn brought
me to an apartment full of young men with plenty of wine, cigarette smoke, and assorted canapés. I met Dudek, a pleasant Canadian, and others whom I have forgotten except for John
Kasper, a tall, gaunt, hook-nosed poet who spoke pontifically
and was treated with deference. They urged him to recite from
Pound's *Cantos* and, without further encouragement, with closed
eyes he flawlessly intoned Cantos 45 (Usura), 35, 36, 51, and
others on request—like a priest droning the liturgy.

When the conversation resumed, a dark handsome Italian
with a Van Dyke beard asked if Pound had a greater influence
on my work than Williams. I replied that neither had influenced
my style but that Williams had given me courage to speak in my
own voice. Slavish imitation was the surest way, I said, to the
second-rate shelf. "And Pound's ideas?" he said sharply. "Don't

you think his literary and social criticism are the greatest of the century? The *Cantos* are *The Divine Comedy* of our age."

"They're terribly funny," I said. I went on about Pound as a master of sound—*melopoeia*—but not sense. In fact, I said, as a thinker he was a windbag, like his hero, Mussolini.

"You must be a Jew!" sneered the Italian. "You're twisted."

"Descended from Jesus Christ on my mother's side," I said.

"Only a Jew," he muttered menacingly, "would dishonor Pound."

"Only an idiot," I replied, "would worship him."

He was very large and young and took a giant step toward me.

"I'd be glad," I said, "to pull out your beard hair by hair."

He stopped. "On my father's side," I snarled, "I'm descended from Attila the Hun." I took a step toward him. Bullies and bigots brought out the worst in me. I was restrained by Dudek and Blackburn, two very nice guys. What were they doing among a bunch of Fascists anyway? Some time later Kasper drifted south and made rabble-rousing speeches against racial integration and got jailed repeatedly. He and Pound were mentioned in news reports as master and disciple, giving rise to the not unfounded suspicion that Pound was in part responsible for Kasper's actions. He had also been publishing Pound's political and economic tracts via his Square Dollar Press. His unsavory adventures may have caused the delay of Pound's release from St. Elizabeth's Mental Hospital.

48

Ezra Pound

Some twelve poets had been approached by Ruthven Todd to contribute a holograph poem each for a project at Atelier 17, an engraving studio founded by the British master engraver Stanley Hayter. Among them were T. S. Eliot, Ezra Pound, Marianne Moore, William Carlos Williams, W. H. Auden, and Dylan Thomas. I was one of two lesser knowns.

Each was to be illustrated by a master painter, sculptor, or engraver, Mirò, Picasso, Klee, Hayter, and so on, all using William Blake's copperplate technique rediscovered by Hayter, working with a buren. For some reason, which I have forgotten, Ruthven delegated me to contact Pound, who accepted. About that time, in the summer of 1952, I visited Black Mountain College, where, as guest of composer Lou Harrison, I spent a few days and gave a reading. I met some of the new avant-garde poets, writers, composers, and painters of the day.

The colossal Charles Olson, six foot eight, towered and boomed in a mighty voice. Through Williams, who was regarded as a god, my reputation had preceded me, and Olson introduced me to his class: "We have with us today the distinguished young poet Harold Norse." I believe I read "The Railroad Yard" and distinctly recall Fielding Dawson, a very attractive teen-aged blond wearing dungarees, and Francine du Plessix (later Gray), a striking dark-haired slender young woman in a black raincoat. I also got to know Franz Kline, who was outgoing and intense, just beginning to paint his black-and-white calligraphic canvases, some of which he showed me in his studio. Besides Lou Harrison there was John Cage and the young dancer Remy Charlip, who had been a student of mine at Cooper Union and then a close friend of Lou's. All were present at my reading. I left to meet Pound at St. Elizabeth's, where I was to pick up his holograph. Our correspondence consisted of a note from me requesting an appointment and his monosyllabic reply: When? Signed EP.

In an oil-burning old Packard I'd bought for ninety-five dollars I drove from North Carolina to Washington, D.C., and at St. Elizabeth's asked to see Pound. "Mr. Pound can't be seen. He is not well today," said the receptionist. "Come back tomorrow." Having only two dollars and nowhere to stay, I told her I had an appointment with Pound that afternoon and had driven up from the South to see him, but could not stay overnight. She plugged in the doctor and said, "There's a young man here who has traveled all the way from the South to see Mr. Pound, doctor." The doctor was unmoved; I left.

49

Living Theatre

In August 1951 the Becks leased the Cherry Lane (preceded by their Theatre in the Room, the idea for which John Cage and I are credited in Judith's *Diaries*) and fulfilled their dream of the Living Theatre. D. wrote the music for Kenneth Rexroth's *Beyond the Mountains*. The program began with Stein's *Ladies' Voices* and Picasso's *Desire Caught by the Tail,* in which John Ashbery and Frank O'Hara, in bunny costumes, buggered each other onstage (simulated). John Cage, Merce Cunningham, and Johnny Myers (manager of Dwight Ripley's Tibor de Nagy Gallery) were opposed to Rexroth's plays: they detested displays of intense emotion. I considered the plays archaic, melodramatic verse and spoke of a poetry stressing natural speech and cadences.

With growing resentment, bitterly complaining that the Becks owed everyone money, D. moved back to our apartment from theirs. I'd written a piece for the program and attended the premiere of *Beyond the Mountains,* December 1951, but had no idea how unprepared they were. In the opening scene the dark stage lightens gradually as Phaedra (Judith) is borne in on a palanquin agonizing over her love for her stepson Hippolytus; moaning, "I freeze! I burn! I am hot! I am cold!" Judith giggled. Who wouldn't? The audience burst into laughter. Her giggles continued until she screamed, "Pull down the curtain!" which convulsed them even more: there *was* no curtain. She was hauled kicking and screaming offstage.

I believe the fault lay with the pretentious script. Judith, who had sparkled in the Stein plays, was perhaps unconsciously critical of the stilted dialogue. On the other hand, her giggling was an old problem, like that of many actors, including Laurence Olivier, who in youth had been afflicted with this strange form of self-mockery. In her *Diaries* Judith admitted she was experiencing "all forms of violence." Under great stress in her new theatrical venture, she became overbearing. With my teaching job at Cooper Union terminated, I was broke and had no idea that the Living Theatre was bankrupt. When D. confronted her backstage with a demand for payment after the last performance Judith slapped his face. D. threw her to the floor; scrambling to her feet, she grabbed a four-hundred-dollar flute from the poor flautist standing nearby and tried to hit D. on the head with it. To save his silver flute the musician struggled with her for its possession, whereupon she sank her teeth into his fingers, drawing blood. He ran off with his flute and injured hand as Judith rushed at D. screaming, "I'll kill you! I hate you!" While she was being restrained by a big brawny youth, D. spat in her face. Seeing me advance, the man took a menacing step toward me. That did it. Burning with indignation, I fetched him a clout in the stomach. More surprised than hurt, he didn't retaliate. "Is this your utopian revolution?" I screamed at the Becks. "Pay their wages!" I stormed out.

No one was more shocked than Michael Fraenkel, who had returned from France on a visit. When we invited him to the show we had no idea he'd get an unscheduled dose of *théâtre vérité*. The year before he had seen us "operating on a high level," as he put it, and could not believe our behavior. Six months earlier, on June 23 and 24, we were reading the Isherwood translation of the *Bhagavad Gita,* choosing "the way of not hurting any living being," as Judith wrote in her *Diary.* "How could I harm them?/. . . Evil they may be,/Yet if we kill them/Our sin is greater," said the *Gita.*

Something died in me that night; I felt betrayed. I couldn't explain it. Pacifism, for which D. spent three years in prison, didn't work. Filled with hostility and aggression, Judith and D. were living a lie. Like the liberals they detested, they were self-righteous do-gooders, yet how could *they* create a better world? If, as Gandhi said, the *Gita* is "the story of the conquest of evil by purity," we all had a long way to go.

The year before I had bought the colonial farmhouse with a hundred acres of woodland—a refuge for us all in Canterbury, Connecticut. That summer, after a few days in the country with D. and the Becks, I found that a rural commune with emotionally troubled companions was not the answer; despite good intentions, a neurotic utopia is just another failed society.

*   *   *

The artesian well had to be pumped and purified. The fire department took care of the former, but nobody would descend the sixty feet or so into the dank, foul-smelling well on whose slimy surface dead muskrats floated. I volunteered.

Our neighbors, the Ames family, lent me rubber hipboots and slung a bucket attached to a thick rope over the side and tied another around my waist. With leather work gloves I grabbed the rope and, rung by rung, climbed down the metal ladder. The Ameses turned out en masse to watch what none of the men dared to do. Some big woodsmen from a shack up the road also came to watch. It was considered dangerous. Shaking their heads firmly, the men said, "I wouldn't do it, no sir. I'd rather pay someone for that kind of a job."

The bucket was lowered into the foul interior. From below I watched the sunny world disappear into a narrowing hole of light. I was to tug twice at the body rope if I felt dizzy or faint. The rungs, covered by a green mossy slime, were extremely slippery. It was hard to keep a foothold or grip. As I neared bottom I could make out, with the aid of a flashlight, bloated corpses on the stagnant water, which stank so bad that I had a sickening spell of vertigo and nearly tugged the rope. Instead, I grabbed a rat, but it slipped away, leaving its slimy skin in my hand. I grabbed it a few more times before I could hold it and then dumped it in the bucket and tugged the rope. The bucket disappeared overhead and was lowered again. The stench was so nauseating I grew faint. But I got all the rats, gave two sharp tugs, and felt the body rope tighten. Clutching the rungs I made my way back to the upper world, met by grins and congratulations as I took a few deep whiffs of fresh air and nearly passed out. The country folk regarded me with respect. Even the Becks looked at me with shining eyes. I was a hero. Judith handed me a beer and a cigarette, which tasted of life and warmth as I gulped down the brew and the smoke. Julian untied the knot and ceremoniously buried the dead creatures in the garbage pit.

That night I watched with amusement as Judith grew sentimental about the "poor moths" circling around the flame of the oil lamp, flirting with death. Julian shooed them away, sneaking up to catch and deposit them outside the house. After shooting squirrels in the eaves I had resolved never to kill again, but these pacifists never succeeded in conquering or transforming their violent feelings. Not only D. came to blows with Judith in De-

cember 1951. In her *Diaries* she records that in January 1952
"four people have been moved to strike me: Milton, Maurice,
Richard, Julian. I look in horror at what I provoke." Et tu,
Julian? She also slapped and was slapped by Paul Goodman—
during psychoanalytical sessions that he conducted. "Violent
paranoids," Lore Perls said of the Becks.

But if their pacifism failed, their theatre based on the dis-
semination of that ideal did not. Its success during the sixties
and seventies was internationally recognized and both Judith
and Julian became legendary figures in their own right, influenc-
ing succeeding generations. And, miraculously, our mutual affection survived those cataclysmic upheavals.

50

First Success

A young man called Eddie, whom I had met through
Jimmy Baldwin, was living with José Quintero, a struggling director who, I believe, practically invented off-
Broadway theatre in the Village. In the summer of 1952 Quintero's
first success was with Tennessee Williams's *Summer and Smoke*—
largely due to a radiant unknown actress named Geraldine Page,
who had acted in *The Thirteenth God*, an early play of the Living
Theatre, for which D. wrote the music. Both Geraldine and Quintero had their start that opening night, which I attended. He went
on to direct Tennessee's plays on Broadway and in the movies. I
had no idea Geraldine was so charismatic. I'd thought her a rather
flaky lady in the early Living Theatre days. Backstage I told her
how superbly moving she'd been and she beamed with expansive,
flowery gestures.

"Oh, *thank* you, *thank* you so *much*, my dear! I'm so *excited*! I
think I'll *scream*!" She uttered a high little screech and gasped.
We both laughed in that euphoric way when the sweet smell of

success and youth makes you giddy with wonder and sheer happiness. She had begun to taste stardom as the crowds gathered around her.

Then something happened that gave me a taste of what it would be like to be a star myself. My first accepted story, called "The Hyperbola," was taken by a major New York publisher for an anthology of the best short stories on the theme of homosexuality. The others in the volume were: Tennessee Williams, Paul Bowles, William Carlos Williams, Truman Capote, John Horne Burns, Ernest Hemingway, Paul Verlaine, Gore Vidal, Thomas Mann, Stephen Spender, and Christopher Isherwood. Not bad company for an unknown! I had just begun writing my first stories since my teens. *Commentary*, then a liberal magazine edited by Robert Warshaw, published a second story (for which I received one hundred dollars), and also my poetry and reviews. Then Alan Swallow in Denver, the only publisher to take a chance on Anaïs Nin, accepted my book.

Meanwhile, things were going from bad to worse on Third Avenue. Unable to sleep at night, I slept during the day. Had I been an early riser Isherwood, like Tennessee, would have remained friendly. Christopher phoned and sent a note. One afternoon I was fool enough not to break a prior engagement when he invited me to accompany him to a rehearsal of *I Am a Camera*, a play based on his Berlin stories, which became a musical and then the film *Cabaret*. Thinking I was brushing him off, he never forgave me and snubbed me whenever we met. But in 1977 he broke his silence to praise my book *Carnivorous Saint*.

My luck didn't hold. The New York publisher got cold feet and abandoned the gay anthology. They couldn't "assume the risk," although the authors were among the most eminent and by no means all homosexual; the time was not ripe. I missed the big league.

51

Picasso

I have done many foolish things in my life but the most foolish was selling the Picasso. To this day I regret it. It would have secured my old age. Knowing nothing about business and with no one to advise me, I proceeded along a fatal course that still makes me shudder when I recall it. The truth was, even the low price of storage was beyond my means, but the sale couldn't have been managed in a worse way.

Picassos did not sell well in the fifties. "Cyril Reed" had paid only a thousand dollars for it at the Matisse Gallery. An indigent painter I knew, who had often borrowed but never returned nickels for bus fare, suggested that for a small commission he would sell it to a dealer. I lacked the confidence even to enter a gallery for negotiating a sale. "Harvey Fein" (name changed) had no such qualms. Pale, fair, soft, and languid, he looked like a gargantuan hamster. His gentle gray eyes inspired trust. But, as he himself once put it, he was no Abe Lincoln. With veiled hints, winks, and innuendos, he often confided how some friend's wife had succumbed to his seductions. Though a terrific gossip, he revealed nothing about his financial dealings. His career as an art dealer, which flourished much later, began with my Picasso.

Harvey had no trouble convincing me that he could get a better price than I; almost anyone could. We signed an agreement designating him as my agent and he took the Picasso. He was to call in a few days but didn't; when I rang he promised again to phone but didn't. Too late it began to dawn on me that I had made a ghastly mistake. Then one day he said he had sold it for four hundred dollars. "Is that *all?*" I protested. "It's a good price nowadays," he purred. I never got the whole sum. Every week or two on windy street corners he'd hand me twenty dollars—which is how he became a successful dealer. Sometimes I waited a half hour in a driving rain or blizzard. His liquid eyes melting with love, he'd swear that I'd get the whole sum soon. "Trust me," he said—two words that strike terror to my heart. Friends said he had probably received a lump sum and was living on it as he doled out the crumbs to me.

52

Farewell to New York

My last months in New York were a blur of wild parties and sexcapades. One of these I remember clearly, attended by Paul and Sally Goodman, the Becks, and Chester Kallman, whom I had helped with his shopping the year before in preparation for his departure for Italy (his list of canned goods unavailable in Italy was pages long). He spoke of Ischia, the island where he and Auden spent summers, giving mouth-watering descriptions of the youths who, unlike the canned goods, were fresh and available. Limping on an injured foot, he sulked alone in a corner. Frank O'Hara was drunk and disorderly and Judith clutched my hand and stared with mad intensity as a handsome boy called Bob attempted to steer me to the bathroom under D.'s baleful glare. Trying to avoid a scene, I resisted his welcome attentions in the din of loud voices and rock music. Bob was kissing and groping me when a small, wispy girl called Jeanette drunkenly lurched toward us, grabbed his balls, and shoved her tongue down his throat. In a flash they were on the floor, her legs spread, her skirt over her navel, his big cock the cynosure of all eyes. His jeans down to his knees, he began pumping away, buttocks bouncing voluptuously as Jeanette moaned. Suddenly another young man (who turned out to be her lover) seized Bob and smashed him brutally in the face. Jeanette stood up, quickly arranged her clothes, and joined her lover in bashing poor Bob, whom she had seduced. Bruised and bleeding, he collapsed. Jeanette turned on everyone, screaming, "Sonofabitches! Fuckin' bastards!" She spat as her lover grabbed her roughly and yanked her out of the house like a rag doll. Must be pacifists, I thought. (Jeanette's bitchy violence provoked Paul Goodman's displeasure; he blackballed her from his therapy group. *His* violence took the form of psychological abuse—a cruel Socrates to the young he dazzled.)

One icy winter evening after dinner at the Chambord I accompanied Cyril to the Chelsea. He wanted to see me nude, promising he would only look. As I stood naked before him he fell to his knees and begged me to lie on the couch. He clasped his hands in rapture, tears streaming down his cheeks, but never touched me. I rose from the couch and dressed. "How can I thank you?" he murmured. "Another Picasso?" I was tempted to reply.

As we waited for a cab in the snow Cyril said, "You really pity me, don't you?" I nodded. We stamped our feet and pounded our gloved hands together. "And pity is a form of love, isn't it?" "Yeah." "So in a way you *love* me?" A wave of nausea hit me. Filled with disgust but really pitying him, I said, knowing it would be the end, "Yeah." Cyril yelped with relief. The genie was freed from the bottle. "Well, dear, here's your cab! Cheerio!" He slipped me a fiver for the fare. I felt like a whore. The magic word *love* had been uttered; the spell was broken.

53

The Undersea Mountain

In May 1953 my first book, *The Undersea Mountain*, appeared and received excellent notices in the *New York Times*, *Herald-Tribune,* and in prestigious magazines like the *Hudson Review* and *Poetry.* But Dr. Williams did not go overboard: "Some of the poems are first rate, in fact they are unusually good," he wrote on May 11, 1953. "Too bad you included the ones which are not standouts. . . . If you had made a book of such poems as 'And All The Travellers Return' I would have gone off the deep end, and I always welcome 'Warnings and Promises' [The Railroad Yard] whenever I read it. There are several poems of as excellent a quality but somehow the book as a whole needs a good kick in the ass to make it stand up by itself."

If I had done as he suggested it would not have been published at all. But I needed a good editor. Williams wanted to see me "knock em dead. Start on the next book right away and make every [poem] in it a standout. Your sentences must be more jagged and packed closer with meaning. Think of their sounds also, the consonants are important." I asked what he meant about consonants, but he never explained. He was hopeless on details. He failed miserably on the technical specifics in which the academics excelled.

Instead of starting on the second book I decided to leave America with my mother's help and the money saved from the Picasso, enough for a return ticket to England and a three-month stay. I still had the house in Connecticut, which I rented to the Ameses' son, Harold, with his wife and baby. He was to pay my mother twenty dollars a month rent. I left a .22 caliber rifle, a primitive oil painting picked up for a dollar in a Canterbury farmhouse, and other stuff, none of which I ever saw again—including the house. Their infant son kicked over a kerosene lamp and the oak floor in the kitchen was destroyed in the fire. Nobody was burned. I had my mother sell the house and land—another dumb financial move—and we amassed the staggering sum of three thousand dollars, which included insurance, and I told her to keep it. It was more money than we'd ever seen in our lives. My mother never spent a penny of it.

54

An Evening with Anaïs Nin

In the summer of 1953 I finally met Anaïs Nin. Kimon Friar showed her my first book and her reaction was strongly favorable. "I met Harold Norse, a poet who has great emotional power in a beautiful, disciplined form," she wrote in her diary. Still an underground figure, she was "suffering from . . . ostracism from the American writing scene. I am left out of every anthology, every poetry reading, every magazine," she wrote shortly before we met. To me she was a living legend, not only for her few privately printed, hand-set books but through Henry Miller's famous encomium in his popular book of essays, *Sunday After the War,* which compared her unpublished diaries to the *Confessions* of Saint Augustine, Petronius, Rousseau, and Proust. No major publisher would touch them. Her grief was so great that, in a hospital ward after surgery for a tumor in February 1953, she wrote in her diary, "As the physical body healed, I became aware of the psychic illness once more: the fact I cannot face is that I am a failure as a writer. The publishers won't publish me, the bookshops won't carry my books, the critics won't write about me. I am excluded from all anthologies, and completely neglected. I had to pay for the printing of *Spy in the House of Love,* done by an inexpensive printer in Holland." She was nearing sixty and I knew nothing of her pain when we met. To me she was clearly a writer of genius.

One evening Kimon and I rode the elevator in the Greenwich Village apartment building at 215 West Thirteenth Street to the penthouse where she lived, in high style, with her husband, Ian Hugo, a wealthy Belgian banker and avant-garde film maker. Tall and slender in a long black shiny gown, with fine honey hair piled on top of her head in neat buns, she looked like a Tanagra figure from classical antiquity. Her warmth came at me in waves, genteel and controlled, to be sure. Her interest was conveyed by the intensity of her gaze, a certain eager, questing look, as if in some sort of recognition, a look familiar to me since adolescence, the look of kindred spirits. She offered martinis, which I gratefully seized, needing something alcoholic to overcome my shyness. I remember liking Hugo immediately, a tall, distinguished, middle-aged man with a friendly though formal manner. I nibbled pastries and gulped martinis while listening as Kimon talked with Anaïs, who kept glancing at me. I was surprised by her thin almost childlike voice—it seemed incongruous in an innovative master of a literary genre. There was a submissiveness, a desire to please, to placate, in her doll-like voice that belied the stubborn independence of her writing.

After an exchange Anaïs excused herself, saying she'd be right back, and returned with a copy of *The Undersea Mountain*, my first book. "You have an extraordinary power to express feeling by breaking down the barriers that surround it," she told me. "It is very rare, especially in America. Americans are afraid of feeling, of expressing it. You do it wonderfully." I mumbled, "Thank you." Kimon smiled with the pleased manner of a teacher for his pupil. "Yes, Harold was certainly my most gifted student—with Jimmy Merrill, of course." Anaïs turned some pages and read aloud a few lines from a poem called "Nightfall":

The blue cop on the corner,
his insolence all ruddy and raw,
stamps, and turns his pointed eyes
on children who tear to insoluble shreds
the silver gauze of evening
with the flukes of their screaming.

"This defies explanation," said Anaïs, "yet rings true. It isn't surrealism with its self-conscious postures and identifiable stylistic devices. But it does what surrealism is supposed to do— deal with reality through the unconscious. I think this is a marvelous example." She went on to say that I brought ordinary experience into full dimension by containing the dream quality of the unconscious in the hard surfaces of everyday life. That the words opened up sensations and meanings on many levels. Then she turned to another poem. "In only a few lines you cap-ture music and mystery like a poem by Poe—but completely modern." She read:

And All the Travelers Return

Where the fire-escape puts forth
like a battered bowsprit
a sad geranium or nerveless daisy

that might be seaweed hung on a wrecked hull

the huge arms of the brackish woman
grate on a flaked sill; she is the figurehead
of this dead ship. Lightly the winds
stir the pathetic weeds of her marine hair

as evening lengthens the shadows of
Christopher Street; soon she will disappear
to unseen customary hells,
kitchen where a broth of dullness puffs

like a fat man ascending the walk-up of a friend.
And the quarter moon will slice
steeple, warehouse, crucifix,
and all the travelers return

who are drowned and live in the sea.

I was elated. This was also one of William Carlos Williams's favorites. The rest of the evening was spent in literary gossip discovering that we knew many people in common: W. C. and Tennessee Williams, Harry Herschkowitz, James Leo Herlihy, Jimmy Baldwin, Julian and Judith Beck, Gore Vidal, and many more. She stiffened when I mentioned Harry. "A raw talent," she murmured, "but he is too confused to develop as a writer. He wants to be great but does nothing. Too much theory and too little practice." The subject of Harry seemed distasteful so I quickly dropped it. Jim Herlihy, on the other hand, she adored. "He works hard and I'm sure he'll succeed." I had met Jim through Michael Fraenkel and also found him a joy to be with: witty, lively, and above all generous by nature—something rare among writers. He also possessed social skills equal to his talent.

I would run into him in Rome a few years later, before he attained success with his novel *Midnight Cowboy*.

Anaïs seemed as delicate and fragile as rare china, as if she might break at a harsh or coarse word. But this was an illusion (when we met again eight years later in Paris she seemed earthy). Before I left she gave me an inscribed copy of *The House of Incest*, a small book she had published herself. On the inside cover she wrote in her flowing hand: "For Harold—Such deep simplicity and a flow from sources where accurate poetry is born, in dark passages of courage to *feel*—Love, Anaïs. . . ."

55

Innocent Abroad

In London I was met at Waterloo Station by my former neighbors Walter and Glyn, who had gone British with a vengeance. In two years Walter's *a* had broadened and his scope had narrowed. Glyn had become an untitled nobleman. As the cab headed for their bed-sitter in South Kensington, after which Michael Fraenkel would put me up in his nearby flat, I realized that they too were reacting to the intolerable McCarthy era of persecution and police spies. Gays were entrapped through enticement by plainclothesmen, and freethinkers were accused of being Reds in rabid witch-hunts. Except for Joe McCarthy and Roy Cohn (two unsavory queers who gave homosexuality a bad name and were the worst threat to human rights since Stalin and Hitler, two unsavory heterosexuals), no one in America could have been less harmful to the state than gays. They wished merely to exercise their right to the pursuit of happiness in bedrooms and toilets. Fleeing persecution in the land of the free, I hoped to find sexual liberation in Europe, which had more emancipated attitudes.

As I gazed blearily at the grim, leaden landscape, we came

to the statue of Eros in Piccadilly, still in its scaffolding eight years after the war, a bound and fettered love god in a culture that imprisoned sex. "Stop the taxi!" I cried emotionally. "But we're not there yet," chided Walter, embarrassed before the driver. "I want to get out!" I yelled frantically. We stopped and I leapt from the cab, gesticulating at the low buildings. "It's all human—scaled to our size!" Tears streamed down my cheeks. "That's why we're here," said Walter softly. "No skyscrapers, no bustle."

Lore Perls's words echoed in my ears: "You suffer from environmental stress." Even with Eros bound and gagged before my eyes in the center of London, the old buildings, with not a skyscraper in sight, gave one a sense of coziness, of tradition. On the surface, at least, the atmosphere was decorous, no matter how impoverished life might be (American energy was missing). In their squalid room Walter and Glyn, like the surroundings, seemed unutterably bleak. They dropped coins in a meter whenever they used electricity or water. What a drab world. *Tristesse post bellum.*

That evening they brought me to the Fraenkels, who had two rooms and a kitchen. Multicolored cloths transformed the sitting room into a fortune-teller's parlor. Peacock feathers adorned a crystal vase; gold-threaded Indian drapes clung to the walls; variegated rocks and seashells graced the marble mantelpiece and an undying magenta rose, encased forever in a glass sphere of water, sat on the dining-room table on a black Spanish shawl. This was Daphne's touch—an arts and crafts teacher, she could make a stable look exotic. What struck me most was the absolute hush; no sound broke the crepuscular silence. I was given a small room with a couch, free to come and go as I liked. When my hosts retired I slipped out and headed by taxi for Piccadilly Circus, with the house keys and thirty dollars in my pocket (I left my traveler's checks in the flat). At Piccadilly you could hardly move without tripping over a whore. "'Ow about it, dearie? Give us a kiss!" said one. "She'll give ya the clap, ducky," chirped another. I popped into the nearest pub and ordered a pint of bitters that tasted like warm piss. A youth with bloodshot eyes asked if I was Irish. I shook my head. "Welsh?" "No." "Bloody Scots?" "Sorry. Up the wrong tree." "Yer brogue sounds Cornish." "New York," I grinned. Surprised looks. "Sorry, Yank, meant no 'arm. 'Ow long ya been 'ere?" "Two hours and twenty minutes."

As I ducked out the door a voice at my elbow said, "Pardon me, sir, would you like to see a bit o' night life?" A very pretty boy, about eighteen, with crimson lips and flat black hair fluttered long lashes. "I overheard your conversation in the pub, hope you don't mind." "Let's try another," I said. "I like Yanks, *manly* ones—like you," he said. We entered a small crowded pub and I ordered Guinness stouts. "I'd love it if you came home with me," said Nigel. I hailed a cab and he put his head on my shoulder and his hand on my crotch. When the cab stopped I paid the driver and Nigel fussed with his door key. "Please be very quiet," he said.

We sneaked through the hallway to his room, where I stood reeling in the dark. He shut the door and switched on a lamp. The large room had a fireplace and high molded ceiling. We sat on a couch and he pressed his lips to mine. I went limp. "Pull down your pants," he said, dousing the light. "Turn it on," I said. "Shh," he said, pulling my pants around my ankles. He deep-throated me. I groaned in ecstasy. "Sh," he said. "You don't mind, do you?" "No!" "Sure you don't mind?" *"No!"* Again he began and stopped. "You're sure you—?" *"Noo!"* "Sh!" He went down again.

It was crazy. He kept gasping, "You don't mind?" so I seized his head and held it firmly, but he broke away and gasped, "You don't mind, do you?" There's a limit to good manners. Suddenly a ferocious wall pounding was accompanied by a deep irate voice: "Stop that bloody racket or I'll call the police!" *Racket?* We were *whisp*ering! Nigel was about to stop but I clung and climaxed, wasting no time pulling up my pants. I left him sputtering, "Hope you didn't mind!" and reeled out of there.

The street was deserted. I stood dazed in the spooky fog. Jack the Ripper could be lurking anywhere. Luckily a cab hoved into view. I gave the address and when we arrived reached for my wallet. It was empty. The Dilly boy had ripped me off—most politely. Jack the Ripoff. I brought a traveler's check from my room. "Thank you very much, sir!" the cabbie repeated and I nearly threw up in his face. I had lost about twenty dollars to Nigel—an old trick: the tart delivers as the john is kept in the dark, literally. The shill (a confederate under the bed) skillfully removes the cash. In this case he may also have banged on the wall (*in* the room) threatening to call the police to get me out fast.

My capacity for getting into trouble did not diminish. Next

day I brought back a youth who upset Fraenkel. In order to get to my room I had to pass through the living room. I introduced Kevin, who stared in dismay as Michael droned on about politics. Daphne grasped the situation and called him to the kitchen. "Who is that man?" asked Kevin suspiciously in my room. "A friend," I said. "He's a Communist Jew!" he said with disgust. "He's an anti-Communist Jew," I said. "The woman—she ain't a Jew." "His wife is French-Greek." Trying to crash the stereotype barrier I explained that Michael was a very kind, good person. "He looks like the Devil," muttered Kevin sulkily. "We can't judge goodness by looks," I said. He was sullen and prejudiced but terrific in bed.

"I can't understand homosexuals," said Michael when Kevin had gone. "That boy was a Nazi. Yet you slept with him."

"He was an uneducated working-class boy," I said. "You can't reach him through his mind, only through his feelings."

We were discussing this at dinner. Daphne agreed. "Michael, you can't change people with a lecture."

Michael shook his head. "That boy wanted to kill me. And you slept with him."

I reminded him that straight men and women are attracted to perfectly rotten bastards. Mildred in *Of Human Bondage,* for example. "A destructive, heartless bitch," I said. "If we could control our passions we'd solve everything." Michael stared pensively, pulling at his moustache. "We love Céline the writer and hate Céline the anti-Semite," I said. "He was a Nazi. And what about your pal Henry Miller, who fucked women as if they were pieces of meat? A typical heterosexual attitude."

"That filthy swine!" exploded Daphne. "Miller hates women! Michael did so much for him. Then he slandered Michael."

"Miller's first page in *Tropic of Cancer* is anti-Semitic," I said. "He's callous and stupid about Jews and homosexuals. Yet we love his work. You love Miller, Michael, but he's a thug."

Michael never condemned Miller and I had made my point. Called Boris, on the first page of the book he is described as a rich, ugly Jew. "And I'm as ugly as a Jew," says Miller. Like Ezra Pound, but unlike Céline, in his later years he recanted, abashed at his stupid prejudice.

56

Harold in Italy

I fell in love at first sight with Italy—the languor, beauty, and extroverted friendliness of the Italians won me over completely. I had never seen such fabulous cities as Venice and Florence. One day, while strolling along the Arno in the intense August heat I came upon a breathtaking youth with long silky hair who looked like a medieval Florentine. He was singing "Stormy Weather" in French. His voice was also silky. From a discreet distance I saw him disappear into a bakery and emerge with a bun, which he commenced to eat. I greeted him in French and said he'd been singing a favorite song of mine and he inquired if I lived in Florence. On learning that I was a tourist and writer he said he was studying with the portrait painter Annigoni, who considered him his best pupil. "But you're so young," I said. "I'm nineteen," he said and asked if I wrote in French. "English," I said. *"Ah, êtes-vous anglais, alors?"* *"Non, américain."* Pause. "Well, buster, why the hell cahn't we speak the mother tongue?" he said in a British accent, and we burst out laughing. His name was Donald Cammell; his father, a scholar and friend of Aleister Crowley, had written the first biography of the famed magician.

Donald introduced me to two English painters, both named Peter, whose jaunty air and debonair wit enlivened our visits to the Uffizi Gallery, Pitti Palace, and Medici chapels. When I announced that I was leaving for Rome the following morning the elder of the two Peters, an art professor in his forties, invited me to join them in motoring to Rome. Because they were restricted in the funds they could take out of Britain (which imposed currency restrictions after the war) I had to share the expense of gasoline. I willingly accepted and next day in Peter the Elder's luxurious black Daimler we sped through the Tuscan countryside beneath skies of blue-and-white enamel. The younger Peter, a tall well-knit youth of twenty, had flame-red lips and crinkly curls like the golden fur of a pedigreed airedale. I couldn't keep my eyes off him. He spoke constantly about sex, bursting into boyish giggles, and I confessed to bisexual desires, which aroused his curiosity about the type of men I found attractive. "Twenty-year-old blonds with ruby lips," I said. "You're not going to seduce me, are you?" he giggled. "Oh, I probably shall," I said to a fresh outburst of titters. "I shall fight you off," he said, squirming in the front seat.

When we stopped to relieve ourselves he said halfheartedly, "Promise you won't look." I promised and we jumped into a shallow ditch beside the road where, six feet away, Peter's rigid member jutted straight out, plum-red and pink, his eyes fixed on the ground. At the wheel sat Peter the Elder with averted gaze while young Peter trembled, his penis throbbing beneath the hot blue dome of the Tuscan sky. I couldn't remove my eyes but, unable to crash the inhibition barrier, I made no move. The rest of the trip was spent in sullen silence.

I moved into a room at the rear of a crumbling palazzo on the Via dei Serpenti in the ancient quarter near the Colosseum. Soon I received a breezy note from Donald saying he would be in Rome a few days and could I put him up. We met at the Stazione Termini, took the bus to Canova's *caffè* in the Piazza del Popolo, and Donald spoke of an erudite friend named Edgar he wanted me to meet. This man would introduce me to the *I Ching* and Zen Buddhism; he would also become my first patron and help subsidize my career.

That night Donald glanced suspiciously at the narrow cot. "I'm not queer," he said firmly. "No hanky panky, please!" As I removed my shirt resigned to frustration, he cried admiringly, "God, all that black hair!" "You wanna feel?" I teased. "Christ, no!" "Don't worry," I said wearily, "I won't seduce you." And like a fool I didn't. Next morning I caught him peeping but he quickly shut his eyes—there was, however, a telltale bulge in the sheet. Near the balcony entrance, broom in hand, stood Signora Viola like a toad. Donald's hair lay in silken auburn strands on the pillow, his beardless face, smooth, creamy, rosy and olive, turned toward me in sleep. The old *padrona* left on fat cat feet. Now I'm in trouble, I thought: overnight visitors were forbidden by law. When the landlady vanished, Donald went to the W.C.

and, hurrying after him, I caught a glimpse of an appendage that swept my breath away. He smirked. "Big enough for you? You had your chance, mate!" He laughed and strutted off like a vain rooster! Again I cursed myself for not being aggressive. In spite of their professed aversion to homosexual acts, and though indeed they might be heterosexual, as Donald turned out to be, in general these English boys were eager, at least when young, to satisfy the primal urge with another male, as for generations they've done more or less happily in public schools. But the overtly gay male had to be the aggressor. Admitting the desire was, in my opinion, the basic, if not the *only*, difference between gay and straight. In all other respects we were alike as functioning males.

Later the *padrona* reappeared. *"Eh, signorino,"* she brayed in her foghorn Roman voice, "it's against the law to have a woman spend the night! I could get a big fine. It will cost you one thousand lire." *"Signora,* it wasn't a woman! It was a man. An English friend from Florence." The *padrona* glared. "Don't lie to me, sir. I saw her with my own eyes! A very pretty girl!" "No, *signora,* you'll see. He'll be back later." I could hardly keep a straight face. "He is only nineteen. I can understand your mistake." Her expression turned crafty. In Italy two people in bed, of either sex, means only one thing. "In that case," she said triumphantly, "it will cost you two thousand lire!"

Whenever I visited London, Donald put me up in his Chelsea studio. His first wife, Miss Greece (I forget the year), was a stunning beauty. He became a successful portrait painter but, much later, made a name for himself codirecting, with Nicholas Roeg, the film *Performance*, starring Mick Jagger, and ultimately ended up as a Hollywood director. But that is another story.

"Burton Gray" (name changed) had doleful blue eyes, fair wavy hair, a small blond moustache, a meager rickety frame, and a dry New England voice. His scaly complexion betrayed a lack of vitamins A, B, C, D, and the rest of the alphabet. We lived in the same seedy flat; he was the first person I met in Rome, via a letter of introduction from Lou Harrison. His room also had French windows opening onto a balcony with a W.C. Royal palms and umbrella pines grew in the yards beyond which stretched church domes, rooftops, and towers. Piled on top of an upright piano with worn ivories were neatly arranged heaps of music scores (he was a twelve-tone composer). A few books stood on the marble-topped dresser, torn wallpaper adorned the walls. My room was small and bare, but I paid the same amount of rent.

Burton (who'd lived in Rome five years) warned me to avoid the Piazza Colonna for changing money. Instead of lire you often got a packet of shredded paper. The best black market, he said, was the Vatican. I took the bus and showed my passport at the gate to the Swiss guard, who winked at me. I grinned at the young blond in medieval costume, his blue silk tights revealing an ample crotch. Like a mechanical doll he winked again, no muscle moving. It was like an operatic scene out of a gay Alice in Wonderland.

In the Bank of the Vatican nuns and priests in black bearing large handbags and attaché cases swarmed like bats, their frocks and habits flapping. Standing in line at a teller's window, I watched religious figures open cases overflowing with currency. It was Big Business; Caesar winked at Christ. I had a glimpse of the wheels of religion churning prayers into money—priests with gangster faces, nuns with power-crazed eyes. What a libretto could be made of this!

57

The Count and Miss McCann

Through Burton I was invited to a cocktail party at the Palazzo Orsini to meet Count Giacinto Scelsi, an avant-garde composer, and his American heiress. It was my social debut. The Renaissance palazzo was on the left bank of the Tiber, across the street from the Ponte dei Quattro Capi, which forded the river into Trastevere, which literally means "across the Tiber." A liveried doorman at the gate greeted us and we proceeded to the building through a gravel drive flanked by spacious gardens. I wore my all-purpose drip-dry electric-blue nylon suit, which I'd had since my college graduation; it never failed to galvanize the beholder. It had a metallic sheen that glittered like a coat of mail and had cost twenty dollars on the ready-made rack at Ohrbach's in Union Square; it weighed a few ounces. As I stepped into the sunlit street that afternoon Signora Viola, happening to see me, bellowed in admiration, *"Elegante!"* I cut a *bella figura.*

Burton introduced me to the hostess, Frances McCann, a young woman with fine blond hair ending in a pony tail (then fashionable), guileless cornflower-blue eyes with a searching look, and a resonant contralto voice. A fellow New Yorker who had spent most of her life in Europe, she moved with a tense but lilting grace. She had an abundance of warmth and succeeded in making me feel at home in the palatial salon with the fourteenth-century fireplace and lofty frescoed ceiling. She introduced me to a small gray-haired man, elegantly dressed in a tight gray suit, who seized my hand intensely in both of his, blue eyes blazing. This was the count whom I'd heard so much about from Burton. He was (as Tennessee Williams would say) of high degree and, according to Burton, might have been quite famous but for his aversion to publicity. He was also Burton's protector, having rescued him several times from illness and starvation. He and Miss McCann would in fact save my life on one occasion and, on another, protect me from certain incarceration.

The count introduced me to Elliott Carter and Frank Wigglesworth, two American composers, the latter of whom I'd met several times through Lou Harrison. "We played the radio together in John Cage's 'Imaginary Landscapes' in New York," I said. "It's the only instrument I can play, but I practice a lot." Carter was thin and unsmiling, Wigglesworth stout, pink, and jolly. Burton, who hadn't eaten in weeks, looked pale as pasta and thinner than air. A bloated middle-aged woman with a cane and stiff leg said, "You're not looking any fatter, are you, Burton? How do you keep so slim?" Burton, with a wan smile: "Oh, it's not difficult!" Woman, greedily gobbling canapés: "I wish I could lose weight! You are so fortunate! You must tell me your secret." Burton, between mouthfuls of cold chicken and potatoes: "I starve. You must try it sometime." Woman, guffawing: "Jolly good!" Burton sotto voce: "Silly cow! She can't believe it's true." Matta, the Chilean surrealist painter, told jokes and swiveled his hips. "To them starvation is unreal," muttered Burton. "They've never known it."

Burton shocked Wigglesworth by describing how he once took a job cleaning latrines in New York. "Now, was it *really* necessary to take *that* job?" "Yes, I had to eat." "Oh, there's something not quite realistic in all this!" exclaimed the wealthy composer in exasperation. "He says everyone should be self-sufficient," said Burton, "but you mustn't accept jobs beneath your station. My job is composing, but nobody pays for it."

We quit gorging ourselves when a live quartet played Berg, Schoenberg, and Webern. Their music, as always, moved me deeply. The count and Miss McCann were to become my staunchest friends.

58

When in Rome

From the terrace of the Trinità dei Monti, before an obelisk six hundred years older than Christ, I gazed down on the Spanish Steps in the moonlight. Immediately to the left, at the bottom of the *scala*, was the John Keats house, where he died. Overhead the moon flashed like a silver dollar—below, the warm glow of street lamps shed a soft amber light. On the steps of the Piazza di Spagna prowled hunters seeking sex, food, shelter, money. There I found the most beautiful young companions I could desire. Though living precariously I never encountered violence and was happier than I'd ever been in my life. I was in love with Rome. Unlike poor Keats, whose luck ran out, I believed mine would hold—and for twelve years it did. I stayed in Rome six of those years.

The language presented no problem. I had studied French, Latin, and Spanish, had read opera libretti, and had a good ear. As I learned to speak the voluptuous Italian tongue, a constant sensual feast, English began to sound thin and flat. Donald loved to repeat the only word he knew, *grazie,* which rolled off his tongue like Mozart. No matter what was said to him he responded *grazie.* "It gives me deep aesthetic satisfaction," he explained, "just to say the word." *Grazie* never sounded more delightful than when Donald uttered it in his resounding baritone.

Speaking Italian was like eating pasta—the language smacked of garlic, salami, meat sauce, and parmigiana. It was smooth as the olive skin of youth. It made me feel good. Passing a *salumeria* in the Monti, the ancient quarter where I lived, I almost swooned when the dense odors of cheese, bologna, and mortadella, suspended in hempen nets outside a shop, gripped my olfactory nerves. Italian was not so much an extension of the mind as of the body—and, of course, for body language the Italians were unrivaled. In a rich vocabulary of gestures they spoke a lingua franca, the language of the senses.

During those first days, wandering alone in the streets drunk on sights and smells, savoring every crooked, decaying doorway like old wine, lingering over some festering metal grille on a window, or awestruck by an archaic facade, I would turn a corner and feel my scalp tingle. I recognized not only the street but the houses. It happened with astonishing frequency, this feeling of familiarity, as if I had entered a haunting portico in a canvas by di Chirico, experiencing nostalgia and outer-space reality. It was what the surrealist painters caught, the world between the familiar and the dream. On many an afternoon, seated on the lower steps of the Piazza di Spagna before the flower vender's stall, I would see di Chirico himself, large, portly, white-haired, and elderly, stroll before me, majestic, unapproachable, rapt in thought.

I soon discovered that Burton Gray was a wino who drank nightly in the wineshops of the old quarter and composed at his rented piano by day. Based on Schoenberg's twelve-tone scale, his music had a poignant plaintiveness unlike Berg's or Webern's, although the latter was an influential model. Gray's originality stemmed from the influence of American torch songs of the 1920s and 1930s as much as from the German dodecaphonic school. In a reedy, world-weary voice, he sang sentimental songs like "Just Plain Bill," "Someone to Watch Over Me," "As Time Goes By," and so on.

One day I knocked at his door and found him seated stiffly at the piano, eyes glazed and unfocused, fingers slipping on the keys. "Are you all right?" I asked. "Oh, yes! Just a bit vague in the head." Subsisting on a few persimmons a day (costing pennies) and a plate of spaghetti on the cuff at Benedetto's, he hadn't had a meal in three weeks. Ordinarily thin as a stick, he now looked cadaverous. He started to play "Someone to Watch Over Me," crooning in a cracked, wavering voice.

"Excuse me, I'm very stupid today," he said dully. The melodrama was not without irony: this gaunt, moustached man in his forties was also playing Camille and Mimi (*La Bohême*)— the "queer" identified with the fallen woman. "I'm too weak to go out and pick up cigarette butts on the Via Nazionale." (Also playing: the little tramp in *City Lights,* outcast martyr to art.) While receiving monthly checks from his benefactors (an ex-lover in New York or an occasional dollar from his father, an illiterate dirt farmer in Vermont) he could maintain his fantasy, but when they ceased to arrive he faced certain disaster. Highbrow music and poetry had no redeeming commercial significance.

> I began to write at the age of six, with the death of my mother. I am still writing her death, my life. I was alone in the room with her body, a small room in the *campagna,* with only a tiny oil lamp which reflected a tiny light. The walls were black. There was no food. She starved to death. Outside was the brown earth and, beyond, the open sea. The door banged in the wind that came from the sea. I looked down and saw, on the dirt floor, two notebooks, open and blank. Oh! What's this? It is a signal, an omen. It is a command to write. It is my diary. I was only six but I have been filling those notebooks ever since.
>
> I cannot fill them up. It is an obsession. When I get to the last page I begin to read what I have written, only to find the pages blank. The two notebooks are always lying open on the floor, empty, beside the body of my mother.

Mario, Burton's boyfriend, had said this and I wrote it down in my journal. Born and raised under Mussolini's regime, which was five years old at his birth, Mario was a peasant with a gift for storytelling. He was educated, fed, given a job during the war, and at eighteen, when the war ended, found himself in rags on the streets of Rome. At twenty-six (he had taken up with Gray two years earlier) he was still penniless. He recalled the Fascist era with nostalgia as the only time he was free from hunger and humiliation. A Fascist demonstration, Mario told me, would be held in front of the American embassy on the Via Veneto Tuesday morning. It was late October 1953. I had been there about five weeks. The occasion was the attempt by Marshal Tito of Yugoslavia to annex Trieste, which, administered by the United Nations from 1947, was to be divided between Italy and Yugoslavia in 1954, only two months away. Backed by the Soviet Union, Tito sent troops to the Italian border. All Italy was in an uproar. Mario and his friend Sergio, a pink-faced blue-eyed redhead, were galvanized out of their demoralized existence. At last they had something on which to vent their frustration. Sergio was a Triestino; his soles were torn and his threadbare jacket (like those of most of the youth in Italy) was full of holes. "Trieste is mine!" he yelled savagely. "I want it back! It belongs to me!"

I wanted to see black shirts, jackboots, and pompous strutting little duces thrusting out stiff arms in phallic salutes of male power. I didn't want to miss the eroticism of overheated Italian youths aroused by political passions I detested.

That evening from my balcony, where I stood looking up at the clear October sky after a sudden downpour of rain, I listened to Burton playing his beautiful piece "Roman Landscapes" in his room a few doors away. In a style identifiably his—a long, flowing, lyrical line in secundal counterpoint—the exquisite tonalities poured into the dirty backyards and alleys of the slum palazzos. If he survived, I thought, Gray would succeed in spite of himself.

Next evening a friend of his named George returned to Rome from a week in Ischia. A professional photographer who contributed to leading photo magazines, he stayed at the luxurious Excelsior on an expense account. A large, soft, lumbering blond in his forties, he traveled around the world on assignments. He took us to dinner at Benedetto's and when we returned to Burton's room everyone collapsed in a stupor on the bed or chairs, surfeited with countless liters of red wine and a heavy meal of spaghetti with meat sauce, baked veal, salad, bread and butter, fruit, cheese, and espresso. Sergio glanced enviously at George's expensive sports outfit and started shouting, "Trieste is mine! I want it, all of it!" "Will it take care of overpopulation and poverty?" asked Burton. "*No!* But why should Tito have it?" "Oh, shut up," yawned George lazily. "Who cares about Trieste, anyway? I'm *stanco*, or stinko, I don't know which." "What does he say?" inquired Sergio hotly. "He says he's tired," said Gray, "and we can't solve political problems." "My aunts and uncles live there! Are they Yugoslavs, eh?" George rolled wearily on his side. "Sergio, I elect you premier of Italy," he said impishly, "but only if you promise to shut up for an hour and let me snooze." "He's against war and noisy politicians," interpreted Burton diplomatically. "Me, too!" screamed Sergio. "I want peace! But Tito's troops are at the border! Should we wait until they march into Italy? Receive them with open arms?" He flung out his arms, then fell to the floor, dead. Then he savagely stabbed and shot everyone in the room, with grunts and screams. His red hair flamed in the fluorescent light. "You want to go and fight?" I asked. "Yes!" yelled Sergio in English. "*Boom!* Dead! Fineesh!" He fell on the bed beside George. "Well, that takes care of that," muttered George with mock relief. "I'm glad the war's over. I'm sleepy." Burton looked at him quizzically. "These boys are really against war," he said. "They have nothing, they sit in the park all day. But the party offers them an ideal, gives them a sense of national pride. I've argued a thousand times," he drawled wearily.

Sergio nodded in George's direction. "He no like," he said in English. "No, I no like," mimicked George. "Well, why you no give me Trieste, eh! You Americans—you take everyt'ing from us." "Oh, for Chrissake!" said George, sitting up, "take Trieste. I don't want it anymore. I'm tired of the damned town. I'll take Capree. *Vah bay-nay*, Sergio? I'm giving you Trieste for Thanksgiving." "Tanks!" said Sergio sarcastically. "You vairy—eh—*generoso*." His lip curled.

George got up and announced he was leaving. Sergio cast a quizzical glance at him and, when George left, looked even more disgusted, demanding to know why George hadn't helped him, why he was so stingy this time. Last time, ah, that was *bello*! Now he didn't even take him back to a hotel with him. Americans!

59

Fascismo!

At 8:00 A.M. Mario knocked at my door. "Via Veneto at nine," he whispered conspiratorially and disappeared. Groggily, I dressed and shaved, went down to Bosso's for my usual breakfast of *caffè latte* and two jelly doughnuts—*bombe*, as they are called from their shape, big round bombs of dough—and was greeted cheerily by the young Sicilian bartender with his morning-of-the-world smile. *"Buon' giorno, signore.* Cuffee meelk?" "*Sì, per favore,*" I answered. "You like Lana Turner?" he asked. "Beaudeefool." He shaped big bosoms in the air.

On the sports page of the morning paper my eye fell on a photo of the landlady's son holding up a brace of fifty birds. The caption read: "Tonino Moreno, nicknamed 'Poison,' returned from Sardinia with 50 partridges." The item went on about the disappearance of his dog, Viena, which saddened the happy occasion. His deep grief was expressed in his statement: "She cost me 25,000 lire." At this point his mother waddled into the *caffè*.

I (holding up the photo of her son): "The great hunter."

She (booming): "*Sì,* mostly of girls."

As I walked along the Via del Tritone to the Piazza Barberini in the warm October sunshine I admired the faded facades of the palazzos that, although no more than two or three stories high, spread spaciously over a whole block, glowing with luscious shades of burnt umber, cinnabar, lemon, smoky rose, Pompeii red. It was before nine, but the senseless, slapdash Roman traffic was heavy. Autos and filobuses zigzagged wildly like charging hippos through the squares, while the small baaing vespas and lambrettas, like maddened rams, butted in and out of traffic singly or in herds, leaving spurts of sickening exhaust. I made it safely to the Via Veneto, with its luxury hotels and massive, imposing embassies, of which the American was the most impressive.

Truckloads of *carabinieri* (paramilitary police), carbines slung ominously across the shoulders of gray uniforms, slowly cruised the streets. On foot they patrolled in groups, swaggering and scanning the faces of slightly bewildered civilians who hurried on. I gazed at the palm-lined drives and wrought-iron gates of the American embassy, wondering what to expect. As I paused in a little piazza to extract from my pocket an improvised map I had hastily scrawled, not yet sure of my directions, two middle-aged civilians, one short and fat with no neck and a bristling gray moustache, the other tall, bald, suave, and smooth-shaven, pounced on me. No Neck, peering over my shoulder at the map: *"Chi è?"* Who are you? *"Chi è?"* I repeated wonderingly. He flew into a rage. *"Chi è? Chi è?"* he barked like a terrier. In my most American accent for such occasions I drawled, *"Non so."* I don't know. He began to foam at the mouth. "English or American?" inquired the other coolly. "American." "What you are doing here?" "In Rome?" "No, *here*—" he said with a sweep of his hand. I said I was a tourist. He translated this to his companion, who ranted, the gist of which was, "Tell him to get the hell out of here!" Suave One lit another cigarette. "We are the police and better you go away now." I wore my dumb expression. "Why?" "There is danger of manifestation. It must not to be safe for Americans."

With aloof unconcern I sauntered to a sidewalk *caffè*, where I chose a conspicuous table from which I could observe the scene over a cappuccino. For an hour heavily manned trucks appeared but nothing happened. Bored, I left for Piazza Colonna, where I found stormy groups gesticulating and shouting good-humored insults. Suddenly I heard chanting, the crowds surged forward toward the square, and about three hundred students with placards, laughing and smiling, marched toward the Via del Tritone. Police whistles blew shrilly and traffic halted for the students, mostly children ranging in age from thirteen to eighteen, with school books under their arms. A few hotheads called to bystanders to join them but were met with tolerant grins. Crudely lettered placards read: DEATH TO TITO! WE WANT TRIESTE! ITALY FOR ITALIANS! WE ARE NOT AFRAID OF TITO! These messages were scrawled in chalk on buildings along the way: PIG TITO! TURD TITO! Everywhere could be seen the w sign for VIVA! and its reverse, M: MORTE TITO! Death to Tito.

In the van of the procession rolled a truck filled with *carabinieri* looking bored and a trifle sheepish. The students ran about hastily scrawling in chalk m's and w's on automobiles that waited for them to pass. From one of these in the middle of the street a woman jerkily protruded head and shoulders from an open vent in the roof, wriggling through with quick, angry movements, like some irate Judy popping out of her box. In a shrill, strident voice she began assailing the student who had marked her car, waving her arms wildly. This was met by a chorus of boos at which, incensed, she turned her head in every direction, chopping the air with her hands like a puppet and yelling, "Down with fascism!" "Boo! boo!" chanted hundreds of students. "Dirty Communist! Down with Tito!" A policeman rushed forward and muttered something to the driver, who had been quietly sitting at the wheel. He must have panicked, for he started the car abruptly, causing the young woman to jerk backward and almost fall out. The entire street roared with laughter and the procession, which had lost its form, proceeded to regroup good-humoredly and march toward the embassy. I was about to follow when I spotted Mario, who appeared to be in the midst of an argument. A student was yelling at him, "Fascist warmonger!" Mario: "You want peace under Malenkov? Will you get it without war?" Student: "Yes! The workers want peace!" Mario: "So do I. I'm a worker." Student: "You're a lying Fascist!" Mario: "And you're a lying Communist!" "Down with the Fascists!" screamed the student, shoving his face into Mario's and raising clenched fists above his head. Mario tried pushing him away, but the student, believing Mario was about to attack him, hysterically seized his jacket and Mario hit him in the mouth; bleeding, the student screamed and let go. A front tooth rolled along the sidewalk. "Fascist swine!" he screamed and fled. Mario laughed bitterly. "We'd better get out of here, Aroldo," he said. I shook my head sadly: two sides of a coin, equally duped.

For three years I lived in the Monti, Rome's oldest and largest region, created by the popes and stretching back even further to imperial Rome. There, near the Colosseum and the Forum, once lived Horace, Virgil, and Ovid and the emperors and empresses themselves. Only a short walk from my room, I visited the Colosseum nightly, not exactly in the pursuit of history. Among the shadows in the honeycombed porticos of crumbled antique masonry lurked others whose interest was not historical. The Colosseum presented endless opportunities for intercultural relations.

The first week I met a young Egyptian student whose surname was Delila. When we returned to my room, on seeing my hairy chest and shoulders, he exclaimed rapturously, "Delila has found her Samson!" Although a delightful youth with immense black eyes and brows, no more than eighteen and hot as a firecracker, he wanted to see Israel pushed into the sea. If I'd had to choose bed partners on the basis of political and religious leanings, celibacy would have been the only course, but a few nights of harangues about "the Zionist plot to colonize the Middle East" dulled Delila's charms. I did not wish to wake up one morning to find my body hair, if not my throat, cut. I could see the headline: SAMSON PICKS UP DELILA, GETS CUT. As the founder of Christianity taught—and I took him literally for he ought to know what he was talking about—I wanted to embrace equally Arab, Christian, and Jew. If in the name of one God they killed one another, they were all stark mad and deserved the leaders they got. I always believed the best idea was to get rid of the leaders instead of each other, and then to compromise on keeping the peace by electing pacifist, populist libertarians whose records on human rights and constitutional democracy are unblemished. But, then, what do I know? I'm only a poet.

When I told Delila that I was part Jewish, he began to yell, "I've been screwed by the enemy!"

"Well, didn't it feel good?" I said. "If we all got together like that we'd end all hostilities." I never saw him again.

60

Roman Wolf at the Door

Unable to stand the cold at Signora Viola's, in November I moved to a *pensione* near the Via del Tritone that advertised steam heat. It was managed by a chambermaid employed by a kind and beautiful absentee landlady who resembled Norma Shearer. Every night one of the tenants, a man with thick black-and-gray curly hair and a blue jaw—a hirsute Italian satyr from an ancient fresco—brought a different woman to his room. The most heartrending sobs, moans, and whimpers issued from his room opposite mine, as if Bluebeard were torturing his victims before doing away with them. But next morning the women, judging from their radiant faces, looked hale and hearty. He, on the other hand, didn't look too good—he seemed tired and sullen, never exchanging a greeting or even a nod. He was one of those lady-killers who ignore other men, convinced of his mission to repopulate the planet by himself.

The chambermaid, a red-faced peasant from the Abruzzi mountains, a region known for its boorish, blunt inhabitants, was short and dumpy and would burst into my room at all hours to clean or demand the rent. Although I was paying for steam heat, there was none. When I complained she replied rudely, "There *is* heat, it's warm." She was pocketing the fuel money. Before Christmas I warned that I'd speak to the landlady. Seizing my hand roughly, she pressed it to the cold metal. "See!" she cried triumphantly. "It's hot. You just don't understand Italian." I understood her, though. She was a fraud, a liar, and a cheat. She insolently splashed my face with cold water and stomped out.

On New Year's Eve I wandered the streets dodging chairs, empty bottles, shoes, broken mirrors—all sorts of junk hurled from the windows—an ancient Roman custom. Littered with debris, the city looked as if it had been bombed. In a *caffè* I picked up a blond body builder, half French, half Italian, who was bilingual and bisexual. We spoke French, in which I was more fluent than Italian. Over six foot three, handsome in the heroic mold, Hugo seemed so civilized that I invited him to the room (there was no surveillance at night, which was why we all put up with the place). The statuesque giant unveiled a body like the Farnese Hercules—smooth, muscular, massive, flawless. The year 1954 was ushered in with a flame that finally heated the icy cubicle.

After observing the venereal rites of Priapus we dozed off. When I awoke, Hugo was fully dressed, standing by the cot, looking down at me. "How much have you got?" he said flatly. "Two thousand lire," I said. He stuck out his enormous hand. I put a thousand into it, but he rubbed his forefinger and thumb impatiently and grabbed the rest. "Where do you keep it?" he

demanded, none too delicately. "The dough!" The classic statue
had turned into the classic hustler.

When I made no response he calmly opened the chest of
drawers and rummaged about until he got to the bottom drawer,
where he found my stash under the dirty laundry. It was all I
had—my last thirty thousand lire (about forty-eight dollars). As
he pocketed the hoard I rose, but he towered over me and
gnashed his teeth, his grinding jaws making a hideous bony
sound. I fell back terrified as he swaggered out.

The room now seemed colder than ever. Shivering under
the thin blanket, I began to feel hungry. It was 3:00 A.M. I was
broke. An icy terror gripped my gut. I curled into the fetal position and lost consciousness. I seemed to be hurtling at the speed
of light through a long black tunnel, with only minutes to live.
This was the lonely void I had known from childhood, not dis-
similar from going under ether at the age of eleven when my
tonsils were removed. It was the nonbeing I feared, the darkness
at the end of the world. But, no, the end of the tunnel was in
sight, a pinpoint of light that grew larger and larger. I gasped. It
was the electric light bulb overhead. My gut was churning, my
chest heaving.

At about noon as I went to the W.C. I passed Bluebeard in
the hall. He looked terrible. He had black bags under his eyes;
his wiry goat hair stood on end. I figured he'd had a hard night,
too. As usual, he took no more notice of me than of the walls. I
found him repulsive, to tell the truth. He smelled awful. In his
flannel pajamas and backless slippers he looked like an inmate of
a mental hospital, a manic-depressive shuffling down the hall in
brooding self-absorption. What did they see in him?

The only person I got to know at the *pensione* was a young
English Jew called Tom Maschler. Tall, dark, and striking, with a
mane of straight black hair and keen, aware eyes, he was interested in film making. My firsthand accounts of Dylan Thomas,
Auden, and Isherwood impressed him immensely. I said I was
broke and he treated me to jelly doughnuts and coffee. He
taught English privately and had more students than he could
handle. Assuring me that there was plenty of money to be made,
he offered me one or two of them. Furthermore, he said, they
paid a thousand lire apiece. An immensely cheerful and enthusiastic nineteen, he was a welcome relief after the melancholy Burton, infecting me with some of his optimism. I revealed nothing
of my personal life to him.

He was born in Germany, where his father, a wealthy banker, escaped the Nazis with his wife and child and, arriving in England penniless, hired himself out with his wife as household servants to a titled English family. Not only did they survive, but his father amassed another fortune in publishing. Tom had a first-class education and upbringing.

Well, I did get one or two students from Tom, but they didn't last. Something else happened that helped me survive. Meanwhile, Tom gave up dabbling in film making, returned to London, and a few years later emerged in his early twenties as the wunderkind of British publishing, the charismatic editor at Jonathan Cape Ltd. In interviews with leading magazines, he attributed his interest in publishing to his meeting with me in Rome. As the first published writer he had met (while starving I had given him an inscribed copy of my book *The Undersea Mountain*), I had unknowingly steered him into the literary world, firing his imagination with anecdotes about literary celebrities. On meeting again years later in London he confirmed this. Thus, while down and out in Rome, through a chance encounter I was responsible for someone else's hugely successful career. It seems that many times in my life I have been the bearer of fame and fortune to others by some word or instruction that I have passed on. But I haven't always been that lucky myself.

61

Karma Circuit

Looking back in wonder, I suppose the weird cast of characters did not begin at Cinecittà, the Hollywood of Rome. I had acquired a freak collection as impressive as Fellini's and witnessed scenes he hadn't thought of yet. For example, the intellectual Protestant from Urbino: emaciated, bony as an El Greco saint. He earned a precarious existence as an unlicensed guide at the Forum, always in fear of arrest. One night he led me to his "home," as he sardonically called it: a mud-soaked cave beneath the Palatine Hill. By the light of a flickering candle he introduced me to a boy of fourteen in rags, more beautiful than a Donatello, who'd been asleep in the catacomb. The cadaverous Enrico, coughing out his guts, acted as father to the homeless boy. Because he belonged to the tiny Protestant minority in Italy, Enrico was denied jobs for which he was qualified, such as university professor or licensed guide. His doctorate was less useful than toilet paper; at twenty-nine he was dying of ill health and hunger. He had lived in the cave for seven months. The boy was a runaway from an unemployed alcoholic father (another anomaly in Italy) who beat his wife and children. When I think of that freezing cave with its dripping walls, mud floors, and coffinlike stone niches where the two martyrs slept, I am reminded that in these same catacombs lived Christians who were persecuted by pagan emperors. Since then so-called Christians have persecuted each other and everyone else.

On New Year's Day I borrowed bus fare and rode to Cinecittà. Burton had said there were jobs dubbing "spaghetti westerns," just beginning to be produced for the English-speaking market. The pay was twenty-five dollars for a four-hour stint, fifty dollars for two a day, an unheard of sum. Outside the casting office as I sat waiting in a large bare room with about five or six other Americans, I noticed a white-haired man with protruding black eyes staring boldly at me. He was dressed like a burlesque comedian: a yellow beret pulled back over a high forehead, a flashy purple tie, loud green shirt, and shocking pink slacks. Instead of a knot, his tie was looped like a lolling tongue. He wore gilt sandals over white woolen socks.

I was hired and told I'd be notified in a few days. As I was leaving, the Disney cartoon character stopped me. "Aren't you Harold Norse?" he asked, grinning. "I'm Frank Muldoon."

He had aged beyond recognition. I'd known him in my twenties when he was in his forties. We hung out at a midtown bookstore in Manhattan clerked by an Egyptian-American who later became a sly "Oriental" TV-movie villain. Muldoon (name changed) had made a pass at me, which I rebuffed. Shy and soft-spoken then, he was the author of a play adapted for the movies in the thirties, which gave him a lifetime income. During the Depression he had lived in the Mediterranean; he had recently returned from India, which was even cheaper. He supplemented his income with small acting jobs.

We rode the bus back and ate in a cheap restaurant called Greco's, frequented by students and bohemians. Like his clothes, Frank was loud and flamboyant, greeting strangers and breaking into song, out of tune. It was my first square meal in days; between mouthfuls I told him of the New Year's Eve experience.

"Aha!" he cried, eyes protruding like Bugs Bunny, whom he resembled. "You had a dark-night-of-the-soul experience. Our meeting was karmically ordained." He stretched out his hands and chirped, "I'm a yogi! That's why we met. You see, you passed the audition! That's a sign it's working. I can help you."

It was a sign they needed dubbers. A gilt-sandaled Hollywood merchant of dreams and kitsch? But I was grateful for the meal and the wine had gone to my head. "I'm glad I bumped into you again," I said, wiping the spaghetti sauce from my tie. Everyone had *sugo* stains. At Greco's I knew a young Italian doctor named Arturo Vivante whose shirt and ties looked like a butcher's apron (his short stories later appeared in the *New Yorker*). "But I can't see the connection between our meeting and my experience."

He sighed. "Still the same old cynical Marxist, eh?"

"No, Frank, neither a commissar nor a yogi," I said.

"Look, only an hour ago you were broke, now you'll be making fifty bucks a day. You think it's just chance?"

I began to wonder. "I don't know, Frank. I want answers."

His face brightened. "That's better. You're still young— golly, you look great!" he cried admiringly. He told me of a Hollywood party he'd crashed with movie stars and producers. When he began to spout Vedanta philosophy they all laughed at him. He felt sorry for them. "I've come to bring you the light!" he said. "The eternal message!" He'd expected them to lap up his wisdom as they lapped up the booze. The producer who threw the party put down his glass. "Listen, you two-bit religious freak," he snarled, "take your goddamn eternal message out of here before I kick your ass through the door!" Frank told the story to illustrate what a great opportunity they had missed.

In a small but well-kept hotel off the Via Veneto, his cozy little room overlooked a garden of palms, shrubs, and oleanders. As I lit a Nazionali he said severely, "No smoking! It pollutes the soul." He was an ex–chain smoker. He removed his beret and put a book in my hands, by Paul Brunton, about atonement. At-one-ment. Being at one with one's Self. Self (not ego) is beyond duality; ego exists in a state of conflict.

"Suspend criticism," said Frank, "until you've read it." The only metaphysical book I had read was *Varieties of Religious Experience* by William James. Muldoon said, "I meditate every day. If I miss one day I feel dirty, like missing a bath. I'll give you one now." A bath or a meditation? He removed his shirt and had me do the same. "Also your shoes, socks, and pants," he ordered. Remembering his pass at me in New York, I stood uneasily in my Jockey shorts as he spread an Indian colored cloth on the carpet.

"Sit in the lotus position, like this," he said staring at my legs. I did it without difficulty. "You were a yogi in a former life," he commented. (I was a former dancer in this one.) "Now, close your eyes. Concentrate above the bridge of the nose. That is the third eye. Let all thoughts come and go, come and go, not clinging to them." His voice was low and dreamy. "Press your thumb on the right nostril, exhale forcefully, then inhale, press your forefinger on the left nostril and exhale . . . now chant the sacred syllable . . . OOOOOOMMMMM."

We chanted until my head echoed like a seashell. "Now we will bring the kundalini force up from the sex chakra to the third eye . . . the serpent fire will rise and open the head chakra." I saw a circle of light, very tiny, begin to widen, like the light I had seen New Year's Eve. It grew large and blazed like the sun. I felt a sense of well-being. At-one-ment. A warm, tingling sensation in my sex chakra—was it rising?—felt blissful. Slowly opening one eye I saw Frank's gray head gently bobbing up and down on my chakra, which indeed had risen, but not to the third eye. . . .

Two days later I sat watching an Apache chief on a horse and a brave holding the bridle. They had rifles on their shoulders, feathers on their heads, and spoke Italian. It was not Texas but Sicily. *"Allora, andiamo,"* said the chief. *"Ugh, uh keh, capo,"* grunted the brave. "So let's vamoose," said the American seated beside me. "Ugh, okay, chief," I replied. Cut. That was my line for the day. Twenty-five bucks. But as luck would have it, my dubbing career was over. I made twenty-five dollars and was out on my duff. Now, as anyone can see, with a line like this you didn't have to be Laurence Olivier. You couldn't flub if you tried, though I recall that we had to take it twice; I hadn't lip-synced precisely the first time. Your lines had to synchronize with the screen. But the dubbers decided to strike for higher wages, though it was the highest I'd ever earned. It seemed an unspeakably cruel trick of fate. So much for Muldoon's occult crap, I thought.

At this point, however, he came to the rescue with one of his more bizarre suggestions. He owed me one since he had raped me in the middle of a mantra. Although he regarded me as a sex object, he had convinced himself that he had transcended desire (except for the boys in Rome, Taormina, Capri, Ceylon, India, etc.). "I can take it or leave it alone," he said. He gave me the number of a rich Italian lady married to an oil magnate who neglected her.

"She wants English lessons and pays well," said Muldoon.

62

Madame Palladino

She was about fifty, five foot ten with an eight-inch beehive hairdo. Like everything about her, it was black and white. "I want lessons three times a week," she said in English. "I pay fifteen hundred lire an hour. Is that satisfactory?"

I beamed. "Very," I said. She had spoken English while living in London, she said, but needed practice. We began at once. She plied me with tea and pastries and paid three thousand lire for an hour and a half. I could earn enough to leave the *pensione*.

I soon discovered it was not English but companionship she paid for. She had an active social life on the astral plane but was quite lonely on this one. On my arrival at three in the afternoon tea and pastries were served while she regaled me with her latest adventures. The following faithfully represents a day in the life of Mme. Palladino (not her real name) and her wars of good versus evil, virtue versus sin, Christ versus the Devil—a world of religious fiction that made science fiction seem like, well, fiction.

Mme. Pietra Palladino struggles against an astral attack. Invisible enemies, a tribe of magicians somewhere in darkest Africa, have tied her to a stake with a rope around her neck. (She says she almost died in bed this morning, before dawn, of strangulation.) With great gusto she reenacts her martyrdom, writhing and foaming at the mouth as cannibals chant and dance in a circle around her—war paint, feathers, necklaces of shrunken heads—in full regalia, awesome genitals flapping. Mme. Palladino begins to shrink, her face a blur of pain. She gasps, clutches her throat, and sinks to the floor, one bejeweled hand outstretched, frantically clawing the hand-knotted floral-animal silk-base ivory Isfahan carpet. Writhing like a holy roller, she shrieks, "Save me! I'm—ack—ugh—*dying*. . . ." Hardly knowing what to make of all this, I watch her performance helplessly.

Chufo, her repulsive Pekinese lapdog, gets in the act. He is more than a match for man, beast, or devil. Like a female impersonator in a fit of hysterics, he begins yapping in a shrill asthmatic falsetto. Mme. Palladino instantly recovers.

"Oh, my adorable little Chufo, you have saved me!" she croons sickeningly, kissing the scrofulous cur and tottering to her feet. "He was an adept in a former life," she explains. "He reincarnated as a dog just to be near me. He has the soul of a sage and the heart of a tiger." She lights up and takes a deep drag of her gold-tipped Abdullah as the ugly mutt yipes and jumps for joy.

"By barking at the right moment this morning he severed the black magic cord that nearly killed me," she says informatively. "I have many enemies on the astral, you know." She blinks rapidly through a cumulus of smoke, gazing over my head as if she has spotted one of them there. She makes the sign of the cross and describes two wide arcs that join in an ellipse around her body, her metal arm bracelets jangling like chimes. She explains that she must always surround herself with a halo of white light. "It's the *only* protection," she intones, "against black magic."

Unable to see the halo, scry as I might, I can't help wondering if her circle of white light is so effective why is she in constant danger? I don't bother to ask. The secrets of the arcane remain closed to the uninitiated. She tinkles a silver handbell and an ancient moustachioed crone approaches on little flat feet.

"A pot of oolong tea," Madame orders without glancing at her. The hairy old woman dematerializes in a puff of Madame's Abdullah. I keep trying to avoid the dog's bulging eyes, which regard me with damp hostility. Madame dabs at her platinum-streaked Bible-black hair upswept in a lofty pompadour à la Nefertiti. Imperious and leonine, she does in truth bear a striking resemblance to the Egyptian mummy.

"When I was born my mother recognized me at once," she says chattily as if the astral cliff-hanger had never occurred. "I came right back, you see. Wasted no time. She recognized me by the shoulders . . . same every time . . . same shoulders. I was a boy before but haven't changed much. 'Don't worry, Mama,' I told her, 'I'll be right back. Just keep praying.' I had caught the mumps and passed on at the age of forty." I stare at her. "I'll be right back, Ma." As simple as that. Like going to the movies for a couple of hours. Is that all there was to reincarnation?

She puffs thoughtfully at her lipstick-smeared Abdullah—a chain smoker like all psychic ladies—and seems to be remembering something with nostalgia. "I was back in nine months. You see, my only child—a daughter—gave birth to me." My jaw drops. "So your daughter . . . is now . . . your *mother*!" *Should* this woman be running around loose? "Uh, Madame, your daughter—I mean, your mother—well, did she recognize you?"

"Of course! We always do!" Madame is indignant. "We have been reincarnating for thousands of years. It's about time, don't you think, that we recognized each other?" She lights another cigarette on the old one, which she snuffs in an overflowing ashtray of solid platinum. "I was my mother's mother many times . . . and my daughter's daughter. I was my son's son and her . . ."

I'm left far behind. The dog eyes my leg with deep interest. I'm hoping he doesn't possess telepathic powers. If he can read my mind I'm done for. "Why do you think they baptized me Pietra?" demands Madame rhetorically. I shake my head stupidly as she fixes me with an inquisitorial stare. "I'll tell you why. Because they knew I was my brother Pietro, that's why."

Under the withering blast of her intimidating scorn I nod in hasty agreement. This woman hops in and out of bodies like a yo-yo. It runs in the family. They have a gene for this kind of thing. They probably hand down the gilt-edged broomstick. I flash what I hope comes across as an ingratiating grin. But the mutt doesn't buy it. He eyes me cynically. "I can remember all my incarnations," says Madame matter-of-factly, in the same tone one uses for a shopping list. She ticks them off. "In the nineteenth century I was an English duke, cousin to Queen Victoria . . . charming lady, I knew her well. Before that I was Count Bernadotte, Napoleon's great general. I was Joan of Arc, Catherine de Medici, Lucrezia Borgia, Richard the Lion-Hearted. My dog, Chufo, was always by my side—not as a dog but as my counselor and chief of my guards. Once I made him a count. In another life a duke. In ancient Rome I was the empress Livia, wife of Augustus, and as you know, well versed in the magic arts. In Greece I was Hippocrates, the healer. In Egypt, Nefertiti . . . but you can see for yourself . . . same shoulders, eh?" Any fool could see that. The weird old servant tiptoes in with a monogrammed silver tea service, which she places carefully on the glass-topped coffee table, then noiselessly vanishes, twirling her snowy moustache. Madame pours tea and tosses a biscuit to the duke, who snatches it in midair with a nasty click of his teeth.

"You must think me a trifle odd," observes the lady with an expression that bodes no good if I come up with the wrong answer. Remembering that she'd once been Lucrezia Borgia, I regard my teacup with respect. "Oh, no, Madame, not at all!"

"What I have told you must seem very bizarre. But I assure you, *Signore,* every word is true!"

"I never doubted it!" I reply hastily. The duke waddles closer to my left leg, belching slightly and licking his chops. "I've read about such things, but you're the first person I've met who has experienced them. I am honored that you confide in me."

"Ah, what a pleasant young man!" beams Madame, her gray agate eyes glistening with warmth. "Most *simpático! Très gentil!*" She zaps me with the full force of her radiance. I have to admit that she is a very handsome lady, if a bit mature, with considerable animal magnetism, which she knows how to turn on when necessary.

"Yes, yes, Mr. Muldoon told me you have had psychic experiences. He says you were a yogi in a former life. Ah, he is very spiritual, Mr. Muldoon. A bit flashy, however, no? What you Americans call 'Hollywood.' But a kindred spirit."

I grin knowingly, wondering what that fool Muldoon has told her. I gnaw at dry Italian pastry that tastes like chalk.

"Please, eat them all," says Madame. "At my age I must watch my figure."

It is a figure men also watch—remarkably well preserved, she is tall and supple as a gymnast. She sighs, sipping her tea between heftier sips of her gold-tipped king-sized Abdullah protruding from her wrought-ivory Chinese holder like a sixth finger. She is never without it. I have an uncanny feeling that we are back in the early 1920s, that time, in some extraordinary warp, has stopped around then. Perhaps it is the way she wields her holder, like a silent-film vampire; perhaps it's the corny elegance of the all-white room and telephone. Her black satin gown looped with pink pearls is straight out of *The Vamp*. Black satin in the afternoon? Perhaps Madame has for too long been submerged in the ectoplasmic swamps of the spirit world to maintain her link with this one. Her home and her life seem entirely unreal . . . and lonely, terribly lonely. Why else would she hire me to teach her English? She already speaks it. As if picking up my thoughts she interjects, "Ah, yes, I remember China, the Incas, the Hebrew prophets—I was one of them." I nod to show how impressed I am by such Immensely Important Incarnations. Didn't she ever come back as a housewife or hooker? "You've had very interesting lives," I tell her admiringly.

"Oh, everyone has! They just can't remember."

From the corner of her eye she squints over my head as if reading small print in dim light. "I see . . . your past . . . lives. . . ." She speaks slowly, portentously. Her face sets in an inscrutable mask. Hearing a low growl, I glance down. Not two inches from my ankle the bowlegged duke is baring his sharp little fangs. I freeze. Madame seems unaware of my predicament. In fact, she is unaware of everything. She has fallen into a trance. I glance at my watch. The hour, I note with relief, is up. I consider taking my leave, although I'm anxious to collect my fee. Getting paid for drinking tea and traveling on the astral is not bad at all.

"Like a motion picture . . ." she murmurs in the weird voice of sleep. "I see it all. . . . I am Nostradamus. . . . History passes before my eyes . . . war . . . carnage . . . madness . . . genius . . . love . . . gulp . . . power . . . glub. . . . Oh, I love being Alexander . . . the Great . . . and Nap-oh-lee-oooonnn. . . ." Her voice trails off into a low growl. No, it's the mutt. Only an inch away. He's eyeing my leg hungrily. I clear my throat. "Uh, Madame, I'm afraid the lesson is over. I'm sorry but—" She can't hear. She has regressed thousands, maybe millions of years. She is in another galaxy. Her sightless eyes, like agates, remain fixed over my head. For all I know she is now a lust-crazed dinosaur crashing through Jurassic forests in search of a mate. She has abandoned me to the present with the Duke of Chew who, unfortunately, she has left behind, his flat ugly snout pressed firmly against my left calf, his yellow fangs bared in a vicious snarl. I decide not to go just yet. Slowly I begin to place the cup and saucer on the glass tabletop when I feel the cold muzzle against my calf. One bite and I'm lunch. My hand freezes in midair, cup and saucer rattling noisily. My arm is about to drop off like a broken branch. In desperation I turn to Madame. She is light-years away, her eyes as flat as the buttons on my drip-dry suit. Her pampered cur looks ready to chomp a slice of my leg. Just what he has been waiting for—meat! Madame, who is a vegetarian, has steadfastly refused to feed her dog meat. Lots of biscuits, chocolates, pastry, angel cake, but no meat. She boasts that he, too, is a vegetarian. But I know better. Meat, that's what he wants. *Raw* meat. "Help!" I shout suddenly. With an abrupt shudder, she comes to and looks around, dazed. "Ah, my dear *Signore*," she sighs, "I was visiting the Gobi desert." The dog waddles over to her, wagging his rump.

63

Belli, Moravia, Pasolini . . . with a Dash of Williams and an Ounce of Pound

I was hired by the Lion School of English, a British institution, and moved to a small furnished room on the quietest street in Rome, the Via dei Foraggi. I now lived in one of a neat row of red brick houses inhabited by gentility. It was situated behind the Roman Forum but cut off from it by chain-link fences; no tourists or traffic disturbed the peace on the medieval cobblestones. The landlady, an Italo-Rumanian countess with asthma, thinning white hair, and a mottled red face, gasped and wheezed; her tonsured black French poodle, Lupo, also had a wheezy bark. So as not to be disturbed by the bathroom door, she provided a chamber pot shaped like her hat. She spoke English and French and slipped little notes under my door: "Mr. Norse, please do not make *Big Things* in the pot. We do not like. It is very embarrassing and *dégoutant*." I had to be still as a mouse when making "big things" in the bathroom, but Lupo would bark and wake her. The countess expected me, as a gentleman, to suppress this function entirely—as, to judge by her face, she had done herself.

My front room over the street was on the first floor of the two-story house; above me lived a Welsh colleague, "Rhys Davies," with his English wife "Josie," who taught speech and whose father was an Oxford don. No stage or film star had more precise diction. She was a tiny brunette with sharp features, and her icy voice and razor-sharp enunciation inspired awe. She could have made a fortune as a heartless murderess in the movies.

Rhys, a shy, gentle red-bearded man with a shock of reddish bristly hair, seemed utterly mesmerized by her. His voice came from pectoral depths, husky, cavernous, and rumbling. Apologetic in manner, he was conciliatory and helpful, as self-effacing as she was cold and aloof. An odd couple indeed. I used to wonder if the hidden side of each corresponded to the other's public image, for she actually concealed her kindness, as I discovered.

For two years I lived on the Via dei Foraggi, keeping my job at the Lion School and tutoring Mme. Palladino about twice a week, earning enough to survive. In 1954 I began translating some of the sonnets of Giuseppe Gioacchino Belli, the nineteenth-century Roman vernacular poet. Because of its "obscenity" and difficulty his work had never appeared in any other language. My Italian was far from perfect and the obscurities of the Roman "dialect" made the job even more challenging. Seeing a strong similarity between the colloquial speech I grew up with and what Belli heard and recorded in the streets and taverns 120 years earlier, the coarse, vulgar language seemed as familiar as Brooklynese. Both shared racy diction, cynical wit, and irreverent humor. The poems were written mostly between 1830 and 1840. I undertook the task for the sheer joy of it despite derisive comments from Italian scholars and cognoscenti: "It can't be done! Impossible! It has never been achieved!"

Belli, who married a countess, lived in a splendid palace but frequented the streets and wineshops of Trastevere, the plebeian quarter, where a bronze statue of him looms in the square. He listened to how the people spoke, recording it on the spot. He wrote as many as fifteen or twenty sonnets a day until he had amassed 2,279 of them. Without publishing them during his lifetime he became an underground celebrity among the leading writers and critics of his day. Nikolai Gogol, "father of the Russian novel" ("Really the *mother*," said David Magarshack, "queer as Tschaikowsky!"), having heard him recite, proclaimed him one of the greatest poets of any age. Sainte-Beuve, the leading French man of letters, wrote: "This Belli, so utterly unknown . . . original, witty in everything, but best of all in his artist's eye; it seems really that he is a *great* poet." In our own century James Joyce recognized in his work, as Eleanor Clark wrote in *Rome and a Villa*, "a heightening and compacting of language values . . . with no parallel in the novel before *Finnegans Wake*." Joyce and D. H. Lawrence had both tried translating Belli and failed. Into this vacuum I stepped undaunted—the only one, I believed, who possessed the key to the tone and language.

In my little wood-paneled room behind the Forum I began the translations in 1954 and finished them in 1955, some seventy sonnets in all. A Roman boy who spent two nights a week with me did a brisk trade in stolen books. His specialty was dictionaries—God knows where he nicked them—which he was always trying to sell me, though I'd bought a big Spinelli from him. He never understood why I couldn't use more than one. The Italian-English dictionary was not, in fact, enough. I needed a Roman-Italian one to provide a glossary of modern *romanesco* and also one for early nineteenth-century slang; but I never found these. The young man, however, proved of great help; he was better than a dictionary and more fun. I'd ask the meaning of obscure words and phrases, which he'd promptly explain with amorous illustrations, in Italian and *romanesco,* to the best of his ability, which was considerable. Then, checking for accuracy, I'd question Burton and Mario, who would offer corrections. When interviewed on my method of translation I'd respond, "I had a dictionary in one hand and a Roman in the other."

This, of course, was best understood by Pasolini. I'd met him through Alberto Moravia, who wrote the introduction to my Belli translations for American publication. The master of the contemporary Italian novel, Moravia was also well informed, civilized, and a brilliant observer of people and politics. He was very tall and handsome, with iron-gray hair, a sort of Laurence Olivier look alike, with a limp from polio early in life. His wife, Elsa Morante, was also a distinguished novelist. But Pier-Paolo Pasolini, who was openly, defiantly gay, something unheard of in those days for a public figure, was an enigma who intrigued me. Moravia told me that he was indisputably the most gifted Italian poet of his generation. So when we were introduced at Rosati's in the Piazza del Popolo, as the four of us sat over coffee at a *caffè* table in the sun, I was silent and intimidated. Moravia told him of my Belli translations and the introduction he promised for the eventual book. I thought of the tales that circulated in Italy about Pasolini: how he drove about in his sports car picking up gangs of tough teen-age youths, whom he'd bring to deserted places or cheap hotel rooms—even to his home, where he lived with his mother—and indulge in orgies (presumably, not in front of her). Otherwise his life was middle-class, though he was a Communist.

Pasolini's demeanor put me off. While he was only in his thirties, his face was pinched, drawn, and cold, his cheeks sunken, his lips thin and cruel. Where Moravia was outgoing and affable, Pasolini was taciturn and brooding. He did not smile and mostly looked away. I was chilled. Handsome youths strutted about, casting calculating looks in our direction, perhaps recognizing Pasolini.

Finally, with unmoving lips, he asked how many sonnets I had translated. About sixty, I said. With no change of expression he asked if it was possible to do it in English. "In *American* English," I said. "We have a similar vernacular in New York. In part influenced by Italians." We spoke Italian; I don't recall him speaking English at all, whereas with Moravia I spoke only English. This was long before Pasolini had created his films.

Because of his politics and sensationally publicized homosexuality, he was largely persona non grata in the mainstream of Italian life, both feared and hated. I had no idea of the greatness of his creative powers, but because our tastes in youths were similar, and because I wanted to get to know him, I tried halfheartedly to open him up. He didn't say much to the Moravias either; they soon left, although both were devoted to him. Alone with Pasolini, who sat in sullen silence, I also decided to leave.

Subsequent meetings at Rosati's were hardly more successful. He always looked preoccupied, sunk in thought. When a few articles concerning the translations appeared on me, with my photo, in various leading Italian magazines in Milan and Rome, Pasolini, who saw some of them, showed interest. "Do you think you'll find an American publisher?" he asked. "It's mostly gutter language. Americans are squeamish about this." I replied that small presses would do it because they were ignored by the media. The *Hudson Review,* a prominent, influential academic magazine, had gone entirely overboard in its enthusiasm for the translations and kept asking for more. William Carlos Williams had hailed them as a masterpiece and promised a preface.

When I informed Pasolini that the printer of the *Hudson Review,* a Catholic, refused to print the poems, since they were offensive to him for their "obscenity" and antipapal stance, he asked, "Then it won't appear at all?" "On the contrary," I said. "The magazine will wait until the contract expires and find another printer." I read to Pasolini from a Williams letter, which I happened to have with me: "The translations . . . of G. G. Belli are superb! . . . a masterpiece. . . . It is wonderful of the editors of *Hudson Review* to be so loyal to you under the circumstances. . . . This translation must not be allowed to die unpublished in English. . . . Pound will be shown your translations at once. . . . [They] have gone to my head, they are so skilfully done and . . . so worthwhile in themselves that I can scarcely contain myself" (November 15, 1955).

I told Pasolini that within ten days he wrote again: "Pound spoke slightingly of the man and of your translations, that they were not rhymed, etc." The translations were, for the most part, rhymed assonantally as well as in *rime riche.* In other instances the rhyme was slant. "He never acknowledges anything as good unless he, der grosser Ich, has had a hand in bringing it to the world's attention," wrote Williams angrily. "I have been frequently nauseated at his pretensions. . . . God damn him to hell" (November 26, 1955).

"Moravia has told me about this," said Pasolini. "Of course, we are not qualified to judge the translations, but Williams certainly is. He is perhaps more equipped than Pound, whose Fascist fanaticism blinded him in many ways to just about everything."

This was the longest speech Pasolini ever made to me. I was astounded. I agreed and told him the *Hudson Review* contract with the printer ended in December 1955 and they would publish twenty-six sonnets in the April 1956 issue, with my introduction. Moravia's introduction for the book, which would not appear in the review, dealt with the life and times of Belli.

64

Arrivederci, Roma

I had been in Italy almost a year when I left Rome for a few months on my thirty-eighth birthday, July 6, 1954. An Associated Press photographer, speaking *romanesco*, showed up at the Fontana di Trevi and took three photos. The first caught me tossing a coin over my left shoulder into the fountain. In another, I crouched beside my bicycle, pumping a tire in last-minute preparations. In the third (all poses were directed by the photographer) I squinted up owlishly from my notebook, as if surprised in the act of creation—as if I've done my *best* work crouching beside bicycles! The caption would read: "American poet leaves Rome on bicycle tour of Italy" (I was already famous for translations I had only recently begun).

My German bike, *Wander,* was loaded with a couple of unwieldy rucksacks that I had unprofessionally tied with rope and that kept slipping from the baggage rack. In khaki shorts, Raymond Duncan sandals, a thin yellow nylon shirt, and black beret, I bade farewell to the baroque fountain, to Neptune and his attending Tritons on their plunging horses, and to my two friends, Burton the composer and Mario, the handsome Italian engineering student I had fallen for that summer.

As I pedaled through the madcap traffic and passed San

Giovanni in Laterano, with the black beseeching hands of Saint Francis reaching out from the square opposite, I ceased feeling the heat and chaos and in a short time was in open country, on the Appian Way, cycling easily and beginning to feel the elation that comes from cutting oneself loose from familiar routine. Much as I loved Rome, it was a relief to leave the massive churches, palaces, and monuments behind. My body, not a machine, was my engine of locomotion. I possessed both strength and endurance.

As a poet and writer convinced that "chance" is more revealing of reality's pattern than any order imposed on it by preconceived ideas, I would be free to experience what the average tourist, in his regimented way, entirely misses. For three months I would encounter, firsthand, the peasant, the laborer, the tradesman, the professional, the aristocrat, in every part of Italy and Sicily. I even found racism among Italians, though in a mild form: in Rome, for example, I was warned about Sicilians. "They are not Italians, they're black." I ignored such myths. In fact, in various towns of Sicily I found more blue-eyed blonds and Celtic types than I did in Rome. The river, the sea, the plain, the mountain, wall, tower and castle, the bust, the vase, and the coin—all would cohere in a vital landscape, shedding light on history. Topography and people would fuse.

This remarkable journey made more than three decades ago I documented in a three-hundred-page manuscript, written on the spot, excerpts of which appeared in various magazines and which, one day, I should like to see in book form. One incident, macabre, absurd, and grotesque, was interwoven with my life in Rome.

Agropoli is on the Gulf of Salerno, situated magnificently among the soft hills that give to ancient Paestum, with its Greek temple columns, and the neighboring countryside a lush, timeless quality. It is the highest point in the area, which is what the name—acropolis—means in Greek, for this is Magna Grecia. At sunset the hills turn apricot and peach-gold, the farms, orchards, and vineyards glow in neat apple-green rectangles and squares.

On the main street of the rural village I found a *locanda* (Italian flophouse) with clean white cots in a spacious room and a wood balcony over the noisy street. The peasant family who owned it belonged to that strange tribe often encountered in Italy who, regarding foreigners as deaf mutes from outer space, believe that to be understood they must shout. Until I produced my passport we had no difficulty understanding one another in Italian (though they spoke only the local dialect). I learned the price of the bed, what floor it was on, what hours they kept, and that meals were served in the restaurant downstairs. In fact, they assumed I was a northern Italian, having requested not my passport but my *documenti.* When I produced a foreign passport the old woman shrieked, *"Un americano!"* as if I'd instantly metamorphosed into an extraterrestrial. From that moment nobody understood a word I said. She stuck her finger at my mouth and then at her own, yelling *"Man-gia-re?"* Eat? Her daughter, surrounded by squirming, squalling kids, gaped in astonishment.

The head of the family, an old peasant with a red face, cropped gray hair, and wrinkled farmer's neck, roaring in terrible English, informed me that the Americans did not bomb Salerno; Pennsylvania, unlike Italy, is rainy and foggy; Italy has the best climate and most beautiful language in the world. He had picked up his broken English in the independent republic of Pennsylvania. For the benefit of his family he pretended to a perfect knowledge of English. Cocking one eye to see if they were listening, he clutched my passport in purple knobby fingers, mispronouncing every word as I filled out the I.D. form.

"Yor-a fader ees-a name-a ees-a blok-a?" he yelled.

"No!" I yelled back. He pointed in the passport to the word *black* under "color of hair." I pointed to my name. He blinked. Then he said in Italian to his wife, "Eh, they don't understand."

The meal was surprisingly tasty—spaghetti with a good tomato sauce, a slice of roast beef with boiled spinach and a glass of local red wine and Fontina cheese, all for about 250 lire or 40 cents. It was the same price for a bed.

For the next few hours I wrote in my notebook, then ascended and chose a cot in the stifling heat. There was no one else in the room except for an inert form under a bed sheet. Waking before dawn, in the dim light of a tiny bulb I saw a naked youth (the other occupant) with dark curly hair and olive skin. He was playing with himself. With a pounding heart I rose as if heading for the W.C. and passed his cot. He stared casually. Knowing how natural Italians are about physical functions, especially in the south, I lingered at the foot of his cot. "Very hot," I remarked, which in Italian as in English has a double meaning. "Very," he said. I sat beside him. "Perhaps we can have a good

time together?" He nodded. *"Va bene,"* he said calmly. We spent a
delightful hour relieving each other of man's most pressing
problem, and were none the worse for it. Learning that I was an
American, he inquired if he could visit me in Rome. We exchanged addresses, the usual formality, and I learned that he
was a stonemason and native of the region. His slender form was
that of an ephebe on a Greek urn. I gave him a few hundred
lire, which he accepted with a nod.

In October when I returned to Rome, one evening my doorbell rang and there stood Luciano, asking if he could spend the
night. He didn't have to persuade me. In the morning he asked
to borrow a thousand lire (the standard request) with the excuse
that he wanted to find work in Rome. He returned several times
and then, one evening, he arrived accompanied by an ugly, sin-
ister-looking man of about twenty-eight. This, he said, was his
brother, Ugo. He was sallow, hook-nosed, with pointed ears and
a harsh voice. Luciano, Ugo asserted, had fallen ill and could
hardly walk. I was sorry to hear it, I said, but he looked fit to me.
No, said Ugo, he had a severe pain in the groin and needed an
operation at once. "What's wrong?" I asked. Ugo leered knowingly. "From what you did to him," he muttered ominously.
"From what *I* did?" "You drained his lifeblood. Crippled him." I
laughed. "Anyone can see that he's perfectly healthy. What's all
this about?" Luciano doubled up and clutched his groin, but he
was a lousy actor. He looked as if he were scratching himself.
"The operation," said Ugo, "costs sixty thousand lire." So that
was it! "I don't believe you," I said. Ugo's face darkened. "We are
poor, you are a rich American. You can get the money." I rose to
my feet and so did they. "We can wait until you raise it," said
Ugo generously. "Can you wait until next week?" I asked. Their
faces brightened. *"Sì, sì,"* they chorused. "Can Luciano bear the
pain until then?" I said. "Oh, *sì,*" said Luciano, nodding vigorously. The mere promise of money had effected a miraculous
cure. "Then, if you'll excuse me," I said, "I am busy. As you
know I'm a *professore.*" Before leaving, Ugo, who was no more
Luciano's brother than I was, could not resist making threats. If
I did not produce the sum he would denounce me to the police
for committing unnatural acts, he warned.

In reality, a *denuncia* from either of us would incriminate the
other. In the eyes of the law Luciano and I were guilty of a crime
against nature. Thus began a bona fide Italian imbroglio with

the purpose of monetary gain. The repulsive Ugo and his menacing air appalled me. I had no intention of submitting to blackmail. The polymorphous-perverse Luciano, like any Italian boy of the people, was used as a pawn in the game of extortion. Lacking the nerve to concoct such a fantastic scheme himself, he remained passive and bewildered throughout the absurd charade. He fidgeted, smoked, stretched, cracked his knuckles, twiddled his thumbs, yawned. I was resolved to remain firm. Not one lira for blackmail. I was very sorry, however, that Luciano was lost to me.

A few days later my doorbell rang. Peeking through the shutters I saw Ugo looking up. A war of nerves had begun. At all hours my bell would ring with frightening insistence. One night as I was passing the Arch of Septimius Severus—the Forum was deserted as usual after dark—he was waiting. Alone, I'd always felt uneasy there, fearful of being mugged; now I was face to face with a half-crazed desperado who might stop at nothing.

Ugo roughly demanded to know when I would have the money and I told him that a rich friend promised to lend it to me. "When?" he barked. "Next week." He described what he would do to me if I didn't hand it over—my cheeks, nose, and throat would be slashed. I excused myself, showing none of the fear I felt. He followed me until I reached the Via dei Serpenti and ducked into Burton's hallway. Mario believed it was a bluff—no derelict would go near the police—but in a fit of frustration and rage he might draw a knife and slash me, he said. He offered to "take care of him."

I could no longer wander freely about in Rome. Wherever I went, even in the crowded sectors of the city, I'd catch sight of Ugo stalking me, darting behind the pillar of a colonnade or a parked car. His clothes were filthy and ragged and his posture bent. I realized that he was a psychopath.

One afternoon I blurted out the story to Mme. Palladino. When I described Ugo she cried, "Ah, the nose, the ears, the eyes—he resembles his master, eh?" I wondered what she meant. Then it dawned on me: she was talking about the Devil. She actually believed the myth, despite her wealth and social sophistication. Her religious mania had made her stupid. Since I had offered no motive for Ugo's behavior, omitting mention of Luciano, she believed he had materialized from depths even lower than the Roman slums. To her, poverty was punishment for evil behavior.

Mme. Palladino began working white magic, believing that

he'd vanish in a puff of smoke. He didn't. He faded away quite slowly, in fact, but before doing so managed to create a lot of mischief. He had taken to lowering the sum more realistically until it was down to a thousand lire and, meeting with no success, a hundred lire; but I refused. If I capitulated I'd never get rid of him. He then threatened to call my landlady and expose me. I countered by threatening to notify the police. Enraged, he swore he would cut my throat. Then one day the landlady burst into my room. "Mr. Norse, I don't know what is going on here," she wheezed indignantly, "but I don't like it. I run a respectable house and you were highly recommended—"

"Countess, please explain what you are talking about."

"Mr. Norse, it is too disgusting. I received a telephone call from a—delinquent—who told me about the filthy things you did—with his brother—" She gasped for breath. "Scandalous! Like Oscar Wilde! It must stop at once or you must leave!"

Her morality was entirely Victorian, which is to say mythic fantasy (the real world is ruled by fantasy perceived as fact). I replied reasonably, "Countess, your informant is a psychopath, a crazy man. I don't know him. When I refused to give him money he said he would tell lies about me." This stopped her for a moment. "But how did he get my telephone number?" she asked (I received messages on the countess's phone). I said he had stolen it from a friend. Luckily, she was convinced. Though they are frequently less harmful than truth, which is no match for lies, myths, and prejudice, I dislike lies; but in this case it was clearly necessary to exercise my fertile imagination.

Still having to deal with the madman, I told the story to Frances McCann, who suggested that I supply the missing piece of information to Mme. Palladino, to whom I had introduced her. She believed the psychic lady had to know the truth if her exorcism was to be effective. She didn't think she would react as the countess did. After all, she was a sophisticated lady. But the count was not so sure. "Signora Palladino is morally a bourgeoise like the countess," he said, not unkindly. "She is conventional."

And so one afternoon I told Mme. Palladino everything, how I had met Luciano in the *locanda,* what happened, and all the rest. She listened quietly, then rose to her feet. "I cannot believe these terrible things you are telling me," she cried in agitation. "I thought you were—a nice man. You are a monster, a degenerate! You swallow babies!"

She was even worse than the countess. She began to harangue me like a fundamentalist preacher. My soul was going to fry forever in hell. She went on about swallowing babies, flecks of spittle gleaming on her lips. I thought, She rages because she craves sex but can never admit it to herself. What if she knew the truth about her friend Muldoon? Respectable people spend their lives blind to the truth, believing false notions, which they expect others to believe, thus creating the hell we inhabit.

I didn't need Mme. Palladino's hocus-pocus anyway. Having seen me with Mario, the sleazy Ugo faded out of my life. Mario was a very tough and burly-looking Roman. Where white magic failed, the implicit possibility of brute force did the trick.

65

Other Voices

The Lion School of English was my sole means of support. With an entirely British staff—I was the only American—it occupied a large old palazzo on the Via del Babuino. I remember a blond woman named Penny Singleton who, like Josie Davies, had beautiful upper-class diction. She led a study group of Italians to New York once to practice their new linguistic skills and when, a fortnight later, they returned I inquired how it went. *"Wa-at?"* she squawked in a jarring, raucous voice. "That's what we learned in the Bronx," she said.

There was a large, overweight brunette married to a teacher many years her senior, whose authoritative presence produced in her a remarkable effect. Her contralto voice would become a cringing whimper and she'd sound like a baby. Fear of daddy constricted her vocal chords. Everyone pretended not to notice, but it caused much comment among the staff—speculative rumors about whips and chains, black pantyhose, paddles, and so on abounded.

I had been at the school about a year when a new recruit was hired—an Oxford scholar, said Davies, and we were lucky to have him. He turned out to be a very shy man, about twenty-eight, with fair thinning hair and a cowlick. When we were introduced he looked away, addressing the wall, his face red with embarrassment. I could never determine whether he was smiling or frowning. I saw no other expression on that tormented, perpetually averted face. In an unrelieved state of excruciating shyness, he seemed deeply ashamed of something. He stammered, nodded, and looked away, his purple lips quivering.

Whenever I encountered him in the hall or at staff meetings his pale blue eyes were evasive and his frowning smile seemed an admission of guilt. He spoke to nobody. About three months after he was hired he failed to appear at school. Days passed. The headmaster, Samuel Deering, a heavy man with a light wit, went around with Davies to see what they could find. They returned pale and shaken. "My God! It was *awful!*" Sam muttered. He was found, when they broke into his room, with his throat cut, a long razor by his side. They also found a mass of daily letters from his invalid mother indicating that she had received every penny he earned. He had starved himself to support her. On the floor beside his outstretched hand was a letter from a relative informing him of his mother's death.

66

The Duke and Duchess Caetani di Sermoneta

The Caetanis were the last of a noble line tracing their origin to the nurse of Aeneas, Gaeta, for whom the ancient coastal town between Rome and Naples was named. In the heart of Rome, at 32 Via Botteghe Oscure, not far from the Palazzo Venezia, lived the duke and duchess in a grand palace. They had two castles, one at Ninfa and the other at their ancestral seat, Sermoneta. The duchess published an international magazine in English, French, and Italian, called *Botteghe Oscure*, to which I had contributed some poems. She paid handsomely and it was a mark of prestige to appear in the voluminous, expensively produced five-hundred-page biennial. Big names jostled lesser knowns. When I was first invited to the palace to meet Marguerite Caetani (who in 1954 was still a mere princess before her husband, in his nineties, inherited the ducal title on the death of his brother), we had corresponded, owing to her enthusiasm for my poetry. All we had in common was a love of poetry and American birth—she was a member of the wealthy Philadelphia Biddle family.

In her eighties, frail, with white hair, a delicate voice, and a languid air, she wore a loose, cream-colored gown, rather like an Indian sari, with a silvery shawl around her throat. Her pendant of precious gems glittered in the afternoon light from the massive windows. Her voice was musical and she had a habit of referring to everything as "amusing" or "not amusing." As we stood in the vast drawing room I could not believe that anyone *lived* there. Such a room (full of precious art objects) I had seen only in museums like the Pitti Palace, the Uffizi, the Vatican, and so on. Liveried servants slid around silently bearing silver trays with refreshments. I thought this life existed only in history books.

To say that I was not awed would be a bold-faced lie. The room was about three stories high and a city block long. You don't just say, "Nice place you've got here." I recall speaking of Dylan Thomas, whom we both knew—she had published a great deal of his work before it appeared in book form—and recounting a few anecdotes about him in New York, which she found "amusing." I mentioned my friend David Gascoyne, some of whose most important work, such as "Night Thoughts," if I recall correctly, first appeared in her magazine. I told her how in London he had taken me to meet T. S. Eliot, who was not at home, and Kathleen Raine, who was. I said that David, with his magical poetic gift, could if he willed it introduce me to William Blake. This she found "most amusing." Then I told her of my current involvement with translating Belli. "Oh, my husband would be very interested in that!" she said. "No one has ever done it." She asked to see the results and I hesitated. "Oh, you needn't be afraid of shocking me," she said. "I read Joyce's *Ulysses* in the twenties." I then told her that I had no copies of the complete three-volume edition for the task and we made an appointment so that I could see theirs. She said that her husband would be glad to meet me and discuss the project.

I returned a couple of times and copied some of the sonnets.

She was part of literary history. Her first magazine, called *Commerce,* in the Paris of the twenties, was edited by Paul Valéry, with André Gide as assistant. Before I left she said, "You must visit us at Ninfa sometime." I had always wanted to be a guest in a castle; now that wish would come true.

On July 13, a week after my birthday, a valet delivered a handwritten note from the duke:

> Dear Sir, My wife writes that you would like to examine again that edition in 3 volumes of Belli's sonnets. Would you mind to come and see me any day between 10–12½ in the morning, and I'll be pleased to lend to you the edition you mention. With my best regards,
>
> Yours truly,
> Caetani di Sermoneta

Thanks to the Caetanis I was able to get on with the job. Then, fortunately, John Becker, an American who lived with his family in the palace (I'd met them at Frances McCann's), having heard about the translations, presented me with the rare three-volume edition, which enabled me to proceed at my own pace on the difficult enterprise. Such patronage kept me going.

Again I entered the palazzo, took the wrought-iron grilled elevator to the second floor, and a liveried butler showed me to the drawing room. The duchess came forward and introduced me to her husband and left. The duke stood six foot four, his full head of hair completely white; he had a long rugged face and a big aquiline nose. He spoke excellent English in a deep voice. His wife's great love was literature; his was music. He had composed an opera that had never been produced and his one wish, before he died, was to see it performed. Ninety-four when we met, he had known Wagner, Verdi, Debussy, and no doubt Ludwig II, "the mad king" of Bavaria who sponsored Wagner. He must have been among the nobility and royalty who attended the world premiere of the *Ring* cycle at Bayreuth—he was born around 1860— and might have known Proust and Wilde. I was staring at a slice of nineteenth-century history in an ancient ducal palace.

We sat taking refreshments from the valets in scarlet livery as the duke began the conversation. "Ah, my wife tells me you're translating our Belli." I smiled. "Um, that's quite an achievement, you know. And Moravia has done the introduction?" "Yes." "Most impressive, really. It's never been done, you know. Well, actually, it's considered impossible." "Yes," I said, "but the difficulties are not insurmountable." "Perhaps not. In the right hands, it could indeed be remarkable. But, really, um, certain *words*, well, used in Roman society—they simply are *not* used in polite society, are they, in English-speaking countries?" "No, but times are changing." He looked thoughtful. "Ah, yes, like Henry Miller. But I *ahsk* you, how would you translate our Roman word *fregnaccia*, for example? To us it just means *big bad cunt*." "Cunt," I said. "It would never *do* in a reception room," he said. "No, but they'd love it in the bedroom," I said. He roared with laughter. Then with a twinkle in his eye: "They would, wouldn't they?" he said, and proceeded to belt out some of the filthiest, most ribald profanities of Roman slang, asking for the American equivalents. He seemed to enjoy this immensely. "I don't believe I've ever had such a conversation before," he said. I saw his hand tremble and his eyes glaze over with a look of fatigue. When it passed in a few moments he said, in a weary voice, "What a bore, old age. Well, thank you so much and good luck with Belli."

I never remembered him as old. He was full of enthusiasm, of the joy of life. His forthrightness put me immediately at ease. I had never regarded wealth and station as superior to genius or talent, but mingling with the Caetanis I saw, for the first time, that ironically enough I had something *they* longed for as much as I longed for the comfort and security I never had. I can best explain it, perhaps, by a historic example. King Ludwig II stood in awe of Wagner rather than the other way around. All Wagner needed from him was support. And Ludwig was the one fabulous monarch whose life was transformed by Wagner's creative power to exalt and transport. The boy king was young enough to be captivated by the godlike transfiguration one experiences in Wagner's music dramas; he was young enough to defy his court and become Wagner's patron. Nor was he mad: this was a fiction of the powers behind the throne to conceal his homosexuality. Thus, whatever my gifts may be, as an artist I felt equal to any king—or queen, actually.

As I chatted with the duke in his regal surroundings I realized that he had sent for me because of a lifetime quest; it was said that he had always yearned for artistic power and sat enthralled before those who possessed it. If indeed I had the magic to bring Belli to life in English, he recognized it as a gift he never possessed. He realized his wish to hear his opera before he died—I heard it played on RAI, Italian radio. It was a lovely mélange of his models, Debussy and Wagner; muted, misty, and mediocre, it lacked an original voice.

Meanwhile the painter Harvey Fein, who had conned me out of the Picasso, showed up in Rome with his beautiful Italian wife, Rosa (name changed)—a golden blonde from Trieste whom I had met in New York. She had film-star beauty—tall, elegant, with flashing emerald eyes and an exquisite peach complexion, a blend of Sophia Loren and Gina Lollobrigida. Her family had fled Italy during the Mussolini era and she grew up in New York. I liked her immensely but refused to speak to her husband. They both protested his innocence and finally, more out of desire for their company than belief in his integrity, I yielded until another episode led to a disastrous conclusion.

Harvey still borrowed money for bus fare, yet his apartment was luxurious. One day he said archly, "I've rented the small bedroom to a friend of yours and his boyfriend." It was Christopher Isherwood. "He isn't staying long—maybe a month. They quarrel incessantly, loud, screaming fights. He says he likes it, it keeps him interested." I ran into Isherwood and his new friend, Don Bachardy, then nineteen, but received only a curt nod.

When I walked around with Rosa the young men went berserk in the streets—they hissed, whistled, called, and cooed. Her mouth and chin set resolutely, she disdainfully ignored them. But Italians are not easily discouraged. Only my presence prevented them from approaching. I asked how she managed to walk around by herself. "Oh, sometimes they pinch my ass," she said. "They try to touch my breasts. But I get rid of them." "How?" "I've found a way." She told me that when she stamped her foot contemptuously and shouted, *"Via!"* (Beat it!) they were so offended that where all else failed wounded vanity succeeded.

As for Harvey, he never learned Italian except for a few phrases in an American accent. To my utter astonishment, before long he was living at the Caetani castle in Ninfa! It still seems incredible. With his languid, easygoing attitude, not to mention his dreamy, liquid eyes and boyish blond hair over his brows, he instilled confidence.

So it turned out that my few days at Ninfa were as the guest of Duke Harvey Fein, lord of the castle, and his lady, Rosa. Oddly enough, they looked the part. Some renovation was under way and the duchess had placed the castle at his disposal for the summer. I floated around under a spell, hearing Debussy's *Pelléas et Melisande* in my head, especially at night when I peered from my turreted window at the moon over the hushed countryside. For the first time I felt the princely sensation of power and grandeur. I explored every niche of the castle, but most vividly I recall the dungeon, where I found heavy chains in the twenty-inch stone wall and an inscription by a hapless prisoner that read something like: "In the year of our Lord 1519, victim of cruel deceit, I, Guglielmo R. rotting in these chains for 20 years, am to be beheaded at dawn, proclaiming my innocence to the last." It was chilling. Absolute power is fine if you happen to be a duke, but the prisoner might have been me after Duke Harvey had embezzled my property.

Harvey soon fell into disgrace, but instead of a beheading, he began working for Frances McCann, to whom I had introduced him. Her chief interest—like that of her friend Peggy Guggenheim, whom I met at Frances's palazzo with her team of Lhasa terriers—was contemporary art. Frances opened a gallery on the Isola Tiberina, called the Rome–New York Art Foundation, and put Harvey in charge. Within weeks he was discharged. Frances murmured of unprincipled behavior.

67

The Duffel Coat

Because my hand was in nobody's till it was always empty. I had no one to blame but my mother—honesty was not the best but the worst policy. It was the surest route to the poorhouse. I applied for a Guggenheim Fellowship to translate hundreds of Belli sonnets, with recommendations from William Carlos Williams, Karl Shapiro, Allen Tate, Kimon Friar, and E. E. Cummings, who warned that his recommendation was "the kiss of death." He was right; the Guggenheims allowed me to freeze almost to death. I sat typing with frozen fingers, not removing my woolen socks for fear of frostbite.

That February of 1956 an icy wind from Siberia blew steadily for ten days from an arctic cold front over Europe. The papers predicted it would last at least another week. Rome had the heaviest snowfall in fifteen hundred years, since the time of the emperor Justinian, the one who blamed homosexuals for earthquakes. Since he couldn't outlaw earthquakes he outlawed homosexuality, the first ever to do so in Rome. Thus persecution of gays began with as much sense as it has ever made. As usual, however, the Romans took no notice either of the cold or the law, especially since the priesthood was predominantly gay. *E fresc' un po'*, said the Romans—a bit cool; but cold? Ridiculous. It never snows in Rome. The media always exaggerates (the snow lay three feet high in the streets but the Romans, like the Flat Earth Society and the creationists, were not a people to allow something so stupid as a fact to alter their convictions).

On February 9 with numb fingers I typed a letter to Williams requesting a preface for the Belli book, which as yet had no publisher. On February 15 Williams accepted and enthusiastically offered to interest Random House and, if that failed, James Laughlin of New Directions. In the same letter he described a reading he had given in Newark the previous night, "a commercial engagement to advertise a brand of pianos." The small audience, he suspected, was made up "mainly of teachers from a nearby normal school" and though "friendly enough" were "totally uninformed on what I was talking about. . . . I feel like a stranger. No doubt that is the way they think of *me*, a wild man who is totally incomprehensible."

My friend and patron, Edgar, whom I had met through Donald, was a wealthy Armenian, two years my senior, and one of the most cultivated people I've ever known. He had initially paid my rent so that I could get started on the Belli translations without interruption, but was in Buenos Aires, where summer was in progress. He had promised to send a duffel coat (his family owned an international textile business, based in Argentina), but delayed interminably. Physically hardy, like most Americans in Italy I walked around in light summer wear. The mild climate was nothing like the arctic New York winters. But that year was different. I was beginning to cough and sneeze when, at long last, a notice from Customs arrived. On one of the coldest, windiest days I set out for the *dogana* in a distant part of town unfamiliar to me. It required three bus transfers and each time I had to wait in the wind and snow for the arrival of another bus in a deserted area. On one of these changes I waded through freezing slush to the next bus stop, two blocks away. Having no boots, I wore my usual Hush Puppies and got soaked to the bone.

When I finally arrived at Customs I wandered through endless drafty corridors in a vast warehouse trying to find the right section. Then, having found it, I waited until the package was located. At this point my nose was running and my head spinning. A bored official said that I had to pay six thousand lire to retrieve the package. This was preposterous. No mention of payment had been made in the notice and I had no money. He shrugged. "*Signore,* I just work here, I don't make the rules." I was in a catch-22—if I left and borrowed the money I'd be too sick to return for the coat. If I didn't return it would be impounded. Feeling deep resentment for faceless bureaucracy, I stood indecisively; the inaccessible, elusive duffel coat became the symbol of my plight.

The customs officer, not unkindly, asked what was inside and I said, "A duffel coat." "Is it new?" "It's my old coat." I was surprised at how easily I lied, trying to get that coat. He sighed. "Well, in that case," he said scratching his head, "it will cost only three thousand lire." His indifferent tone led me to wonder if, like most situations in Italy, this was negotiable. The right rhetoric could do it: the magic word was *mamma.* With passionate conviction I told the moustachioed little man in the blue suit and badge that my mother had sent it knowing how I suffered from the cold . . . oh, yes, it's not cold, but still . . . she was thousands of miles away and wept with concern about my well-being. As an American journalist I write beautiful things about Italy; I wouldn't want to spoil it with an ugly story—that is, you understand, about being unable to retrieve my old coat because of red tape.

His expression softened. Darting furtive glances around him to make certain that he was not overheard, he muttered, "*Signore,* why didn't you say so? Take the package and go. But don't tell anyone, *capito?*" I grabbed the package, thanking him profusely. "Eh, *via, signore*. Go, go!" I flew out of there and tore the package open at the entrance, donned the thick tan woolen coat, pulled the hood over my head, and felt safe. But it was too late.

When I got to my room an envelope from William Carlos Williams lay on the bed. It contained the preface. In the accompanying letter he wrote: "It has been a pleasure to write this for you on a work which fascinates me. . . . Wish I could flip myself over there to have such a man as you to take me round the town. I saw Rome with my brother 50 years ago and later with Floss and often think of those days with intense longing." I was breathing rapidly and beginning to perspire. As I read his preface twice, the words swam before my eyes. I had a strange, detached feeling, as if I were about to float, to levitate. He said significant things and—was it possible?—implied I was a genius. He spoke of the American idiom as "one of the greatest of modern languages waiting only for a genius of its intrinsic poetry to appear. . . . It is in the measure of our speech, in its prosody, that our idiom is distinctive. That Harold Norse has as birthright." I felt myself rising and floating in the icy room. . . .

"*Eeeeeee* . . ." Thin and piercing, from a great distance, the sound reverberated in the darkness. Where did it come from? It went on and on. I opened one eye. The light dazzled me. I saw a face, blurry, and shut my eye. When I opened my eye again it was still there. The chambermaid, mouth wide, was screaming. I shut my eye, heard voices, and opened both eyes. Two blurry faces, the countess and the chambermaid.

"Is there anyone I can telephone to come to your assistance? You can't stay here like this! My maid thought you were dead. You gave her a fright. You should be in the hospital."

I whispered Frances McCann's number and all went black again.

I believe the doctor arrived that day—three days after I'd returned from Customs. I had been in a coma the whole time, hanging by a thread. For three days I had gone without food or medicine. There was blood on the pillow, I was coughing and spitting blood. The doctor, sent by Frances McCann, examined me and shook his head in disbelief. "*Signore,*" he said, "I don't believe it. You have overcome bronchial pneumonia in three days without food or medicine. You must have had the strength of three men." I noted the tense he used and almost fainted. "The worst is over, but you must take great care to restore your strength," he said. "You are weaker than a baby."

Frances McCann and the count had saved my life. Every day the count's chauffeur arrived bearing food and medicine. I remained in bed for weeks, unable to get up except to use the bedpan, about which the landlady grumbled constantly. It disgusted her. Anything physical disgusted her. Sex and turds were the same to her. She wasn't religious, just prudish. Clearly, I had worn out my welcome, but she was impressed by the chauffeur, the limousine, and my titled friends. A beautiful young baroness from Brescia visited me during my convalescence and the landlady fluttered and wheezed with approval. The food prepared by Frances's cook was wholesome and delicious: baked chicken with fresh salads and cooked vegetables, nuts, fruit, and cheese. But I felt no stronger; my energy seemed permanently drained. When I stood up my legs buckled. I was thirty-nine but doubted I'd reach forty.

68

Florence

Spring came, oleanders and almonds bloomed, tourists arrived. And the *Hudson Review* appeared with my Belli poems and introduction. I left Rome and the little room and the tomato-faced countess and went to Florence at the invitation of an acquaintance I had met in Rome.

In Italy those involved in the arts were primarily antiquarians, arch-conservatives who zealously guarded the Old against the New, which was viewed as a threat by incompetent craftsmen to destroy the enduring values of the masters. Artisans, copyists, and archivists, they believed themselves the only true artists, regarding imitative skill as the measure of artistic achievement. Florence was the fortress of this parochialism and Pietro Annigoni, the portrait painter who had "done" Queen Elizabeth II, was revered as the greatest living master. He alone, it was said, possessed the technical secrets of the old masters.

In Florence even the streets were museums. In the Piazza della Signoria, under the statues by Cellini, Michelangelo, and Donatello, in a kind of mystical void—one-pointed fixation on the Dead Creator—one partook alfresco of communion pastry and espresso at *caffè* tables. There shall be no other God, etc., repeated like a mantra, like White Russians longing for the czar. In America Williams was struggling to bring to poetry the measure of living modern speech. In Florence the Old Guard said, "Picasso can't draw, Dali is a fake, Joyce a joke, Stravinsky is tone-deaf."

Into the household, or I should say stronghold, of precisely this type of rabid fanatic I fell with a dull thud. Geoffrey Tyndall (as I'll call him) was one of these zealots. When we met in Rome through the gentle Edgar, who knew him casually via the Anthroposophical Society, he was so engaging on the surface that I snapped up his invitation to stay with him in Florence to recuperate. There is no better convalescent home: except for sex, Florence is Italy's Sleepy Hollow. Nothing much goes on there. Dying of boredom was a legitimate concern.

But relying on the kindness of strangers is not the best way to conduct one's affairs. Tyndall, who was my age, just forty, had inherited a considerable fortune from his deceased father, a professor of music for whom he bore only contempt. In their native Rochester his father had provided him not only with a private income but with the best musical education money could buy. World-famous musicians played in his musical salon. Geoff's allusions to them are revealing. In his snobbish, provincial voice he would honk disparagingly, "You couldn't move without tripping over a fiddling Jew. I studied the flute because I associated the violin with the yids. Father, who had no Jewish blood, *adored* them." "Jesus had no gentile blood," I said, "yet you adore *him*." He smirked. "He didn't play the fiddle," he said. Then: "There's not one great Jewish composer or painter."

"Mahler, Mendelssohn, Offenbach, Ravel, Chagall," I said. "Not to mention Wagner, whose real father was Ludwig Geyer, the handsome blond actor and dramatist. A German Jew."

But reason is no match for prejudice.

Swallowing my pride, choking on it, I grinned and clowned. This tactic diffused the sick provocations, the ugly slurs. He thought Picasso was Jewish because he was short, dark, and cunning. In spite of it all, however, Geoff was humane. Without hes-

Above, the "Pillbox" and terrace on Posillipo, over the Bay of Naples, 1959, where Julia Chanler-Laurin changed my life one sunny afternoon by offering me an apartment on the Île St. Louis in Paris. On a clear day you could see Vesuvius. Sir Harold Acton lived next door in a sugar-white villa. PHOTOGRAPH TAKEN BY ME, AUTHOR'S COLLECTION

Left, the Duke of Windsor walking the plank of Onassis's yacht *Christina* to welcome his cousin Pat and me (rather frostily). I took two snaps, of which this one is slightly unfocused; the other is in my archives, Lilly Library. *Right,* with Gregory Corso (left) caught by a street photographer in front of the Cathedral of Notre Dame, Paris, 1959. AUTHOR'S COLLECTION

Above, with James Jones (lighting a cigarette) during the *vernissage* for my exhibition of ink drawings called *Cosmographs*, in the *cave* of the English Bookshop, 42 rue de Seine, Paris, 1961. *Below*, crowd at my exhibition—the drawings were hung by the Greek sculptor Takis, not only on the walls but also on the ceiling to indicate space travel. COPYRIGHT © BY MARTHE ROCHER, AUTHOR'S COLLECTION

Above, in the *cave* with Takis and drawing by
Greek artist Minos Argyrakis, which somehow
presages the angelic devil or bastard angel, long
before I dreamed it up in San Francisco
COPYRIGHT © BY MARTHE ROCHER

Right, with Anaïs Nin in the English Bookshop at
her book party for *Seduction of the Minotaur*, approximately 1962 COPYRIGHT © BY MARTHE
ROCHER

Above, with my friend Mohammed in Arcila, Morocco, 1962. I'm wearing a *taguiya* and my dove-gray princely djellabah that Achmed Yacoubi bargained for, on my behalf, in Arcila.   PHOTOGRAPH BY PAUL BOWLES, AUTHOR'S COLLECTION

Below left, in Athens, wearing my Moroccan *taguiya,* 1964. *Right,* in Gstaad, 1965, trying to recover from hepatitis.   PHOTOGRAPH BY CHARLES HENRI FORD; PHOTOGRAPH BY A FRIEND, AUTHOR'S COLLECTION

Group photo at Caffè Trieste, North Beach, San Francisco, 1975. Left to right: Lawrence Ferlinghetti, Minette and Pete LeBlanc, Howard Schrager, Allen Ginsberg, me, Jack Hirschman, and Bob Kaufman.   COPYRIGHT © BY DIANA CHURCH, AUTHOR'S COLLECTION

Caffè Trieste. Left to right: Allen Ginsberg, me, Jack Hirschman, Michael McClure, Bob Kaufman.   COPYRIGHT © BY DIANA CHURCH, AUTHOR'S COLLECTION

Above left, in front of my first apartment in San Francisco, near the East Bay Bridge, 1973. This photo, in high contrast, was on the cover of my *City Lights* book, *Hotel Nirvana,* and also in *Carnivorous Saint.* It was also hung at the Beat Generation Poets Exhibition of the M. H. de Young Memorial Museum in San Francisco, 1974. *Right,* this was taken by Frances McCann in San Francisco, approximately 1975. PHOTOGRAPH BY NEIL HOLLIER, AUTHOR'S COLLECTION

Below, with William Burroughs on the patio of our living quarters, after our 1980 reading at Naropa Institute PHOTOGRAPH BY MICHAEL KELLNER, AUTHOR'S COLLECTION

Left, with Allen Ginsberg after the reading. *Below,* reading at Naropa with Allen Ginsberg and Peter Orlovsky, left. *Bottom,* Allen introducing Burroughs (at table), who started off the reading. I'm at right. PHOTOGRAPHS BY MICHAEL KELLNER, AUTHOR'S COLLECTION

Left, hotel balcony in Barcelona, October 1978
PHOTOGRAPH BY DAVID WENTWORTH,
AUTHOR'S COLLECTION

Below, in the *City Lights* offices, 1980. Left to right: Robert Duncan, David Gascoyne, Mrs. Gascoyne, Lawrence Ferlinghetti, me. COPYRIGHT © IRA NOWINSKI

itation he'd help the old and the blind cross the street, and on one occasion I watched him give mouth-to-mouth resuscitation to someone injured in an auto accident until an ambulance arrived. Once at the risk of his own life he rescued a man from a burning building (presumably without asking first if he was Jewish). He was full of contradictions. When he wasn't a dogmatic boor, he was a bawdy sensualist. In private he loved profanity and licentious behavior; in public he was conventional. But he *was* a racist.

In the grim, impregnable fortress of a massive fifteenth-century palazzo he owned a spacious top-floor apartment that was like a wing in a castle, where he reigned like a Renaissance duke; it had floors of polished Carrara marble, high vaulted ceilings, authentic quattrocento furniture, tapestries, chandeliers, paintings, and vast fireplaces. I lived in the maid's room facing the heavy oak entrance doors; tiny and bare, it had a small window on the court. The structure stood imposingly on a street behind the Arno and the Ponte alla Carraia. A Bechstein grand kept in prime condition (a master tuner arrived from Stuttgart four times a year to tune it), dominated the drawing room.

I don't want to give you the idea that Tyndall was a monster. He was rich, spoiled, and autocratic—but not evil. He embraced the weltanschauung of Rudolf Steiner, the clairvoyant metaphysician and founder of anthroposophy, whose astral voyages through time and the cosmos were spectacular. But it did not temper Tyndall's burning resentment for his father. It turned out that the crowning blow to Geoffrey was that most of the money was left to his married brother because, when his father lay dying, Geoffrey refused to return home for a reconciliation.

In Florence he pursued in secrecy an erotic life that, I assure you, was far from riveting. Mine, on the other hand, was so rich and strange that it kept me there, and since this furthered my convalescence, I was willing to put up with anything, even Tyndall. An accomplished grumbler who said no to living art, he retreated into the past, believing music ended with Bach. Donald Cammell's father, a scholar and poet, was convinced that poetry ended with Tennyson; to him Yeats, whom he knew personally, was an abomination. He believed another friend, Aleister Crowley, was a greater poet who wasted himself on the black arts. Such were the types I saw in Florence.

One day I met the foremost English translator of Dostoevski, David Magarshack, a Russian Jew whose family fled the Revolution when he was sixteen and became British subjects. As we paused before a house with a plaque commemorating Dostoevski, who had written *The Idiot* there, on the street facing the Pitti Palace, I said, "He must have *lived* in the museum."

David Magarshack smiled. "I doubt that he ever noticed it."

"You mean, he ignored the museum entirely?"

"Yes. He was interested only in his characters."

The greatness of Dostoevski versus the smallness of the antiquarians. He was more alive in death than they were in life.

But Tyndall's dinners were great. My after-dinner conversation kept him laughing and he stuffed me like a goose on the best fare available in Florence, taking offense if I offered to share the cost or didn't devour every morsel. Edgar provided me with a small allowance to defray costs, such as the token rent, during my stay. Edgar's interest was my work, Tyndall's my friendship. We had sirloin and tenderloin steaks medium-rare, exquisite pastas such as green tagliatelle and spaghetti alla bolognese, abundant salads, and the best Tuscan wines and gourmet desserts. In the fifteenth-century dining room those candlelight dinners (the tapers custom-made of pure beeswax from Tyndall's favorite candlemaker) were unforgettable. He also displayed a formidable technical knowledge of the music of the past.

It was in this atmosphere that I wrote a long poem in four sections called, appropriately enough, "Florence," but did not send it to Williams. The poem dealt with the Florentine cinquecento, and I was troubled that the style and treatment had a patina of the past that would arouse Williams's anger. I sent it to *Poetry* magazine, where it was accepted and published. To Williams I wrote complaining that "I keep seeing the little Fulbrights, like spots before my eyes, upon whom America lavishes so much money for dubious scholarly pursuits . . . a deader, less imaginative group of cephalopods would be hard to find. . . . Me: 'What do you do on your Fulbright?' Reply: 'Just fuck. There's a nice German girl I'm keeping on it, if you must know.'"

69

Benidorm

With the onset of winter I left Florence and settled in the hamlet of Benidorm on the Costa del Sol just north of Alicante, on the southeast coast of Spain, the warmest spot in Europe. Except for a few Scandinavian women and children it was quiet and deserted. The Guardia Civil, with their carbines, gray uniforms, and black patent-leather tricornered hats, were a grim lot. This was Franco Spain. For 45 dollars a month—240 pesetas—I had a tiny room and three meals a day in the run-down Pension España. A small balcony overlooked palm trees and the beach. At night the owners, an old couple and their parents in their nineties, closed all doors and shutters and huddled around a shortwave radio for the news from Paris, where they had worked for twenty years—four generations concerned with their loss of freedom in Spain.

In this town lived renegade German Nazis who bought up real estate hand over fist. Once I got into an argument with a Spanish pharmacist who had fought for Franco and tortured and killed his own friends in the town. He was not liked. He kept insisting that Americans had no great writers like Cervantes or Dante; he pooh-poohed Whitman, Poe, and Melville, scorned Hemingway. But when I mentioned Ezra Pound he said, "Ah, yes."

When I repeated the conversation to the old pension owner he made a face as if he had stepped in dogshit. "He's like the woman in a story about our great poet, Quevedo—you know what the name means?" "Yes, it means 'what do I see?'" I said. "Right. He lived in the royal palace and one day he was relieving himself by squatting on the floor of a palace room when a grand noblewoman came in unexpectedly and exclaimed in horror, 'Quevedo! Quevedo!' So Quevedo looks up at her and says, 'She knows my name but she doesn't even know the word for shit!'"

In a letter to Williams in January 1957 I asked if he had seen my poem sequence "Florence" in the November 1956 issue of *Poetry*. His response (January 24, 1957) swept me off my feet. He couldn't place it within any category that he knew and at first he felt disturbed. The effect, he thought, was to show the superiority of the past over the present (not my intention), but then he grew rhapsodic:

> Your vision and stress upon the savage masculinity or maleness of the old masters is a masterly observation. That poem in which you speak of it . . . is frightening and will be totally ignored. They will not know what to do with it, it will be buried. It must not be because nowhere in my life or reading has an image been so vividly presented. I have never seen anything like it. . . . It is really a masterpiece.
>
> But as in any other masterpiece it incurs responsibilities. You can't repeat it. Are you going to change your style to conform to it? . . . For you can't ignore what has been done. You . . . are standing at a crossroads of your life. This poem is a beginning or an end. . . . What you have done in this poem is too beautiful to ignore. . . . [It] has to stand alone. [He is referring to "The Square."]

The Square

In the Piazza della Signoria
the old palace with its fountain
and rash statues tall as buildings
heavily tell of male dominion

crushing Hercules brushes the sun
over his shoulder, and David his neighbor
from his encounter with the slain
giant, in repose, marvel of promise

and Neptune, third colossus, crown
a home of pigeons, white above spray
and bronze goatmen with flapping phalli
pawky lips and fish-hook beaks

primed in the tilt of thigh and hoof
—the sexual cry in hoarse bronze
clanging over cobblestones—
the loggia witnessing the silent

drama, from its chocolate gothic
barrel-vaults, Cellini's dream
Perseus, gorgeous with the gorgon
head, aloft, sinews rich

and limber over the female
demon, then the raped women
—what cinquecento madness led
the masters to such virile pride

in a bold access of the blood
carving all but the will aside?
(from The Dancing Beasts *[New York: Macmillan, 1962])*

In this poem I record the fascinated repugnance with which I regarded these works of the Renaissance, realizing that such lust and madness for power was based on an indomitable will to crush, to destroy—trampling on women. This I could never abide—at all times my mother remained on my conscience as a martyr to such injustice, which I voiced in the poem constructed, as Williams said, "uniquely . . . seemingly from the quatro cento [*sic*] . . . most carefully studied for an especial effect." He was right. I wanted the ambivalence of attraction and repulsion to show through the horror of sex used as a weapon by dominant males of the past five thousand years.

"Sometimes I think your place should be in NY, not Europe. Then again I think just the opposite. What the hell have I to do with it, you're the judge of what is best for you." Thus Williams began a St. Valentine's Day letter to me on February 14, 1957. Was I his valentine? He loved me like a father and slapped me down when he thought I needed it. He wanted me to snap out of my European idyll, to participate in the events that were shaping a revolution of style.

The cause of this outburst is a movement that began in San Francisco among a group of young (not so young) poets who are beginning to make their way at

present in New York. They are headed by Allen
Ginsberg, Jack Kerouac. . . . The reason I speak of that
gang now is [they are] . . . headed for Italy. Look for
them in a month around Florence or Rome, 4 or 5 of
them including a poet named Corso. . . . A feature of
the united front that these men present is that they are
all Zen Buddhists, one of their most influential members is at the present time living in a monastery in Japan
[Gary Snyder]. . . . I hope you meet at least one of them
for they know what they are about and you would enjoy
meeting them. But. Right at this time when you yourself
have just struck a lead [it] may not be profitable to dwell
too much on Allen Ginsberg and his gang.

I was astonished, for I too was practicing Buddhist meditation. My friend Edgar had given me a book published in Ceylon
called *The Way of Mindfulness* by Bhikku Soma. He also sent me
the name of a German Buddhist monk in his eighties to whom I
wrote for advice while practicing meditation. The effect on
me of learning that Allen Ginsberg was doing this in New York
was electric, not to mention that he had become a leader in a
literary movement. I had just had an out-of-the-body experience—the only one since the age of fourteen. From the ceiling I
saw my body on the cot. *(I became the sound of a barking dog, of
clacking palm tree fronds, of pounding surf: subject and object merged,
observer and observed were one.)* A separate reality. I had lost my
physical I.D.

From April 1957 to January 1958 Tyndall and I put up with
each other again after my return from Spain. It ended more or
less as I had expected. No words were exchanged, nothing vulgar, you understand, merely a frozen silence followed by a formal note: *Please vacate by Saturday. Someone will be moving in.*

The atmosphere had chilled for some time. Once he had
invited to dinner a black woman composer who had come to Europe to perform and write on a Guggenheim Fellowship. Tyndall, who had never succeeded in gaining a performance of his
compositions, which were few and sterile, made vicious racial
slurs when she left. "Did you notice her scrummy hands? Made
for washing laundry and dishes, not playing piano. Did you see
how the black nigger in her came out when she had enough
wine?" Spite and envy consumed him. He felt compelled to de-

grade those he envied. I introduced him to two young black men, one of whom, my bed partner, he seduced, befriending the other, but disparaging both behind their backs; I found this contemptible. But they believed him, not me. Until then Tyndall's sex life had been as interesting as a limpet's. What impressed my friends was his ducal home, his class.

As the atmosphere grew charged with conspiracy and intrigue, matters worsened, involving some business about the sale of Renaissance paintings through Harvey Fein, who showed up fatter, shadier, and richer. I was kicked out with my one suitcase.

Harvey never believed Tyndall was queer. "How do you know?" he would ask skeptically. "There's nothing queer about him." I had lost my black boyfriend to Tyndall and had often seen them romping naked in bed when the door was ajar. Besides, we had shared confidences during the year I lived with him. But Tyndall's closet was a fortress as impenetrable as his prejudice. His deception fooled even me while I lived with him until months had passed and, as he put it, he wiggled a finger out of his hole testing the atmosphere. His armor was the toughest I'd ever seen.

70

Victor Emmanuel Monument

While visiting Rome in the summer of 1957 I phoned John Ciardi, the poet and poetry editor of the *Saturday Review*, who had published two poems of mine. He was living on a Guggenheim grant with his wife and children in a sumptuous apartment on the Janiculum. On my few previous visits I found him cordial, but now he shouted rudely into the receiver, "Where the hell are you?" "In Rome." "When did you arrive?" "Just now." "Well, turn around and go back!" he yelled. "What?" "Haven't you *heard*? The Italian police

are looking for you! The American embassy is looking for you!
You'll be *arrested*! If you don't want to get deported, stay out of
Rome!" "Have I killed or robbed anyone?" I grumbled. "What
the hell is this all about?"

"Listen, you've got twenty-four hours to get out of the country. They may not let you return—at least not until it blows
over."

"Until *what* blows over, for Chrissake?"

"All right, your last poem in the *Saturday Review* about the
national monument? It almost got my ass kicked off the magazine! And out of Rome! The Italian consulate in Washington has
been screaming at the American consulate for days!" His voice
shook with anger. "I'm not publishing you anymore," he added
nastily.

"Would you mind telling me what crime I've committed? I'd
like to know before I become a fugitive," I said sarcastically.

His voice grew less strident. "The government considers
your poem political fodder for the Commies. A black eye for the
national image. If it hadn't been ten days before elections nobody would have given a damn," he said bitterly.

"Well, sorry," I said, "that *you* didn't time its publication well.
I didn't intend to upset *your* stay—or mine."

I did not appear in the *Saturday Review* again. I'm sure the
reader would like to see what an internationally dangerous poem
looks like. You may never get another chance. You are hereby
warned that the following contains language and material that
may be offensive in nature:

Victor Emmanuel Monument (Rome)

The marble typewriter or "wedding cake"
is large enough to shelter in its side
several armies; as it is, they keep
a squad of bersaglieri *there, the hand-*
picked of all Italy, the flower to guard
this monsterpiece. In scarlet fez and blue
pom-pom halfway down the back, like birds
of paradise they strut, their bodies hard
and flashing flesh by sunlight or moonlight
with all the brilliance of the male panache.
And this is all they have to do. What else

on seventeen cents a day, in Italy?
Any night by the white marble ploy
discover them in whispered assignations
picking up extra cash from man and boy.

Auden was wrong when he wrote that "poetry makes nothing happen." All depended on whether the Communists would see it and make political capital of it. If they didn't it would blow over. I never knew I had such political power. But I had to get out of town. So I visited friends, told the story to much good-humored laughter, recited the poem to bursts of applause, and got drunk.

71

The White Goddess

Late that night I attended a party at Mitty Risi's. Mitty was an Australian painter with a little white house on the Isola Tiberina in the tiny square that looked like an opera set. When I arrived at the smoky, noisy party I drank myself into a stupor, telling the crowded room what had happened. Mitty, a striking woman with scintillating blue eyes and patrician features, took me by the arm and introduced me to the Australian ambassador, a white-haired distinguished-looking gentleman who said he didn't think I had too much to worry about, but if I knew anyone with a yacht it would be a capital idea to cruise beyond territorial waters for a few days. I was about to respond that I knew nobody with a yacht when a rather apathetic English voice drawled, "I have one and would be delighted to host a writer on board." I turned to face a slender young man, not much taller than I, with a flaming red beard and brick-red frizzy hair. "My name," he said, "is Pat Ryan. I'm leaving for Fiumicino in five minutes, if you care to come along." He was the nephew of the Australian prime minister.

So, at about three in the morning, I found myself in the soft leather seat of a fire-engine-red MG roaring to the port of Rome at 105 miles per hour on a deserted tree-lined road with a total stranger. Pat was suave and unflappable, qualities I've always admired. The speed, defiance of danger, submission to chance, and the tone of assurance exuded by the bearded madman at the wheel as we plunged through the night were zany but not dull. At last I had escaped the insufferable ennui of Florence.

That morning I climbed from my bunk to the deck, where Pat, in a grimy Basque shirt, soiled dungarees, and rope sandals, looked like a dock rat. He gave me a similar outfit and we made a scruffy-looking pair of deckhands. I learned that his wife, with whom he had come to Italy, had returned home to bear their first child. He missed her terribly and had considered returning until I showed up. An aspiring writer, he wanted to learn from a published one but informed me that at sea the captain is the law and his orders must be obeyed. "Aye, aye, sir!" I said.

The boat, a thirty-foot launch with two masts and an engine, was called *Dwynwen*—"the White Goddess" in Welsh, Pat explained. Looking over the starboard side I cried in astonishment, "Pat, have you seen the name of the boat beside us?" It was called *The White Goddess*. "She must have docked last night," he said. Out of curiosity we leaned over the port side, where another craft had pulled in. It was called *Anahid*. "That," I said unable to keep the awe from my voice, "was the name of the White Goddess in Asia Minor!" We stared in wonder. "Well, you're the poet," he said. "Excellent augurs, doncha think?" "Yes, it's like being given supernatural support for my poem, which rocked two consulates and one shaky editor. Perhaps she's telling me to get on with my work." "Jolly mystical," cried Pat. "Like coming up with three cherries at Las Vegas," I said, "only rarer." We swabbed the deck and Pat suggested coffee and *bombas* at a port *caffè*.

72

I Meet the Duke of Windsor, King Edward VIII

It was a small port. The Italians, as usual, were extremely friendly, and a few youths in T-shirts and shorts who seemed to know Pat approached, calling him San Giovanni Battista because of his beard and thick unruly hair. His clothes were greasy with motor oil, but he *did* look like a Renaissance saint. As we left Pat suddenly cried, "Hello! There's the *Christina*! Onassis's yacht. She must have also docked last night." A few hundred yards away loomed the massive white ship. "She may not be the White Goddess," said Pat, "but in the real world she's a powerful symbol. Oh, my cousin's on board. Let's pay him a visit." "What's his name?" I asked. Pat stared. "The Duke of Windsor." "You're putting me on," I said. "Not a-tall," said Pat coolly. "We aren't first cousins, more like eighteenth cousins. Let's go see coz." "Like *this*?" "Oh, don't fuss! We're at port," said Pat. His sangfroid never deserted him. "We look like stokers," I said. "For goodness sake, relax!" said Pat. "That's an order!" "Yes, *sir*!" I stood at attention and saluted. Pat laughed. "How do I address him?" I said. "You don't. He addresses you. He *was* the King of England. Call him Your Grace." Everything had changed so rapidly into Wonderland that I expected to wake up in the maid's room in Florence like Cinderella. Pat spoke to a liveried flunkey and we waited. I thought it *was* a dream when I saw Pat looking up—on the gangplank, inches from me, was ex-King Edward VIII of England.

The former monarch glanced at me when introduced and nodded. I snapped two photos of him with my Leica. He wore a dove-gray summer suit. It was like looking through the Palomar telescope at a distant star. He was a very frosty duke, his brow furrowed with concern, his eyes a pale watery blue. Gone was the dash of the cheery young Prince of Wales whose playboy photos were familiar to me in the tabloids I had read as a boy—playing polo and golf, falling off horses, diving from yachts, standing on his head. He had wens on his face, deep lines, a yellowish waxen pallor, indicating a bad liver: his complexion was no doubt jaundiced by rivers of alcohol and rich food. His eyes looked pained. His hair was a faded gray rather than blond. He appeared more or less embalmed. After they had spoken awhile he nodded to me and returned to the ship.

73

Ventotene

At noon we hauled anchor and soon reached extraterritorial waters. We sailed south in the turquoise sea with cavorting dolphins that accompanied us for miles. The sea, sky, wind, and sun, the flashing gemlike waves, made me think of the White Goddess: she'd been especially kind to arrange a meeting with royalty after the raw deal I'd had over my innocent poem. We sent up a libation of red Chianti during lunch, casting the dregs into the Mediterranean with a toast. "To Dwynwen-Anahid, the White Goddess!" As we skimmed the dazzling waves with a southeast wind in the sails and the white scud gleaming, I felt wildly, joyously free.

We docked at various ports on the southern Italian coast such as Foggia and Bari, at one of these picking up a blond Oxford student who was given a bunk opposite mine. Before retiring to his cabin Pat said stuffily, "No buggery aboard my vessel! That's an order!" The boy blushed to the roots of his flaxen hair while I turned crimson with vexation. So the "bohemian" Pat who met the Duke of Windsor in a wharf-rat outfit was just as puritanical as a fundamentalist! The student, however, who was snobbish and opinionated, didn't like me much, but around dawn I caught him peering at me with a hankering look. I wisely suppressed an impulse to climb into his bunk but cursed Pat for being a damn fool.

Somewhere along the journey we dropped the student and sailed into the wild blue yonder. I criticized Pat's scribblings and gave him exercises, at which he worked diligently. But his style was stiff and labored. Once we sighted a three-masted schooner and, using his field glasses, Pat said, "I think I know that ship." Within hailing distance he called through a megaphone, "Ahoy!" and the skipper called for identification. *"Dwynwen!* Pat Ryan, Australia!" Pat said, "Let's board her!" I felt like a pirate clambering up the gray hull.

The owners, a family of ancient Britons in their eighties and nineties, were archaic and autocratic. Lacking wit and humor, they spoke only of practical matters. The patriarch reminded me of John D. Rockefeller, Sr., a mummified corpse in a serge suit and captain's hat. He sat in the conning tower. From time to time an old woman called officiously, "Skipper!" The crew consisted of teen-age Spanish boys clad in bikinis who during lunch hour dived from the deck into the mirrorlike sea about a hundred feet below, their skin a liquid coffee-bean brown in the merciless sun. I half expected to see the color flow like ink when they emerged, their black hair sleek as seals' as they shook the water from their heads. The ancient mariners kept droning on of how they hired them in Malaga or Alicante, where they came aboard to work for meals and a few pesetas. Some caught stealing were put in the brig. Most, however, were so glad to be eating at all that they caused no trouble. The old woman kept referring to one boy as McGill and I thought it odd that there was an Irish or Scottish boy aboard until I realized this was her pronunciation of Miguel. I quickly developed a dislike of these heartless bores, so lacking in humanity they treated people as commodities to be used for profit. She was convinced that "all foreigners speak English behind our backs." She would have been mortified to learn that she was a foreigner.

When, much to my relief, we were once more on our way, we headed for Ischia. In Auden's wake, by the mid-fifties the isle had become an Anglo-American literary colony. Dylan Thomas's widow, Caitlin, was a regular, and had already scandalized the clergy with her drinking bouts and affairs with local boys.

As we sailed north, Pat wore a bewildered expression. "I seem to have made some miscalculation. There's an island ahead, but it's certainly not Ischia." He kept consulting maps and charts as a tiny island hoved into view. It seemed made of papier-mâché, consisting of black igneous rock with weird lumpy contours, like the petrified lava of an extinct volcano, rough-hewn yet smooth in texture. Through the glasses we could detect no sign of life. "This must be one of the Ponza islands," mused Pat. "I think I see a port, but nobody's there." "Maybe it's deserted," I said. "No, I don't think so," said Pat. "In fact, if anything, it's a prison island." I began to feel uneasy.

At about five in the afternoon we noticed through the binoculars some men moving toward the dock, their numbers increasing as they watched us cruise slowly into the harbor. With a sense of misgiving we realized that they were indeed convicts, clad in drab gray regulation outfits. "Maybe we ought to turn around and go back," I muttered, my courage failing. "No," murmured Pat a trifle irresolutely, "that would be an admission of fear." "Better safe than sorry," I mumbled. It occurred to me that we might be taken as hostages. They stared (did I fancy it?) with a mixture of curiosity, envy, and lust. Definitely lust, the way men look at women. If all those dark handsome young men staring in glum silence made Pat's blood run cold, it made mine boil with fear and desire.

As we dropped anchor and cast the lines at the mooring, one of them, unable to restrain his curiosity, said, *"Inglesi?"* *"Australiano,"* said Pat, pointing to himself and then to me, *"Americano."* They looked us over appraisingly. "Why are you here?" said one with the face of a cutthroat. "We lost our way to Ischia," we explained. Pat said nonchalantly, "I would like some coffee and would be happy if you were my guests." Instantly the young men broke into smiles and swarmed around us. It occurred to me that Pat had a considerable amount of money in a safe on board—some of them looked like expert safecrackers. We followed them to an outdoor *caffè* on the port with the mouth of a cave behind it. The owner also looked like a convict. We sat answering a barrage of questions about America and Australia. They all wanted to emigrate. When we informed them that both countries had been settled by convicts and refugees, they were amazed. Since I spoke Italian I did most of the talking, interpreting for Pat. One young man said eagerly, "Do you dance?" "A little," I said. He seized my hands and pulled me to my feet and began whirling me around to a jukebox with 1940s tunes in a sort of Lindy hop crossed with a tarantella. A big muscular youth seized Pat by his slim waist and twirled him around, much to his annoyance, like a stick of wood in the man's hands, brittle, unbending. "Serves him right," I thought, "for being so incorrigibly straight. This time he must conform to native customs." Indeed, Pat soon began showing signs of enjoying himself. As others cut in for my hand I found myself the belle of the ball, so to speak. Dancing with convicts on a prison island and meeting the Duke of Windsor did not happen every day.

As the sun sank behind the mountainous rock we were whirled into its bowels through the mouth of the cave, sweating and panting, until the music faded out of earshot. My first partner, who kept reclaiming me from the grasp of others, had skillfully waltzed us into a remote silent nook. Alone in the groin of the cave, our arms entwined around our waists and behinds, his breath, quick and hot on my face, inflamed me further. He was transported with pleasure as he pressed against me and removed my shirt in the muggy grotto. I dismissed as paranoid a moment of doubt about being murdered after he had taken his pleasure, but when he kissed my lips, face, and neck with unrestrained passion I threw caution to the winds. He removed his shirt, stuck it in his rear pocket, loosened his belt and mine, moaned when our pants fell to our ankles, and . . . well, you know the rest.

When we emerged it was dark. The others had disappeared. He kept clutching my hands, saying he was sorry I had to leave in the morning. I said I felt the same way. About nineteen, he was a lean, smooth Neapolitan beauty with thick black curls, long lashes, and huge brown eyes. I had an urge to remain on the island.

Back on the yacht a nonchalant Pat was cooking dinner. "Did you have a good time?" he asked. "Yes, very!" I said. "What about you?" "Oh, this big bloke kept insisting that we go into the cave but I absolutely refused. He seemed very upset." "Naturally! You rejected him cruelly." I grinned. "Well, I'm sure they have each other," he said. "They look like a bunch of buggers."

I slept well and early next morning prepared to haul anchor as a small group saw us off on the dock. Blearily, Pat looked around—he had been drinking a lot of whiskey to steel his nerves against the bizarre situation—and caught sight of the tall con who had first grabbed him. "I'm sure I dahnced with him lahst night," said Pat. "I hope Elizabeth will forgive me." "Oh, she will," I said, "given the heroic defense of your virtue."

We could not understand the island. There were no guards, no women, nothing but young convicts. It seemed so easy to escape by sea. Then a strange thing happened. Two suspicious-looking characters who had been eyeing us asked in terrible English if we were going to Ischia. I nodded. "You take-a me an'-a my frien'." Indicating Pat I said, "He's the *capitano*." Pat said, "Sorry, we can't." "Why? We not prisoners. We visit cousin. We from Ischia. We show you how to go." "I don't like the look of them," muttered Pat. "I got good American frien' in Ischia," pursued the man. "You know Owden? Chest'? Very *famoso*. Me frien'." This was too much. "He knows Auden and his boyfriend, who went to college with me," I told Pat. "This is the most absurd moment of an absurd adventure." "Well, Auden and your friend Chester don't seem terribly discriminating about their island connections," muttered Pat. I explained that Auden was more careful, but Chester was profligate. With some misgivings we took them aboard, but they turned out to be harmless and helped in steering to Ischia.

74

The Heavenly Twins

I remember Pat saying, "Let's look up Mitty. She has a house on the hill." We ascended and found Mitty in a modish straw hat and blue silk bathing suit, looking cool as usual, even in the scorching heat. "Ah, the Heavenly Twins," she greeted us. "Castor and Pollux arrive from their sea journey to escape the wrath of the Roman gods." She gave us a look of approval. We both wore black watch caps and clean dungarees with our laundered Basque shirts. I was tan as a berry and Pat

was flaming red. Mitty was a good sort, but I sensed her loneliness; it was almost tangible, something with which I was very
familiar. A divorcee, and of a certain age, she was, I believe, still
in love with her ex-husband, Nelo Risi, an Italian film maker
whom I liked. She seemed, in her heroic fashion, going from
yacht to yacht, palace to palace, and party to party, almost coming apart at the seams.

We left Mitty and descended to the American bar (the ubi-
quitous Harry's?), where a wild-looking red-headed woman
lurched toward me, shot glass in hand. "Dah-ling, what's your
name? *Come si chiama?* Speak English? Have a drinkie on me.
Don't be bashful." It was Caitlin Thomas. The last time I'd seen
her, with Dylan at the White Horse Tavern, she'd snarled, "Another little friend of Dylan's, are you?" Taking me for an Italian
seaman, she was trying to pick me up. As she entwined herself
around me I faked an Italian accent but after a while I said,
"Now, Caitlin, I'm not a piece of Italian trade, I'm Harold Norse,
one of Dylan's little friends, remember?" She recoiled in horror
as though I had deliberately disguised myself to deceive her.
"Sorry, I can't scrape off the tan or stop looking like an Italian
sailor, can I?" I said, grinning. She had typecast American poets
as bland academic poufs and bores, but I didn't fall into the slot.
She grew silent and I told her I had to board the "ship."

The Communists did not win the elections, and I returned
to the mainland. My poem had at least repaid me with some of
the more bizarre episodes in my life. Oh, yes, Auden was on the
island, but Pat never met him. I made a quick visit to his little
whitewashed villa, where I tried to make conversation, but he
just scratched his dog's belly as both grunted like pigs. It was the
only response I got from him. Like Tom Drew, the British seaman, I realized that he had me on his list; neither Wystan nor
Chester would ever speak to me again.

I ran into Elsie, Chester's lifelong friend from Brooklyn College, who told me that Wystan, coming from a swim the previous
afternoon, had fallen on his face in the sand and begun to sob.
"Oh, Elsie, I'm so miserable! Why *cahn't* I express my feelings to
anyone!"

75

Last Days with
William Carlos Williams

Dr. Williams was the best thing that ever happened to me. In the forties and fifties he had, to a great extent, been overlooked, ignored, and underrated. Unlike most poets, the best and the worst, he lacked the pathological narcissism that beguiles them into psychotic delusions of grandeur—he was not grandiose. When in August 1958 I wrote, calling him a great poet, he replied, "I never have pretended to be the distinguished person that you picture." This unheard of modesty was so refreshing that I thought perhaps he was really unaware of his own stature. This turned out to be true.

Having no idea, of course, that we'd never see each other again, I visited Dr. Williams several times in the summer of 1958 during a brief stay in New York. Five years later he died. Decades would pass before I realized what a pivotal role he had played in the new poetry. Unwavering in his aesthetic beliefs, he altered the course of American poetry.

"I'll experiment till I die!" he cried during one of our last meetings.

In early April I had a warm reunion with him and Floss, who served homemade rhubarb pie with bottles of cold beer in the garden at the back of the old gray house. Williams looked much better than he had five years earlier, though this was to prove deceptive. He inquired after my "staunch mother"—he admired the courage and fortitude of working-class women, whose babies he had delivered.

But in spite of his innovative genius, Williams was not an inspired talker. Unaccountably inarticulate, he was unable to express adequately his perceptions and discoveries. Displeased with some new poems I had written in Italy, he said so. "You never wrote this way when I first saw your poems!" he exploded. "Nothing about them indicates that they're from the present age. They might have been written in the time of Ovid or Lucretius. The meter is from ancient Greek or Latin."

"Maybe that's why the *Paris Review* accepted them," I replied.

"Maybe so. That's what they want, what the established magazines want. But it's the wrong track. It's academic."

It was the same old struggle: part of me craved acceptance by the establishment, part wanted to overthrow it. We argued and ranted but ended in a stalemate. Before I left that evening he put the original manuscript of *Paterson 5* into my hands as we stood by the door. "It's dedicated to Floss so this is her copy. Take good care of it."

"I'll guard it with my life," I said, and meant it. I remember the trip back by bus and subway, as I clutched the precious typescript, reading it with shock and bewilderment. The innovations of structure, line, rhythm, and word usage sounded rough, rugged, and often flat. I missed the thrust of the work, its colloquial advance into new terrain. Perhaps he was right; I had stayed in Europe too long and lost touch with the present.

That night and the next day, obsessively reading *Paterson 5* again and again, baffled, exhilarated, thrilled, and repelled, for some of it seemed banal and obvious, I tormented myself trying to understand what he was telling me as a man and as a poet. Experimentally he was light-years from what I was doing, but on one level I could identify completely: I had been close to the material of the poem all my life and, in such poems as "The Railroad Yard," had hit a similar idiom to express ordinary scenes in a fresh way. What I learned from *Paterson 5* was the courage to go on in my New York vein. And this is precisely what Williams hoped I'd do.

To limit Williams's contribution solely to a shift in emphasis from "literary" to colloquial speech would do him a grave injustice. He did much more. He moved English, via American, into a new modality, that of the plebeian, shifting it from centuries of aristocratic and middle-class culture to the idiom and cadence of the common man and woman, whom he loved. The task was completed by his disciple, Allen Ginsberg, in *Howl,* a sensational poem that extended Williams's influence farther than poetry, until then, could have hoped to reach. By the sixties it began to reach millions. A new subculture was born, uniting with the black civil rights movement and, at the end of the decade, with gay liberation. What

Williams had started was by no means confined to poetic technique. It was nothing less than a cultural revolution, a language for several generations of protest and social change.

Of course, in 1958 I could not have foreseen all this any more than he could. About a week later, I brought back his manuscript. He had attacked my new poems but wrote me, saying, "Who the hell am I to reject work of yours? Come back at me having read *Pat.* 5 and give me the Hell I undoubtedly deserve." To my undying shame I must admit that I did just that. I said I didn't like it, that it was ragged, loose, a falling away from live experience. I was really stung by his harsh criticism and lashed out at *Paterson 5* (he had also praised highly some of my poems for being beautifully written but not his "kind of poetry"). About two months later, back in Europe, I recanted and wrote that "I was too concerned with licking my wounds to give you a really fair comment." He reached great heights in the poem, I said, and ought to do *Paterson 6* as a finale, dealing with metaphysical and spiritual elements. In a letter dated September 2, 1958, he says, "I'm interested in what you say of a possible *Pat.* 6, I never thought of going on into a still wider dimension and don't relish it. Well, we shall see." He goes on to praise my new poem for being completely without inversions, its rhythm "very satisfactory to my ear."

I had finally turned the corner. In a week I would be teaching in Naples and writing a new kind of poetry, the kind Williams would unreservedly admire. I was free at last to allow my natural voice and rhythms to emerge. I had left New York for Italy on my forty-second birthday, and thanks to Dr. Williams, it proved a turning point in my career. If he was a late bloomer, so was I. And so was Whitman; it seemed that Americans who had to learn to write naturally in the common tongue first had to unlearn the teaching of the schools.

Before I left, Williams told me that Pound was to be released from his long incarceration and would spend a night with the Williamses on June 30. Did I care to meet him? After a moment's hesitation I said, "No thanks." "You're right," said Williams. "I don't know why, but I still can't turn him away. God knows he's impossible. But I've known him all my life, if that's a good enough reason."

I was to leave for Italy on July 7 and mentioned it in my long letter of June 27 about *Paterson 5* and the current poetry scene. Williams's reply about Pound's visit, dated July 2, for some reason arrived at my New York address after my departure:

Ezra Pound was here, his party of 5, including Dorothy his wife, spent Sunday night with us, Flossie on the couch in the living room. They left yesterday afternoon. . . . Thanks for your letter. If you can come out on the 4th at the usual time we should be able to say something intelligent to each other by then. At least we can greet each other amicably by way of farewell. Poor Pound has had to withstand the whole country's hatred, we don't have to bear that Albatross about our necks. Your comments about *Pat.* 5 amount to just this in my mind, I am not today the man I was ten years ago. I am not for that reason alone dead. The theme has gone on into a higher bracket: that of the mind where all physical characteristics become ambivalent, take whatever characteristics the poet may assign to them. Whatever worth *Pat.* 5 may come to have in contrast to the other parts of the poem, I could not afford not to have written it.

Between my letter and the arrival of his, forwarded by my mother, I saw Williams one more time. I felt rotten about what I had said—the long work put him among the immortals, and I was sniping at him when, in his last years, he most needed support. I wanted to clear things up, especially since I had no intention of ever returning to America. It wasn't until I arrived that I realized how upset he was about Pound and me. Warm as ever, he told me that he had been horrified by Pound's vanity and beliefs. He thought he was, after all, insane if megalomania to the degree in which he possessed it could be called madness. He described how Pound came up the walk with his wife, Dorothy, and a retinue of followers and mistresses. Pound walked into the house talking, sat with shut eyes as his entourage listened in respectful silence, and after a long monologue on his familiar themes of economics and politics, rose suddenly with a look of suspicion, went to the big table, and raised the cloth for a peek underneath. Then he went to the front windows, parted the curtains, and peered out anxiously.

"What's the matter, Ezra?" said Floss sharply. She had never liked him and would not stand for his conceit and nonsense. "Nobody's hiding under the table or on the lawn."

"The Jews," said Ezra, "it's them Jews—they're following me."

"That's baloney!" snapped Floss. "A lot of hot air!"

Taking no notice, as if he hadn't heard her, Pound went on,

seating himself. "If they don't get me tonight, they'll get me on the boat. Won't be safe until we land in Italia. They'll torpedo the boat." He closed his eyes and off he galloped on an anti-Semitic harangue, hotly pursued in his imagination by the nefarious Jews, thirsting for revenge against decent right-thinking anti-Semites. Thoroughly disgusted, Floss maintained minimal civility as hostess while Bill, unable to stomach the spectacle of a totally deranged Pound, disappeared to the front porch. At last Pound opened his eyes, as if from a trance, looked around, and inquired in surprise, "Where's Bill?" "On the porch," said Floss coldly. She went out and found him sitting on the steps in the dark, wringing his hands. "Come in," she said. "You'll catch cold." Then she added sarcastically, "Ezra misses you. He has nobody to insult."

This is the story as I've remembered it with dismay for thirty years. I was right not to have been present. He might have found me skulking under the table with a .45.

Subsequently, the unrepentant American Fascist embarrassed the Italian Social Democratic government on his arrival at the port of Genoa, where the press was present and photographed him with his hand raised in the Fascist salute from the deck of the *Cristoforo Colombo*.

76

To Naples with Love

The American Studies Center, part of the United States Information Service program, was on the third floor of an old palazzo in the Largo Ferrantina a Chiaia, behind the Villa Communale in Naples. It faced an enormous crumbling palazzo inhabited by slum dwellers whose courtyard resembled an opera set. Trucks unloaded fruit and vegetables and, at dozens of stands, all kinds of food, flowers, clothing, and sundry items were sold. Narrow little alleys, with shops and ruined entrances to tenements, wriggled and squirmed tortuously this way and that. Old women, children, and youths burrowed in and out like armies of demented ants.

The palazzo (built by Joseph Bonaparte and once inhabited by Lady Hamilton) had the appearance of an embassy with its flaring marble staircase, statues in niches at each floor landing, vast rooms with crystal chandeliers, lofty frescoed ceilings, and Pompeii-red damasked walls. The other floors were occupied by wealthy Neapolitan families. Only a block away, on the Via dei Mille, were large villas inhabited by some of the city's wealthiest families. In Naples, slum tenements and palaces jostled one another in noisy coexistence. Errand boys on bicycles rode by warbling *Guaglione* in sweet tenor voices. I remembered that the great Caruso came from one of these sleazy tenements.

The director of the school, John Hagy Davis, a young man of twenty-nine, had been living in Naples for many years. The only son of Maude Reppelin Bouvier (the sister of Jacqueline Kennedy's father), he grew up close to his cousin Jackie. He had a Ph.D. in philosophy from Princeton and one of the most lucid minds I'd ever encountered. As a lieutenant/junior grade in the navy, he'd served with the Sixth Fleet in the Mediterranean in the early fifties, when it was a peaceful American lake, literally "Mare Nostrum." Then he studied at the Croce Institute on a Fulbright grant and fell in love with Naples, immersing himself in the Neapolitan world. At twenty-two he witnessed the stark poverty of the slums (the ancient *bassifondi*), and what people had to do, and become, to survive. Instead of horrified retreat he abandoned for a while his books and romantic illusions, learned the dialect, got to know the natives and their problems, and had the will and compassion to identify with the plight of the lowly and disadvantaged. When he became head of the USIS school his humanity was proved by his deeds. He would eventually achieve distinction for his biographies of the Bouviers, the Kennedys, and the Guggenheims.

We first met at the bar of the Hotel Excelsior in Rome. I needed a job and an American poet I knew, who was teaching at the school, arranged the meeting, although she wasn't present. We hit it off and I got the job. With thick black hair and dark good looks he was often taken for a Sicilian don or Neapolitan *signore*. I was taken for an Italian film actor, especially when I grew a Lautrec beard.

As I sat in his office for a briefing, he said, "The school personnel is full of weird characters. I hired them out of pity and because they work for less than anyone else. It's not exploitation—just the opposite. No other institution in the city will take them. They'd starve. Our errand boy has a prison record." He nodded in the direction of a shifty-looking man in his fifties who stood by as if waiting for orders. "In Italy, that slams the door on you forever." Davis rested his gaze on a man who sat with one leg thrust stiffly before him. "Our carpenter and jack-of-all-trades there, whom we call the Maestro, is a cripple, has a stammer, and suffers attacks of amnesia." With gray-black hair parted in the middle hanging down to his shoulders and a tragicomic expression he looked like an *opera buffa* clown. When I made this comment Davis said, "That's a keen observation. He was a successful opera singer with important roles at the San Carlo. He also taught singing. During the war a bomb fell on his head—*literally*! How he survived is a miracle. He spent years in the hospital, lost a leg and his memory, and began to stammer. I found him in a *caffè* where he begged for a job two years ago. He's been with us ever since. He sleeps here. The school is his home."

The Maestro entertained high hopes of marrying an American woman and living in the States as a retired gentleman—on her money. He corresponded with one Liberty Belle Cotton in Alabama, who answered his passionate outbursts of operatic love with equally amorous spirituals. The Maestro's missives, penned by Davis, bore cagey inquiries (smuggled between flowery images) into her financial status. He did not want to believe she was black, as was clearly evident from her photos, and referred to her as *pellerossa,* a redskin. He had procured her name from a Lonely Hearts agency, one of Italy's thriving industries. To the Italian bachelor this was the American Dream.

Then there was the fair-haired overweight young lady with the haughty blue eyes and a face that might have been painted by Piero della Francesca had it been less fleshy. She sat disdainfully aloof behind the reception desk. At that moment she rose to carry some papers to another room and I was shocked to see one leg in a brace; also a cripple, she walked with a rolling lurch.

"Our secretary," said Davis, "is Countess ———, the daughter of the Fascist ex-mayor of Naples. They're the leading family in this part of the world, one of the oldest and noblest in Italy. Her father was, and still is, a fanatical Fascist—he bet everything on the wrong horse. They're broke."

I had arrived in mid-September 1958 and vividly recall that in his office John had a copy of Jack Kerouac's first novel, *The Town and the City,* just published by Scribners. "Have you read this?" he asked. "I think he's a major talent, another Fitzgerald, perhaps." Davis had immediately seen the significance of Kerouac. I hadn't read it and he went into a perceptive critique of the book, revealing a keen grasp of contemporary writing. In Davis, a fellow New Yorker, I had found a friend.

Many of the students were bored, lonely old noblewomen who wanted to be amused. Exchanges like the following were common. "Professor, would you say that your Walt Whitman has the stature of a *Dante?*" "*Marchesa,* would you say that Jesus Christ has the stature of a Buddha?" "Ah, I see. Very entertaining, professor."

I got along well with most of the staff and the students, but being glared at daily by the countess disturbed me. Her frosty demeanor and sullen discontent got on my nerves. Every attempt at civility met with hostile silence. Once as I was telling John about my experiences with the Duke and Duchess Caetani in Rome, he was suddenly called out of the room for a few minutes. Glaring from her desk with a flushed, angry face, the countess hissed, "Mr. Norse, do you always give yourself such airs?" "*Contessa,* do you think only *you* are entitled to give yourself airs?" I retorted. But there she was, impoverished nobility, while I, a no-account American, hobnobbed with the Roman Caetanis when she didn't have a palace or castle to her name. It was insufferable. But I wasn't crazy about Fascists anyway. Call it poetic justice.

I didn't mention the embarrassing episode to John. Although I was accused of social climbing, the truth was, I never sought out the rich and the titled—they sought me out. If they liked me for my talent and personality, I in turn valued them for their qualities. I was no snob. Embittered by her misfortunes, the countess had been brought up to detest Americans and the democratic form of government and must have loathed her subordinate role as secretary for former enemies.

Nancy Whicker, John's wife (his then fiancée), was a lovely young southern debutante and concert violinist, delicate and high-strung. I spent hours at their apartment discussing books and music and swapping anecdotes. Some of our most enjoyable times were spent at the Villa Vergiliana, a rambling estate at Cuma with a vast library, where classics scholars from all countries came to do research. Virgil, it is believed, wrote parts of *The Aeneid* in the nearby Phlegrean Fields. John was administrator of the villa, and he and Nancy often spent weekends and holidays there.

They had a pet lion called Aeneas who was under two years of age and therefore could be legally kept as a domestic pet. Upon reaching the age of two, however, he would have to be destroyed or given to the zoo. Meanwhile, the villa enjoyed absolute freedom from thieves and prowlers. I remember John entering the cage of the roaring beast, who, like an oversized kitten with a gravelly voice, reared on his hind legs and grappled with him.

"Do you want to scratch his head?" John called. "I'll let him out." "No thanks," I said hurriedly. "I'll watch you scratch him." "He's perfectly safe," said John, "although he plays a bit rough sometimes. He doesn't know how paper-thin our skin is." "I do," I said. "His tongue alone can break the skin when he licks you," said John. "I hear lions are very unpredictable," I said uneasily. "Yes, when they reach adulthood. They're okay until two. That's when they begin changing. But we've grown so attached to each other that I'll feel lousy when the time comes."

When John and Nancy left him alone the lion would moan like an abandoned child. "We were his mother and father," John told me years afterwards. They'd had Aeneas since he was a cub. They also had a marvelous cook called Umberto, whose meals, consumed with local wines, Falerno and Lacrima Cristi, were delicious. Where but Naples would you enjoy a wine called the "Tears of Christ"?

John told me that occasionally he'd excavate in the garden searching for shards of ancient Greek pottery. One night an American classics professor fell into one of the pits John had dug. His screams went unheard for hours. Luckily they found him, but next morning he left. "It's so much more appropriate," said John as we laughed about it, "to have a poet here than one of those sour Wasp classics scholars we always have to put up with."

I was invited to spend a week during Christmas. We went down to the ancient Greek acropolis and famous cave of the Sybil at Cumae. What was once a powerful, prosperous city was now an open plain along the sea. Near the Sybil's grotto two headless female statues seemed to be holding a conversation among the weeds and grasses—as if they hadn't lost their heads. The cave itself had many niches and fissures from which the beach below was visible. It was quite eerie, evocative of vanished mysteries, of something important to the world that had passed away forever. You felt like shouting or hooting, half expecting that instead of your own echo some other voice, from the ancient past, would respond in riddles and runes. I wrote the following:

> *Gibbered at Cuma*
> *in the cave*
> *sprang thru weeds*
> *cool silence*
> *echoed*
> *long white beach*
> *whispered & hissed*
>
> *But the niches were empty*
>
> *Where is she now*
> *with her answers*
> *or did I hear*
> *a scream*

The neighboring peasants reacted to the lion with fear and loathing. They complained that the roaring terrified their sheep at night. Dogs barked and howled, the peasants trembled in their beds. They lived in dread that the lion would escape and devour their flocks and children. But John managed, from time to time, to allay their fears. He himself, as the animal grew, had some close calls. Once the great claws ripped John's arm to the bone and, I believe, his chest was torn. This had been in play; the lion never attacked him. I could see the genuine love and affection between them. Aeneas was truly like a playful kitten. But finally the sad day came; the Naples zoo called for the big cat.

I recall visiting the zoo and finding Aeneas behind bars. His mournful roars filled the air for miles. To the dismay of the onlookers, John stuck his hand in the cage. I too was uneasy until the beast bent his huge head and gently licked John's hand!

77

The Pillbox

I lived in a tiny modern pillbox built of concrete, perched precariously on a cliff over the Bay of Naples, with a stupendous view. Called Posillipo (meaning "pause from pain"), the hillside was full of tropical foliage and old mansions with a hint of decay not unlike our own southern, postbellum sort. The chief feature of my otherwise featureless room, apart from its semicircular row of windows offering a spectacular view of Vesuvius and the bay, was the concrete terrace stretching from my glass door, about thirty feet long and twelve feet wide at the entrance forming a triangle. It was wider and longer than the room, which formed the apex and would have been claustrophobic without it. The Pillbox cost $45 a month; I earned the then princely sum of $150 a month.

Directly below lay the rocks and the sea; the street was above. I overlooked the sparkling bay from a considerable height. I enjoyed walking up or down the hill on the stone street stairs past decaying mansions engulfed by banana leaves, bougainvillea dangling from tufa walls, and thick spiny fico d'India jutting bladelike into the sky. At night from my windows I could see lights glowing like stars on the slopes of Vesuvius and the festooned chains of light bulbs on the anchored ships. Beneath the terrace waves lapped the rocks.

Dans la nuit du tombeau, toi qui m'as consolé,
Rends-moi le Pausilippe et la mer d'Italie. . . .

Posillipo had long been a favorite of the ancient Greeks and Romans, who carved out caves from the igneous rock, making smooth, sensuous golden grottoes everywhere, with houses and terraces open to sun and sea. My address, Via Posillipo 38, Grottaromana (which means "Roman cave"), bore testimony to its history. Sometimes, as I lay alone at night, the sound of the waves drove me crazy. I felt marooned, imagining I was in a lonely lighthouse, far from civilization.

By day, however, it was the reverse. Naples swarmed with life, especially with *scugnizz'* (small street boys) and youths who dogged your footsteps, trying to sell everything from cigarettes, fountain pens, and watches to themselves or their sisters. "My seester, meester? My brudder? You like-a me? Chip. Me like-a you." They were naturally amoral and attractive but could be treacherous; you never knew what you might get into. One followed me for about a half hour on the Via Caracciolo and, finally realizing the futility of his trek, stuck out his hand and pouted.

"Meester, you owe me two hundred lire."

"For what?" I demanded in astonishment.

"Eh, for wearing out my shoe leather."

Naples is the original Third World. The street boys boasted that during the war they bought and sold American sailors. The drunken sailor would wake up in some back alley, stripped bare. One story tells of a stolen American battleship, spirited away without a trace—sold, it was said, for a good price! It is a fact that after the Allied invasion the boys defeated the Nazis by incredible feats of bravery and cunning. They lived on rats in bombed-out rubble and tunnels. Mere children, their courage helped turn the tide against the Germans.

But each transaction was also a pitched battle—with the grocer, tobacconist, cabbie, *portiere,* and vendor. Constant vigilance against *freggatura* (deception, to put it politely) was a prerequisite. My Florentine friend Giorgio, who visited me for four days, was horrified by the trickery. The natives repelled him and he couldn't understand the dialect. I had to translate from Neapolitan to Italian!

The poet who had introduced me to John Davis was a nervous wreck. Each scene with a cabbie or *tabacchaio* who shortchanged her caused the veins to stand out in her neck as she screamed. But the Neapolitans, interpreting this as just another bit of theatre, like their own, in the ongoing saga of the lira, remained unmoved. "You misunderstood, *signora,* I said two thousand not one thousand lire. You don't understand our dialect." At this she would almost burst a blood vessel. "Cretin!

What am I speaking if not Neapolitan?" she'd screech. "I will not pay one extra lira! I'll call the police!" Usually the man would accept the price, already high. To drown her sorrows she drank heavily and would pass out, sprawled on the floor, thighs exposed. Finally, to everyone's relief, she married a sober Italian engineer and went to live in Rome.

I loved to wander along the bayfront promenade on the Via Caracciolo, a wide, blindingly bright thoroughfare where the bay sparkled in the sun. Near-naked youths leapt about on rock jetties between the water and the promenade, singing, shouting, and scooping up handfuls of squid and octopi and dumping them into buckets. Their lean bronzed bodies glistened like metal sculpture in the dazzling light. They smiled and shouted to me.

One day I was adopted by a shabby youth of about sixteen wearing ragged pants, battered shoes, and a soiled brown shirt. Salvatore was handsome and olive-skinned but uncommunicative. When I offered him three hundred lire to get something to eat, he regarded me with a hurt look in his great dark eyes. He didn't want money, he insisted, he wanted an American friend. I had been in Italy long enough to know the special, esoteric meaning of the word *amico* and felt a thrill of excitement. Refusing the money was objective proof of his sincerity in that part of the world (though it could be construed as aiming for higher stakes). As if on cue, while we sauntered aimlessly along the crowded walk, he offered to share with me some "pleasures"—*divertimenti*—and motioned to follow him. With a tightness in my stomach I went along until we reached the *funiculare,* where I paid the fare and we boarded the train.

About halfway up he signaled to get out. As we stood on the deserted platform in the cool dim tunnel, watching the train disappear uphill, I felt uneasy. Without warning he seized me with such force that for a moment I thought he wanted to hurl me to the tracks below. Instead, with great excitement he unbuttoned his pants and mine, ran his hands all over my body and pulled me to a bench, where we both quickly climaxed.

The sound of the returning train brought us back to the real world. Barely rearranging our clothes in time, we stepped inside with the bored nonchalance of people in trains. As I looked at the other passengers, wondering what they would think if they knew what had just happened on the platform, I realized that sex, in this volcanic environment, was like hunger, a natural need to be shamelessly filled. Even children did it without shame. Everyone in this part of the world was, in Freud's phrase, "polymorphous perverse," by which he described pubescence. But if all indulged in sex it couldn't be more perverse than hunger. Even the dictionary, defining *elemental,* says: "basic and powerful, primal: as hunger and sex are *elemental* drives." The term *perverse* was a puritanical judgment of nature, but the act itself was clean and sweet as a Neapolitan song. Perhaps this is what stimulated their vocal chords and made them sing like birds. It was common knowledge among opera buffs that in the old days Italian tenors, before going onstage, performed *fellatio* on the firemen in the wings (it was said to lubricate the vocal chords). In Italian the word for "fireman," *pompiere,* and the slang for "blow job," *pompino,* are cognate. Language preserves with accuracy certain truths that, through hypocrisy, remain unspoken.

Suddenly Salvatore intruded upon my musings; he seized me roughly and shoved me out the door to another platform before we arrived at street level. Again I had a moment of paranoia. Would he pull a knife, try to steal my money? But the moment we were alone again, he thrust and ground his pelvis against mine and feverishly kissed my face, neck, and mouth with moist hot lips. His breath, like his body odor, was sweet, with a faint garlicky tang, the fresh fragrance of Italian youth. Garlic and parmigiana lend a distinct bouquet to the healthy masculine odor in Italy.

With soft moans Salvatore licked my body and throat and another wild session ensued, after which tears welled in his velvet brown eyes. Hugging and kissing me intensely, he mumbled something I couldn't understand. I was so moved by this youth's passionate involvement with a total stranger (whom he had seduced from first to last!) that I had difficulty keeping back my own tears.

Out in the dazzling sunlight again, I pressed fifteen hundred lire into his hand (less than two and a half dollars). He thanked me profusely and said that he would use the money to depart for his village in the Campania and give it to his parents, who were poor peasants. I believed him. He was a real country boy. After five years in Italy I knew the type—motivated by his feelings, honest in a naive, unequivocal way. He started crying again and kissed me on the mouth, as members of the same family do in southern Italy. If interchange of deep sexual feeling means anything, we had certainly become family by our spontaneous act of union. He was my brother, my *amico*. We were now bound by love.

In a large flowery hand Salvatore scrawled on a scrap of paper his name and address. "Write to me," he said. "I will never forget you." He wiped his tears. *"Ciao, amico mio, ciao."*

78

Sir Harold Acton

From John Davis I learned that the multileveled cluster of small rooms and terraces had been built by a gangster whose dance floor, on street level, had once been a noisy meeting place for organized crime. It was now remarkably peaceful. Goldfinches warbled in the foliage and I never saw my neighbors. Gennaro, the *portiere*, a scheming, conniving, deceitful son of Naples, showed up to collect the rent or extort money. But once, unwittingly, this old *caffone* did me a good turn. Next door to our complex was a whitewashed stucco villa of which Gennaro was also the *portiere*. On questioning him I learned that the occupant was "an English milord." One day not long afterwards, Gennaro arrived with a calling card from Sir Harold Acton inviting me to tea. I could scarcely believe my luck. I'd heard about his antics when, as a young Oxford student in the twenties with Evelyn Waugh, Auden, Isherwood, and others, he was allegedly the inspiration for Anthony Blanche in *Brideshead Revisited*. He had conceived, it was said, the original idea for the novel. I learned later that he had lectured in English literature and taught for seven years at the National University of Peking, where he was involved with the Chinese classical theatre.

Acton ushered me into a spacious room and poured tea. A tall bald man in his fifties with a courtly mandarin air, he spoke in a hushed, measured voice, touching his fingertips together and taking small mincing steps, as if in carpet slippers. He was a Roman Catholic of a noble British-Italian family; his ancestors had figured prominently in the wars of the Bourbons, who bestowed a title in gratitude. A main thoroughfare along the Naples waterfront was still named Via Ammiraglio Acton. In England the family was in the peerage.

Gennaro, he said, had told him that an American *professore-scrittore* lived next door and he was eager to make my acquaintance. After discovering that we knew people in common (Auden, Isherwood, Spender), he told me of his abiding interest in working with the Catholic charities program for street-boy rehabilitaion—something with which he had been involved for years, through donations and volunteer work. I had never before seen so many waifs and strays living on the streets, I said. He sighed, regretting that it was typical of Naples, but said that much was being done by the church to alleviate their condition. His air of piety contrasted sharply with a sort of implicit naughtiness, nothing more tangible than a nuance in voice and gesture, nothing actually said. With a sort of clerical air he moved and spoke ceremoniously, as if eternally administering the wafer and the wine, as if life were a blessed sacrament. Yet the thought persisted that all this religiosity was more pagan than Christian— like the annual *festa* of San Gennaro, patron saint of Naples, where the dried blood of the saint, kept in a reliquary urn, miraculously liquefies once a year to assure good crops and fortune. In Naples pagan elements have never died. The priests were aware that, had the liquefaction not occurred on schedule, San Gennaro would have been violently discredited by the mobs that annually attend this dramatic insurance policy. They were never slow to revile or demolish a plaster saint who does not deliver the goods.

I told Acton of some scenes I had witnessed in the city, such as a man and twelve-year-old street boy who, several times a day, squeezed into the narrow space between the stone walls of two adjacent buildings on a crowded street, obviously assuming they had remained unobserved. Acton wore a Mona Lisa smile. "The Madonna is never far away," he intoned. "The flesh and the spirit impinge upon one another lightly here."

"Isn't this what draws northern Europeans like a magnet?" I said. "They take a holiday from guilt in the seamy streets of Naples and the pagan islands."

"The lure of the sun and the flesh," he said, "will always draw them here. It acts as a narcotic to the sensually deprived."

"D. H. Lawrence treated this frankly and openly," I said.

"To be sure. A very strange, mousy little man."

"You knew him, then?"

"Ah, yes. And his German *frau*, Frieda. An odd combination."

"What was he like? Formidable, no doubt."

"Oh, no, no, not at all! *She*—the baroness—was formidable. *He* uttered scarcely a word. At least not to men, especially of the upper classes. He was overconcerned about his plebeian background. But women found him irresistible. Men could not understand why. He had a hesitant, thin, squeaky little voice. Quite ineffectual. But, apparently, with women he became quite fierce." Then he added with an arch smile, "At least, verbally."

Acton obviously knew what he was talking about. Later I discovered he was a scholar-writer with fourteen published books, including *The Bourbons of Naples,* a historical work.

"Did you see him often?" I asked.

"Oh, yes. Here and in England. He was made much of in London. But he was always the same—shy, withdrawn, intense."

Once again, through the eyes of those who knew them, I saw how false myths and legends were perpetuated by ardent admirers of famous artists, in the belief that the fictitious creation and the person are one and the same. The famous men and women I knew were nothing like the public imagined them. They were prey to the same fears and insecurities, the same vanities and shortcomings, as others. I don't suppose anyone could have been more self-deprecating than William Carlos Williams, yet he was one of a handful of great modernists, including Lawrence, in our century.

79

Classic Frieze in a Garage

I t was in the Pillbox in 1958 that I wrote the poems that won Dr. Williams completely. Almost overnight, from the time I arrived, my style changed. It had a lot to do with the good doctor's teachings, but the al fresco life of Naples and Lawrence's free-verse poems also had much to do with it. I felt as the impressionists must have felt when they left the studios for the open air. "Very satisfactory to my ear," wrote Williams, September 2, 1958. "Let's not talk about the 'variable foot' as long as you write in this way." Toward the end of the year he sent an inscribed copy of *Paterson 5* and I sent about twenty-five poems I had written in November while sick with the flu, plus an earlier batch. I received a rave dated January 30, 1959:

> Something has come over you, these are the best you have ever sent me—I haven't finished reading them but the first 2 or 3 in this batch are superb. All sense of straining has in these three poems disappeared from your writing and your control of the language has blossomed like a flower, a sense of ease has taken possession of you which I have never before seen in your work. I'll get Floss to read me more as soon as she can be captured. I am delighted to be able to write in this way, it makes me as happy as I hope it makes you.
>
> [Two days later] My first impression has been confirmed, Floss read the poems to me and she enjoyed them as much as I did, especially the first, the *Piccolo Paradiso*, that will stand up anywhere among the best poems of our times. . . .
>
> You have breached a new lead, shown a new power over the language which makes theories of composition

so much blah—save that they open the artist's eyes to what is going on about him to record unchecked by academic rules. Your freedom in the measure is worth all the rest to me.

I had written Williams on December 12, 1958: "I find I am striking a style. . . . The old world and the new . . . I actually saw, on a street in Naples, the incredible juxtaposition—in an old garage where mechanics were welding & greasing & blowtorching cars—two huge classic friezes, hardly the worse for wear, stood proudly and majestically over the Fiats, the mechanics & the gasoline!"

"Classic Frieze in a Garage" had won his instant praise. The whole group would appear in underground magazines in the States, and two, less stylistically daring, in the *Paris Review,* and later in a Penguin Modern Poets volume with Charles Bukowski and Philip Lamantia. I had finally achieved a stylistic breakthrough.

80

Madame Laurin

I had been teaching in Naples for about six months when I met a remarkable woman at Frances McCann's new apartment near Castel Sant'Angelo. Frances had thrown a party in my honor to introduce me to some new friends of hers, particularly Mme. Laurin. This blueblood—large, stout, with frizzy orange hair and a florid complexion—resembled many another American matron in her fifties, waddling stiffly about, peering from steel-rimmed specs with blue-eyed alarm at the dangerous world. But if Julia seemed vulnerable in public, in private she was a commanding personage. Her upper-class quasi-British accent and compelling style—a mix of gossip, anecdote, information, advice, psychology (Jungian), and occult lore, at which she was adept—made her an American blend of Mme. Blavatsky and Eileen Garrett; all three were look alikes. She was in fact a theosophist and, as Tennessee Williams would say, a lady of high degree. A great-granddaughter of John Jacob Astor and direct descendant of Peter Stuyvesant and of English nobles who beheaded Charles I, she was a puritan with a sense of humor. When Henry Miller's *Tropic of Cancer* first created a stir, she pitched her copy (after reading it) into the Seine. "Dirty book," she said, "but funny." Born and raised in Paris, she kept American nationality while living most of her life in France. She was also related to William and Henry James.

I signed a copy of my first book and she became an ardent admirer. When I left to resume teaching in Naples she followed me. I soon fell under her spell but didn't know she'd fallen under mine. (I was a short New York poet, a combination she found irresistible.) She was sentimental about New York and America—from a distance. Her father, Robert Chanler, was six foot six ("I loathe tall men!" she'd say), lived on the Hudson River, and had a house on Sutton Place, where he built a connecting passage to the Barrymore house so that he could more easily reach John, his drinking companion. "He was very intimidating. He'd sit in the front row at Broadway plays and heckle John Barrymore. 'All right, Bob, come and show us how it's done!' John would shout, and Father would attempt to climb the proscenium amidst a chorus of boos and cheers. Next day the tabloids would carry the story. He always made headlines for scandalous behavior."

In the twenties she did collages with Max Ernst, inspired Blaise Cendrars, who was in love with her, and visited Gertrude Stein's famous salon on the rue Fleurus. "What a voice that woman had!" she exclaimed. "But the baby talk got boring." Alexander Calder married her niece, while she had a *mariage blanc* with an American that remained unconsummated—he loved boys. Her second husband, Gabriel Laurin, a French painter from Aix-en-Provence, was an intimate friend of Darius Milhaud, Max Ernst, Albert Giacometti, and so on. He figures in Cendrars's fictional masterpiece, *L'Homme foudroyé,* as the leader of a gang of young hoodlums. A hero of the French *Résistance* during World War II, he had a hook instead of a left hand and became a famous Nazi killer during the Occupation. Cendrars, who had lost his right hand in World War I, called Laurin his "right-hand man." Mme. Laurin bore two girls, and when the Germans occupied France she escaped to Lisbon and boarded a refugee ship that was bombed during the voyage, but she and the girls safely disembarked in New York. The other passengers, Jewish refugees, were not so lucky. When they were denied entry into the United States (Roosevelt's policy), the ship sailed to Canada, where it was also turned away. This time they were blown up by the Nazis—no survivors.

When she arrived in Naples, red-faced and fearful of the sun, I knew nothing about her, had no idea where she lived. With her daughter Pauline, who was twenty-two, she took a room in a second-class *pensione* (she never lived extravagantly) and visited me at the Pillbox. She'd sit in my canvas director's chair in the shade while I sunbathed in swimming trunks on the reclining deck chair. Pauline fidgeted, goldfinches warbled, the sea sparkled, and the sun dulled my mind in the intense heat.

Why had this society lady taken such an interest in me? She had certainly not come to Naples, a city she abhorred, for the sun, which she couldn't stand. As the days passed an answer finally came. I had confessed to being bored with Italy and suddenly she said, "I want you to reply to this question without thinking, right off the top of your head. What city in Europe would you choose to live in if you were offered the chance? Quick!" "Paris!" "Splendid. You have an apartment waiting for you there!"

For some time I had felt lost, stuck in a backwater, caught in the past. For creative stimulation Paris was unequaled, but beyond my means. Evidently the *grande dame* was also bored and lonely and needed company. She had an apartment, she said, on the rue St. Louis en l'Ile that she no longer used—small and quiet, perfect for a writer. She needed someone to live there (it contained rare objets d'art from China), but I had to leave as soon as possible. When I told her the semester ended in three months she rose impatiently. "I wouldn't wait too long if I were you," she said. She asked if my friend Edgar would take care of my living expenses and I assured her he would. "It's a deal," she said.

I soon discovered that she was at her best when arranging people's lives—a sort of social Diaghilev, an impresario who could divine the perfect move for others, but, when governed by whim, which sometimes swept through her like a tornado, she could cause consternation and damage. Then her interference was viewed in a more somber light as meddling. But I'm getting ahead of my story; happily, at that moment, it turned out to be the perfect move. And John Davis cooperated as soon as he heard about it. As I recall, he took my class himself to complete the semester.

81

Dancing with Polanski on the Paris Express

In her letters Julia threatened to revoke the offer if there was further delay, so I spent only a few days in Rome. On a sunny afternoon in May 1959, I stood on the platform of the Rome-Paris Express at the Stazione Termini, bidding Edgar, who financed the trip, good-bye. He would send a small monthly stipend to cover expenses so that I could write without financial pressure. I now had two patrons (they never lavished money on me, just enough to get by) and vowed that my new work would repay their kindness.

Arrivals and farewells with Edgar were memorable experiences and this departure was no exception. On the platform we kept quoting Nerval, Rimbaud, and Lautréamont and I quoted a moving poem by Po Chu I on friendship. "That's culture," he said with glistening eyes, "when we have world literature at our fingertips." A few feet away a good-looking man with straight blond hair and bangs was passionately kissing an incredibly beautiful girl of about sixteen. We decided they were in the movie industry, she looked like a starlet and he, although no taller than Edgar and I, might have been an actor. "I *say*, isn't she absolutely smashing!" murmured Edgar. "Yes," I replied, staring at the young man. The lovers were oblivious of everyone. I don't know what went through Edgar's mind when he gazed in rapture at beautiful women, but I was sure it was no different from my feelings when dazzled by attractive young men. I suffered from chronic sexual malnutrition, feeling sex-starved most of my life. Like John Keats, I couldn't forsake the flesh for the spirit—to me they were one; my spirit suffered when body and soul went unappeased. ("Those who separate body and soul have neither," said Oscar Wilde.) The young satyr nibbling the nymphet's cerise-tinted lips would, I thought, agree. The electricity crackling between them could have run the train.

Finally, whistles blew, conductors shouted "All aboard" in Italian, and I boarded the sleeping car. The blond rushed into the same compartment and we hoisted our valises into the overhead baggage rack. We both stuck our heads out the window and waved—I to Edgar, he to the dark-haired siren. Then we sank into our economy seats wedged between old Italian peasants as the train pulled out.

"Are you going to Paris?" he asked in Italian and I responded "*Sì.*" We soon discovered we weren't Italians and lapsed into English. He was a Polish film maker who had been working in Rome but had met with no big success and was going to Paris to try his luck. His name was Roman Polanski. He, too, he said, was Jewish.

With his childlike blue eyes, caressing voice, and histrionic gestures, he was very engaging. In the way of travelers looking forward to a long dull journey, we found that we had many things in common. For instance, we had both been ballet dancers. To illustrate this, he jumped up and executed some pirouettes, which I promptly matched in the moving train, to the astonished delight of our fellow passengers. Although I was old enough to be his father I had the resilience and suppleness of a youth and he took me for thirty (he was in his twenties). Except for catnaps during the long night at the end of which we had become old friends, we talked each other's heads off. He gave me a phone number in Paris and said he was usually at the Deux Magots, the best-known Left Bank café. Occasionally I ran into him there, looking scruffy and despondent. As time passed the train ride receded into the distance, lost in the terminus of time. I forgot about him until he achieved fame as a film director, which increased with the tragic murder of his wife, Sharon Tate, by Charles Manson.

82

Paris in the Spring

I arrived in Paris eager to sink into depravity, to become dissolute like Verlaine, the *homo-duplex* between Satan and God, deeply spiritual yet immersed in wine, absinthe, hashish, opium, and sexual marathons with both sexes. Paris offered everything I needed. I was a poet, not a priest. But instead of the promised land for a wanton life of bohemian dissipation, I found myself in the backyard studio of Mme. Laurin's proper stone house in Boulogne-sur-Seine—a *banlieu* (suburb) of Paris where forced chastity almost unhinged me. Rue Thiers was a quiet street in a respectable suburb and *numéro* 9 was like an artists' colony in which I was the artist. I had artistic freedom, no financial worries, and no life.

Mme. Laurin had the rare faculty of nurturing artists with the skill of a gardener tending plants. By virtue of her magical and imaginative faculties she was a real muse (though getting on), yet as the weeks passed I couldn't help wondering why the Ile Saint-Louis apartment was never mentioned. I craved the youth and ferment of the Latin Quarter, in the center of things, not the dull, conventional suburbs, without a touch of Paris life. When on occasion I'd casually inquire about the flat, my hostess would reply vaguely, "Oh, the young man hasn't left yet, doncha know."

On my first day she introduced me to a big elm tree in the backyard. "This is Henry," she said, patting its bark affectionately as if it were an animal. *"Bonjour,* Henry," I said. A bough swayed in response. "He is the presiding spirit of the garden," she said, "which is full of elementals. And this is Annabelle, who is very old and wise." A big white chow with an almost black-purple tongue panted in the sunny warmth of the yard. When I patted her head she wagged her rump and licked my hand. "You've passed the Annabelle test," said Mme. Laurin as we crossed to the trellised wooden studio, on whose brown facade a riot of roses bloomed. "Well, here's where you'll live and work. Nobody will disturb you, not even the cleaning woman." I put down my two traveling bags. "If you miss anything, call Antoinette. She never fails to find things." "Is she your maid?" I asked. Mme. Laurin grinned. "You might call her that. She's an elemental whose power is finding lost objects." "My power is losing them," I said. "I'll certainly need *her* services."

So there I was, with a tree, a dog, and a spirit. I had to call Antoinette almost at once. I couldn't find my traveler's checks, which I kept in a suitcase—the wrong thing to do, anyway. Starting to panic, I muttered, "Antoinette, my traveler's checks, *please!*" Within minutes I found them in the pocket of a pair of blue jeans. From then on she has never let me down. I was tempted to clap my hands and say, "Antoinette, a beautiful youth, *please,* between eighteen and twenty." It might have worked.

Even if the meals had been decent I'd have made trips to Paris, but the culinary arts were not among Mme. Laurin's accomplishments. She was a vegetarian who regarded food as a nuisance. Her idea of nutrition was Cheez-its, Chesterfields, and Coca-Cola. She grew stout on Cokes and pastry. I frequented cafés in St. Germain des Près afternoons or evenings. I'd take the Métro at Porte St. Cloud in Boulogne, change at La Nuette, and get off at Odéon. For twelve centimes I'd buy a croissant, for fifty centimes a café crême, and a ham sandwich for sixty-five centimes: twenty-five cents for the meal, thirty-five with two beers. Paris was wonderful for the impecunious. Today the coffee costs three dollars, and with a croissant, ham sandwich, and tip it comes to around ten dollars in the cafés.

During the three weeks I spent at Boulogne with Julia—we had shifted to a first-name basis—I experienced some baffling psychic phenomena. One afternoon as we sat in the living room talking, I heard the clatter of rapid footsteps on the stairs. "Oh, Pauline is coming down!" I said. I turned and saw no one. With a peculiar knowing expression, which I would come to recognize, Julia also turned to look. About five seconds later Pauline ran downstairs, but with absolutely no sound! "Auditory precognition," Julia said. "Nothing unusual."

Twice I had severe headaches and each time she stood behind my chair, passed her hands over my head, without touching me, and the headaches disappeared. She would wash her hands afterwards, saying that without this precaution the healer was in danger of absorbing the pain or illness into her own body.

As Edgar had talked interminably of anthroposophy and Rudolf Steiner in Rome, Julia revealed the world of theosophy, explaining the finer, invisible planes within the dense physical body. I listened with a mixture of wonder, curiosity, suspended disbelief, and skepticism. These finer states of material existence, she said, were the etheric, the astral, and the mental. They all exist simultaneously, interpenetrating one another—the dream and waking world—independent yet overlapping. Through clairvoyance it is possible to contact the higher plane, she said. But I wanted to contact the lower plane.

83

Erotic Versus Esoteric

At the end of three weeks I announced that much as I appreciated metaphysical enlightenment I was feeling uncontrollably erotic: wouldn't I be better off in a hotel in St. Germain? Julia leapt to her feet, clapped her hands twice, and shouted, "Pack your bags! No wonder I've been smelling centaurs and goats for weeks! *Quel horreur!*" She pressed some francs into my palm. "Take a taxi, go straight to the apartment—it's ready— and tell the young man to get in touch with me. Give him this note."

She was in no danger, but I didn't want to offend her by saying so. Besides, she already knew in which direction my libido lay. A slight, curly-haired blond young man in his early twenties, speaking fluent French and American English, smiled when I handed him the note, picked up some clothes, and left. Sorry to have dispossessed him, I put down my bags and looked around. The flat was small but cozy, with rare Oriental objects and antiques. A narrow stairway led upstairs directly to the living room, behind which a king-size bed filled the tiny bedroom. It was at the rear of a leaning gray stone house with four stories, some five hundred years old. I don't recall a kitchen, but there was a cookstove and bathroom. A small window in the living room overlooked an air shaft. Dark, quiet, with a musty odor, it was perfect for me.

I was lucky to have a separate entrance independent of snooping *concierges*, rumored to be police spies. After some exciting but brief sexual encounters I found what I was looking for. Even now when I think of Tim Reilly (name changed) once again I relive the pleasure of that *affaire du coeur*. It lasted about a year and was the high point of my sentimental attachments in that city of nymphs and satyrs. I could have gladly spent my life with him.

I ran into him in a Left Bank bar sitting on stools before the zinc counter. With a sort of defensive pride he said he wrote poetry and stories and knew James Jones, the novelist, who praised his talent. Jones was a real writer and a real man, he said as he guzzled his beer. The trouble with most writers, he confided, was—they weren't *real* men, they were "fags." Uh oh, an ugly American, I thought bitterly—but he was beautiful—so he'll gore Jews and Negroes next. I stood up. "Hey, where the hell ya goin'? Did I say somethin'?" Grabbing my arm, he seemed perplexed. "Just when we're gettin' acquainted," he grumbled. "True," I replied drily. "All right, fuck off," he snarled. "Who gives a shit!" He looked so absurdly hurt when I left that I couldn't get him off my mind. Perhaps his boorishness concealed feelings very different from those he revealed. I decided to find out.

Next day I returned to the bar, half hoping to find him in a less stupefied state. On the same barstool he sat moodily staring into a beer. When he saw me his face lit up with a big happy grin. "Hey, it's the poet," he exclaimed, "lemme buy ya a drink!" When he wasn't drunk he oozed Irish charm—without homophobic slurs. We discussed Fitzgerald and Hemingway, both of whom he worshiped and were, like him, from the Midwest. He was twenty-two, with flaxen curls, a high forehead, soft brown eyes, and exquisitely chiseled features. He resembled the young Dylan Thomas in the Augustus John portrait and Lord Byron. Trim and muscular, he was about five foot eight. His father was a U.S. senator, but Tim wanted to be a writer. "Which is why I'm here," he said. "Jim Jones is my teacher. Well, anyway, he crit-

icizes my work. It's like learning from a living Hemingway." I
told him that William Carlos Williams had written the preface
for my second book. "Which ought to be out any day now," I
added. Tim was duly impressed. He asked if he could read some
of my work. I wrote my address on a slip of paper. "You live
near Jones! He's on the Ile de la Cité."

A few days later the doorbell rang and a voice bellowed from
the stairs, "Hey, is it true you're queer? That's what they say in the
cafés!" He stomped into the room belligerently, his breath reeking of booze. "Well, maybe they're right," I said, my gut con-
tracting, "and maybe they're wrong. What business is it of yours?"
"I wanted to know if—if it was true." His voice wavered. "Did you
come to find out for yourself?" I sneered. "To fuck or fight?" I
spat out the phrase. In panic I thought of Julia's priceless antiques
smashed in a drunken brawl. He looked bewildered. "No, I don't
wanna *fight*! I'm—I'm half *queer* myself!" He blurted this out as if
plunging into icy water. "May I sit down?" I nodded. "You sure
sounded like you wanted to bash my head in," I said, still trembling. He looked genuinely amazed. "Hell, no!" "Then why do
you behave like a queer basher?" He slumped in the chair. "Believe me," he said, "I'm not!" He stared soulfully, lustfully at me.
"I'm actually three-quarters queer," he said.

That afternoon, evening, and the following day we were never
out of each other's sight for a moment except to run down to the
little shop across the street for cigarettes, sandwiches, and coffee.
Once the air was cleared of the dread of exposure, he was a
wonderful, inexhaustible lover. From that day his tenderness
never wavered, he lost his belligerence entirely. "You're a real
man!" he'd say, to which I responded, "It takes one to know one."

His hypocritical contempt for "fags" was a masculine coverup.
Heavily armored against social disapproval (his muscles were
plates of bronze), his only crime against nature was to hide it. "Even
sodomy can be sane and wholesome," said D. H. Lawrence,
"granted there is an exchange of genuine feeling." We had plenty
of that to burn; it overpowered us, increasing daily. It was a
nurturing feeling that gave us peace, a deep sense of fulfillment,
healing and balancing us. I had known it so rarely in my life that I
could have lived with him forever. But it was not to be.

Around that time a most extraordinary thing happened. I had
arranged to meet Julia at American Express, near the Opera,
where she would make a financial transaction, after which we'd go

to a nearby café where we liked the pastries. I wore a nylon summer shirt, tan chino pants, and my fedora and, perspiring freely, kept mopping my brow with a handkerchief—it was a very hot July day. When I entered American Express I was struck by the deafening roar of hundreds of voices from a mob of tourists—it was the high season—and, spotting Julia with her back to me at a teller's window at the far end of the floor, I began walking toward her. As I did so the roar of voices ceased abruptly and an eerie hush fell over the place. Slowly making my way through the silent crowd, I experienced a sensation of unreality. From a distance of about fifty yards Julia turned, with her knowing expression, and nodded. The moment I was at her side the roar resumed. "Julia?" I said questioningly. "Yes, I know," she said with her wise look.

"How do you explain it?" I asked while we waited for our coffee and pastry in the café. I told her I'd had such experiences all my life. As a teen-ager I could feel the charged hush when I walked into a schoolroom, theatre lobby, or restaurant, all eyes suddenly turned on me in astonishment.

"It's psychic energy," she said. "They look but don't know why. You are an archetype, an elemental condition, a dream image. They react subliminally—as if a centaur had trotted into a bank. The crowd acts from the collective unconscious."

"But I wasn't doing anything except mopping my brow," I said.

"It has nothing to do with what you are thinking or doing. It's like a time warp, a shift of consciousness."

"I felt a current between us," I said, "though your back was turned. I felt as though we'd galvanized the whole place."

"Oh, but they didn't connect it with us."

Nobody could have been more representative of American heterosexual masculinity than James Jones. He was short but with the face and build of a heavyweight boxer, all muscle. Soon after Tim introduced us in a bar, we were having drinks one afternoon with Gregory Corso in our favorite watering place, Les Nuages in St. Germain. Jim's driver's license had been revoked for a year for drunken driving. At one point he asked me, "Do you like boys or girls?" I said I preferred boys. Gregory, who was by no means above a little fag bashing now and then to assert his top-dog status, asked him, "Have you had any queer experiences?" "Sure," bellowed Jones in his gruff voice, "many times. Have you?"

"Naaah," lied Gregory. "Did you like it?" "Yeah, very much," Jones growled. "The only thing I didn't like was, when you kiss, the other guy's beard scratches. But after a few experiences I kind of lost interest. I just happen to like women more."

I admired Jim Jones for his fearless honesty. He was the only straight man I knew who didn't cover up or misunderstand. He was the boy with the courage to say the emperor had no clothes. Corso was all coverup, pose, rationalization. Jones was unafraid of the truth. Unlike most writers, he wasn't a liar. I still miss him. I introduced Julia to Jim and his wife, Gloria, when their first baby was born and they got along beautifully: the baby is now a writer.

A young French-American nobleman, André de la Rochefoucauld (a direct descendant of the great French writer), also drank with us at Les Nuages. His mother was American. Although only twenty, André had the same forthrightness as Jones. Once he said to Corso, whose nose was running, "For God's sake, Gregory, wipe your nose! You're disgusting. You look like a street urchin." Helpless before such candor, Gregory complied.

I got to know the *Paris Review* and *Merlin* magazine bunch— Nelson Aldrich, Austryn Wainhouse, and, only briefly once, George Plimpton; most of them hung out at a café called Le Trianon.

84

A Gray Ghost

I ascended the winding staircase of the nameless little hotel where I found nobody in the dark smelly halls that reeked with the pungent odor of feet, urine, and disinfectant. No answer at room 15, *premier étage,* so I left for a nearby café, the Tabac St. Michel, and stared at tall, thin, frozen-faced men at the other tables. One of them might be William Burroughs. I didn't know there were so many gaunt pokerfaces in Paris. Corso had described Burroughs and told me to look him up. It was late June 1959.

"Man, you've never met anyone like him! He chopped off his little finger to prove a point. Jack and Allen say his novel's gonna blow America's mind. There's nothing else like it." In his late twenties, Gregory was slight, boyish, and winsome.

I tried again and again at room 15 and decided to give up, when the door swung ajar. In the doorway stood a tall, cadaverous figure in shirt sleeves, a naked light bulb casting an eerie glow behind him. I introduced myself. Friend of Allen and Gregory.

"Yeah, man?" There was no change of expression. After a long pause he rumbled, "Well, come in."

Room 15 was not much larger than a walk-in closet: a cot, two chairs, a table, a battered portable typewriter. Black marker drawings on white typing paper (twisted brain-shaped labyrinths) writhed on gray walls. He motioned me to a chair, took the other, crossed his bony legs, and proceeded to ream his fingernails with the end of a match, the classic stereotype of the "drug fiend" in the silent movies: taut parchment skin, pale impassive features, bladelike lips, expressionless eyes. So this was the man who was writing "the endless novel that would drive everyone insane," as Ginsberg had written in his dedication to *Howl*. He looked as if he had driven himself insane. But even under these conditions I could sense the power of the man, the iron-willed personality behind the inscrutable mask, a mastermind—head of a gang of cosmic crooks, perhaps, about to burgle his way into the ancient secrets of the universe? It made conversation somewhat difficult.

"Living in Paris?" he mumbled.

"Yeah. Just came here a month ago."

Silence.

"From where?"

"Italy. I've been living in Italy."

Silence.

"Italy?" A faraway sepulchral voice, slightly disdainful.

"Yeah."

Silence.

"Don't . . . like . . . Italy."

"Oh, I like the people, the sun."

Silence.

"Hate . . . the . . . sun."

"Uh, haha, well . . . *Paris* is great!"

Silence.

"Never . . . go . . . out." Silence.

The room was hot and stuffy. He sat hunched over, digging at his nails. Had he lost track of my existence? I wondered. I too fell into a sort of catatonic state. Finally, I saw that I had to break the silence or get out of there, so I began an interminable monologue, spinning weird tales heard in the quarter, quoting Eliot and Pound, putting on a performance. He kept staring at his nails. I rose and began edging toward the door. He looked up. My mouth shut as his eyes, naked, vulnerable yet penetrating, indicated that he'd heard every word. In a slow, panning motion he took me in from head to toe like a laser beam minutely X-raying every inch of my body with those piercing blue eyes. Then, very slowly, back again from my toes to the top of my head. Click. Click. Registering every detail. I felt like an overexposed negative pinned to the wall by a giant lizard. He got to his feet and opened the door. "Yeah, man, nice to see ya," he drawled in a deep hollow voice. "Come back again."

Even as a forty-five-year-old junkie, unknown and obviously at the end of his tether, Burroughs had a magnetic presence.

85

The Horrors

The Mistral Bookshop on the rue de la Bûcherie across the river from Notre Dame was, like Gaït Frogé's Librairie Anglaise on the rue de Seine, a place where English-speaking writers met. Spacious and quiet, with tables on the sidewalk where you could sit and read and drink coffee, it was owned by George Whitman, an eccentric American who claimed descent from Walt Whitman (who was, of course, childless). You never knew when George was joking or serious. Sometimes he was just plain crazy. He went around with a brown canvas rucksack on his back. Once he greeted me on the street with a punch in the belly. When I returned the blow he gasped, then spoke in a civil manner as if nothing had happened. But he had a big heart and his sprawling two-story building, a combination bookstore and youth hostel, was always filled with young transients who slept upstairs, where George had beds and a vast cavernous refrigerator stocked with food and drink for the people passing through. In return for his hospitality they worked and did chores for him. He always invited me to lunch or dinner. When George wasn't abusive and insulting, which he could become without warning, he was generous and helpful. Tall, thin, bearded, and sandy-haired, of an indeterminate age between thirty and sixty, he was the subject of strange rumors, wrapped in a cloak of mystery: he was a secret agent for the Russians, a spy for the CIA, a multimillionaire eccentric, Walt Whitman's illegitimate grandson, a closet writer taking notes on everybody. In fact, George spoke fluent Russian, had lived in the Soviet Union, and disappeared unaccountably for days at a time, leaving some of the young people in charge of the shop. Nobody knew where he went. It satisfied everyone's need for intrigue. George also gave book parties for famous writers like Anaïs Nin and Lawrence Durrell (George took a photo of us once).

At the bookstore I met a young British mathematics student on holiday from Cambridge for the summer. His name was Ian Sommerville. I invited him to my apartment on the Ile Saint-Louis for dinner. Not the least bit literary, he worked for George because he could meet people and sleep at the Mistral. He had come to Paris to learn French but intended to return to England shortly with no plans to revisit Paris. Among the Beat writers he had heard only of Kerouac. He was wholesome, highly intelligent, with a good sense of humor and an endearing personality. He had straight coppery-blond hair combed flat and was rather attractive, but a provincial Yorkshire accent and mumbling speech made him difficult to understand. His hair sometimes stood up as if electric currents were shooting through it.

After I'd been seeing Burroughs, who was trying to kick heroin, for about six weeks, he asked, "Where do you go to meet people?" Although he didn't say so, he needed a helper-companion. "Well, Bill, one place is the Mistral," I said. "I met a nice-looking English kid who works there, but he's not my type." "I've never been able to pick anyone up there," he said. When I described Ian his eyes lit up. "The kid likes older guys," I said.

Though he rarely ventured farther than the Café St. Michel, Burroughs began to hang around the bookshop. On August 24, with a literary acquaintance who had pestered me to meet him, I knocked at his door and received a shock. The door flung partly ajar and in the dim light stood a tall thin figure stripped to the waist. "Bill?" I said hesitantly.

"Hey, man, Bill's kicking and I'm taking care of him," said the figure in the door. It was Ian Sommerville.

I was stunned. "I thought you were Bill!" I exclaimed.

"Everybody does," said Ian. "I'm a replica." He kept the door partly ajar without inviting me in. I felt a twinge of displeasure. "Well, I hope Bill pulls through," I said, thinking it incredible that Ian was now Bill's companion.

"Bill can't see anyone," he said in a friendlier tone, as if to make up for his initial abruptness. With a quick nervous gesture he swept back his damp hair. "I can't tell you what it's been like, man, it's been fuckin' unbelievable. I never want to go through this again. Hallucinations, convulsions, freakouts, the edge of insanity. But it's been worth it; he's getting well."

In *Naked Lunch* characters are superimposed on one another—they replicate. I could only explain the mirage my acquaintance and I had seen as a projection of Burroughs's image onto Ian.

A couple of weeks later Ian told me that Bill had gone to London for Dr. Dent's apomorphine cure. Ian had the air of someone transformed by some shattering experience. He was high-strung, moody. "I've spent a season in hell," he said. The only poetry he'd read until then was Rimbaud. While nursing Burroughs he read *Naked Lunch*. "I had to hang on to my sanity by my fingernails," he said, "and they're bitten down to the moons." His delivery grew so rapid and nervous that I could catch only fragments of his long account of what had transpired.

I gathered that Burroughs was reliving the characters he had invented and the drug experiences he'd had in Mexico and South America; that he metamorphosed into the very horrors he had created: Willie the Rat, Mr. Ugly Spirit, the giant centipede, Pantapon Rose, and many more. Identities spilled over and merged, new characters were born full-grown from composites of others. He assumed each monstrous shape in rapid succession, his voice and features undergoing startling changes like some demented ventriloquist. Through him the world of Hieronymus Bosch had emerged with a twentieth-century accent. He raved, ranted, raged, retched, and groaned. He thrashed about in fits and convulsions. It was a bit much for a rational eighteen-year-old British math student, used to the cloistered walls of Corpus Christi College. Yet Ian Sommerville had proven equal to the task of bringing about the junk cure of perhaps the most haunted American literary genius since Poe. Ian became his nurse and companion, lover and collaborator. And so it happened that I was the agent of not only Burroughs's cure but also the first lasting love affair of his life.

Ian moved into the hotel and Burroughs became a new man; gone was the sinister junkie who, on one occasion, told me, "I could watch my best friend die in agony and not feel a thing." We saw each other more often and he kept urging me to move into the hotel at 9 rue Gît-le-Coeur. "For a dollar a day you get a room, gas ring, linen, and cleaning service if you want it," he drawled. "And you can bring in tricks. Can't beat it, man." He passed me a joint. "If Madame *likes* you," he added, expelling the smoke.

A spying concierge was the norm, always ready to stop you with a beady eye and a buzzer like a cattle prod if you tried sneaking in a pickup. Fortunately, the indomitable Mme. Rachou, blue-haired and iron-willed, liked me and in April 1960 I moved in.

86

The Beat Hotel

The hotel stood about halfway between the Quai des Grands Augustins along the Seine and rue St. André des Arts, an ancient part of the Latin Quarter. A thirteenth-class establishment among the peeling gray facades cracked and cancerous with age, it had a musty bar with a brass rail, cuspidor, and zinc counter behind which, handling accounts, serving beer and wine, and keeping an alert, watchful eye on the comings and goings in that dim bistro (into which bright daylight never seemed to filter through the lacy white curtain), Mme. Rachou presided. She had worked hard all her life and bought the hotel with her savings around 1930. As a girl of twelve she had served tables in a country inn at Giverny, frequented by Monet, of whom she was a favorite.

"Whatever happened to the young Monsieur Pissarro?" she once inquired wistfully. Tiny and toadlike, Mme. Rachou habitually wore a stern, formidable expression of "inflexible authority," in Burroughs's phrase. But she had a soft spot for artists and writers and could even be charitable when their checks were delayed. She reserved for us her special beaming smile, which because of its rarity was unexpectedly warm and radiant.

We were indeed an extended family, living and working together as an artistic community, sharing ideas and convictions, propelled by the excitement of discovery in groundbreaking stylistic experiments. It was a creative, once-in-a-lifetime opportunity, a three-year high, which can only happen by "chance" and can never be repeated. *Chance* was the key word of the experimental mode.

"The law of chance, which embraces all other laws and is as unfathomable to us as the depths from which all life arises," wrote Hans Arp in 1917 during his early Dada experiments, "can only be comprehended by complete surrender to the Unconscious. I maintain that whoever submits to this law attains perfect life."

Well, I can't say that we attained perfect life at the Beat Hotel, but if for the artist perfect life can be defined as living in a community of fellow artists, with constant creative activity (you could even draw on the walls) and the freedom to come and go as you please while satisfying the appetite of the flesh (which van Gogh saw as the motor of artistic energy) and, last but not least, to have all this in Paris when you were still young enough to subject the body to long bouts of sensual explorations and dissipations, then we lived the perfect life. Not until it was all over, years later, did we realize how unique it was. We smoked marijuana and hashish just as a century before Baudelaire, followed by Rimbaud and Verlaine, had done. We were equally unhampered by legal interference, for the drug laws in Paris were lenient then. The acrid odor of cannabis seeped from every door and keyhole and floated into the nostrils of the police across the street who guarded the living quarters of an ex-police chief on the death list of the FLN (the Algerian Liberation Front). Some mornings I awoke to loud explosions and shattered windows opposite mine. They never got the police chief, but they ruined my sleep.

Bombs always went off at an ungodly hour. Like Keystone Kops the *flics* frantically ducked into our hotel bar for a quick one to steady the nerves. With her special brand of hauteur Mme. Rachou, her raised eyebrows bordering on contempt, made them crawl with respect. She exerted a power before which the police appeared helpless. There was some French mystery about all this that I could never fathom (like Mme. Defarge, who made the nobility quail as she knitted their doom into her woolen caps). With a dignity unmatched by *grandes dames* she was all working class.

One night, when a horny young *flic* on duty followed a sexy American girl entering the hotel around 1:00 A.M. and tailed her to her room, instead of the blond beauty he was confronted by the toadlike little lady with the blue hair. With a withering look she growled in the dim hallway, *"Monsieur, que voulez-vous ici?"* (Sir, what are you doing here?) He slunk out, defeated.

Through a separate entrance, with a freedom rare for Paris, residents came and went as they pleased. But if there was a spot of bother, Mme. Rachou—equipped with a special radar or clairaudience, not to mention her light-control panel, which brightened or dimmed for each room, measuring minutely the amount of electrical energy being used and sending a code message to Madame—could "hear" a strange footstep or creaking door four flights up. A note of danger or disruption and she would suddenly appear, white-gowned and stonefaced, a hooting apparition. Madame's electrical system was incredibly sensitive.

Young people came to stare at the crumbling facade, hoping to catch a glimpse of a famous Beat writer. One morning, wearing a red plaid lumberjack shirt as I kept up a prolonged clatter on my Olivetti 22, I happened to look out the window on one of my breaks and spotted some youths huddled together on the street below. They stared with burning interest, which gave me an electrical charge that must have lit up room 9 on Madame's panel. I moved to the table for a Gauloise and returned to find them still gazing reverently upward. I gazed reverently back at them. Finally I opened the French windows. One of them waved shyly. I waved back. Gathering courage, he called in a German accent, "Are you Jack Kerouac?" I might have known. "No," I called, "but almost. Won't I do?" They didn't laugh. "Is Kerouac there?" asked another. "He's hiding in the closet." "Is Allen Ginsberg there?" "In another closet." They stared and lumbered off with hankering looks, still convinced that I was Kerouac. They would tell their friends they had seen and talked to "The King of the Beats" at the Beat Hotel.

Gregory Corso and I experienced an even funnier scene at a sidewalk table at the Mistral Bookshop as we sipped coffee. Three neatly attired young men emerged and stopped in their tracks. They hastily withdrew to one side, whispering animatedly. Then, turning and staring straight at me and ignoring Gregory, one said, "Excuse me, but aren't you Gregory Corso?" I was becoming all the Beat Generation poets wrapped in one. I was about to introduce him when Gregory said quickly, "Yeah, that's him." Keeping a straight face, I inquired, "Where are you from?" "England," said another, beaming. "We're on holiday from Oxford. Oh, I say, Mr. Corso, we would very much like your autograph." "Well, to be quite frank," I said, "it would be forgery. You see, I'm not Corso, he is." I nodded at Gregory and their faces fell. Signals swiftly passed among them. Then the first spoke sharply. "We don't believe you! And we don't think it's very decent of you, Mr. Corso, to poke fun at us." "I didn't say I was Corso," I protested, "you did." "Don't believe him!" yelled Gregory. "He's lying! He *is* Corso!" "I'm not! Corso is lying. He's the *real* Gregory Corso!" They were furious. "Well, we know *you're* Gregory Corso," the first one persisted haughtily, "and we think you're very disagreeable. As for your *friend*"—he sneered—" he's a little American *bore!*"

They left in a huff as we doubled up with laughter.

87

A Fleabag Shrine

I n the late fifties and early sixties everyone, it seemed, was fascinated by the flaky Dream Palace "when it was home for most of the writers and painters who were the vanguard of the Beat Generation," wrote *High Times* in 1978. "Allen Ginsberg, Peter Orlovsky, Jack Kerouac, William Burroughs, Brion Gysin and Harold Norse were the seminal hipsters at the funky hotel."

Kerouac first stayed there in 1957. He slept in Corso's room in the garret—number 41—and wrote: "As I lay there on the floor he makes love to Nanette all night, as she whimpers." *Time* magazine called it "a flea-bag shrine in a section of Paris where passersby move out of the way for rats." *Town,* a slick English magazine, called it "a sleazy surrealist hideout where a new lost generation adds to the thousand and one nights of Paris." It ran photos of Burroughs, Corso, Gysin, and myself with a story on each. *Life* wrote lurid accounts and *Esquire,* with more accuracy, documented the place as a slice of literary history. "Maybe Harold Norse was prophetic," continued *High Times,* "when he said of the Beat Hotel in 1963, 'the flea-bag shrine will be documented by art historians.'"

The experiments with cut-up writing and tape recorders that we did at the hotel, made famous through the works of Burroughs, have percolated down into pop rock, New Wave, and punk lyrics from David Bowie's *Diamond Dog* to the Clash, and into such films as *The Man Who Fell to Earth* by Nicholas Roeg and *Performance* by Donald Cammell (his first film), influenced by Burroughs after I had turned Donald's attention to *Naked Lunch* in Paris. The experiments have permeated many other aspects of our culture in ways it would be impossible to trace.

In 1960 and 1961 I worked on my cut-up novel, *The Last Word,* which came to about 280 pages. Burroughs kept cheering me on. If he saw me sitting at a café table he'd mutter, "Aha, goldbricking, eh?" I'd feel guilty and go upstairs to work on the novel. Opium and hashish and sex kept me going. In August 1963 on my way to Rome and Athens I left the manuscript behind in two suitcases in the storage room of the hotel attic (under the watchful eye of Brion Gysin, who promised to guard it like a dragon) with my notebooks and other papers and the rare three-volume edition of the Roman poet Belli, whom I had translated. On my return all had vanished mysteriously and I was left holding a fifty-page fragment. Still, via the mystique of cut-up, it seemed to form a complete, highly charged text on its own. It was first published in 1975 as *Beat Hotel* in Carl Weissner's German translation by Maro Verlag in Augsburg (now in its tenth edition and still selling in German-speaking countries). Burroughs wrote the foreword to the 1983 American edition. Since the Beat Hotel is now part of the mythology of Beat and cut-up history, I think a few words from Burroughs are in order. (He sliced random pages of my work into *The Soft Machine* and *The Ticket That Exploded,* appearing in echoes and permutations throughout his subsequent cut-up works as leitmotifs. Why not cut Burroughs into this memory tape?)

Foreword by William S. Burroughs
to *Beat Hotel*

It is with pangs of nostalgia that I read those on-the-spot notes from 1960 to 1963, composed by Harold Norse in the now-famous Beat Hotel at 9, rue Gît-le-Coeur in Paris. The hotel had no name, just the number. . . .

Things were happening in every room. People were writing, painting, talking and planning, and Madame Rachou presided in her little bar with the zinc counter. In a room adjacent to the bar and separated by a curtain, Madame gave occasional lunches, usually for the local inspectors of the police, with whom she always maintained good relations—so her clients were spared searches and harassment. However, the "police of foreigners," the immigration police, made passport checks from time to time, always at eight in the morning, and would often take some guest away whose papers were not in order. The detainee would be back in a few hours. . . .

We were well on the way to launching a literary movement, complete with *copains* and enemies. (It is said that André Breton, dictator of the Surrealists, wrote and answered twenty abusive letters a day.)

Harold Norse was among the first to apply the cut-ups. I recall my enthusiasm and laughter when Brion and I read *Sniffing Keyholes.* "What a gas!" Brion exclaimed, and coming from him that was high praise indeed.

Harold also applied the principle of randomity implicit in cut-ups to painting. I was so impressed by the results that I wrote an introduction to his Cosmographs. I remember we had a discussion as to whether the method should be revealed. After some demurring Harold agreed that our basic postulate, *Poetry for all,* dictated that the method be revealed and explained in my introduction.

Harold moved into the hotel at this point, quite a distinction since Madame Rachou was very mysterious and arbitrary about who she would let into her hotel. "She has her orders," Brion always said. And if her orders said NO, you didn't get in and that was that.

For the next three years I saw Harold on a daily basis. He had, like Brion, Ian and myself, become permanent party at the Beat Hotel. We held constant meetings and conferences with exchange of ideas and comparison of cut-up writing, painting and tape recorder experiments, the latter carried out under difficult circumstances.

Madame's electrical system was of an unbelievable sensitivity—*une sensitivité incroyable*—and she could tell by consulting her switchboard if someone had smuggled in an illicit hot plate or was overloading the current with a hi-fi set. In order to play the tape recorder, all the other lights had to be extinguished. . . .

It seemed as if things would go on forever at the No Name Hotel, and then quite suddenly it was gone. Madame Rachou retired, Corsicans bought the hotel and installed telephones. The hole-in-the-floor toilets went the way of the zinc bar. In some rooms private bathrooms were installed, which was unheard of in Madame Rachou's day, when one had to give advance notice of a bath so that the water could be heated, and there was, of course, a surcharge.

It was a magical interlude, and like all such interludes, all too brief: "The things we have never had remain: it is the things we have that go. . . ."

We are indebted to Harold Norse for recording the strange interlude in which he played a pivotal role at 9 Rue Gît-le-Coeur . . . Street Where The Heart Lies.

January, 1983

Random associations come to mind: the stinking hole-in-the-floor toilet on each landing where you squatted on a porcelain footbase and reached for shredded newspaper, a place you didn't want to linger in; someone kept making off with the paper and Burroughs, infuriated, left a sign: TO THE NAMELESS ASS-HOLE WHO RIPS OFF THE PAPER—STOP! . . . Bud Powell would be carried in on the nod, almost OD'd, into anybody's room, once mine, to be laid out on the bed like a corpse. . . . Mezz Mezzrow visiting his son, Milt, on the top floor, endured humili-ating insults from his offspring, I never knew why. . . . Corso in one of his rabid mad-dog seizures brought the young son of Mondadori, the Italian publisher, to my room to witness a char-acter assassination, screaming at me, "You never influenced a generation like me and Allen!" and when I mentioned this to Burroughs he sneered, "He's been telling me the same thing. I told him not to bother coming back." . . . Brion refusing to help me kick opium, calling down the stairwell, "I've been through it with Bill and don't want to share the horrors again!" "Red hot ants are crawling under my skin!" I screamed. "Get an anteater!" yelled Brion heartlessly. . . .

88

Sniffing Keyholes

After Mme. Laurin had given me notice as impetuously as she had installed me into her flat (her daughter needed it, she said briefly), the affair with Tim Reilly also ended abruptly. For months he had obsessively doodled women's breasts and vaginas. "If I don't find a woman I'll go nuts," he'd moan. Then suddenly he left for an American woman and I drowned my sorrow in the pissoirs. I missed Tim badly. After he had lived with the woman for less than a year, I heard he was going nuts again—when the Sixth Fleet hit Paris. Once he visited me hinting at sex but, foolishly I must admit, pride held me back. That was the last I saw of him.

In February 1960, before moving into the Beat Hotel and after leaving the apartment, I began doing ink drawings and cut-up poetry at the Hôtel Univers on rue St. Grégoire de Tours next door to Edouard Roditi. He had often put me up at number 8 where, he said, Théodore de Banville had rented a room for Rimbaud.

Shortly after I moved into the Beat Hotel in April, I wrote "Sniffing Keyholes," a sex/dope scene between a muscular black youth called Melo and a blond Russian princess called Z.Z. I felt I had broken through semantic and psychological barriers; hashish and opium helped with the aleatory process.

My experience of breaking new ground alarmed and exhilarated me. For a while I believed I had lost my reason but didn't consider it a great loss—the mind works in mysterious ways. Actually, word, image, and perception come together in a simultaneous jumble, not, as grammar and logic would have us believe, in a linear structure. I telescoped language in word clusters in a way James Joyce had pioneered, but with this difference: I allowed the element of chance to determine novel and surprising configurations of language. John Cage had done it in music, Pollock in painting. When I showed it to Brion Gysin he raved, "You've done something new! It's a gas! Bill must see this right away!"

Bill Burroughs came down to my room. "Well, Harold, Brion says you've written a very funny cut-up. I'd love to see it." In his fedora and topcoat he sat at the edge of my bed reading the piece, exploding in little sniffs and snorts, his equivalent of lusty guffaws. "This is marvelous," he said, looking up. "You must show it to Girodias." Maurice Girodias, owner of Olympia Press, had published *Naked Lunch;* his father had published Henry Miller's *Tropic of Cancer.* But I wasn't so sure he'd go mad about a few typewritten pages of cut-up. Burroughs disagreed. "I'm calling him right away to get you an appointment."

A day or two later I trekked over to the office a few blocks away on the rue St. Séverin. I was right. Girodias read it and thought it similar to Burroughs. He wanted to see more but didn't sound enthusiastic. "He missed the point," snorted Burroughs. "He rejected *Naked Lunch* the first time it was offered to him." "Sniffing Keyholes" remains the centerpiece of *Beat Hotel.*

Burroughs had introduced me to Brion Gysin, a resident American painter in his forties with four previous nationalities (he was born in England), who had spent most of his life shuttling between Paris, New York, and Tangier. He had long sideburns, was tall and spruce with close-cropped sandy hair and a ruddy pink complexion riddled with purple squirming capillaries on his nose and cheeks that looked like frostbite. He had the voice of an actor, with polished diction, and flamboyant show-manship. He had owned a posh restaurant in Tangier called the Thousand and One Nights, with lavish Oriental decor, musi-cians, magicians, and dancing boys. Burroughs liked the dancing boys and the pigeon pie but cast withering looks in Gysin's direc-tion, snarling, "That guy's probably got a phony von in front of his name." In the fall of 1958, about six months before I arrived in Paris, the two men ran into each other on the Place St. Michel, and Burroughs, always the junkie, muttered, "Wanna score?" Gysin, who'd never won Burroughs's interest before, moved into the hotel and from then on they were inseparable (the hotel had been discovered by Allen Ginsberg in 1957).

One day in the summer of 1959 Gysin had a lucky accident on his drawing board. He unintentionally sliced through a pile of newspapers while cutting a mount for a drawing and, his curiosity aroused, pieced it together at random, read the newsprint across, and burst into laughter. The results were funny yet meaningful. They sounded like code messages from a Ouija board. Some months earlier he had mentioned to Burroughs his idea of apply-ing to writing the principle of collage, which painters and film makers had been doing for half a century. The idea was not new. In the early twenties the dadaist Tristan Tzara announced at a surrealist performance that he would create a poem on the spot for the audience. He cut up a newspaper, threw the pieces into a hat, shuffled them, and picking out pieces at random, read them aloud. It caused a riot. André Breton, the surrealist strong man, expelled him, but Tzara had created a new literary idea—to use, not reject, the results of chance. Forty years later Gysin discovered and Burroughs developed the technique they called cut-up. A literary movement was born in the hotel.

Tzara still wandered around the Café de Flore and Deux Magots—a small white-haired ghost searching for someone he never seemed to find. We were introduced on three occasions, but he pretended not to know me. Ginsberg fared no better. As we sat together at a terrace table Allen called, "Tzara! Yoo hoo, Tzara! Hello! It's Ginsberg!" We were rudely ignored.

The mind shifts irrationally from association to association, without control, in past, present, and future, all existing at once in a mosaic pattern, which is what cut-up writing reflects. Exactly one hundred years after Lautréamont wrote in 1860, "Poetry should be made by all," cut-ups appeared in book form with *Minutes to Go*, the first published texts by Burroughs, Gysin, Corso, and Sinclair Beiles. The method is simple: pick a text, any text—Shakespeare, the Bible, *Moby Dick, Newsweek,* a letter. Type a page from one of these and one or more of the others. Cut down the middle, cut each of these down the middle, place section 1 beside section 3, and 2 beside 4: these now make a new page. Read across and type the results. You have a new text ungoverned by your conscious mind. You are now a writer. This was the first method for doing cut-ups, which later became fold-ins, without scissors. Edit and change as you wish. The results may be good or bad.

We believed we had a new vision and method to express a new dimension of consciousness. Gertrude Stein had cut words from their associations and meanings; Burroughs cut words from their manipulative power over beliefs and actions, thereby undermining thought control by disrupting the traditional use of language, destroying social and religious prejudices and false teachings. This, of course, was the mystique; but the effect, like that of mind-expanding drugs, was psychedelic. It made mind changes.

There was, of course, considerable messianic zeal about all this, mostly on the part of Gysin. I arrived at the hotel too late to participate in what was already top secret: the closely guarded collaboration on *Minutes to Go.* I recall visiting Burroughs around Christmas 1959. Corso came to the door and rudely turned me away, saying that he, Burroughs, and Gysin (whom I had not yet met) were busy. Burroughs hurried to the door and gently explained that they were working on something. Despite his reputation for steely coldness, he usually behaved with courtesy and consideration, unlike Corso, who had the delicacy of a barracuda. Later I found out that they were collecting their final texts for *Minutes to Go.*

Even before I was installed in the hotel, however, Burroughs had taken me up. I had begun painting at a suggestion from Julia Laurin. I threw colored Pelican inks at random on Bristol paper and washed them off in the bidet with startling results: a series of maplike drawings of outer and inner space in the most vivid colors and minutely precise details, as if they had been meticulously drawn by a master hand. Yet my hand never touched them. I allowed everything to happen, letting the laws of chance take over, acting as a medium through whom these colors, shapes, and designs could flow, dictated by whatever forces reside in the unconscious. With the feeling that I was charting new territory in the visual arts I worked compulsively, calling the results "Cosmographs"—cosmic writings. I was no draftsman, but I was an artist.

When I showed them to Burroughs (before I had done "Keyholes") he was so enthusiastic that he wrote the introduction to my first one-man show, which opened a year later in March 1961 at the English Bookshop, 42, rue de Seine. I had in fact been offered a show by two galleries but chose the Librairie Anglaise because it was a hangout and the owner, Gaït Frogé, was a friend and supporter who had also given a book party for me the year before. Burroughs credited me with discovering a new genre in painting. Brion Gysin kept calling me *maître* and actually kissed my hand once or twice. I had received the ultimate acclaim from the cut-up chieftains. Here is Burroughs's introduction to *Cosmographs:*

> The ink drawings of Harold Norse are charged with a special intensity of messages from unexplored areas spelled out in color. These are maps of psychic areas, that is to say they have a definite function. Art for its own sake is no longer a tenable position. The artist is a map maker and his work is valid in so far as his maps are accurate. Poetry is a place. The drawings of Norse map a place. And anyone can go there who will make the necessary travel arrangements. Poetry is for everyone. Painting is for everyone. Harold Norse reached the place of his pictures by a special route which he is now prepared to reveal so that others can travel there. So that others can reach the same area on paper or canvas or mixing colors in the street, you can paint anywhere. Pick out the blues as you walk and the reds and greens and yellows and mix them according to the method of Harold Norse and you will reach the area where painting occurs. What is painting? What is writing? Art? Literature? These words have no meaning now. This is the space age and we need precise maps of space areas. Only the painting and writing that gives us precise maps of some psychic areas serves a function at this intersection point of word and image that we call Present Time.

The sleazy rooms would have been depressing had it not been apparent from the start that something rich and strange was going on. The walls that summer were acting weirdly. Instead of being exclusive, shutting in and out, erecting a barrier or frontier, as walls are supposed to do, they behaved like electromagnetic fields, carrying words and messages—from *whom*? Later, when I met some of the young writers in the hotel who showed me their writings, we found whole word clusters and images, as well as style, astonishingly similar, often identical.

Was all this pure chance? Whatever the explanation, extrasensory perception cannot be ruled out. Cut-up and considerable magnetism from Burroughs, Gysin, and myself generated light and heat for new areas of writing. I got electronic effects through psychokinesis, entirely unwilled, with a primitive one-speed tape recorder by simply reading some of my cut-up pieces and Belli poems. The machine took over and provided eerie effects, perfectly matching the content. Upstairs, where Brion, Bill, and Ian experimented with sophisticated techniques on the big eight-inch reels, they could do no better. I still have my two-inch reels to prove it. The machine acted with a mind of its own and was never wrong. But, then, I've always had a psychokinetic relationship with mechanical objects: watches, TV's, radios, cars, cameras, you name it. They get nervous breakdowns at my approach. My relationship with cameras has lasted all my life. It is a rare photographer who can get a good picture of me without something going haywire. But the tape recorder was user-friendly, at least with me.

89

The Bidet School of Art

*L*ife magazine interviewed me and their photographer, Loomis Dean, shot me in a ballet leap among my ink drawings suspended by magnets and wires in the *cave* by the Greek sculptor Takis (the story was bumped in New York). John Ashbery, poet and art critic (later for *Art News*), reviewed it in the Paris edition of the *New York Herald-Tribune,* March 22, 1961: "Harold Norse, 'beat' American poet, shows his highly-attractive 'Cosmographs' at the English Bookshop. Painting with colored inks on wet paper, Norse produces fantastic webs, maps or labyrinths, and strange combinations of iridescent color." At the Café de Flore Ashbery told me that my drawings had inspired him to begin painting, which he had always wanted to do. When I said that like my cut-up fiction and poetry it was based on aleatory techniques, he exclaimed, "I've been doing it for years! I pore through the dictionary, books, and magazines, pick out words at random, and string them together." He scoffed at the "newness" of the technique when I told him what we were doing at the hotel. "Tzara did it forty years ago," he sniffed. "I did it in my teens and twenties," I said, "using the dictionary, but destroyed it." "It certainly works in your painting," he said.

The show was an artistic, social, and financial success. *Le tout Paris*—the most exclusive, snobbish, aristocratic clique in Paris—attended. Among those impressed was Henri Michaux. *"Très bien, vraiment, mais il faut aller plus loin, plus loin!"* he said cryptically. James Jones and Mme. Laurin were at the *vernissage,* as well as distinguished painters, some of whom made appreciative noises, while others remained aloof. Julia bought a drawing and Jones bought two. When Allen Ginsberg arrived at the end of March Peter Orlovsky, with a long face, said, "I must tell you, we don't like it." They didn't like cut-ups either. Though at first Corso participated in the cut-up technique, he and Allen felt threatened by the random use of language. Their identity as poets was at stake. (It's interesting that Ashbery, who later achieved the pinnacle of poetic success, did so precisely with the random means they feared and rejected.) "You can't please everybody," muttered Burroughs with lofty indifference.

I was interviewed and written up in the major French newspapers and magazines, including *Figaro.* Best of all, the drawings sold well. My rich young American boyfriend bartered his Fiat 600 for two drawings and a little cash from me. I had my first car! When I introduced him to Allen Ginsberg he began to babble, "You're my god! I can't believe it! I'll tell everyone back home in San Francisco that I *spoke* to you!" Allen replied, "Relax."

Stoned on hashish, like most of the others, I lost control when a Dutch painter, Guy Harloff, mad with envy that I, a poet, had a show when for years he had tried without success to have one, threatened me. He was six foot seven and I five foot four, but when he insulted me on the steps of the *cave* (I was on the upper step) I pinned him to the wall with my arm on his throat. His eyes bugged out and he would have suffocated had Norman Rubington, an American painter and writer, not intervened.

Years later in Athens I heard that a new group of painters in Paris, calling themselves Cosmographers, had founded a school based on my method. I immediately christened it "Bidet Art." After all, as an innovator I'd have been ungrateful not to mention the part played in the creation of my drawings by this toilet appliance, which possessed the symbolic significance the urinal had for Marcel Duchamp; furthermore, the bidet had produced cosmic effects—thereby affirming in art the function of objects despised because of stupid moral prejudices. I proved that if Alice could enter the fourth dimension through the looking glass, I could do so through the bidet.

90

Naked Bunch

Gaït Frogé threw a party for me, attended mostly by writers and painters, including Corso, his girl friend Jean Campbell (the Campbell soup heiress), Allen Ginsberg, Peter Orlovsky, and my rich boyfriend Tom Donovan (name changed), who supplied the champagne.

Tom was not only rich but handsome. Once he took me to Kitzbühel to ski (though I could barely stand on ice skates). He got more exercise dodging the rich young ladies who slalomed onto their fannies when they caught sight of him than he did on the ski slopes. Had they known what went on beneath the goose-feathers of our quilt, they would have poisoned my muesli.

"God, those silly bitches won't leave me alone!" he fretted, unaware that he behaved like a "silly bitch" himself.

Peter Orlovsky, stoned on hashish, sidled over. "Take off your clothes," he said. I glanced nervously at Allen, who stiffened. "Come on," urged Peter. "I wanna see you naked. I wanna blow you." Allen blanched. Friendships have ended for less. "Sorry, Peter, I'm not stoned enough." "*Get* stoned," he said. Straight friends egged me on, yelling, "Take it off! We wanna watch Peter suck it!" I smoked more hash and guzzled more Pfeiffer-Heidsieck. Peter slipped out of his sandals, dropped his jeans, and stood naked. As I peeled I heard Gait mutter to her lover, Norman Rubington, "Now we know. Short and thick, like the rest of him." There was a burst of laughter. I reddened. "It's not short," I said, "it's shy." More laughter. "I'll be right back," said Peter, heading for the bathroom. "Don't go away—I wanna see it grow." Allen stood up, stripped, and drew applause; after all, he started the Beat myth of public nudity. He planted himself like a sentry before the bathroom door and crossed his arms on his chest, bristling. His body language spoke loud and clear: "There will be no blow job tonight!" Some men, followed by several women, stripped and soon everyone, except for Corso and Jean Campbell, was dancing nude. Peter emerged and ignored me, for which I was grateful. Allen relaxed. I was relieved.

A Greek friend, Minos Argyrakis, called out, "Harold, let's see some Hindu dancing!" and the music obligingly shifted to Ravi Shankar on the sitar. I had on occasion entertained them by sinuous arm and head movements and intricate mudras, which I had studied in my early twenties. Now, like a temple dancer, I did the Dance of Siva that I learned from Jack Cole (who popularized East Indian dancing in swanky night clubs like Spivy's and the Rainbow Room, then in Hollywood movies). Photos recording the event, including Allen and Peter in the raw, were taken.

91

Naked Lunch

In 1959 Burroughs had accepted an invitation to read sections of *Naked Lunch* at the Mistral Bookshop. Corso and I completed the program. When the day arrived Burroughs didn't appear. He was junk-sick. He sent a tape of his reading from the opening pages of the novel. The tiny audience, mesmerized by the deep, hypnotic voice and black humor, sat spellbound. This was his first reading; it was entirely appropriate that a disembodied voice should create the hallucinatory climate of fear, horror, and fun.

Later, when the landmark book appeared, Gaït Frogé threw a party at the English Bookshop. I was surprised at the small turnout for such an important event. There was no fanfare whatsoever. That evening Burroughs came to my room and handed me an inscribed copy with disarming warmth and shyness. "This copy is for you, Harold," he said, standing in his topcoat and trilby, his back to the window that faced the street. I accepted it gratefully and read the inscription: "For Harold Norse, ally and accomplice, with very best wishes." The talk turned to Ezra Pound, whom he disdainfully dismissed as "a pompous windbag."

Gysin was not the only one at the hotel involved with magic, although he spoke a good deal about scrying with a crystal ball, which hung from the ceiling in his room, and peering into the armoire mirror to see transmogrified faces, past lives, etc. One afternoon as I sat in Burroughs's room with a friend of his, he offered the usual tea—boiled water in a battered aluminum saucepan on the gas ring, poured into a grimy cup containing tea leaves. As he stood behind me, suddenly I felt something pierce through the top of my head, as if a heated ice pick had been plunged into my skull. So severe was the pain that for a moment I thought I'd pass out. I turned to see Burroughs standing over me with fiendish glee, his steely blue eyes boring like a laser beam through my scalp. He turned immediately to speak to his friend, who, seated beside me, was unaware of what had happened.

That evening I mentioned the episode to Brion. "What was he doing?" I asked anxiously. "He looked as if he wanted to kill me!" "Oh, he was just practicing his Death Ray," laughed Brion, "and apparently, it worked!" "I don't think it's funny," I grumbled. "I thought Bill liked me." "He does! He tries it on all his friends!" "I'd hate to be his enemy!" I said. "Oh, he turns on a minute amount of power. More than that and you're dead! You should tell him it worked. He'd be delighted."

92

Baboon Zonk!

Brion Gysin was a master storyteller. I offer one of his typical yarns as a taste of what, at any hour of the day or night, you might expect if you partook of his kif or hashish, liberally offered in room 25.

"On mescaline the first time—this was in Tangier—I experienced the power of magic. I was going to do it right—not eat anything all day, take an enema, a purge, a bath, a real purification so that I'd have a pure mescaline kick. It's quite a job to instruct twenty-one Moslem servants that you are to be left entirely alone all day—no telephone calls, no business, nothing. Not even if the palace burned down was I to be disturbed. I told them that if I walked through the house they were to take no notice of me, to act as if I were invisible. They were rather used to strange things from the master, so they got the message.

"Well, the whole room started to move, to breathe, to come alive. Doors and windows creaked, panels opened in the walls, a

puff of smoke burst from the floor, and a strange being stood
before my eyes. It was everything you ever read about—
Cagliostro and Paracelsus and Michael Scott—real sorcery. As I
wanted to see the effect outside, I and my friend John, who
brought the stuff, went out and decided it would be great to look
at animals. We went to see this rich woman I knew who had a
mad house, like a zoo, with every kind of animal—mongooses,
cobras, monkeys, apes, birds, ocelots. Once I opened a door in a
cupboard and hundreds of *owls* flew into the room. She had an
African mongoose whose whole body, upright, was smooth and
firm, feeling just like a tremendous prick when you grasped it.
Well, we walked into a garden—it was a vast estate, just outside
Tangier on the mountain—with pits for wilder animals, like lions
and tigers, and all sorts of jungle-type arrangements, and we
came upon the baboon, which I had seen before. He was tied by
a long chain to a tree where he could hop onto a suspended
automobile tire that was his swing.

"Now, this baboon was actually a nasty, ferocious animal if
you got near him, so the length of chain was just enough to keep
him from getting too far from the tree, and yet not so short that
he'd be unhappy. When I got close enough, perhaps too close,
for John was warning me to step back, I suddenly caught the
baboon's eye—*wham*! Dead center! And he caught *mine*, the same
way. I looked *through* him and knew that *he* was a baboon, that *I*
was a man, and that at that very moment, for the first time, he
felt his *baboonhood* and *knew* I was his superior. And man, that
ferocious animal, in that split second when we looked at each
other, just turned upside down and fell to the ground like a
stone. The baboon *zonked*! He was dead before he hit the
ground. John looked at me strangely.

"As we passed a datura tree he said, 'Pluck a blossom.' I
picked off one of the large bell-like flowers and for a second it
lay fresh and alive in my palm, with the thick juice still oozing
out. Then *zing!*—it shriveled up and shrank and almost disappeared. We looked down at the grass—wherever I walked it
withered, died, took on the color of hay, as if frostbitten. There
was a well that I used to gaze into and watch the water lilies
floating on the surface. This time, when I looked in, I could see,
in the dimness, all the water lilies begin to breathe, as if struggling against closing, and then slowly they all closed like a hand
clutching for air. It was an immense power I had, for I could *see*

into the life of all these plants and animals. Then there was this something *else* that destroyed them. For the first time I understood how *real* magic is. Don't believe this jazz about all magic being superstition and old wives' tales and ancient history. It's real. *Now!* It was *always* real!"

But the real magic, I thought, was in Brion's gift of storytelling, of mythmaking. He had the rare ability to weave a spell, to bring alive in a compelling, if not always convincing, way his experiences on drugs, his encounters with the rich and famous, his vast body of historical and artistic learning, skewed by some vulgar prejudices, like his hatred of women and Jews. The baboon story was, after all, a Technicolor Hollywood cliché of special effects from *Sinbad the Sailor,* the *Arabian Nights*—once you were out of range of his voice. His work as a painter and writer never had a wide appeal, though his collaborations with Burroughs won him a reputation. Indeed, the spell he had cast on Burroughs is no doubt his greatest accomplishment. As a conversationalist Gysin was second to none. At the time of his death in Paris in 1986 at the age of seventy, he had a cult of devoted fans that included rock stars, film makers, and New Wave punk artistes. He had become a legend, a guru for explorers of the New. And he even received the title of *chevalier* of the Legion of Honor from the French government just before his death.

93

Saroyan, Chagall, Nin, et al.

My first Paris book party was held in 1960 at the English Bookshop for the publication of my Belli translations. Norman Rubington did an attractive full-window display. His own books, successful detective-fiction spoofs, with his witty collages and captions, were published by Olympia Press under his pseudonym, Akbar del Piombo. I was astonished when William Saroyan, whom I had never met, came into the shop and, in a shy, humble manner, requested my autograph. He approached hesitantly, holding a copy of my book. "I would be honored," he said, "if you inscribed your book to me." I could hardly believe my ears. "The honor is entirely mine, Mr. Saroyan," I replied. I wrote: "For William Saroyan, a great writer and boyhood hero." From what I'd heard and read about him the humility was out of character. The gossip circulating around Paris dealt mostly with his compulsion to gamble and lose vast sums of money. Although I hoped to see more of him I never did.

Every day at the little shop across the street from my old flat on the Ile Saint-Louis, when I had bought my newspaper I'd often stand face to face with another customer, Marc Chagall. He was a very little old man with sparkling sapphire-blue eyes and white hair. His expression of wonder and curiosity seemed permanent. Sometimes we'd bump into each other in the shop and, like a couple of Charlie Chaplins, we'd apologize with courtly grace. "Oh, *pardon, monsieur!*" I was too shy to speak to him, but one day the French proprietor, a man in his fifties, approached and said in French, "*Messieurs,* three champions meet together today—in art, sports, and poetry. I was a champion welterweight boxer!" We all laughed heartily and Chagall, addressing me in French, said, "You are a poet, then?" "An American poet," I said. He raised his eyebrows and in good but accented English, replied, "Ah, I knew it! You must make a poem about this!" I returned to my flat and wrote "The Ballad of Marc Chagall."

Anaïs Nin turned up at the Mistral Bookshop. I hadn't seen her since I had left New York seven years earlier. She was staying at the posh Hotel Crillon on the Place de la Concorde. Her world of wealth and comfort was strikingly different from the bohemian squalor of the Beat Hotel. As we strolled along the quay I was astonished at how young and beautiful she looked. Far from being the untouchable, fragile, queenly figure that Henry Miller and Harry Herschkowitz had portrayed, she was down-to-earth, matter-of-fact, and vulnerable. She even seemed unsure of herself. I recall that this startled me—no other major literary figure I had met behaved with such evident insecurity. As we discussed Harry, who, she said, almost traumatized her with his romantic insistence on reliving the relationship she had

had with Miller, she giggled like a shy schoolgirl before a teacher. I was mystified at this side of her personality, so "out of sync" with her reputation.

It was a sunny spring—or perhaps summer—afternoon, and we strolled in leisurely fashion from the rue de la Bûcherie to the *quai* opposite Notre Dame. "I was never the precious, exalted lady that Henry portrayed," she said earnestly, "but I was no bohemian either. My manner of dress and bearing seemed aristocratic to him, but it was consistent with the way I was brought up. He was surprised that I was not shocked or offended by his vulgar language, both in writing and speaking. But I was not a prude. I believe in the power of honest expression and have always disliked euphemism where plain speech would do."

"Well, in his essay comparing your journals with Saint Augustine's *Confessions,* he made a goddess out of you," I said. "And that image stuck." She tittered. "Yes. But in many ways I am as earthy as Henry. I don't use vulgar language because it isn't part of my background and it would be false of me to do it." She said she had written erotic stories—another surprise.

Harry had depersonalized her entirely, accepting the goddess image and worshiping this bogus idol that existed only in his imagination. When he expected her to be his muse and lover she refused. His reaction was psychotic. He kept turning up, threatening suicide or to take her life; he spoke with overwrought frenzy, imitating Antonin Artaud, with whom he identified (Artaud had fallen in love with her and was rejected because she feared his madness). When Harry arrived in the lobby with a gun she called the police. By the time they appeared he had vanished. He never bothered her again, but the memory still unnerved her. She was anxious to convince me of his emotional dishonesty but, knowing Harry, I needed no convincing. When I told her he had died of multiple sclerosis she looked pensive but offered no comment.

She said that I appeared fleetingly in her journals. Pleased, I mentioned that in each other's lives we both appeared fleetingly. I still have some photos of us and of Sylvia Beach (publisher of Joyce's *Ulysses*) at a book party given by Gaït Frogé for Anaïs's novel *Seduction of the Minotaur.*

94

Ginsberg in Paris

When Allen Ginsberg arrived in Paris in March 1961 en route to India with Peter Orlovsky, it was our first reunion since I had left New York almost eight years earlier. Corso and I were strolling on the Boulevard St. Germain to the Deux Magots when Allen and Peter appeared. The three rushed into each other's arms in an emotional embrace, after which Allen barely nodded and off they went!

A day or two later while I sat on the terrace of the Deux Magots, Allen and Peter showed up and sat beside me. Allen apologized for the incident, explaining that he hadn't seen Gregory for some time. His warmth and sincerity won me over, especially when he asked if I had a copy of his new book, *Kaddish*, which I hadn't, jumped to his feet, threw an arm around me, and said, "Let's go to La Hune. They have it there!" At the international bookstore near the Deux Magots, Allen bought a copy and wrote on the title page: "For Harold Norse, in fond memory of 1944 New York subways, with Love, Allen Ginsberg." This he wrote so that the words formed a circle with a heart in the middle; he made me a gift of the book with a quick kiss on the mouth. I melted completely—the shell of the crab is thin, the flesh tender, and the heart huge: but beware the nippers. For the rest of his two-month sojourn in Paris we saw a lot of each other.

One sunny day as we walked down the rue de Seine toward the quay, I said, "Here it is a fine day in Paris in the spring, and I've got a toothache."

"Haiku!" said Allen, raising a forefinger to the sky.

He asked if I wished to accompany him and Peter to a meeting with Artaud's former mistress, Paule Thévenin, whom they were to interview with the intention of learning something about the intimate life of the great French poet who had influenced us so powerfully in the forties and fifties. I accepted enthusiastically. At a café on the Boulevard St. Germain several blocks from the Deux Magots we awaited her arrival. Finally, just when we had decided that she wouldn't come, a tall dignified woman with long, straight black hair, dark olive skin, and a hawklike gypsy face haughtily approached our table. Allen and I rose to our feet and I was introduced to Paule Thévenin, who glanced at us and took her seat without a word. She scarcely seemed to take notice of us. When Allen summoned the *garçon* she ordered a Vichy or Perrier and, eyes fixed on the glass, sipped it. She spoke no English and Allen began, in passable French, to ask questions about Artaud.

ALLEN: Did Artaud sleep with many women?

THÉVENIN (frostily): Certainly not!

A: Then you were his only mistress?

T: Yes.

A: Was he in love with Anaïs Nin?

T: She says so.

A: Then Artaud was faithful to you?

T: I had no reason to doubt it.

A: Was he very sexual? Did he demand a lot of sex?

T (indignant): Certainly not! He was not interested in sex.

A: You mean Artaud was abstinent?

T: Of course! His work, his intellect, dominated his life.

A: Was it because of impotence?

T (bristling): Artaud was not impotent, no! But he put his strength into his work! (She has become progressively irritated.)

A (persistent): Perhaps his illness was the cause.

T: *No!*

A (gently): Did he write at all hours or did he have a fixed routine?

T: He worked always, without stopping. He had the greatest mind in France. He was not insane. He was far ahead of everyone.

A (gently): Yes. It's true.

PETER: Ask her if he jerked off.

A (pause): My friend wants to know if—did Artaud masturbate?

T (her lips curl): Never!

P: Ask her if he ever made it with boys or men.

A: My friend wants to know if Artaud liked men or boys.

T (rising to her feet): Not at all!

She turned to go and, without bidding us goodbye, stomped off indignantly, as if she had wasted her time.

The meeting lasted longer than I've indicated here, but I can't remember all the questions. I was put off by her contemptuous attitude, her hauteur, yet admired her powerful personality and commanding presence. It's true, we all wore beat-up jeans, Allen's and Peter's hair was long and unkempt, and Mlle. Thévenin, of an older generation, may have regarded us as riffraff. Peter's blunt naivete had even crashed the language barrier. Like Tristan Tzara, she was probably not much impressed by American writers. Also, like many wives or mistresses of great men, in her fanatic devotion she believed all others inferior. The delicious story of James Joyce's wife was too good to be true, but it probably was. When the unlettered Nora Joyce was asked what she thought of Marcel Proust on the only occasion when her husband and the great French novelist met, she said, in her Galway brogue, "Marcel who? Sure, when you've been married to the greatest, you don't remember the small-fry."

I remember sitting with Henri Michaux on the terrace of the Bar St. Michel. He lived a block from our hotel and was questioning me on Burroughs and Ginsberg, about whom articles were appearing in the French media. I had met Michaux in Rome some years earlier at the salon of Frances McCann and the count. He was tall and bald and looked like a French bourgeois (he was actually Belgian), but his remarkable book about his mescaline trips, *Miserable Miracle*, was one of the influential works of the new drug culture just beginning to appear. I spoke glowingly of Burroughs and Ginsberg and their groundbreaking books in which consciousness took a quantum leap through experiments with ayahuasca, mescaline, peyote, mushrooms, and the new psychedelic drug, LSD, which they pioneered with Timothy Leary. Michaux, in his sixties, sighed. "No more mescaline for me," he said. "I nearly died. I nearly lost my mind. I don't even drink coffee. Only this." He pointed to the orange juice on the table. The sidewalk was crowded with promenading youths. I realized that he had gotten too old for drugs and that, one day, this would happen to me. I lit a Gauloise. "The hardest thing to give up," he said sorrowfully, "was cigarettes." I inhaled the smoke deeply.

95

The Dreamachine

Without Ian Sommerville's scientific imagination and expertise Gysin could not have realized his Dreamachine, which provided a drugless high when staring into a slotted cylinder with a light bulb inside, rotating at a fixed speed on a turntable. And without my prodding and editing, as he admitted, Gysin would not have produced his first writings on cut-ups, which have now become the handbook for the method. It also resulted in his novel *The Process*. In his writings and interviews no mention is made of this indebtedness. Terry Wilson, in a biographical piece on Gysin in 1981, speaking of the Beat Hotel experiments, writes: "The important collaborators on this mission were Gysin, Burroughs, Sommerville and Balch. . . . Other white American compatriots residing in the Beat Hotel were, as Gysin says, just about ready to collapse with a whimper or run screaming for the police in the face of all this."

If, at Burroughs's insistence, I had not moved into the Beat Hotel, if I hadn't hounded Gysin to write about cut-ups and edited them and gotten them published, would he have written at all? If I hadn't mentioned Ian to Burroughs, would he have had a lasting cure when previously all cures had failed? Would Brion have had a Dreamachine? Or his Permutations (poems) recorded by the BBC, and so on?

"Only you ever encouraged me to the point of bullying, Harold," wrote Brion in a letter dated April 9, 1970. "You're responsible for THE PROCESS. It grew out of that time you set me to writing something and I obeyed you. . . . I summon you to stir up a controversy and save me on this writing course you set me on, Harold Norse, when you were sitting down there in Room Nine on your rotting vegetables."

Here is the actual history of our collaboration. One day Gysin asked me to look at an old novel he had written in the forties or fifties. He had no faith in it and wanted my opinion. I read the manuscript and agreed. It was wooden, stilted, didn't flow. The characters were one-dimensional, the style conventional.

"Look, why don't you write something about your relationship with Burroughs and cut-ups?" I suggested. "The way you talk."

At first he resisted. My opinion of his novel had confirmed his self-doubt. He said despondently that he didn't think he was a writer. He also felt he had failed as a painter. It took some coaxing to break through this sense of failure and despair, but after weeks and months of dogged persistence and bullying I finally succeeded. About a month later he came down to room 9 with a bulky manuscript.

"You're responsible for this," he said as if I'd thrown up on the floor. "Now clean up the mess." He placed it in my hands. "It's *your* idea. Do something." He looked skeptical.

I blue-penciled it. I deleted, slashed, revised, condensed, rewrote. I made suggestions in the margins. It was major surgery, a Caesarian. This was our baby. The operation was a success. In successive stages he'd show me the rewrite and again I'd edit. The final result was a colorful story of his relationship with Burroughs and the genesis of the cut-up technique. He christened it, at last, fondly: "Cut-Ups: Project for a Disastrous Success."

"Now what?" he said. *Evergreen Review* was publishing my poetry, and I sent "Project" and "Cut-ups Self-explained" to them and they were taken. Another section, "The Pipes of Pan," I sent to Ira Cohen for the first issue of his magazine *Gnaoua* in Tangier. It appeared with Burroughs's excerpts from *The Soft Machine*, Ian's permutated photo experiment "Mr and Mrs D," and my cut-up fiction "Sniffing Keyholes." The four of us appeared together for the first time. I did not run screaming for the police.

In the first flush of his enthusiasm for my catalytic role in getting him started as a writer and novelist, Gysin promised that if a book of his writings that I midwifed was ever compiled, he would dedicate it to me. A few years later in London, 1967, he visited me at my flat and said, "My novel, *The Process,* is being published by Doubleday, but I'm not dedicating it to you."

I didn't ask why. I already knew. No good deed goes unpunished. He was editing me out. The same way he treated his mother. When she arrived he said, "I can't wait for her to go." I was surprised to meet a gentle old woman whose diction was perfect.

She was a drama coach; Brion was a drama queen. She had sent him to the best schools, but he hated her. When she died he said, "I'm glad the old bitch is dead at last." I was horrified.

96

A Small Guffaw

I'd climb the winding staircase to room 20 to visit Burroughs and he'd come to my room. Every night he saw Ian in room 15, where he'd kicked the habit with Ian's help. It adjoined mine by a wooden door that couldn't be opened on either side. I'd hear Burroughs's voice rumbling on for hours accompanied by Ian's incessant giggling. Then one night the four of us got together in Ian's room to hear sections from Bill's new manuscript, *The Soft Machine,* which was his first book after *Naked Lunch,* and also his first novel using the cut-up technique. We turned off the light and turned on by candlelight. The hash pipe circulated quickly, each of us taking deep drags and coughing violently as it seared our lungs. My head exploded. Burroughs began to recount his experiences in Mexico and South America. It held us spellbound. I saw before my eyes through the smoky haze in the candlelight an old Peruvian Indian, a shaman, a sick junkie. The scenes and characters of *Naked Lunch,* which had been put together for publication in this room, came to life.

When Bill began to read from *The Soft Machine,* I witnessed for the first time the awesome magic of the cut-up medium when employed by a writer of genius. After he finished, I sat stunned—and stoned. Brion leapt to his feet and knelt before him, grabbing the hem of his overcoat and kissing it repeatedly; then slobbering over his hand he gasped, "Master! master! You've opened the door, mmm, mmmmm, to a new consciousness!"

Burroughs coughed. Or was it a small guffaw?

97

El Hombre Invisible

I often sat in silence with Burroughs for hours sipping beer or coffee at a table of the Tabac St. Michel, watching the strollers. I felt comfortable not having to make conversation. Years later I discovered that I was sitting with "a silent, starving, skullheaded Chinese on the banks of the muddy Yangtze—a man with no words, no ideals, and no beliefs: Burroughs' ultimate persona," which was what Gerald Nicosia, who interviewed him for his definitive biography of Kerouac, *Memory Babe,* wrote. When he underwent depth analysis in 1944–45, seven or eight separate characters were discovered. Among these were a "nervous, possibly Lesbian English governess" and much farther down the digs "the doctor found an old Southern sharecropper sitting on the banks of the Mississippi, catching catfish." I sat on the Left Bank of the Seine with all of them. I felt sure a riverboat gambler and circus magician were among the bunch. How well did I know Burroughs? He was an archaeological find but I was no archaeologist.

The topmost layer of his alternate personalities was the St. Louis renegade whose grandfather had invented the adding machine (the big money never came their way; the inventor received only a small amount of the shares, which Burroughs's father sold in the twenties). This was the companion whose anecdotes, mimicry, dry wit, and deadpan delivery, especially of one-liners, were as good as any comedian's. He was a cross between the frozen-faced Buster Keaton and the flamboyant W. C. Fields. His brand of black humor was similar to the con man comic's, but behind his folksy earthiness Burroughs possessed a first-rate intelligence, a vast store of knowledge, and a uniquely macabre imagination.

"His persona constituted by a magic triad of fedora, glasses, and raincoat rather than by a face, his first presence is that of a con man down on his luck," Paul Bowles once wrote of him in Tangier. In Paris, instead of a raincoat he wore a topcoat, under which was the perennial three-piece suit and tie. If he had no face he had many faces. In repose his eyes were extinguished, leaving only the husk of a face. Once I was talking about the Eastern spiritual discipline of making the mind blank.

"Allen's always going on about attaining an egoless state in meditation," he said. "That's easy. I can do it anytime."

"Just like that?" I said. "Without meditation?"

"Yeah, I can leave my body behind like a shell. Wanna see?"

He stood up, stared at me with a fiendish look, and *sput!* out went his eyes, dead and vacant, his wan face featureless as an Egyptian mummy's. All consciousness seemed sucked from his brain. I grew uneasy. "Bill?" I called softly. "Bill?" Nosferatu, thousands of years old, stood before me. I recalled that for an entire year in Tangier he slept in his suit, socks, shirt, and tie without removing them. To the Spanish boys he was known as *el hombre invisible*—the invisible man. Finally a dry nasal voice rumbled, "See what I mean?" I told him the story of two magicians trying to scare each other. After the first went through his repertoire of terrifying tricks, the other's turn came. "Boo!" he said. I had Brion and Bill in mind.

In summer the boulevards were full of wandering youths with long hair and beards (just coming into fashion), clad in threadbare leather vests and tight jeans, guitars slung on their backs. Many were too young to grow beards, but all affected the guise of student outlaws, the picaresque persona of François Villon, showing contempt for mercantile society. For the most part they came from bourgeois families and attended universities. They hitched rides, smoked dope, drank beer, and hung out in specific meeting places. One of these was a murky run-down bar called Chez Popoff on the rue de la Hûchette, a tiny narrow street of Dixieland and modern jazz clubs, where youths dumped their packs on the dirty floor and stood around in silence or mumbled impassively. Mostly Dutch, German, and Scandinavian hitchhikers, they panhandled and slept on the quays in bedrolls.

One hot afternoon as Burroughs and I sat without exchanging a word for over an hour, watching them rambling on the boulevard, he suddenly drawled, "Not a good fuck in the whole generation." After another gulp of beer he added in a low snarl, "They make it with their guitars."

He was right. They seemed chronically bored, lobotomized, inert. Occasionally I met some of these youths at Popoff's. Since they always needed a place to sleep I'd bring some to my room to spend the night. One eighteen-year-old cornsilk blond called Harry the Head from Amsterdam was a cute, talkative boy full of wild energy and charm, not at all the type Burroughs had so accurately pilloried. Because of a sex position he taught me, for which he displayed an insatiable appetite, I recall him vividly. "I am bee-sexual," said Harry the Head and proceeded to astonish me with inventive sex play. During the two nights we spent together we enjoyed every minute of our frolic, but needing to push on with his trek across Europe, he left. He would now be forty-three, exactly my age at the time. Another remark he made fixes him in my memory. "Look," he said pointing at his nude body as we lay in bed, "new body." Then pointing at mine: "Old body." If he's alive he may be saying this to some boy of eighteen, but in reverse.

I recall our excitement when Burroughs returned to the States at the invitation of Dr. Timothy Leary at Harvard, then a professor of psychology conducting his early experiments with magic mushrooms, or psilocybin, as the synthetic was known. Burroughs was among the first to take the drug, but he'd had a bad experience, initially at the hotel, and again in Cambridge. After taking LSD he had another unpleasant experience and sneered, "That bastard wants to control the minds of the next generation." For a while he disliked Leary.

He was not a bad prophet. As early as 1960, when *Naked Lunch* had been cleared of obscenity in an American court of law, he foretold the breakdown of censorship within five years. As for consciousness-expanding drugs he saw that all Leary had to do was step into the vacuum created in the minds of the young by their disaffiliation and control them. Burroughs's work was based on the premise that all mind control by authority is evil. The cold war, the Bomb, and the Berlin Wall had done their damage; the young would have no choice but to turn their backs on their parents' ugly and violent world. It would be an easy matter for the psychedelic guru to take over their minds with his formula, "Tune in, turn on, drop out." The Beats had rejected Mammon and looked into mind-altering drugs and metaphysical disciplines like Zen and Vedanta. Sexual liberation from puritanical restraint, the pursuit of ecstasy through the crotch, and sentimental anarchy had begun to manifest itself widely in the States. The era of permissiveness had begun. But dropping out on drugs could lead to disaster.

98

Sex and Dope

I had a large mirrored armoire and chest of drawers with a marble top full of strong spices and herbs such as valerian, sage, basil, rosemary, and thyme. "It smells like a goddamn country garden!" Corso would yell, making a dive for my assortment of over-the-counter drugs, as well as pot, hash, and barbiturates, on which I'd been hooked since my mid-twenties. I'd hide everything when he knocked; nothing was safe from marauding Gregory, who was known to devour mouthfuls of pills without regard for their contents or owner. Once while visiting Edouard Roditi we waited in vain for him to return (how we got in remains a mystery, for his concierge was one of the worst in Paris—an invisible spy behind a hidden window near the staircase). Gregory ransacked the medicine cabinet in the bathroom, found a bottle of pills, and without reading the label (he couldn't read French anyway) spilled them into his palm and swallowed them without water. Years later when I recounted this to the Italian translator Fernanda Pivano, she gasped, "Those were epilepsy pills! They could have killed him!"

When I told the story to Edouard he laughed. "Well, they couldn't have killed him," he said, "but in such large doses it causes you to lose all your teeth!" Perhaps that's how Gregory lost his.

I was horrified at his reckless abandon with drugs. At least I exercised caution. Yet he persistently said of me, "Harold Norse can't pass up a drugstore." It was true. I was a pillhead. And thanks to Burroughs, I became a junkie. I'd been interested in opium since my twenties, when I'd had some morphine shots after a minor operation for an anal fistula. When I told Burroughs that I suffered from constant colds and attacks of *la grippe,* he said, "I've got just the thing for you, Harold. Eubispasmes." "What?" "Opium, man. Black pills. You can get them over the counter at any pharmacy in Paris. Cheap. They're laced with codeine. Little box called Eubispasmes." "But what has that got to do with sore throats and runny noses?" "Coats your cells, man, makes them impregnable. No virus would *dare* bore a hole through your cells."

When old *brujo* Dr. Burroughs prescribed he knew what he was talking about. So I ate the little black Eubies like candy and remained free of coryza (as Paul Bowles called it) all winter, to my immense relief. I could write in peace without a runny nose, cough, or sneeze. I could smoke dope, cook my exotic chicken-and-rice dinners, for which I had become famous in the hotel, and go out in all kinds of weather. I had elaborate Technicolor dreams and sat at the typewriter for hours without discomfort from cold or damp. But when spring came I was hooked.

At night I cruised café bars like La Reine Blanche and Le Royal in the heart of St. Germain des Prés, both frequented by artists and gays. In 1962 in a cut-up piece called "Flash of Machine Faces" (now in my novel *Beat Hotel*) I described the scene: "On the boulevard hard searching thru neon trees & fluorescent cafés . . . shlepping from St. Michel along the pissoir route to the Flore . . . the cold whipping into makeup of hopefuls at terrasse tables. . . . Across the street at the Café Royal . . . the Youth swindle . . . blade-sharp hustlers . . . sweeping coiffures, every dyed hair counted, every advantage price-tagged."

One night I brought home a young Vietnamese known as Ping-Pong. He was a regular at the Tabac St. Michel, but, since he usually had some beautiful French girl in tow, we assumed he was unavailable—a false assumption, as I proved. Thanks to my opium habit I projected unusual self-confidence, and next thing I knew the sensational sinewy Ping-Pong was in bed beside me for the night, lured no doubt by the promise of hashish. Burroughs was impressed.

"How did you manage that, Harold?" he asked with some awe.

"A piece of cake," I said, grinning. He enjoyed my blow-by-blow description of my night playing Ping-Pong.

The pissoirs were a sure thing. For two thousand years they had provided sexual relief for the male population. It is said that André Gide and Jean Genet used to cruise them. The most attractive men could be had for the asking in those smelly shrines to the god Priapus. They offered varieties of religious experience that no church in Christendom could compete with (orgasm is surely the most immediate and universal form of union with God). But, after the war, heeding the shrieks of horror from shocked American ladies who found them malodorous and disgusting, Mme. de Gaulle prevailed upon the general to pull them up by the roots, thus destroying an ancient subculture. Is nothing sacred to the barbarians?

There was also the Piscine Deligny, a swimming pool on a barge moored on the Seine. Everyone lay around, men and women, sunbathing on the hot, red-lacquered wooden boards, clad in bikinis that left little to the imagination. You jumped into the pool and came up with a boy in your arms and popped him into a locker reeking with the heady, pungent brew of jockstraps and sperm.

After kicking the habit Burroughs was shy and insecure. *Naked Lunch* began to attract attention, not always favorable. *Time* attacked the book mercilessly, disparaging him as a degenerate homosexual. But at the obscenity trial that followed, Norman Mailer testified that Burroughs was, perhaps, the only living novelist in contemporary American fiction who might be said to have genius.

At a party we attended together given by James Jones we met William Styron and my old friend James Baldwin. Burroughs stood ramrod stiff, never removing his trilby, wordlessly staring with lips clamped shut in a taut thin line. After futile attempts to engage him in conversation, the others gave up. He stood beside me downing martinis in a state of acute terror to judge by his looks. It was his introduction, so to speak, to the competition, and he couldn't have met nicer guys. Yet he was petrified.

After his cure he consumed four fifths of whiskey daily and smoked pot, but I had no idea that addiction had taken such a toll psychologically. I never again saw him so insecure. Further recognition brought poise and self-assurance.

I remember Brion and Ian assisting in Bill's social rehabilitation, helping with the transition from the reclusive, sociopathic junkie to the celebrated man of letters. As we all continued living at the hotel for three more years until it changed hands, I watched the successful metamorphosis. He became relaxed and, though not demonstrative, a loyal friend. Without literary success I have no doubt that he would have slid back to the drugs that made it possible to endure the unendurable: being a misfit in a dishonest world.

99

A Distant Episode

In the fall of 1961 I left Paris for Tangier. Burroughs had told me to look up Paul Bowles who, he said, would be helpful. So when the old Yugolinea freighter steamed into the dock from Gibraltar, I had every intention of getting to a telephone straightaway. I looked over the railing with great excitement at the dusty finger of Africa jutting into the straits, my first foothold on the dark continent. And, to be sure, I had never seen anything like the sight that greeted my eyes. Throngs of swarthy turbaned men in rags and bare feet swarmed on the docks below, jabbering and gesticulating wildly. It seemed more like the Middle East or India than my idea of Africa. I felt like a visitor from another planet.

When I descended the gangplank, they rushed me, screaming and shoving to get at my bulging nylon flight bag. They didn't look like porters to me. Incredibly ragged and threadbare, these sad untouchables of the Arab world were toothless, crippled, pockmarked, and mangy. I realized I was conspicuous in my light blue Dacron suit, which gleamed in the sun like shot silk. I intended to get to a public phone and ask Bowles's advice about hotel accommodations, but I saw only an arid waste that stretched beyond the docks with no sign of Tangier. My heart sank.

Clutching my bag with sweaty hands, I set my jaw. Two "guides" in Western dress, speaking atrocious English, attached themselves to me and began to shout and shake their fists at the dock men, who angrily jabbered back at them. For a while I thought there would be a free-for-all, but soon we left the tattered beggars behind. Now I would have trouble shaking off the "guides." Burroughs had warned against these con men.

Invisible from below, the town lay high above a gray embankment wall, accessible only on foot by stone street stairs leading steeply upward. The "guides" kept urging me to surrender my bag, conveying not too subtly the information that I would remain at some risk—from them, presumably—if I proceeded alone.

"Meester, you know, Tanjer ees vairy dangerouse. Not can walk alone wit' baggage, you unnerstan'. You go wit us, hokay."

Disoriented by the stark terrain and the throaty Arabic language I doggedly followed. When, puffing and sweating, we reached the town overhead, we entered a crowded square that resembled a nineteenth-century opera set.

"Meester, you buy coffee. Sit. Then go to cheap hotel. Only minutes."

The fat one, called Jimmy the Guide, had a jagged keratoid scar on his bulging forehead, which gave him a sinister look. I had no choice. I wanted a hotel as fast as possible. We drank black coffee and mopped our faces and necks at a café table. Ali, the other guide, was a mixture of cunning and depravity, with the blasé air of Peter Lorre, whom he resembled.

We set out through dark winding labyrinths thick with veiled women in laundry bags (as it seemed to me) and with men whose eyes peered from hooded heads. I worried that I would end up minus my flight bag, clothing, and traveler's checks, or worse, minus tongue, eyes, ears, nose, and throat. The trek seemed interminable. When we finally left the casbah the sunlight blinded me. Then we were attacked by packs of small street boys screaming, *"Money! Dirham! Baksheesh!"* They tugged at my sleeves and trousers, making a terrible row. The "guides" shooed them off and we entered an Arabian Nights palace. The walls and floors were of colored mosaic tiles interlaced with intricate patterns, over which were strewn exquisite rugs. The ceilings

must have been forty feet high. This was certainly not the cheap
hotel they had promised, only minutes away (but minutes are
merely a figure of speech in the Mediterranean).

A quiet man, who may have been the maître d', approached,
gracefully touching his lips and heart with his fingertips when
the "guides," nodding in my direction, said something to him. In
these sumptuous surroundings I began to relax. We took our
places on a richly-textured Oriental carpet, seated cross-legged
before an embossed metal-topped table with intricate, lacy,
wood-paneled legs that looked like teak. A waiter placed before
us a pitcher of green tea and a beautiful nargileh from which we
took deep puffs. I held the harsh, searing smoke in my lungs a
moment, then coughed it out.

Sinuous Arabic music wound its repetitive patterns within my
brain and inner ear. Couscous was served steaming in a silver
tureen, full of almonds, raisins, spices, and large succulent chunks
of baked chicken. I fell upon the food voraciously as the music
seeped out of the walls, the carpets, the arches. . . .

It was evening when we left the palace. The last strands of
flame in the pale sky faded over the minarets as the muezzins
wailed to a crescent moon. It gave me a deep feeling of peace. I had
paid for our repast, too stoned to know or care how much, and
once more we were engulfed by the mysterious medina. Then a
rising wave of pot paranoia swept away my euphoric state as we
trekked through the nearly deserted mazes. (Paul Bowles's story
"A Distant Episode" had made an indelible impression on me when
I first read it in the *Partisan Review* in early 1947. Now I found
myself in a situation not unlike that of the professor [to my mind] in
that terrifying tale. The naive but educated Westerner, who is a
language scholar, finds himself in the Sahara doing research on
"variations of Moghrebi" [the Arabic dialect of Morocco], is captured by nomadic Reguibat tribesmen, who cut out his tongue,
throw him into a cage, dress him in a costume made of the bottoms
of tin cans strung together, and exhibit him on their wanderings as
entertainment, like some dumb animal or subhuman idiot, a spectacle for the laughter and derision of illiterate tribespeople.)

Intensified by the aftershocks of strong hashish, my mind
fixated on the horror of Bowles's Moroccan tale. The "distant
episode" had come disturbingly close. In this deserted terra in-
cognita I could be robbed, maimed, forced into slavery. No one
would ever know.

But the "guides" deposited me, stoned, paranoid and disoriented, at the Hotel Carlton in the Socco Chico, the little square we had first entered (ages and ages ago). They got ten dollars from me, which I surrendered without a fuss, relieved to be rid of them and their ministrations.

The Carlton was a dump, with carpetless, creaky wooden floors and dismal, drafty halls. It was so dark that you literally could see nothing when you entered. Your eyes had to grow accustomed to the dimness. Dog tired, I was about to fall asleep in the shuttered, musty room when I heard a soft knock. Jimmy the Guide stuck his scarred mastiff head inside the door.

"I get you good kifi, yes. Vairy cheap."

"How much?"

"Not worry."

"Well, I worry."

"Ten dollah. Cheap."

"No."

"Wan kee-low. Fi'dollah."

"That's better. No good, no pay."

"Hokay. You see. Vairy nice."

He was back in ten minutes with a plastic bag that included leaves, seeds and twigs. It looked like a great bargain. I paid and he left wreathed in sinister smiles.

Every morning I phoned Paul Bowles, but Jane always answered. I thought it odd that each time she put me off in the same way, repeating the same questions. She did not remember that we had been through it all before.

"Hello. May I speak to Paul Bowles?"

"Who *are* you?"

"A friend."

"Yes, but *who*? Don't you have a name?" She always forgot it. I didn't want to mention my name again because I thought she was prejudiced against me, but she would insist.

"Harold Norse."

"Oh . . . the name is familiar . . ." The vague voice hesitated, sounded dubious; then, heavy with suspicion: "Do *I* know you?"

"I don't think so."

"Well, then, what do you *want*?"

"I want to speak to Paul."

"But we don't *know* you."

"Paul would know me, if I can just—"

"If *I* don't know you, I'm sure Paul doesn't either."

"Would you please tell me when I can reach him?"

"No-o, I couldn't do that. . . . If we spoke to *everybody* just off the boat. . . ."

"I'm not *everybody*! We have lots of mutual friends. I'm a writer—"

"Oh, everybody's a writer! Everybody has friends."

I ticked off some names: Burroughs, Corso, Ginsberg . . .

"Friends!" her voice dripped sarcasm. "They are not *my* friends!"

"Let Paul be the judge of that. They told me to look him up, if you don't mind!"

"But I *do* mind!"

At this point I'd swear, unable to control myself, and hang up.

Then, about a week later, when I had abandoned the prospect of ever softening Jane up, she suddenly relented.

100

A Special Way of Seeing

Some twenty years after my visit to Tangier, and ten years after her death, Jane became posthumously famous. She is now compared with Colette, Doris Lessing, and Gertrude Stein, admired as an amalgam of Zelda Fitzgerald and Louise Bryant. New generations worship her for her flamboyant, witty, bohemian life-style, her uniquely original prose.

"The greatest writer of our century in the English language," rhapsodized Tennessee Williams in his memoirs.

"One of the really original pure stylists," said Truman Capote.

And, most recently, William Burroughs, writing of Denton Welch, said, "I think the writer to whom Denton is closest is Jane Bowles. Both . . . are masters of the unforgettable phrase that no one else could have written . . . each has a very special way of seeing things."

At Jane's death in 1973, she had an imposing list of establishment admirers, but not a wide reputation. Now she has both.

What was Jane like when I knew her? Certainly unlike anything this post mortem adulation would suggest. I saw not a glamorous legend but a disturbed, ailing woman, desperately unsure of herself. As for wit, there was little evidence of it. She was petulant, fussy, irritable. Bohemian? Suburban seemed a far more apt description. Her background was clearly one of ease and privilege. In fact, both Paul and Jane Bowles (by contrast with all the other writers, mainly Beat, whom I knew at the time) seemed conventional in their social life, dress, and behavior. Whatever their intellectual and artistic attainments or political philosophy, they exuded a distinctly cosmopolitan air of "café society" New Yorkers.

The Beat writers never referred to Jane's work. But what is even more curious, Paul never spoke of it either. I assumed it wasn't worth mentioning. Paul, on the other hand, was highly respected as a precursor of the Beats; his novels and stories dealt with altered states of consciousness through drugs and themes of incest, "under-age" homosexuality, and other taboos long before any mainstream American writer dared to touch them. I can understand in retrospect why Jane must have felt so completely obscured by Paul's fame and by his friends—although Paul surely could not be held responsible for such feelings. She did much to create her own isolation and neglect. In fact, without Paul's constant badgering and encouragement and, not least, his superb critical eye, there is evidence that she might have produced even less than she did.

Small, lame, morose, and anxious, Jane led a claustrophobic, hothouse existence, full of phobias. Whenever I saw her—and I never saw Jane without Paul—I was struck by the peevish tone with which they pursued, during an interminable colloquy, the subject that never changed: what they would have for dinner. This bizarre ritual, carried to the point of absurdity, was an obsession that they must have secretly enjoyed, although I can't imagine why.

Jane's apartment, situated on the floor above Paul's at the Inmueble Itesa, an apartment building in the Marshan (European quarter), was neat but featureless, lacking the taste and character, not to mention the fastidiousness, that marked Paul's existence. Like Jane herself, the place looked rather plain, with bare light bulbs and dowdy furnishings in the Moroccan manner. Each time, upon arriving, after I had steeled myself in advance against a comatose hour or so, sometimes even longer, my appearance was invariably greeted with the same complaint.

"You only come here with Paul. You *never* come to see me."

To this I had no answer; the accusation was just. But it was also unfair. It did not occur to her that when I arrived in Tangier she had discouraged me from doing this. Yet with a note of anguish in her voice, she would cry irritably, "*Nobody* ever comes to see *me*! You're Paul's friend, not mine! Everybody is Paul's friend! I have no friends! I used to have them, but nobody comes anymore."

Paul would respond to this tirade as he responded to everything: with irrefutable logic.

"Janie, you know that's not true! There's Sonya and Narayan and Ellen to start with. And there's David and Isabelle and Ira. There's Tennessee and Libby—"

"Paul, stop it!" she'd protest, looking more injured. "You know very well what I mean! All the literary people who come to Tangier look *you* up. They're not interested in me!"

"Some of them become your friends too, like Ira."

During such arguments she would cast baleful, accusing glances in my direction, which only succeeded in making me feel more uncomfortable. She would sulk awhile with a look of defiance, her crippled leg protruding straight out in front of her, as she'd slouch against the wall like a disgruntled waif, peering at a hostile world from behind horn-rimmed spectacles. Having vented her irritation on the subject of being abandoned by everyone, she'd watch Paul intensely, both of them puffing cigarettes, and then he would broach the subject for which he had come: what they would have for dinner. Almost immediately their faces would assume the rapt expression of players in a game of chess, while I nodded over a book or magazine.

Once I asked Paul whether she was mentally ill. He said she wasn't, but that she had never been the same since her stroke.

In the background hovered Cherifa, Jane's companion,

tight-faced, hostile, chain-smoking, a silent spook in trousers, her thick black hair bound tightly at the nape. She was extremely withdrawn, hard-looking, and masculine. I can't recall that Cherifa ever greeted us or said one word, though Paul and I would stop in to see Jane quite often before we set out, with my friend Mohammed, on some trip or other in my Fiat 600, around the countryside or to small, sometimes distant, villages where we visited cafés and listened to white-turbaned musicians play and sing their native music, a custom that was rapidly dying out, said Paul, and would probably be extinct in Morocco in one more generation.

101

Les Liaisons dangereuses

When I asked about Cherifa, Paul said she had poisoned Jane. Jane, on the other hand, would never give her up. She felt protective of Cherifa, believing that in spite of Cherifa's selfish character, she was like a child who loved and needed Jane. Paul loathed Cherifa and was convinced that she was waiting for an opportunity to poison him, too.

"She has actually threatened me," he said, "on many occasions. 'Paul, I'm going to kill you.' She would say it coldly, when Jane wasn't around."

It was a Charles Addams household, and these sophisticated Manhattanites lived in constant fear for their lives. Yet in some perverse fashion they seemed to be enjoying themselves immensely in this backwater North African port, at the mercy of superstitious illiterates who could not read a word they wrote. The Bowleses formed the closest bonds with them, making them part of their intimate personal life, and refused to give them up. Paul had done exactly the same with Ahmed Yacoubi, whom I got to know quite well. Yacoubi also feared and hated Cherifa.

As for Jane, she disliked (was jealous of) Paul's friends—especially Ginsberg, Kerouac, and Corso. They had preceded my visit to Tangier by a few months. It was very likely that when I announced over the telephone that they were my friends, she lumped me with them and set herself against me. She may have resented them because, as a writer, they ignored her. One thing is certain: she could not have disliked them for their behavior—she was notorious for creating public scenes herself. She had a knack, Paul said, of livening things up in restaurants and cafés.

In time Jane's attitude toward me softened. Paul put it this way: "Well, you know Janie. She has pro-Norse days and anti-Norse days. Mostly, I guess, anti-Norse days."

At some point I lent or gave Paul a copy of my most recent book, *The Dancing Beasts,* published earlier that year by Macmillan. He made a complimentary remark and indicated that Jane also admired it. I think this established me in her mind as a poet she could take seriously. Shortly after she had seen my book Paul reported, "Janie says if she had to choose between you and Gregory as poets, she wouldn't be able to because you're both equally good. But if she had to choose between you as people, you'd win, *faute de mieux.*"

"A Pyrrhic victory," I muttered.

Paul, who was usually cheerful and brisk, and whose resentments (not so near the surface as the vulnerable Jane's) were mitigated by his inexhaustible fund of humorous anecdotes and odd information, startled me once by grumbling quite sullenly when Tennessee Williams arrived, "Tennessee doesn't come here to see me! He's only interested in Janie. He wouldn't even bother to come to Tangier otherwise. They positively *adore* one another."

He commented peevishly that they had an almost mystical union, believing that they alone among American writers possessed a rare poetic sensibility.

"An alcoholic *participation mystique*," Paul observed drily.

102

Tennessee in Tangier

That summer of 1962 Tennessee Williams arrived, moonfaced and florid, one arm hugging a bottle of whiskey, the other outstretched in greeting on the busy thoroughfare between the Socco Chico and the Café de Paris, where he was headed. As I descended the inclined street toward my hotel, we met head on. "Harold! *Harold!*" he shouted effusively. "Paul told me you were here! C'mon, baby, let's have a drink! Let's go to Jay Haselwood's!" Haselwood's bar was frequented by the Anglo-American colony.

Tennessee's large blue eyes, barely focusing despite several operations, still had a trace of strabismus and looked more watery and fishlike than ever. Also fishlike was the way he kept gasping for air as he talked, his speech thick with drunken exuberance. Now in his fiftieth year, he had aged considerably since I had last seen him, a few years earlier, at what he called his "naughty rumpus pad" in Rome, where, as I recall, the rooms were painted brothel scarlet.

Since I had a prior engagement I could not accompany Tennessee but said I'd be at the beach the following day with Gregory Corso.

"Oh, is Gregory here? Remarkable boy! I'm very fond of Gregory. Let's meet on the beach around noon!"

Before Gregory's arrival I had moved to the Hotel Villa Muniria, a run-down stucco building in the casbah. I had a dark, gloomy room on the ground floor, entered from an unkempt garden by French doors. There was a narrow bed and nothing else. The walls were a murky repulsive green. I had one suitcase and a small spirit stove with camping equipment. The adjacent room was occupied by Corso. The proprietress, a fierce old Frenchwoman, had been a whorehouse madam in Hong Kong.

When Paul first came to see me there he exclaimed, "This is Bill's old room! When he occupied it empty Eukodol bottles, garbage, and manuscript pages littered the floor. The pages blew into the garden with every breeze. Madame swept them away with the trash. Hundreds of pages must have been lost."

When Paul inquired about the pages, Burroughs muttered laconically, "That's my work!" Tight-lipped and poker-faced, Paul mimicked him perfectly, burring the *r*. The "work" was *Naked Lunch.* "I never cleaned or dusted the room," said Burroughs much later. "Empty ampoules and garbage piled up to the ceiling."

103

A Game of Chance

I had only thirty dollars and put off my return to Paris. One night Gregory said he knew how I could double or triple the money. I responded skeptically, "I'm all ears." We would play at the gaming tables, he said, his eyes beginning to shine and mine to lack luster. "You can't lose!" he argued, trying hard to convince me.

All I had to do was lend him five dollars, he said, while I played the rest myself. If we lost he promised to repay the sum I put up from his next monthly check from Grove Press—for the novel he was writing. I was convinced. We donned suits and ties and, resembling a couple of Italian gangsters, advanced in high spirits on the casino. I turned in my cash for chips and followed Gregory into a spacious room with a green felt table and whirling roulette wheel. It was like a movie set: gilt decoration, showy furnishings, crystal chandeliers, haughty dowagers in diamonds, stern old gentlemen in tuxedos puffing cigars. Handsome croupiers (were there ever any plain ones?) impassively twirled roulette wheels.

With me behind him Gregory marched resolutely to a table.

We took seats and placed our chips on the green felt. Gregory's five-dollar pile looked ridiculously small. I hardly dared raise my eyes at the croupiers or the patrician players, whose air of cold hauteur was chilling. But if I was self-conscious Gregory was not. He grabbed some of my chips, placed them on a number, and hoarsely muttered instructions to do the same. Nurturing a secret conviction that I had beginner's luck, I placed my entire sum on a number and lowered my eyes in silent prayer. The wheel spun. When I opened my eyes I watched my number come in.

"You've got the luck!" cried Gregory. "Go for it!"

He scooped up more of my chips as I placed the rest on a number and won again. "Great! Great! Don't stop now!" exclaimed Gregory. The old ladies and gentlemen glared. Emboldened, I risked all a third time and as my number came in I grew euphoric. The world began to shimmer and shine. Five times I won in succession as the other players glowered and placed larger and larger sums on the table. On my sixth win, Gregory, the seasoned gambler, stared at my pile of chips and whispered hoarsely, "You can quit now if you want to. Wanna quit?" I still felt lucky, still had that magic feeling. Like a great athlete or musician, swept along on the path to glory, I was following a rhythm, a destiny. I had the *power*. Luck, grace, intuition—whatever it is. And when it comes it doesn't always stay. I felt that the two of us together exerted a powerful force field, although that night the luck did not rub off on Gregory. It was my moment.

Studying the red squares with the black numbers, I took my time before the next move. Like a magician about to pull something out of a hat, I was the cynosure of all eyes. The players watched furiously. Very deliberately, I put my chips, all of them, on number 7, the month of my birth, the number of my moves. Sweat poured down my flushed face and neck. Then I sat back, blowing thick clouds of cigar smoke into the room, loftily smug in my cheap Dacron suit with the tiny moth holes and cigarette burns.

With abrupt angry movements the old men and women placed large sums on the green table, all eyes glued to the wheel. The white ball came to rest—on number 7.

Gregory leapt from his seat, throwing his arms in the air like an Olympic gold medalist. Our team had won. The others shook their heads in shock. For the first time the thought crossed my mind: perhaps I should quit. I sat looking at some three thousand dollars. Enough for a prolonged stay in Tangier, in a good hotel or apartment. Or I could return to Paris without financial problems. But the inner voice, persistent, urged me on.

As I slowly began to move my entire pile onto another number, waves of electricity sparked through the room. From the other gaming rooms hushed crowds came and gathered around the table, murmuring in awe, with expressions of disbelief and wonderment, waiting breathlessly for what would happen next.

When, for the eighth time, the croupier pushed everything my way—around five thousand dollars!—there was a chorus of oh's and ah's. Now the churning feeling in my gut urged me to leave with my winnings. But, swept along in some trancelike euphoria, with the languid movements of a sleepwalker on the edge of a rooftop high above the city, as crowds breathlessly watched, I began pushing all my chips onto a number, holding my breath. Only the sound of the little white ball clicking in the wheel could be heard. As it slowed to a stop it hovered one number away from mine on the ridge between them; and then, as I realized with a sinking feeling what I had done, I could not believe it when the ball barely tipped over and made it into the slot, my slot, for the ninth time in a row.

I sat dazedly staring at about ten thousand dollars.

I had defied the laws of probability. But did it merely boil down to the psychology of being a winner or a loser? I believe this is too simplistic. There was something else, something peculiar. It had to do with the reason I gave up chess in high school, after having beaten the chess team, including the teacher who had taught us the game. I had already proven my skill, and winning seemed gross. I did not enjoy the sensation.

So when an inner voice told me to cash in my chips I did not obey. While beads of perspiration rolled down my face and neck and my gut churned and the little white ball came to rest for the tenth and final time on the wheel of fortune, a great cry of triumph rose from the throats of the onlookers and intense relief swept the casino like a cool breeze following a heat wave. (It is not true that all the world loves a winner. They hate and envy him, they wish him dead.) The croupier broke into a tight little smile, his first since I had sat down to play. I had lost everything. But, curiously enough, I too felt a sense of relief, as if a burden had been lifted from my shoulders. I felt free.

One morning we were on the beach with Tennessee, Ted Joans, and a few others, including a beautiful young woman of about twenty called Nazli, whom I had known in Paris. Her mother, an impoverished French countess, owned a ramshackle villa in Nice which, in desperation, she had put up for sale. Nazli's father, an Egyptian painter, had divorced the countess and left them destitute. Nazli dressed like a Rumanian gypsy in colorful but soiled dirndls and makeshift blouses from discarded scraps. She went around barefoot. Her large luminous blue eyes and pale rose complexion contrasted sharply with her lustrous black hair. With her soft voice and upper-class British accent, despite her ragamuffin appearance she exuded sensitivity and breeding, reminding me in her delicacy of Anaïs Nin. Strongly attracted to Nazli, I felt protective.

Like so many other young people, she hung around the Beat Hotel absorbing the cut-up technique and new ideas that we were experimenting with. Burroughs had recommended her work to Maurice Girodias, publisher of Olympia Press, who was so impressed with her innovations, not to mention her beauty, that in an issue of *Olympia* magazine she was represented by a long poetic play and full-page close-ups, giving her the look of a glamorous new star. Later her work appeared in a volume of experimental writers, published by John Calder in London.

On the beach I introduced Nazli to Ted Joans, who, for some reason, took an instant dislike to her. He looked down his nose and said disdainfully, "Oh, another of them pushy little Jewish girls who hang around famous writers, huh? You *are* pushy, baby, aren't you? A pretty little New York Jewish girl."

Easily intimidated, Nazli softly protested, "No."

"Oh, come on! Don't lie about it! Admit what you are! There are worse things, you know."

"Well, I'm not."

"You're ashamed of bein' what you are! It's obvious, girl, so why don't you admit it?"

"I'm French, not Jewish. And I've never been to New York."

"French, eh! Well, well, but you speak mighty fine English, doncha, girl? Where'd you pick up that classy accent, huh, baby?"

"In England. I went to school there."

"Smart little beatnik girl. Do you always hang around famous poets and writers? Cancha tell we're busy? We can't be pestered all the time by groupies, see!"

Nazli turned to me desperately for support. I took her aside.

"He's excited at being with Tennessee," I said. "He's just showing off." She was on the verge of tears. She had hoped to

sell her watercolors to tourists on the beach but Ted had fright-
ened her. He had been one of the original beatniks around Jack
Kerouac in Greenwich Village, had been praised by André
Breton, and was perhaps the best black American surrealist poet.

I took Nazli by the arm to meet Tennessee. "This young lady
has some interesting watercolors that you might like," I said.

In a white linen suit and Panama hat, his perennial cigarette
holder gleaming in the sun, he smiled distantly. I nudged Nazli,
who was petrified. Her hand shook as she handed him a sheaf.
Thoughtfully he examined each one, humming to himself and
murmuring, "Mmm, very nice. Yes, very nice." In a grandiose
manner he handed them back and said, "Well, honey, they're
lovely but we're broke today. Come back some time when we've got
some money on us." With a mournful look in my direction, Nazli
slunk off, defeated. I couldn't help thinking that if she had been a
pretty boy he would have found his pockets and his heart full.

Tennessee requested my company at the boathouse, where
he could escape the noonday sun. In the deserted refreshment
room, facing the straits where we watched the whitecaps curling
below, he kept humming softly the same tune, with a dreamy
faraway look in his eyes that I remembered from our Provincetown summer almost twenty years before. He had always lapsed
into these moody silences, usually indicating preoccupation with
something he was writing. When I inquired about his recent life
he looked even vaguer and, more loudly, sang, "Should I reveal
exactly how I feel?" It was the same old tune.

Finally, after an endless pause, I mentioned that I was practically stranded because Gregory owed me some money.

"Oh, I'm sure you'll get it!" he exclaimed vehemently.
"There's no malice in that boy, none at all!"

He plunged into another silence while I marveled at his
touching faith in Gregory. Leaving him to his melancholy brooding—he was completely unreachable when he was like this—I
recalled the late summer of 1944, when he had been as vulnerable and unsure of himself as Nazli was now. He had the same
frail, waiflike quality that made people want to protect him, to
soften one's voice in his presence. You were afraid that if you
spoke too loudly or harshly he might break. As if he were made
of glass. "Poor Tennessee," we said.

Now he was often callous and insensitive, even going out of his
way to hurt and humiliate friends, deriving some perverse satisfac-

tion from such crass behavior. Asking him for a handout was hopeless. In an aggrieved tone he would immediately complain, "People think I'm loaded. They think I'm a millionaire. I just manage to live comfortably, that's all." This was patently absurd.

The only thing that had never changed about him was the dreamy, faraway look. Otherwise, he bore no resemblance to the obscure, painfully shy young playwright I had lived with two decades before.

104

In the Hub of the Fiery Force

I left Tennessee in the boathouse and returned to the group on the beach. During a pause in the conversation I whispered in Gregory's ear that I needed the money he owed me. His features contorted with rage, he leapt to his feet, shouting abuse. Humiliated in front of the others, whose poor opinion of me was legible in their hostile faces, I scrambled to my feet and stumbled off. I thought of Tennessee's remark that Gregory had no malice in him. How could so eminent a playwright know so little about people?

That evening there was a nervous knock on my door and Gregory sheepishly entered. "Man, I'm sorry. Really sorry. I just can't control myself. You gotta believe me."

Tears sprang to his eyes. He flung himself on my bed and leaned forward, head in hands, and began to weep. Thunderstruck, I sat up while he hunched over the foot of the bed.

"Why do I goof with people I love?" he sobbed. "We've had great times together, remember? I don't want to put you down."

Although still nursing hurt feelings, I couldn't help being moved. Beneath the ruthless character assassin was a guilty child who, like his victims, also suffered from his sadistic behavior. But as his most recent victim, I was still licking my wounds.

"Gregory, that was incredibly unfair," I said warily. "I asked for the money you promised to repay and got insulted before others."

"I know, I know. I can't help it. That's what hurts. I don't know what comes over me. I always goof. Man, I'll take care of the money, don't worry. The check hasn't arrived yet. We're friends?"

He stuck out his hand. I nodded. He hugged me and left.

As the days passed Gregory gave no sign of honoring his promise. Again, as we sat on the *terrasse* of the Café de Paris, where he was eating a large slice of angel's food cake and drinking coffee, I mentioned that I was broke. And again, as if the scene in my room had never happened, he jumped to his feet and threatened to push the cake with its vanilla icing into my face. I think the same cast of characters was present. I almost punched him in the nose, but I left.

Again a contrite, shamefaced Gregory came to my room in tears, but this time I said that I was neither his father confessor nor his mother superior, and that I was not going to put up with any more nonsense. He could, I suggested, relieve himself of his guilt by repaying the small sum of thirty dollars, if he was so concerned about saving our friendship.

I never got the money.

105

A Dove-Gray Princely Garment

I was forced to sell my burnoose to Paul for twenty dollars. It was a dove-gray princely garment that had belonged to a sheikh, for which Ahmed Yacoubi had bargained on my behalf in the souk at Arcila. When Paul first saw the *silhem* he inquired, "Where did you get it? It's a very fine robe!" When I told him that Ahmed had bargained an hour in the hot sun and dust on a dirt road in Arcila, and got it for twenty dollars, Paul said, "That's a very good price. If you ever want to sell it I'd like to buy it. I'll certainly give you twenty dollars for it."

"It's a deal," I said, "but I don't think I'll ever sell it."

I now took him up on the offer.

"What do I need another djellabah for?" said Paul, looking noncommittal. He was seated on a hassock puffing his cigarette, dangling the holder at a rakish angle. "I've got twelve djellabahs."

"But you *said* you'd buy it if I ever wanted to sell." I was shocked that he had forgotten.

"Well, it *is* a beauty. How much are you asking?"

"Thirty dollars."

"I really don't need it," said Paul. "Besides, Janie wouldn't let me. She'd be furious. She says I've been spending too much recently."

He continued puffing his cigarette and blinking rapidly, his thin pale face slightly perplexed, as he often looked when disagreement arose. Of all the people I had known in Tangier, I had been closest to Paul, whom I liked and admired immensely, and knew to be completely trustworthy. I couldn't believe that he, too, would break a promise. I had reached the door when he called my name. I turned, startled to see him trembling all over. He had risen to his feet and his voice shook. He said he would honor his word and buy the burnoose. "But you're asking ten dollars *more* than you paid for it?" he said in an outraged tone. I sold it to him for twenty.

"I hope Janie doesn't find out," he said guiltily.

Sometimes I thought that living in the Arab world most of his life had sharpened the shrewd, relentless bargaining skill that lay just beneath his cool, composed, New England Yankee demeanor.

My entire stay in Tangier was made unforgettable by Paul. Though we did not reveal much about our inner lives, as I got to know him better I began to see him on a gossamer tightrope (stretched like a silken spider's thread over an abyss) poised in a precarious balance between desperate angst and sheer delight.

Once, when we went together with my friend Mohammed to a mountain village called Jajouka, where the ancient Greek Pan ceremony was still performed annually by the native priest-musicians, the music of which Paul recorded, we watched him pre-

pare for sleep in the adjacent cot. He plugged both ears with
stopples, placed a packaged blindfold over his eyes, and swallowed sleeping pills. I, who could not sleep without barbiturates
and stopples myself, realized that Påul was even more troubled
about losing consciousness. He may even have detested noise
more, if that was conceivable. I recognized a fellow-equilibrist on
the tightrope between being and nothingness.

Better than anyone I knew, however, he filled the void with
music and conversation, producing endless pleasure. Once he
took me to a town called Chaouen where we sat in a ramshackle
café made of weathered gray boards on an unpaved dirt road.
We watched young dancing boys in shimmering female costumes, multicolored, while old men lounged on pasha pillows
smoking kif and hashish with their long-stemmed, segmented
sebsis. With sinuous erotic movements, their smooth arms brace-
leted with colored beads and gleaming metal adornments, heads
crowned with ornamental bands around white turbans, the boys
danced and sang. Between nine and fourteen years old, their
dark eyes heavily painted with kohl, their lips and cheeks
rouged, they were incredibly beautiful. Everyone sat transported, relaxed and happy, smoking cannabis, while the musicians never let up their nasal wail and hypnotic sound of ouds
and wooden flutes.

From time to time the boys sat on the laps of the white-
bearded old men (like an old Persian print), who fondled them
tenderly, feeding them sweets, kissing and caressing them, and
giving them money. I had never seen such an affectionate interchange between generations—this was mammal nature herself,
the unspoiled natural condition of the human primate, unin-
fluenced by false preachings. Here was a tiny remnant of a by-
gone era, stashed away in a remote corner of North Africa, off
the beaten tourist track, keeping alive what once had been widely
prevalent all over the eastern Mediterranean, from Turkey and
Byzantium to Morocco, an irrepressible instinct allowed to express itself openly. For this sight alone I would have been eternally grateful to Paul Bowles.

"Dancing boys must behave like women in every way to
arouse the man," Paul explained. "That is the point of the dance.
This is how they earn more money—the goal of it all. Like other
boys in Morocco they are not a bit effeminate. It is merely
custom, a highly stylized ritual." I felt like Lawrence of Arabia,

like an adventurer. "It won't be around much longer," said Paul, a trifle ruefully. "It will be gone by the end of the century."

In a sort of uneasy cease-fire I was sitting one afternoon in Madame Porte's tearoom with Paul, who had bought my burnoose, and Gregory Corso, whose default on a loan had caused me to sell it. We were drinking tea and munching cookies and chatting as if nothing had happened between us. Suddenly Jane appeared, disheveled and wild-looking, her hennaed hair sticking out like a fright wig. I'd never seen her in public before. She stormed over to our table with blazing eyes.

"Hypocrites!" she shouted, waving her arms about. "You're nothing but a bunch of hypocrites! All three of you! Only yesterday you were at each other's throats! You didn't have a good word to say for each other! Now *look* at you! Sitting there all chummy! Having a tea party! Mealymouthed hypocrites! That's what you are! Have you no shame? My God, how can you face each other? How can you face yourselves? And you call yourselves *friends*! Is that what you are?"

We sat there, sheepish and stunned. Madame Porte's was the only respectable, middle-class tearoom in Tangier, frequented by proper old English ladies. We liked it because it was quiet and European, a respite from the teeming Moroccan bustle and noise outside. As we grinned sheepishly the old ladies, in their neat, stuffy attire, sat rigid with shock. Jane, who had a very resonant, expressive voice—at that moment electrifying—glared at us and then wheeled on the ladies. They quickly lowered their eyes and sipped their tea in mortified silence. Without another word, Jane turned and, dragging her stiff leg, hobbled out.

Next day, with only twenty dollars to get me through Spain and back to Paris in my little Fiat 600, I made preparations to leave. It was nearly noon. Groggily, I prepared brunch with some Quaker oats I'd found in an open box on the dusty floor. I had never covered it and had no pantry or refrigerator. I stirred some water into the oats and idly watched it puff for several minutes on the alcohol stove, then poured some milk into it and began to eat. Something crunchy and tasty was mixed with the oatmeal. Peering into the box I saw what I took to be tiny chocolate chips. Ah, Nesselrode, I thought vaguely. Then it dawned on me. The last time I had seen Nesselrode was in my boyhood in Brooklyn. I examined the package—not a word about

Nesselrode. Puzzled, I closely scrutinized some dry oats in my palm; then suddenly knew. Mouse shit. Tiny black pellets of mouse shit.

I spat and gagged in horror.

I pulled on my pants, tore upstairs to the hotel telephone, and frantically dialed Paul. No answer. I dialed Jane. Thank God she was home. In great excitement I sputtered out what had happened.

"Jane, I need a doctor at once! I've swallowed mouse shit! Yes, I said *mouse* shit. Maybe rat shit! No, I didn't *know* what it was! I wasn't trying to commit suicide, Jane. I was just eating oatmeal for breakfast and tasted something that I thought was Nesselrode. My God, what if I get convulsions? Spasms? The bubonic plague? Yech!"

I choked, retching with disgust.

Jane made sympathetic noises, saying she knew all the European doctors in Tangier. She told me to drive over while she phoned them. I leapt into the Fiat, sped to the Inmueble Itesa. Jane greeted me with a shot of whiskey, which I gratefully gulped. She told me her Swiss physician, Dr. Roux, was out. In the sweltering heat we raced to another doctor—also out. We drove from doctor to doctor, but not one was available. It must have been around 120 degrees Fahrenheit. Sweat poured down my face, armpits, and crotch. Jane was a marvel of patience. I don't know what I'd have done without her. She suggested that we return to her place, noting that I hadn't exhibited any horrible symptoms so far.

"You probably sweated all the poisons out of your system," she said, handing me another shot glass at her apartment. "You must have avoided any dire effects by boiling the oats. You'll live, so relax."

I wasn't so sure. But by then the panic had begun to subside. It was more than an hour since we had set out on our quest, and a few more shot glasses brought on a rush of warmth for Jane. Her concern, her reassuring tone and manner, and above all, the feeling of *gemütlichkeit*, a homey New York feeling that I liked so much in Paul, melted me with gratitude. Furthermore, she had behaved sensibly, something I had never expected of her.

"You don't know how grateful I am," I began. "If it hadn't been for you—"

"So stop kvetching," she interrupted with a wry but charm-

ing smile. Suddenly she became a real person. Until then I had
seen her as only a neurotic, compulsive invalid. "If you still think
you need a doctor this evening, we can probably get Dr. Roux—
if she hasn't expired from heat prostration."

That evening in Paul's apartment he told me that Jane had
been hysterical with laughter all day. "She phoned everyone she
knew in Tangier, telling them how Harold Norse ate mouse shit
for breakfast thinking it was Nesselrode. And how, on the hot-
test day in memory, you shlepped with her all over town for a
doctor, finally getting drunk at her place. And how sentimental
you got over Janie, probably because you never thought she had
the sanity and presence of mind to be of assistance in a pinch."

I was flabbergasted. Was there one writer in the whole world
that you could trust? While professing sympathy to my face, Jane
couldn't wait to laugh behind my back.

In disbelief, I asked, "She said all that?" Paul nodded.

"But if I hadn't boiled those damn oats—"

"Oh, you'd still be around to tell it. Haven't you heard of
people eating rats during wars and famines? They didn't always
boil them." He passed the kif pipe imperturbably. "They ate 'em
raw," he said, after coughing out the green smoke. "And they
survived."

"Do you think Jane knew that?"

"Who knows what Janie knows or doesn't know?"

"Not even you?"

"Certainly not me."

"Well, it was mean of her to make fun of my predicament."

"Why? You were in no real danger. And there was no malice
in it. She loves situations like that. Well, you know Janie, she—"
He put down the kif pipe and slapped his forehead. "I'm forget-
ting what I wanted to *say*! Lost in the middle of—a sentence. I'm
kiffed!"

He started laughing. Then I began to laugh. I laughed and
laughed, at myself, at the whole nutty episode, at Jane and Paul.
I couldn't stop. It was a splendidly relaxed feeling. I was stoned,
glad to be alive, to be sitting with Paul again, perhaps for the last
time. What a fascinating year it had been! But did I really know
Jane Bowles? Or Paul for that matter? Did I know *myself*? Anyone? Everybody—friends and enemies—the world—weren't
they, we, all of us, gaga? Absurd? Wasn't I weaving a rope of
sand?

106

Palma de Mallorca

D ressed to pass Spanish customs inconspicuously, with the twenty dollars from the sale of my burnoose to Paul Bowles and my boots stuffed with a kilo of pot (trouser legs tight over the boots), I drove my Fiat onto the ship. On disembarking my heart sank. I watched customs officers perform a body search and carefully probe the cars for hidden compartments. Ahead of me a well-dressed woman watched as they cut open the lining above the windshield of her car. Jesus, the jig is up, I thought. Quaking in my boots with enough kif in them to put me away for life (we all had American friends languishing in Spanish, Greek, or Italian jails for possession of cannabis), I broke into a cold sweat and wondered how I could have been so stupid as to risk my freedom for so little. It was sheer madness.

Finally an agent stuck his head through the window. I stared at vacant brown ox eyes and a small black moustache, resting my hands on the wheel to steady them as he perused my passport. "You are American?" he asked in English. "Yes." "You wish to stay in Spain?" "No. I'm going to Paris." He returned the document and touched his visor politely. *"Bon voyage, señor!"* I sped off vowing never to try anything so foolhardy again.

In Torremolinos I looked up a *real* smuggler, Berthold Hansen (name changed). A tall soft overweight Swede from Minnesota in his late twenties, he had hair so blond it was almost white. In fact, everyone in the house was platinum blond. "I feel as if I've stepped into a Strindberg play," I said. As a raconteur Bert was almost as good as our friend Ira Cohen, who was almost as good as Brion Gysin. In later years Ira developed a surreal individual style in poetry, at times as remarkable, but different from, the surrealist Philip Lamantia, who was then living in Churiana, a village north of Torremolinos. Bert had made a fortune smuggling gold to India and was now engaged on some new enterprise. He had befriended a distinguished British scholar in his eighties and his wife, nearly ninety, who was slowly dying. Bert's story about her is unforgettable.

"She was so witty and charming that I never tired of her company," he told me. "We used to laugh a lot. Then one day she said, 'Bert, there's very little time left. Please bring my husband.'" Before complying with her request he asked, in their usual bantering tone, "Is there anything else I can do for you?" The wizened old lady gazed at him longingly. "Yes," she said. "All my life I have loved the magic and thrill of the sex act. I've missed it a great deal. Before I go, I can think of nothing that would make me happier." He hesitated, repelled by the mummified wrinkled face, then unzipped his fly. "Give me head, baby," he said. A beatific smile crossed her lips. Ten minutes later when her husband arrived with Bert she was dead—peacefully smiling.

"What was it like being sucked off by an old lady?" I asked.

"Terrific! Gums are even sweeter than pussy."

As I've always said, straights have no shame.

The old scholar's current girl friend was an Englishwoman in her thirties whom I'll call Cynthia. When I tried to sell her some kif she reached into a large canvas bag, extracted a plastic baggie with about two kilos, and said, "It's like carrying coals to Newcastle. We get all we need from Tangier for the price you paid."

Years later Cynthia married a young American poet I had met in Paris who died in Nepal, where they had a son. In 1979 in Amsterdam, where I gave a reading at the One World Poetry Festival with Burroughs, Gysin, Patti Smith, and Ira Cohen, I ran into Cynthia. She told me that the boy, who was nine, was in Katmandu being brought up by Buddhist monks, who had pronounced him the reincarnation of a self-realized spiritual master.

In Palma I stayed with Ruthven Todd, who had taken up residence there. Unfortunately my bedroom was over the main thoroughfare and, since Ruthven spent most of his time in the bars, I quickly grew bored with the heat, traffic fumes, and noise, and decided to leave. To raise cash I was forced to sell Ruthven one of three Moroccan blankets, which, he gleefully told his friends, was a steal. The day I packed my bags he stuck his head in the doorway, his graying black hair awry, horn-rims perched on his snub nose. "You'll wanna meet Rabbit before you go. Everyone does." "Who's Rabbit?" His whiskey-slurred speech was hard to understand. "Robert Graves, for Chrissake," he said. "Oh." I didn't much care. "Don't be silly," he said. "Nobody comes to Palma without meeting him." I shrugged. His poems had never moved me.

107

Deyá

On a fine day in July, Ruthven and I rode through the din of clattering trams and smelly exhaust, leaving behind the tourist trap of the capital, with its colony of retired British alcoholics and their cheerless arrogance. On the road winding north up the coast we passed Valldemosa, where Chopin and George Sand spent their unhappy winter of 1838–39. ("Frederic, there's blood on the keys!") Then we climbed a winding coastal road and soon reached Deyá, a fishing village of about five hundred inhabitants on the slopes of a rocky part of the island. Its main street is tiny. I recall only one small café with nobody to be seen in the afternoon heat.

At Graves's compound, "Canelluñ," we entered a white-washed courtyard blazing in the sun, with bougainvillea-draped walls. Ruthven introduced me to Graves's wife, Beryl, and a teen-age daughter and several other women. The heat and somnolence were awful. Just as I wondered whether Graves would show up, he suddenly appeared, a very tall white-haired old gentleman in a large straw bonnet, open summer shirt, khaki shorts, and sandals. He was impressive-looking with a prominent lopsided nose and pained gray eyes; but his mouth, fixed in pursed disapprobation of the world, was primly puritanical—unpleasant, soft, bitter.

"I saw Clare Booth Luce yesterday," he said. "My God, how that woman can talk! Distressingly glib. But short on poetry. For the first time in my life I was rendered absolutely speechless. 'Why read poetry?' she said. I was so shocked I couldn't answer. So I've offered twenty-five pesetas to anyone who can. So far nobody has won." Graves paid no attention to me, but I blurted out audaciously, "Why look at a tree?" He stared with sudden interest and surprise. "Yes," he said expectantly, "but that's answering one question with another." "Because," I said. "The twenty-five pesetas are yours!" he exclaimed, and then added, "But I haven't got it on me at the moment."

I never got the reward, but it was "friendship at first sight," to borrow a phrase from one of his poems. Needless to say, I had made a dramatic entrance into the Graves household. He took me up with enthusiasm. As the others vanished indoors and the heat grew more intense, I saw him wilt. "It's siesta time and I'm going to take a nap," he said. "I'll only be a couple of hours." Ruthven and I nodded. "Ruthven tells me you have a new book. Have you got it with you?" I gave him *The Dancing Beasts*. "I'll get you the manuscript of my recent love poems," he said. "You can't take it to Palma, but it's short enough to read here." He went in, returned with a thick sheaf of poems, then disappeared into the house.

I sat alone in the sun-drenched patio attempting unsuccessfully to go through the manuscript, but the love poems failed to excite me. In fact, they added to my somnolence. I wandered off to the tiny plaza, where I sat at a table outside the café hoping that a few coffees would revive me. In a daze I looked up and saw a familiar woman sauntering toward me in the isolated street. I recognized Mrs. Luce. Haughty, cold, formidable, and patrician, she had honed her tongue to the sharpness of a steel blade. Well, well, I thought, no wonder even Graves was speechless.

In the late afternoon I found Ruthven drinking indoors. He said Graves had requested our company in a couple of days. I left the love poems on a table. "You made quite an impression on Robert," said Ruthven enviously. "How do you know?" I asked. "He said so. He's reading your book and is very impressed."

On our return two days later Graves greeted me warmly. "I've read your book twice," he murmured. "It's very, very good, very honest, absolutely no cheat. You will go far. Please, sit down." He said much more that I couldn't catch; his soft-spoken rapid Oxonian speech fell on my deaf left ear. He insisted that I call him Robert and invited me into his study, which was very small, with some books and a desk facing a window over a garden with orange trees and shrubs.

In 1959 Graves had experimented with hallucinogenic mushrooms and inevitably the conversation turned to psychedelic drugs and their effects. He pulled out two huge tomes about magic mushrooms by R. Gordon Wasson and his wife, Valentina. "In the fifties I directed the authors to the sources in Mexico for the mushrooms," he said. I was fascinated by what I saw: big colored plates that can only be described as phantasmagoric visions of otherworldly forms, plantlike, humanoid, animal and mineral, rich and strange, ranging from the paradisiacal to the diabolical. He would point to specific plantlike humanoids and say, "I've been there," or "I've experienced this." When, in May 1960, he took the synthetic form, psilocybin, and, like Burroughs, had a bad reaction, he gave it up. He did have a mystical experience from which he made the decision that the Muse, "the natural poetic trance," meant more to him than any "induced by artificial means." By the time we met in July 1962 he was through with drugs.

Jerry Robbins's name came up and I told him that when young we practiced ballet together, that I had known his sister, and that I had a similar Brooklyn background. He looked surprised. "But—you're not Jewish? You're Irish or Scots, aren't you?"

"I *am* Jewish," I said, "mostly."

"But you haven't got the nose!"

I found it hard to believe that a man like Graves would fall for such an obvious stereotypic fallacy.

His brows knitted. "But you're not—homosexual?"

"I *am*," I said, "mostly."

He looked a little dashed. "Well," he said, reassuringly, "it's no problem. I know someone who can cure it quickly."

Auden would have replied, "Oh, goodie!"

Graves spoke of his Afghan friend, Idries Shah, a Sufi spiritual leader of thirty million followers, who would return to Deyá in a few days. By means of occult symbols he had extraordinary success in "curing" homosexuality, among other illnesses, said Robert. "In fact, it's easy to cure, quite easy."

The irrational had reared its silly head.

Meanwhile, unable to sense my reaction, for I gave no outward signs of chagrin, Robert changed the subject.

At the foot of the table in the large dining room sat Idries Shah with twelve others, all talking, heartily drinking Spanish wine, and stowing away a delicious *paella* for lunch. At the opposite end I sat at the right hand of Robert (at the head) and Ruthven opposite. All the others were women of the Graves menage. After a while Shah called out, "Robert tells me you've been in Tangier. My father stays there."

"Yes, I met him," I said, "at the house of some friends."

"Oh? Who were they? Perhaps I know them."

"An Indian prince called Narayan and his wife, Sonya, a Georgian princess."

"I don't know them. What did you talk about?"

"They have monthly discussion groups on metaphysical and occult subjects in their home."

Idries Shah had a loud assertive voice with a British ruling-class accent. About thirty-five, he was swarthy, of medium height, with thick black hair and a large aquiline nose.

"Did my father participate?" he asked.

"Oh, yes, he was the guest speaker. The group is small, usually five or six people, in a tiny house at the edge of town. The Kamalakars are very poor. Sonya sold her false teeth to buy a birthday present for her daughter, who's a ballerina in London."

"What did you discuss with my father?"

There was something about his tone I didn't like.

"We discussed meditation and I spoke of Krishnamurti."

He fell silent, then inquired, "What did you say about him?"

"Oh, I asked why it was necessary to follow any spiritual dogma or religion when, as Krishnamurti says, all authority wields power over the mind and enslaves it instead of freeing it for the experience of self-realization."

All of a sudden Shah interrupted and began attacking Krishnamurti as a false prophet, a teacher of platitudes with a simplistic approach to something complex and beyond the grasp of most, who needed the discipline of a traditional system of religion. As he went on at some length I realized, with horror, that he had no knowledge of Krishnamurti's thought and was, in fact, bluffing. Even if he was Graves's mentor I couldn't just sit there listening to a misleading put-down of Krishnamurti. But I observed decorum.

"Well, I've listened to what you've said, but excuse me if I mention that Krishnamurti speaks much more simply and to the point—his sentences are clear and precise, conveying his ideas unambiguously. Your objections are fully answered in his talks." This little speech was received in total silence. Then Shah rose to a half crouch, pounded the table, and shouted, "I don't know who you are or what your purpose is but I will *not* be interrupted and I don't have to sit here and be insulted by *you*, my friend!" and stormed furiously out.

Thunderstruck, I watched Robert rise with a look of perplexity and hurry after him as, one by one, everyone left the table, Ruthven last. Alone and feeling like Jesus deserted by the apostles I sat rooted to the spot, thinking, "I've done it again, I've upset everybody, but what was I supposed to do—sit here while Shah rambled on without knowing what he was talking about?" Just then Robert stuck his head in the doorway with a troubled look.

"What went wrong?" he said. "I have no idea!" I replied. He disappeared again. Ruthven came in. "For God's sake, go out and patch it up!" he said. "They're in the garden." "Patch *what* up?" "Nobody knows. Robert doesn't know. Just say something, anything. Apologize. Say you're sorry." "For what?" "*I* don't know." He left and I got up and sauntered out. I saw them by the rock wall at the far end of the garden, deep in conversation. Shah sat on the high wall dangling his legs like a schoolboy. They fell silent at my approach. With sincerity, I said, "I'm very sorry for what happened, though I don't fully understand it."

Shah stared, brazen-faced. "I don't have to accept your apology, my friend," he sneered. "You Americans think everything can be settled by friendliness and goodwill. Well, you're wrong. I am not interested in your goodwill. I don't believe in your democracy or equality. We are not equal. I couldn't care less about what you think."

I was being insulted. I shot a look at Robert, towering over me with a fierce, anxious expression. I turned to Shah.

"In that case, I'm no longer sorry. I've wasted my time."

I turned and strode off.

Days later, I'm sitting in the little deserted square in Deyá. The hot sun beats down on my head. I'm calm and relaxed on the sun-drenched café terrace, reading a book. All of a sudden Idries Shah appears, approaches with a grin, and seats himself beside me. "How are you, my friend? Robert tells me that you are a poet with a following. I had no idea. I should like to see your book. He admires it very much."

I am astonished. Nothing pleases me more than high praise in high places. It means my work has broken down doors, dissolved enmities, crossed impenetrable barriers. Unlike the princely Shah, democracy and equality mean everything to me. "Not until the sun excludes you do I exclude you," said Walt Whitman to the prostitute in "Song of Myself." I have always honored this commitment, with prince or pauper. Poetry brings the mountain to Mohammed. I watch Idries peruse the book. "Listen, Robert tells me you'd like to work with me on your homosexual tendencies. I'm busy but willing to give you two sessions—one should be enough."

It's preposterous, but I smile amiably. "When do we begin?"

"Right now. I live down the street at the Posada."

We enter a handsome gray wooden dwelling that belongs to Robert. I take a seat in the dim shuttered front room. It is cool and quiet. "I'm going to flash some symbols on cards for a split second," says Shah. "You are to draw them exactly as you remember them."

The whole thing takes less than an hour. "You're cured!" cries Shah, standing up. This must be the world record for a sex change, I tell myself. I thank him and walk out, a new man. Rehabilitated. I can't wait to get back to Palma and pick up one of those blond Swedish girls in the bars. I'm so fired up I jump into my car, step on the gas, and—a peasant boy grins at me on the road! I almost run into a tree, but instead we end up together in an olive grove. I return to Palma incurably addicted.

In the days that follow, Robert unaccountably cools. Alone outdoors, without warning, and in a most disagreeable tone, he says, "The trouble with you is, you think too much. Your prefrontal lobes are overdeveloped." We're on the gravel outside the compound. The accusation is absurd. But *anything* I say will be discredited. His tone is final. He makes a few more sadistic, unfair remarks. "Why do you Americans smoke only half a cigarette and throw it away?" he says peevishly. "You're so wasteful." "Because," I reply, "the nicotine collects in the lower half." He turns and walks off. I feel mugged. Condemned without a hearing. I don't even know why. Friendship senselessly ended just when it began.

108

The Isles of Greece

I returned to Paris in the summer of 1962 to find that the Beat Hotel had been sold to Corsicans, who had begun renovation. Most of the denizens had fled; Burroughs took up residence in London, while Gysin and I, going separate ways, were the last to depart in June 1963. From Paris my odyssey took me to the home of Odysseus. There for three years I lived among the lotus eaters on the enchanted islands—Hydra, Poros, Crete, Madouri—and in Athens. It was everything a lotus eater could wish for: donkey boys, a naval academy, young fishermen dancing together in tavernas, bouzouki on the jukebox, delirium on cannabis and retsina. I did Zorba's dance, the *sirtaki*, with suntanned youths, wearing a jasmine in my ear and a gold ring in the lobe (macho in Greece), and spoke demotic Greek. I had a long affair with Eileen (as I'll call her), an ex-nun from Seattle, but mostly I was involved with the native boys. It was too good to last. In the end I must have eaten a bad lotus. In fact, I ate quite a few before disaster struck.

I had learned to dive from the rocks into the harbor, paying no attention to the floating turds; in the restaurant we had to shout at the waiter who served our spaghetti, "Not with your hands!" as he scooped it from the pot with grimy fingers. The lotus boys and donkey boys were not always clean either. And the local sawbones used dirty needles. I turned brown with jaundice.

An epidemic swept the foreign colony. A little-known Canadian poet who owned a house in Hydra also caught it but quickly recovered. His name was Leonard Cohen. He played the guitar and sang folk songs in a beautiful voice and we read each other's poetry aloud. We also exchanged our books with inscribed copies. "For Harold Norse, True Poet," he wrote in his copy of *The*

Spice Box of Earth. I showed him my cut-up "Sniffing Keyholes" and spoke of the experiments at the Beat Hotel. A week or so later, as we smoked pot on his white terrace in the sun, with trembling hands Leonard gave me some freshly written type-script pages. "I owe this to you," he said, "thanks to your key-holes." He watched nervously as I read. It was the best innovative prose I had seen since *Naked Lunch.* It became Leonard's novel *Beautiful Losers.* Two years later he achieved fame as a folk singer.

The isles of Greece. No wonder Lord Byron couldn't tear himself away. There the sensual life is fulfilled. But if, as Goethe observed, the loveliest sunset is boring in an hour, sex and beauty become enervating too. I was a hedonist, not a sybarite. If pleasure is good and pain bad, too much of either can destroy the soul—and the body. But who wouldn't rather die of plea-sure?

Before I got hepatitis I had stayed on a private island called Madouri, owned by a friend, the Greek surrealist poet Nanos Valaoritis. There was nothing to do but sunbathe, wade in the blue-green water, and write poetry in the old mansion. The is-land was an exquisite gem in a chain of islands owned by Aristo-tle Onassis, who wanted Nanos's island to complete the chain. Daily he sent a launch with two white-liveried servants for the Russian princess who was a guest of Nanos. Her father, whose sister had married the archduke Boris, the czar's brother, had been Onassis's friend and gambling buddy in the casinos at Monte Carlo before he died. The princess did water-skiing ara-besques like a ballerina, a tall blond Venus in the blue glare of the Mediterranean. She was a Farrah Fawcett look alike, a natu-ral blonde, a real Viking, and Jewish on both sides. Her mother was an American millionaire, her father's family the first Jews accepted at the court of the czar. Her aunt, the archduchess, was a great beauty. The princess herself died in mysterious circum-stances, in a Buddhist monastery in Nepal, where she had be-come a monk. So much for stereotypes about Jews.

A six-foot-eight giant would also arrive in a launch and in a hoarse, reverent whisper would say, "My master wishes to buy Madouri." "But it's not for sale," Nanos would respond. Per-plexed, the man would reply, "But Mr. Onassis *wants* it!" "*I* want it—it's not for sale." "Name the price!" the giant would whisper hoarsely.

One day Nanos said, "We are invited to dinner on the *Christina* at Skorpios by Onassis. He is wooing me because of the island. He won't get it, but we can have a marvelous dinner. Greta Garbo will be there." I couldn't believe my ears. "That's the night I promised Taylor Mead I'd be in Athens for the showing of his films!" I said. "I gave him my word." "Are you crazy?" said Nanos. "You'll never get a chance like this again." But I couldn't break my word.

When I arrived in Athens and told this to Taylor he gasped, "You passed up Greta Garbo to keep your *word*? On Onassis's *yacht*? I don't know anybody who'd have done that. I wouldn't!" I won Taylor's undying admiration but have regretted it ever since.

It was while I was living in Athens that I had the affair with the ex-nun. She was good-looking and a great talker and could hold listeners spellbound discoursing on Malcolm Lowry's novel *Under the Volcano*. She knew more than the scholars did.

Irving Rosenthal arrived with a letter of introduction from Ira Cohen in Tangier asking me to help Irving find a place to live. At first I liked Irving and tried to be helpful, offering suggestions and warning him about getting mail at American Express, which delayed or lost it. I also warned about boys in that area.

"Avoid Papaspyros, Constitution Square. They're hustlers. Best places are Omonia Square, where country boys hang out, and the streets or marketplaces, like flea markets and so on." He looked offended. "I prefer meeting someone socially," he objected prudishly. I felt rebuked for being indelicate. He asked about lodging and I suggested the Kronos Hotel, where I introduced him to Charles Henri Ford. But it was too expensive then for Irving. I told him that I was spending the summer in Hydra and he could have my one-room dwelling in Plaka at the foot of the Acropolis. He was interested and showed up the next day, looking approvingly at the bare stone walls, the spartan furnishings: a chair, table, cot, toilet. It was little more than a cave in a rock.

"This suits me perfectly," he said, "for finishing my novel." Eileen and I were happy to help. I said I'd sublet it for what I paid, twenty dollars a month, at no extra charge. "It's the cheapest you'll find in Athens." "When are you leaving?" he said. "In two days." "Can't you make it sooner?" Eileen and I exchanged looks. "No. By the way, I'm offering this deal provided that I can spend the night once a month. I have a sleeping bag." His face fell. "When I'm working I don't like being disturbed," he said firmly. "If I took your house I might not let you in."

"In that case, Irving, I'll have to think it over," I said. The deal was off.

When I returned to Athens and ran into him I was cordial; he seemed gentle but detached, indifferent. He had a room in a private house and when I passed on the street he'd be looking out the window and call my name. When next I saw him Charles Ford and I were going to a reading by the first Greek surrealist writer, Andreas Embirikos, a charming white-haired man we liked and admired. Irving came along. We debated whether to walk or take a taxi. Tired, I chose the taxi, but he wanted to walk. We rode.

When Irving moved into the Kronos and finished his novel, Charles said, "I'm sure he wants to see you. He likes to control, but he's changed my life. I'm more prolific."

His room was pleasant, clean, and well lit. His white shirt hung over his trousers as he washed his feet in the sink. He made no effort at conversation, nor did he respond to my attempts to do so. When he had cut his nails, he lay back on the bed with his head propped on an elbow. "You offended me when I arrived in Athens," he said. "You didn't treat me with respect." "Wasn't I helpful?" I said. "Every encounter with you was a knife chop," he said, stony-faced. "A series of knife chops." "I don't understand," I said, fascinated by the lizard eyes. "Yours not to understand," he said imperiously. "Yours to blow trumpets or be silent." He went on with a litany of my sins: I had come five minutes late to an appointment. I argued about the taxi when he didn't want one. Worst of all I was responsible for the Great Mail Tragedy. "You gave me the worst advice anybody has given me here. You told me not to receive mail at American Express. This caused a great disaster. My landlady returned it to all the senders."

Many writers and artists think they are God, but Irving was the only one I knew who convinced others of it. I had the weird feeling as he lay on the bed denouncing me that he was attempting to mesmerize me. Charles (who photographed teen-age boys) had said, "I do everything Irving tells me to. I can't have sex with my models, Irving won't let me! I'm serious. *He is God!*" God was at this moment cutting his toenails. If Charles, who picked up shoeshine boys as models and bedmates, had lost his mind, I had not. But Irving—what was I to make of *that* one? How could Charles fall under his spell so completely that he gave up sex?

But arguing with God is futile. This tiny Caligula fixed his snake eyes on mine and told me that he was not interested in me or my writing, it left him indifferent. He said, "You have no moral force!" At Charles's insistence that Irving would welcome me after all the misunderstandings, I had mistakenly expected a rapprochement. What had I done except refuse to be manipulated? When I asked why he thought I had come to see him he replied, "To come to terms with me!" in a tone so grandiose and exalted that I stood up to go. "I think you'd better leave," he said redundantly. As I neared the door he added spitefully, "I've put a hex on you." I turned. "I'll throw it back," I said, "it will boomerang." "Well, there's no point in continuing this," he said tiredly. "I will lift the hex when I see fit."

Charles said, "I have great admiration for Irving's book. It's a step further than Burroughs. Better than Genet. It's like nobody else. He's like Lautréamont." Then he bestowed his highest praise: "Only thing I know like it is *my* journal."

When Grove Press rejected his novel, Irving got Allen Ginsberg to badger Grove, threatening to jump out the window if they didn't publish it. They capitulated.

109

London

I spent the next three years wandering about northern Europe in quest of a hepatitis cure—Heidelberg, Zurich, London. All failed. In 1967 I lived in St. Mark's Crescent, Regents Park, London. With Edgar's support I had a beautiful flat with a fireplace. Since I couldn't get about, my friends visited me there. Donald Cammell, who had become a movie director, was shooting Mick Jagger's first film, *Performance*. He kept inviting me to the set to meet Mick, but I had to decline. I was exhausted, down to 120 pounds. "The starved look is fashionable," said Donald, "very mod." It was the era of Twiggy. Another visitor was Stephen Spender. But I was so disabled by the liver ailment that I wasn't very good company. That year Leonard Cohen became famous.

A small press in London published my book of poetry *Karma Circuit,* which became a cult book in the counterculture there. I was also offered publication in the prestigious Penguin Modern Poets series. Actually, the Penguin editor, Nikos Stangos, offered me a volume of my own, but we thought it would sell better in the successful series. It did. Stangos had asked what two poets I would like to share the volume with; I chose Charles Bukowski, whom nobody had ever heard of, and Philip Lamantia, whose work he knew. It appeared in 1969. The *London Times* raved about my work: "A really striking 50 pages of exultant poems . . . magnificent lyrical celebrations. . . . The thunder and glitter of technical achievement can only accelerate the tuned imagination."

During that year I saw a lot of Burroughs, who was living at Duke Street, St. James. He had gotten hooked on Scientology. From my experience with Dianetics in New York I had reservations about it, regarding it as a mind-control system. I told Bill about my illness and that my Dutch boyfriend had stopped sleeping with me and was going to marry an Australian starlet. Following the principles of Scientology, Bill believed the liver disorder was linked to the emotional one, caused by an engram—a mental picture in the reactive mind of an unconscious incident in the past that contained pain.

"This is the compulsive reexperiencing of emotions not appropriate to the present time situation," he explained. We sat in his study with an E-meter on the table and two tin cans attached to electrodes. I held a can in each hand and he asked questions. If anxiety was aroused, the needle would move; if the needle floated, it meant the old incident that caused the anxiety was defused, you were free of the unconscious pain and compulsion.

He brought me to headquarters to meet the head man there, offering to pay for my being cleared at the center. "I'll take care of it, Harold, so go ahead." I was very interested in a cure.

When Bill forgot to pay the few pounds (I couldn't), threats for nonpayment, which I ignored, piled up. I'd get strange messages: IF YOUR DEBT IS NOT PAID IMMEDIATELY YOU WILL BE

SUBJECT TO SEC CHECK. . . . YOU ARE NOW A NON-PERSON RE-
QUIRED TO REPORT TO THE CASTLE FOR CORRECTION. . . . PACK
YOUR BAGS IMMEDIATELY. YOU ARE TO FLY TO VALENCIA AND
REPORT TO SEA ORG FOR EXTREME LIABILITY. It was like a comic
operetta about a mad dictator. I wrote Burroughs:

> In my previous letter I wanted to avoid any misunder-
> standing such as your finding yourself under an obliga-
> tion you hadn't originally intended. The auditing
> sessions for me are a lifeline at a time when my survival
> is threatened. Devouring the literature and working
> every day with it & with auditors, am hoping for re-
> leases, relief from Reactive Mind fuckups. Reduced by
> sad effects, suppressive persons, I see a rapidly dwin-
> dling spiral in which "the individual decays." Disturbed
> though by some of Hubbard's word-lapses like redun-
> dancy in definition of engram: "a mental image pic-
> ture"—tsk tsk, Ron. No clear arrangement seems to
> have been made, according to the guy at the financial
> end, about payments. I wanted you to know, before it
> got out of hand, of the situation—to have your okay or
> stop. I recall you told me you could get me in gratis,
> and then ran into this ambiguous situation.

I wasn't getting better and, after fifteen years of exile, decided to return to the States. The party was over.

Epilogue

Where else would an oil well sprout beside a Stratford-
on-Avon chili joint? Or a Renaissance palazzo with
Venetian columns serve as a fast-food diner and liquor store selling girlie magazines? Where else would junkies,
winos, hippies, Jesus freaks, and body builders rub elbows and
hawk acid, pot, anabolic steroids, and Holy Scriptures? Or

psychedelic love shops nestle beside storefront synagogues and Greek delicatessens? Where do swarms of old Jewish ladies and gents live and die in a dingy whitewashed twenties mausoleum called the Cardiac Hotel (aka the Cadillac Hotel), facing the Pacific, sitting behind plate-glass lobby windows and watching golden surfers whiz by on surfboards, acrobatic boys on skateboards? Where do golden girls in bikinis skim aquamarine breakers like bionic women? Where do superstars of the iron game parade on Muscle Beach?

In Venice, California, of course.

As I conducted my first transaction at the Security Pacific Bank the teller looked up from her cage. "Are you English?" she said admiringly. "No, I'm from New York." "Oh, you have such a beautiful English accent!" she cooed. I not only felt like a foreigner, I sounded like one: clipped, brisk, international. But I was home.

Home. My mother, now seventy-five, had come from New York to the farthest western edge of the continent because it was cheap, sunny, and warm. Home was one room and bath in an old apartment house on Paloma, over a narrow dirt road running south called Speedway, a half block from Ocean Front Walk, called the boardwalk. Home was Social Security, an old-age pension. She sat on the benches with the other old ladies croaking to one another. She had the same flat, defeated, grating, monotonous voice, the same cheerless tone. Their straw bonnets shaded pale skin from the subtropical sun; they commented sarcastically on hippies, winos, one another.

In the evening the ferocious sun flattens on the horizon, a violent slash of scarlet, and the moon, in all its changes, comes up red, the red moon of the Pacific rim like a ripe buttock in the engulfing darkness. But they don't see it. Their eyes, sclerotic with distant traumas, look inward. They speak of the betrayal of sons and daughters, of long-dead spouses. They speak of illness. They speak of food. They trust no one.

My mother was wrinkled but said, with a coy laugh, "I have natural beauty, dear. I'm not like the other old ladies." It was true. Her baby blue eyes still sparkled, if with less luster, and in spite of the lines her face retained a piquant prettiness. But it was marked with tragedy, with poverty. All her hopes and dreams had been crushed long ago like dead leaves. TV could not save her from loneliness; but without it she might have gone altogether mad. It pained me to be around her, but I lived in a room on another floor, which she had held for my arrival. And to my shame and guilt, she paid the rent. I was home.

About a month after my return, approaching the corner of Arizona and Ocean Avenue at Santa Monica, a few long blocks from where I lived, I saw Paul Bowles in a spruce white suit on his top-floor terrace at the Shangri-La Hotel. I waved and he waved back. The last time I had seen him was in Tangier, six years earlier. When I stepped into his room he said, "I had no idea who was waving to me, but waved back." After a while he touched a button on a tape recorder and I realized he was taping our conversation. I can't remember a word. He was teaching for a year as Distinguished Professor of Literature at San Fernando Valley State College. A few days later Christopher Isherwood showed up in his rooms but ignored me, still unforgiving for what he considered The Slight—of twenty-five years ago. At sixty-five Isherwood looked a handsome forty-five. Vedanta and vendetta agreed with him.

I remember walking with Bowles on the mall to the cleaners: he picked up five immaculate summer suits. He dressed like a dandy and was chauffeured to college by a student in a black sedan. The student kept speaking with admiration of William F. Buckley, of his erudite vocabulary.

Venice, however, was a run-down community. The canals stank, the oil pumps bowed like skeletal tyrannosaurs, the beach-front bungalows and hotels were dilapidated. Long-haired hippies, dirty, shabby, and broke, roamed the boardwalk panhandling, making the *V* sign for peace, dropping acid, drinking, smoking pot. Everything was attributed to karma, energy, vibrations in venereal Venice.

I had just missed the Summer of Love in 1968 by weeks. The young were euphoric, mellow, and gorgeous. They had turned on, tuned in, and dropped out; they kept their mind and body available in a funky paradise of drugs and sex. Vietnam had brought in its wake license and incense, sitars and guitars, cross-dressing, love beads, black light, sound and light: the psychedelic revolution. It had brought Bob Dylan and the Beatles, Joan Baez and Leonard Cohen. Only blocks from my tenement lived the old man who had written a book about the Beat Generation, *The Holy Barbarians,* which I had read in London. His name was Lawrence Lipton and he would become a friend and supporter. Even he wore the fringe of hair on his bald pate long.

Police cars prowled Speedway and the boardwalk. From my third-floor window I watched as the "pigs," sensuously patting, palping, groping crotches, seemed unable to keep their hands off the blue-jeaned boys. The beach front held a derelict generation in its torpid arms. A mile inland, blocked by the sea air, the smog ceased. The climate was mild, as sluggish as the dropout youth. But beneath, always about to erupt, lay discontent and despair. You could read the violence in the broken bottles, the overturned trash cans—held back like the smog, but in the air.

I had chronic fatigue, diarrhea, and insomnia, weighed 128 pounds. My mother knew nothing of this. Had she known she would have made my life more miserable, blaming and nagging me. In the sterile, unlovely room, dubbed "the clinic" by my new friends, I felt more like a patient than a tenant. It was all windows, furnished with a sofa, small table, two chairs. The bed was concealed in the wall. Off to the side the kitchenette was like a tiny lab. The red brick building resembled a ship with iron-railed catwalks on the outside, from which you entered the apartments; and the old ladies were like inmates of a nursing home. The only tenement, it towered over the bungalows on the street.

Every morning when the black postman arrived, a fierce old man came charging from his basement apartment. "Goddamn him, what's he doin' here anyway? Up to no good, I'll bet!" he'd grumble with galloping paranoia. The postman ignored him. When I took my mail the old guy was convinced I was stealing it. Was he a shell-shock victim of the Great War? Rumor had it that he'd been a wino. Then one morning I passed his wife on the way to the washing machines in the basement. "Why is he always hassling me?" I asked. "Oh, pay no attention to him," she laughed, "he died on the operating table years ago. When they brought him back his brain didn't have enough oxygen." The description fit everyone in the building.

My poor mother was certainly not in her right mind. She had unpredictable spells of acute anxiety. "Look!" she exclaimed dramatically one morning as I stepped into my apartment while she was cleaning. "Look at my face!" "I'm looking," I said. "What is it?" "I've been crying all morning," she said vindictively. "Why? What's wrong?" "What's wrong?" she repeated. "What are all those chicken gizzards doing in the frigidaire?" she said accusingly. "That's poison! I almost died when I saw them." If I answered, the conversation would snowball into accusations, recriminations, tears. Once she cried for three days because she thought I was smoking in bed, though I'd quit three years before. She had seen a dark smudge on the linen, which she mistook for a cigarette burn. Another time she cried for weeks; she'd seen a telegram from New York that she believed was from a son of mine who wanted to come and live with me. It was a sixteen-year-old boy I'd met and had an affair with. She accused me of being ashamed of her and keeping her away from my wife and children.

Then there was Charles Bukowski, a different sort of ruin. We had corresponded for five years but had never met. From his first drunken letter ("Some day a dog will piss on me and I will drink his piss") to our first meeting in my apartment, during the worst storm in the southland in thirty-one years, late January 1969, I knew that a wild Falstaffian ruffian had come to shake things up with more fiction than fact, more fantasy than truth. The wind, the rain, and the sea were thrashing ferociously and the old building shook like a ship on its moorings. He was accompanied by his sidekick, a short overweight rabbinical student called Neeli Cherry (later Cherkovski). Bukowski was misshapen—a big hunchback with a ravaged, pockmarked face, decayed nicotine-stained teeth, and pain-filled green eyes. Flat brown hair seemed pasted to an oversized skull—hips broader than shoulders, hands grotesquely small and soft. A beer gut sagged over his belt. He wore a white shirt, baggy pants, an ill-fitting suit, the kind convicts receive when released from prison. He looked like one, down and out.

Later, his friend Neeli told me how nervous he was about meeting me. "We're going over to meet a great writer," said Bukowski. "Jesus, I don't know what to say to him, baby, he's the best." We had established a mutual admiration and rapport in our letters. His were explosive with pain and humor, an amazing amalgam of wordplay, ripe, earthy, vulgar; his language leapt from the page like a van Gogh, galvanic, whirling, immediate, full of raw violence, color, and light; he was an American Dylan Thomas but bolder, cruder, meaner, more daring, not stuck in tradition. He was more savage than Céline, Miller, or Jan Cremer . . . but he was also gentle.

The man, the drunken writer, would not wear well. He

never tired of bragging and boasting, of clamoring for attention. His competitive spirit, arrogance, and macho pose were irritating. When drunk, which was after 5:00 P.M., he had an insulting mockery in his voice; his aim was to crush others. Before five he was a lamb, literally sheepish with shame and guilt. I believe his hurt eyes got their color from envy and jealousy. He'd shout, "I'm Charles Bukowski. Watch my steam, baby. I'm the king, I'm the greatest!"

For a few months before we met we had long phone talks, full of sympathy for each other. I couldn't see anyone, I wasn't up to it. For his part, he sounded like a beaten man. He complained about not having had sex for two years, about his health, his job at the post office, where he had worked for ten years. "It's triple super hell, baby. The post office is nailing me to the cross. Oh, shit, each day I go to work in a tomblike trance. Even on Sunday. I think of walking into that building and I go mad. Purple seas of Christ! I *am* going mad!" All this in a slow weary drawl, not hysterical, but measured, controlled, unutterably sad.

Prince Hal he called me, the prince of poetry. At first he was careful not to spoil the relationship, but then he'd get drunk. He'd raise his voice and become scornful, derisive. He'd also rack his brains for ideas on how to make money. One way was to turn on my Uher tape recorder and rap. "It oughta be of some interest to dealers, Hal. The two best writers of our generation on tape. Turn it on! Is it on?" "Yeah." "Well, I'm sitting here with Hal Norse, a damn good writer; but I'm Charles Bukowski, number one!" I switched it off. "What are you doing? Is it off? I'm only having a little fun. You know I think you're the best. Turn it on." We'd start again. "This is Charles Bukowski. I'm at Hal Norse's pad. He thinks he's a writer, but don't they all? I'm the king, numero uno!" We never finished that one.

He was so drunk that he spent the night on my sofa. At 3:00 A.M. I had to pass him on the way to the toilet. Slumped in a half-sitting position with shut eyes under the lit floor lamp, he was muttering and chuckling. He opened an eye. "Who the hell are *you*, mother? Jesus, where am I?" Next day he said he thought he was on a ship, shanghaied, and asked about the eighteen-year-old blond cabin boy going by during the night. I said, "You're crazy."

"Ah, you sly old dog," he said, "you and your big bologna."

He believed that I had a harem of boys and girls at all hours under my mother's nose. I wasn't that lucky.

He could also be warm and friendly: "You know, as you walked along the beach with me back to my car, well, I don't wanna sound like a goddamn romantic, but I got a real feeling of human warmth for a change. We're two old dogs, hooked on life. Here in L.A. you've gotta keep the hustle going. If you don't produce, you're forgotten in a month. So, it's good to know you have a friend."

In his '57 Plymouth, which he drove very slowly and cautiously, to avoid costly accidents, he brought over friends and, once or twice, his four-year-old daughter, Marina. He also brought his girl friend, Linda King, a big talented sculptress, a female Bukowski, but better looking, who wrote bawdy poetry and stood up to him. They had raging, screaming drunken fights. He kept saying he would dedicate his next book to me, but he never did. While I was in Europe he'd sent me his weekly column, *"Notes of a Dirty Old Man,"* in John Bryan's counterculture paper, *Open City*. In a letter dated March 9, 1968, he sent me one, "part of which is an almost direct quote from one of your letters; anyhow I hope you don't take offense." In it he quoted two pages *verbatim,* not *almost,* from my London letter in 1968 as I lay dying, I thought, with chronic fatigue from the liver ailment; here's part of it:

> i'm in this fishbowl, you understand, a vast aquarium & my fins are not strong enough to get around in this big undersea city. i do what i can, tho the magic is surely gone. i just can't seem as yet to pull myself out of this cold turkey state . . . no writing, no fucking, no nothing . . . it's going to be a long period of hibernation, a long dark night . . . the sky is black & pink & flushed at 4:40 in the afternoon. the city roars outside. the wolves are pacing in the zoo. the tarantulas are squatting beside the scorpions. the queen bee is served by the drones. the mandrill snarls viciously, hurling filthy bananas & apples from its crotch at the crazy kids who taunt it. if i'm going to die i want to go to california, below l.a., far down the coast on the beach somewhere, near Mexico. . . .

A half year later I landed in Venice instead of San Juan de

Capistrano or some such place, still agonizing about fatigue, still feeling stuck. But what the great European medical specialists were unable to do at Heidelberg, London, or Zurich, with their high fees, blood tests, and tubes stuck down my throat to get samples of my stomach juices, an uncultured female chiropractor in L.A. managed to do in a few short weeks: she began a real cure, costing peanuts. She took me off all medications, including barbiturates, which I'd been hooked on since my twenties (a cold turkey worse than kicking heroin), purged me on a diet of grapefruit for a week (I was climbing the walls and running to the bathroom with a loose bowel), and then, lo and behold, for the first time in four years, I slept; I slept in spite of the noisy old lady in the flat above.

Sleep, sea air, sun, beach, and ocean did what medicine could not do. I was a new man. I read Rachel Carson's *Silent Spring* and Adelle Davis's *Let's Get Well*. I shopped in Santa Monica at Doc Huckaby's health food store for organic fruits and vegetables, envying the young body builders from Gold's Gym, who bought their daily ration of six quarts of milk and two dozen eggs.

After a few months of slow walks on the beach, I purchased a hot French racing bike for eight dollars from a black youth who had stolen it—it must have been worth three hundred— and rode daily on the boardwalk. I began sprinting on the shore, dipped into the waves, and sunbathed.

When a year had passed I felt strong enough for a step I had for some time wanted to take. Three blocks from where I lived the golden boys of the West developed their bodies into shrines at which men and women worshiped. I was pushing fifty-four. My first day at Gold's Gym, feeling nervous and self-conscious among so many gargantuan figures, I stared with disbelief and awe at a young giant pressing about 350 pounds of man-hole-cover-size metal plates, without strain. I continued staring hypnotically even when he got to his feet. He returned my stare and headed toward me.

"Listen," he said in not too friendly a fashion, "ven I am vorking out I don't like people looking. Do your own thing, yah?"

He had a thick German accent and a ferocious scowl. Feeling out of place and put down under the scrutiny of others, I did my five-pound beginner's routine like a ninety-seven-pound weakling. A few days later this same giant was more amiable. He smiled, explaining that his concentration was so great at a work-out that if people watched it put him off. His name was Arnold Schwarzenegger; he had come to the United States a few months before from Austria. At twenty-one he was the reigning monarch of the entire body-building world. His buddy, the phenomenal five-foot-five Sardinian, Franco Columbu, who was an inch taller than I and twice as broad, could speak no English. Since I looked Italian, Arnold asked if I spoke it. I did, and translated for Franco when Arnold wasn't around (they spoke German together). That's how I got to know them. My archives contain a photo of myself and Franco in Gold's Gym. Franco was known in Europe as the Strongest Man in the World.

As I got to know Arnold I discovered that he was intelligent, quick-witted, and skillful with the put-down—backed by twenty-two-inch arms. He was no slouch when it came to culture either. Once he said, "Why is it that so few American athletes appreciate classical music? How many body builders even heard of Mozart? I love Mozart, but here it's not manly to say so." He had a great sense of humor, was mischievous, and loved to upset people by his direct, disarming manner. We used to work out on Muscle Beach, in the outdoor ring maintained by the city, and lie around with the other body builders on the sand, working on a tan.

In two years I had fourteen-inch biceps, a forty-inch chest, twenty-eight-inch waist, a fifteen-inch neck, and rippling abdominals. I weighed 145 pounds. Charles Atlas was right! I could now kick sand—and ass! At fifty-five I was a muscle man; I'd succeeded in pushing the clock back twenty years! Jogging on the beach with Arnold, we attracted stares. "You look good for your age," he said. "How old do you think I am?" "Oh, thirty-six." I had found the fountain of youth.

Once I asked how he prepared for competitions. "You have to psych out your opponent," said Arnold. "I don't care who he is. It could be your best friend. When you're posing on the stage, it's only for a few seconds, you don't have friends." "Not even Franco?" I asked in surprise. "Listen, he is like a brother, but for the title I'll do anything I can to make him look bad and me look good." He told me that before the contest he always used his wits to make his competitors doubt themselves. I thought of Bukowski. They were alike—except that Bukowski worked hard at destroying his body, and did a great job. Is it strange that they both ended up as Hollywood box-office hits twenty years later, one as movie star, the other as writer? I think it was predictable.

Once as we watched an unattractive hooligan with an average build sneering with hatred and envy, which was common at the workout area on the beach, I said, "He's telling himself that beauty is only skin deep." "Yaah," drawled Arnold, casting the guy a contemptuous glance, "but ugliness goes to the bone."

Body building had given me new life. There is no feeling quite like the one after a good workout. In his first film, *Pumping Iron,* Arnold describes getting the pump (the flow of oxygenated blood to swelling muscle, a warm, exhilarating surge of ecstatic well-being): "It even feels better than coming," he said. I can vouch for it. One feels regenerated at any age. This is the arena of man against death, as in a poem, but in this case it's one's own body used as a weapon in a constant duel with time, where the power of muscle is pitted in a daily struggle against man's fate—death and decay.

Bukowski came over with Linda King, who'd put him on the wagon. He had a scraggly grayish beard at that time, bermuda shorts exposing hairless, chalky, soft fat legs. In a T-shirt his paunch touched his lap. Nobody smoked, we drank nothing but apple juice—organic—which I served in wineglasses with twisty stems that Carl Weissner, my great friend from Mannheim, bequeathed to me when he left Venice. Carl was one of the finest, most decent persons I'd known in Europe, or anywhere for that matter. And he was the best German translator of the Beats and raw-meat writers.

We were talking about being an artist. "Writers and artists are selfish bastards," said Bukowski. Nobody disagreed. I dug up a correspondence we'd had for the past two years. It was a scheme of Bukowski's to make money—we'd write letters to each other, sending only the carbons, and keeping the originals for collectors. It was to be published eventually as a book. Like all his schemes it fizzled out because he was too worried about his own rank, too competitive. He said he pulled out because my letters were so much better they made him look bad; I felt it was the other way around. Mine were anecdotal, intense, colorful; his were gutsy, vibrant, caustic, a stylistic event. "All right, baby, there's no competition between van Gogh and Gauguin," he drawled. Presumably, he was van Gogh to my Gauguin. He said I

had only one fault: I had read too much Dante and Shakespeare.
I countered by saying that *his* fault was he hadn't read enough of
them.

Occasionally I visited Anaïs Nin in Silver Lake, a suburb of
Los Angeles, where she lived in a Frank Lloyd Wright house
with Rupert Pole, the stepson of the great architect. It was a
wonderful house made of boulders, with a spacious living room;
it felt alive, like an animal—a *living* room. Anaïs suggested I submit a new volume of poems to New York publishing houses and
compile a list of comments on my work from established authors,
which I did, quoting Baldwin, William Carlos Williams, Robert
Graves, Ginsberg, and others. It made me feel like a venerable
Old Master. When I told her that Robert Giroux of Farrar,
Straus & Giroux had described the volume as "raw meat" poetry,
"although," he added, "the poems are magnificent," she was indignant. "That is absolutely untrue," she said, "your poetry is
racé!" Giroux had used Robert Lowell's designation for
Ginsberg's poetry. At that time poetry fell neatly under two labels: "raw meat" or "cooked meat." I held that cooking deprived
food of its life-giving nourishment. In 1970, however, the major
publishers still got indigestion from Beat, raw-meat writing. Today it has become kosher. "They never had faith in me," said
Anaïs as I looked out of the window at a cat with a live bird in its
mouth. "My French publisher still can't believe that my *Diaries*
are a best-seller in France, where I have won prizes for it. Har-
court, Brace published only twenty-five hundred copies of the
first printing. So I know what you must feel when they turn you
down."

No one who hasn't lived through an earthquake can understand its awesome power. One morning before dawn I was
shaken by a rocking, rolling motion. I awoke thinking I was at
sea; the huge brick building swayed sickeningly, the bed swayed.
I felt a lurching vertigo from the pit of my stomach to my brain.
I rolled out of bed with a deep primitive fear and stood under
the lintel of the room, once divided by double doors. With cold
terror I watched the swinging lamps, the quivering TV, the moving walls. Would I be buried beneath the rubble, die a wretched
death with my poor mother? The building shuddered and seconds later the deep rumble and seismic tremors ceased. Next day

I learned from a friend of my mother's that she had found her ashen pale, her teeth chattering, unable to talk. My mother never spoke of it. In that quake of February 9, 1971, thousands died. We were thirty miles from the epicenter.

In June at the L.A. Airport I saw my Greek friend Nanos Valaoritis en route from his home in Oakland to Greece for the summer. His ten-year-old daughter, Katherine, was clutching a book. I asked what it was. "Oh, it's *Hamlet.* I'm reading it again," she said. "She's read it many times," laughed Nanos. "She really likes it." That's what it means to be the child of a poet-prince-professor. I always envied such children, with all their advantages. "Is she entitled to be a princess?" I asked Nanos. "Only if I claim my title," he said. "But these days it's a bad thing. And in Greece it's better to be a Communist than a royalist," he laughed. "In any case, it goes against what I believe."

Through a romantic involvement with a young German woman I met at Lipton's I found myself in San Francisco for a week in late July 1971. A poet in her twenties, she was a women's libber with a strong, determined mind. With Erika I visited Michael McClure, whose work I admired. He lived in his own home on Downey Street with his wife, Joanne, and their young daughter. I had the peaceful sensation of belonging, of not feeling like a fringe figure.

I also spent an evening at Philip Lamantia's, where Nancy Phillips (now Peters) cooked an excellent spaghetti dinner. We reminisced about Greece, Spain, and Morocco. Allen Ginsberg, they said, was disappointed at missing me but would phone me at Erika's on his return. When they told him of my intention to live in San Francisco, he exclaimed, "Harold will love it here! It's just the place for him!" and seemed genuinely excited about my arrival, they said.

August 2. At 3:00 P.M. Allen greeted me warmly, kissing me on the mouth, at the City Lights Publishing office, at the corner of Grant and Filbert streets. It was to have been at two, but he was delayed in Berkeley and, always considerate, he phoned Nancy to keep me posted so I might not experience doubts about his arrival. We had seen each other last in New York at the Living Theatre's performance of *Paradise Now* in 1968. For about half an hour he took care of his correspondence and other matters at the office. Then he swept me up into his whirligig life. For the next eight hours we rushed around town in taxis to various people and groups Allen was involved with, including the FitzHugh Ludlow Memorial Library, which, at that time, was headquarters for "The Declaration of Independence for Timothy Leary," who was in a dungeon cell, in solitary confinement, in Switzerland, for a few ounces of marijuana found in his daughter's car. At the same time Julian and Judith Beck were in jail in Brazil. I saw a letter from Leary to Allen saying, "We have become Europeans" and that he didn't want to return to the States again.

As we rode in a taxi and saw the hills of San Francisco dotted with white houses gleaming in the sun I exclaimed, "It's like Spain!" "I never noticed that," said Allen, "but which city?" I couldn't answer. Back in North Beach we ate at the Minimum Daily Requirement, a cheap café-restaurant on Grant and Columbus. Warm, friendly, benevolent, loving, Allen brought our food to the table. Lawrence Ferlinghetti had joined us. Allen said he wasn't involved in as heavy a sex scene as he would have liked. He'd been working for a year and a half with Miles, an English book dealer, on selecting the best tapes of all the readings he had given, to make twenty albums of an oral record of his work. There was news of Peter Orlovsky, Gregory Corso, Burroughs, Julian and Judith Beck, Leary, and others. A young guitarist joined us. He was to play the music Allen had composed to Blake's *Songs of Innocence,* which Allen was going to sing at a gay theatre group, the Angels of Light, an offshoot of the Cockettes. We visited their loft later. He asked after Lawrence Lipton, Jack Hirschman, a Venice poet, and Bukowski, whose first collected volume of stories Ferlinghetti was soon to bring out. Allen was bumming cigarettes everywhere for both of us, breaking my six-year abstinence. "Am I fucking you up or vice versa?" he asked. "I think it's mutual," I said. "What do you smoke?" he said. "Anything you do." "No, what do *you* smoke?" "Okay. Camels. No filters." He bought a pack. We were off.

Allen on Monday. Ferlinghetti on Tuesday and Wednesday. McClure Wednesday evening. In a very cordial reception Ferlinghetti presented me with two of his books, *The Mexican Night* and *Back Roads to Far Places,* inscribed, and also with many books of others he had published. McClure presented me with a volume of his plays, *Gargoyle Cartoons,* and *The Surge,* a poem he had published himself—both inscribed. Ferlinghetti was friendly and helpful. I didn't know that in three years he would publish a book of mine, *Hotel Nirvana.* He extended a friendly invitation to visit him next day at the office, which I did. While I was there Allen phoned; I made another date with him and then stepped into the sunlight with Ferlinghetti at the Mediterranean street stair leading steeply up Telegraph Hill to Coit Tower. We had barley soup at the Minimum Daily Requirement, where he said he was going to publish all the Bukowski prose available, six or seven hundred pages, because he thought he was going to be the next big name in literature within a few years. He admitted having missed out on the poetry because he wasn't crazy about it when it appeared in the mimeo mags. He had also turned down Burroughs, Kerouac, McClure, and many others. "I didn't like their work." Well, he was honest, if quirky. He could have continued with the most powerful new voices of the era, but missed a truly great chance.

His own credo he expressed during the conversation: "Most poets talk to themselves." He was a populist. He also said, "The Penguin volume with you, Bukowski, and Lamantia is ridiculous. It's like picking any three poets at random. You have nothing in common with one another except that you're all good poets. The volume with me, Allen, and Gregory at least makes some sense. I didn't want to be in it. I thought Kerouac should have been in instead of me. But the editor wanted me." I disagreed on my own volume. I thought Bukowski, Lamantia, and I shared a surrealist approach to imagery, though with little stylistic similarity.

On December 29, 1971, I left Venice intending to spend a year or two in San Francisco. Almost two decades later I am still there.

I moved into a five-room third-floor flat in a drab old Victorian on Guy Place, a tiny horseshoe street among business-district office buildings, near the East Bay freeway off First Street. The rent was ninety-five dollars a month and it was furnished. I inherited the flat and furniture from a friend, Jan Herman, who got married and moved to New York. It was a lucky find. I stayed five years, until the noise and gasoline fumes drove me away. The walls of my study I collaged with photographs of friends and myself: Tennessee, Anaïs, Burroughs, Allen, Corso, Bowles, and others. Dealers wanted to buy them; one dealer actually stole irreplaceable inscribed first editions when my back was turned. Bukowski had warned of this.

Nanos introduced me to many people, but the first was a young Rumanian poet with a Count Dracula accent, Andrei Codrescu. He was witty and entertaining and, best of all, a fan of mine. "You're very famous," he said, "and should have no trouble publishing your new books. The kids will love you. You only need to give readings and they'll be your slaves. Of course, American slaves are the worst." His clothes looked as if he had raided an army-and-navy store: olive drab field jacket, army fatigue pants, military boots. He had a droopy black moustache and eyes the color of licorice. He gave me an inscribed copy of his recent poems, with a cover photo of himself in a garbage can in the East Village, fashionably dressed in fatigues.

I gave poetry readings at colleges and universities, and read to capacity houses in theatres and auditoriums. Anaïs Nin asked me to read with her in a three-day celebration of her work at Zellerbach Hall at the University of California at Berkeley. Over three thousand people attended. "I can always feel out the audience when I step on the stage," she told me. "This is a very warm, receptive one. Don't be nervous." I was, but when I stood before the microphone and began, I was suddenly free of anxiety. It always happened. Something took over. I was no longer my ordinary self. I felt a surge of power, of superenergy. It turned out to be Anaïs's last major reading before her death from cancer.

In the fall of 1974 the De Young Memorial Museum held a "Beat Generation Poets" exhibition by the artist Peter LeBlanc, featuring ten portraits: Lawrence Ferlinghetti, John Wieners, William Everson, Michael McClure, Bob Kaufman, Lew Welch, Allen Ginsberg, David Meltzer, Robert Duncan, and Harold Norse. Our portraits hung in the museum, our notebooks and manuscripts (including the deceased Kerouac's) were on view in glass-topped tables. On three successive nights we read to overflow audiences: Gary Snyder, Ginsberg, Philip Whalen, Duncan, McClure, Diane di Prima, Kaufman, Meltzer, Everson, and myself. The first night a riot almost broke out because hundreds had to be turned away. There was not enough room. Ferlinghetti stepped outside and quelled the riot by announcing that loudspeakers would be set up so that they could hear everything. The third and last issue of my magazine, *Bastard Angel,* a special edi-

tion with the portraits and work of the poets, served as the catalog for the museum's exhibition. The entire printing of two
thousand sold out.

The young curators of the museum approached me for a
one-hour documentary film to be shot at my flat. It was accomplished, but to this day I have never seen it. I simply lose interest
once a project is completed.

In 1973 Allen Ginsberg won the National Book Award with
Fall of America, published by City Lights, and in 1974 my book
Hotel Nirvana, also published by City Lights, was nominated for
the award. As usual I did not win, but that year I got a National
Endowment Grant for poetry. *Bastard Angel* won two grants and
much praise. Things were looking up.

In 1975 a major reading in honor of my work was held at
Francis Ford Coppola's Little Fox Theatre on Pacific. Among the
poets who read were Ferlinghetti, McClure, Lewis MacAdams,
Neeli Cherkovski, myself, and many others. In 1977 Winston
Leyland, the publisher of Gay Sunshine Press, brought out my
collected gay poems from 1941 to 1976, *Carnivorous Saint.* On
the cover of the *Advocate,* the major national gay magazine, my
picture was between that of Rock Hudson and Sylvester, with a
review and a long article by W. I. Scobie in which I was dubbed
"the American Catullus."

But things did not go smoothly. I've never lived anywhere in
San Francisco without noisy neighbors: overhead three giants in
hobnailed boots stomped, practiced karate, hammered, and
played stereo hard rock at decibels hitherto unknown to man.
When I complained they said it was music, not noise. "Do yoga
and gain deliverance from bad karma," they advised. "Meditate
on peace!" I meditated on murder and moved into a concrete
apartment building in Alamo Square, only to discover that every
night a football game was in progress overhead. It turned out to
be a black whorehouse. There were screams, thuds, scrimmages.
When I complained I was accused of racism. My life was threatened. I moved to Monte Rio in Russian River with a boyfriend
who came into an inheritance and bought a house. At last, peace
and quiet in the country! But the next-door neighbors had two
giant German shepherds that barked all night under our windows. When I complained, the owner, an irascible redneck with
a violent hatred of hippies, queers, and city folk, screamed,
"You're crazy! Go back to San Francisco where you belong!"

We had bought the house from Andrei Codrescu. "It's the only rural area I've seen that looks like Transylvania!" he raved. It was full of Hell's Angels and hippies in 1977. The river was dry and mud-caked from a drought. When I told Andrei that the dogs kept me awake he was offended. He had enthused lyrically about the silence and claimed the property went a mile to a creek—except that it turned out to be a 150-foot lot. I had committed the unpardonable sin of questioning his surrealist license to embroider the truth. On the other hand, when he wrote about the incident in his memoirs, he gloated that his wife, Alice—who made the deal and to whom we handed twenty thousand dollars in cash (most of it my boyfriend's)—had driven a shrewd bargain, for we also picked up the mortgage to boot. I still liked him, however, because like me he was also a half-Jewish bastard; his name in Rumanian, he once confided, means "bastard." If his nerve and panache were Daliesque, so were his dealings with others.

Meanwhile my boyfriend and I had no one to talk to but rednecks and redwoods. One night he lay in bed with a 103-degree fever and I had to drive to the city to read with Andrei and other poets in a high school gym. During my reading Andrei went to the men's room, dragging a beautiful young woman with him; they came out, disheveled, when it was over. I raced back home at midnight to find my boyfriend in bad shape. Next morning, in a terrible gale, he dressed silently, picked up his guitar, and walked out. I was alone with the redwoods and the cold rain.

Two days later he phoned. "Where are you?" "L.A. I'm all right." "What about the fever?" "It was an allergy. I'm allergic to yogurt." "Oh. When are you coming back?" "Dunno, I'm on acid. I drove four hundred miles on it." It was his first acid trip. "I see things differently now. It will never be the same again. I'm gonna stay on acid. It's a cosmic experience. You can't understand—everything else is drab and dull. I've started a new life, the *real* life. What went on before was false." He hung up. Yogurt had altered everything. Nothing would be the same again.

While waiting for the agent in a real estate office to negotiate the sale of the house, I gazed listlessly through the venetian blinds of the back window one summer afternoon. I'd been alone in the country for two years, remodeling the house, writing short fiction for national slick magazines to earn money. Before I left for Amsterdam and Zurich to earn money on readings, *Penthouse* contacted me for fiction. Meanwhile my boyfriend had an apartment in the city with a young pusher he was crazy about. The pusher was crazy about his money. He got twelve thousand dollars in three weeks. My friend sat around burning twenty-dollar bills to show his new friends his contempt for money. As I gazed out the window musing on the Candide-like nature of my life, I saw a little blond boy of about eight or nine brandishing a sizable erection. He was squirming as he inserted it between a small girl's thighs. Both stood upright, underclothes around sneakered feet in the grassy yard. I was struck by the fact that his little face wore a rapt look of eager absorption, not unlike that of an adult engaged in the same diversion. The girl rubbed against him cooperatively with evident pleasure. Then he turned his attention to her butt. She bent over, doggie fashion, wriggling it. I was so fascinated by the spectacle that I started with embarrassment at the agent's lowered voice beside me. "There he is! A regular cocksman, that kid! Hard as a rock, too."

As if sensing something, the boy looked up quickly and saw that he was being observed. With a startled expression of fear, guilt, and shame he hurriedly hitched up his pants and the girl her panties and off they scampered. "Oh, the little rascal!" boomed the agent, a large portly man. Then he roared with laughter. "He's always at it when he thinks nobody's lookin'. That kid's a *real* little man! Y'know, when things get slow around here, like they are now, I close the slats and peek through, and sure enough he'll show up, always with another little girl—or another little boy—to play with like that. He ain't particular."

Should he have reported the boy? Many rednecks would have done so without hesitation. To them the child was a sex offender. He would have been charged with aggravated assault for corrupting the morals of a minor. Since the crime was committed between the agent's and the sheriff's office (across the street behind the yard), a wild chase with sirens wailing and lights flashing through the inner city of Guerneville, which consists of two streets, would have been avoided. The agent could have made a citizen's arrest—he was six foot two and the offender was three feet tall; no contest there. If convicted the boy would have been sent to a mental institution . . . for being a boy.

But since I was neither a redneck nor a lunatic, I thought this was one civic duty we could do without. Nor did I charge the agent with collusion for harboring a criminal on his premises. This did not intrigue me. I considered nature's law far worthier of respect than man's in this case. Civil disobedience seemed the only way to go.

But sometimes at night, I must confess, I awake with a start, breathing fitfully, in a cold sweat, trembling. My unconscious accuses me. Then I console myself that we are all criminals. And I go back to sleep dreaming of a world without stupid laws.

Sometimes it's hard to believe in the real world. Before I left Russian River my neighbor Julie told me something even more bizarre. The nice old woman across the road, a devout Catholic, took a fancy to one of the puppies Julie's bitch had whelped; when Julie gave it to her as a Christmas present she was over-joyed. But Julie soon realized she had made a terrible mistake. The woman beat the puppy unmercifully. She could hear the pathetic yelps and cries. "I never thought she was cruel," said Julie miserably. Then one day while visiting her she noticed the dog wore a woolen coat in the heat of summer and was fearful and hysterical, with his tail between his legs. When she inquired about it the woman said with grim determination, "You know, when I wanna pet him he rolls over and goes belly-up, showin' his privates. Well, I'll break him of that disgusting habit if I have to kill him to do it." "So much," Julie told me, "for religion in the real world."

February 1989. I've lived in the Devil's Quadrangle for eight years. This is the new name for the neighborhood. High crime. Lower rents. Headquarters for heroin in the Bay Area. Four cafés on one block. Seven restaurants. A recent feature story in the *Chronicle* called it the New Bohemia—a funky mix of art, music, and politics. When I moved into the rear cottage on Albion Street it was a peaceful, residential, tree-lined block off the main artery, Sixteenth Street between Valencia and Guerrero. North Mission. The front house, a beige Victorian, faces Camp Street: the first in the settlement of San Francisco.

Three books of mine have appeared since I've lived here:

Mysteries of Magritte, a limited fine edition of poems about painters, and the first American edition of *Beat Hotel,* my Paris novella, with an introduction by William Burroughs. The third, *Love Poems,* a collection of gay poems from 1940 to 1985, is an update of *Carnivorous Saint.* All were very well received. Critics and professors have written glowingly about *Beat Hotel* as a major Beat work. A film honoring Jack Kerouac called *West Coast: Beat and Beyond,* directed by Chris Felver in 1983, narrated by Gerald Nicosia, was shown in repertoire movie houses, such as the Roxie Theatre on Sixteenth, around the corner from where I live. The poets and writers in the film are Ken Kesey, Allen Ginsberg, Lawrence Ferlinghetti, Gregory Corso, Philip Lamantia, Bob Kaufman, Jack Kerouac, Jack Micheline, Peter Orlovsky, Bobbie Louise Hawkins, JoAnne Kyger, Howard Hart, and myself.

Several books have appeared with critical studies on my work, notably *The Great American Poetry Bake-Off* by the poet, critic, and professor Robert Peters (Scarecrow Press, 1979), and poet Neeli Cherkovski's *Whitman's Wild Children* (Lapis, 1988).

For the last three years I've been writing this book. In the previous five years I gave occasional readings in Europe. (The last time I saw Brion Gysin alive was in 1979 in Amsterdam, where we read with Burroughs and Patti Smith; she and Anne Waldman took group photos of Burroughs, Gysin, and myself, but I never received the promised prints.) In 1984 I read again at the Amsterdam One World Poetry Festival with James Broughton and Dennis Cooper. I was offered the top floor of a wonderful sixteenth-century house over a canal by my friend Eddie Woods. My writer's block vanished immediately; I wrote nonstop for two weeks until I left. On my return I was mugged and almost strangled to death in my hallway, lost my voice, twelve dollars, and nearly my life. Writer's block returned.

In the backyard of the adjacent tenement a Latino beggar's opera has been acted out for eight years: whores, pimps, and junk peddlers make noise of every kind and variety. When one group stops, another begins. They do it in shifts. And always there is the sound of garbage falling like bodies with a dull thud, and hammering on metal and wood, the whine of the power saw, the screams of children, barking dogs, and loud "music" pounding into the night.

Meanwhile AIDS, like a medieval plague, has claimed the lives of many I knew and changed the world I knew. I have drawn in my horns, so to speak, become celibate. For two years I had a very young lover and lost him to drugs. Between drugs and the plague there was little to choose. I went underground.

In my teens I had read *Candide,* which left an indelible impression. I've reached the age of Dr. Pangloss in this best of all possible worlds, and find myself hankering for my own little garden to cultivate.

"A poem is never finished," said Paul Valéry, "only abandoned." If this is true of a poem, and it is, then how can we ever finish memoirs? We can't. This is but the draft of a draft, as Melville said of *Moby Dick.*

INDEX